Lighters in the Sky

The All-Time Greatest Concerts, 1960–2016

Corbin Reiff

LESSER GODS

Copyright © 2017 Corbin Reiff

FIRST PUBLISHED IN THE UNITED STATES OF AMERICA IN 2017 BY:
Lesser Gods, 15 W. 36th St., 8th Fl., New York, NY 10018,
an imprint of Overamstel Publishers, Inc.
PHONE (646) 850-4201
www.lessergodsbooks.com

DISTRIBUTED BY: Consortium Book Sales & Distribution,
34 13th Ave. NE #101, Minneapolis, MN 55413
PHONE (800) 283-3572
www.cbsd.com

FIRST EDITION SEPTEMBER 2017 / 10 9 8 7 6 5 4 3 2 1
PRINTED AND BOUND IN THE U.S.A.
ISBN: 978-1-944713-18-8

LIBRARY OF CONGRESS CONTROL NUMBER: 2017940760

To my wife, Jenna

I love you with all my heart

TABLE OF CONTENTS

"That's a hard feeling to describe—being on stage, performing and knowing that you've really got it that night. It feels like God is blessing you."

—James Brown

INTRODUCTION

I remember vividly the first concert I ever attended. September 28, 2005: Nine Inch Nails at Arco Arena in Sacramento, California, with Queens of the Stone Age supporting. I was 16 and a junior in high school. I had spent the entire summer slinging blizzards at Dairy Queen and, having saved up enough money, convinced some friends to go all in with me on general admission passes.

I had no idea what to expect as I entered the cavernous space. The sight of so many people sitting down on the open floor was bewildering. My friends and I carved out a chunk of concrete near the right side of the stage. We sat down and chatted about what songs we hoped Trent Reznor and company would play.

A half-hour after the opening band's set ended, the lights went out and Queens of the Stone ambled into view. I whooped and hollered as the guys grabbed their instruments and kicked into "Someone's in the Wolf." The Queens primarily played songs from their two most recent albums, *Lullabies to Paralyze* and *Songs for the Deaf*. I knew most of the music and was thrilled to sing and dance along with the crowd.

Midway through, singer Josh Homme noticed a burly dude who kept jumping over a small woman near the front barricade. He stopped the show immediately. Homme has the height and build of an NFL tight end, and his threat to enter the fracas got the offending "bro" to back off.

As the last notes of "No One Knows" died out and the Queens took their final bow, I could feel a pit well up in my stomach. Everyone has at least one—if not two, three or four—musical paragons that help them navigate through the horror of adolescence. Nine Inch Nails' albums *The Downward Spiral* and *The Fragile* were the receptacles for my teenage angst. When I couldn't articulate my own deep-seated anxieties and fears, Trent Reznor screamed them out for me with full, vocal cord–shredding fury. The thought of experiencing something so important and personal while surrounded by so many people was overwhelming. I felt like throwing up.

When the lights went down again, I experienced for the first time that euphoric release of the energy from the crowd consuming you. The hours of built-up anticipation explode out in one single scream. Those exhilarating seconds before the music starts, standing in the darkness waiting to be blasted into another dimension, can feel like a lifetime.

Reznor walked out and the audience in the pit surged forward, taking me with them. He didn't say a word. He simply picked up a guitar and launched into "Love Is Not Enough." All around me, bodies collided as the fanatics moshed. I became separated from my friends. I was lost in the moment, going berserk, totally free. The slower numbers like "Hurt" and "Right Where It Belongs" were a temporary reprieve from the madness, but then the band would launch into something like "Wish" or "Head Like a Hole" and the mania would take hold again.

By the time Reznor had snarled his last snarl and screamed his final scream, I was physically and emotionally exhausted. My head was pounding, my feet were throbbing and my back was stiff. I was on the verge of tears, but my heart was filled with a burning desire to do it all again—and soon.

I've attended hundreds of concerts since then. I wouldn't say I've seen it all, but I've seen a lot. I've seen future icons on their way up, big names in their prime and megastars well past it. While I was in the Army, one of the last things I did before I deployed to Iraq was see Depeche Mode at Key Arena in Seattle. One of the first things I did when I came home was see Bob Dylan at McMenamins Edgefield in Portland, Oregon.

After hanging up my uniform, I managed to carve out a career as a music writer, which has greatly expanded my potential to catch live performances. I've seen farewell jaunts, homecoming blowouts, tour kickoffs, private events and full-album performances. I've had beer spilled on me in small clubs, belted my lungs out in intimate theaters, danced through the aisles of basketball arenas, felt the hot blast from pyro on my face in massive outdoor stadiums and camped out for multiple nights at sprawling music festivals. I've seen classic rock, indie rock, prog rock, punk, metal, jazz, blues, pop, rap, trap, hip-hop, R&B, funk, folk, country, new wave, EDM, emo, shoegaze, hardcore, softcore, dance-core and any other -core you can imagine.

There's so much about the concert experience that I find intoxicating. I love the first pang of excitement that wells up inside my chest when I hear about a cool gig. I relish the weeks or months of anticipation. I love the pre-show beer . . . the second and third pre-show beers. I love the post-show recaps and taco runs. I love how all that tension leads up to a single cathartic release when the lights go down, the crowd roars around you and the band walks onstage.

Not every show leaves a mark, but every once in a while, when the energy and emotion being expended onstage translates into the crowd, when the music blasted directly at your face at 100 dB and more finds its way down into the pit of your soul, there's hardly anything better. A concert can change your life. More than a few have changed mine.

Each year there's usually one, maybe two, live musical performances that transcend all others. It's a unique event that forces you to say, "How cool would it have been to have been there?" Rather than make a list of the 50 or 100 greatest concerts of all time, I thought it'd be more interesting to pick out a single performance from each year since 1960 and unpack what made them so special, unique and important. As anyone who was lucky enough to attend such a show can tell you, the sense that you witnessed something exceptional sticks with you forever.

A few types of live gigs have that power. The first is the stacked bill. These are typically mega-festivals like Woodstock, Monterey Pop or an especially fruitful Coachella, where the sheer amount of musical talent overwhelms anything that a singular artist can achieve on their own.

The next type is the big name in a small space. This is a concert that draws a modest crowd in a compact setting—the key word here is "intimate"—and is mythologized in retrospect. Examples include Elton John at the Troubadour in Hollywood in 1970, The Replacements at First Avenue in Minneapolis in the mid-1980s and Elliott Smith at Largo in the late 1990s. Even though only a couple of hundred people were present, everybody and their uncle claims to have been there.

The most common show in this book is the right time/right place gig. Just because a band drops the record of the year doesn't mean it can deliver the goods live. These shows are marked by dynamic, culture-defining artists at their apex, playing with inhuman levels of energy and enthusiasm. James Brown at the Apollo Theater in 1962 is a good example. So are Led Zeppelin at Earls Court in 1975, Queen at Wembley Stadium in 1985, Nirvana at the Reading Festival in 1992 and Kanye West at Coachella in 2011.

Performances intended primarily for television audiences, like The Beatles on *The Ed Sullivan Show* or Elvis's 1968 Comeback Special, have been excluded from consideration. Though they were one-of-a-kind, era-defining live performances, the audience extended far beyond the people who were physically there. This book is about playing for the people on the floor or in the stands, not on the couch.

Each person's definition of what a great show looks and sounds like is different. Some selections may send your fist pumping in the air in agreement. Others may cause you to scratch your head and think, *What the hell was this guy thinking?* I've dug through hundreds of reviews and pored over thousands of hours of film and audio recordings. I've talked to both prominent members of the music industry as well as regular folks. I promise you that my choices weren't made on a whim.

I once asked Bruce Springsteen what makes for a great concert. As a guy who's spent the last forty years staging three- and four-hour musical marathons of intense drama and superhuman enthusiasm, he's an expert on the topic. Bruce pondered my question for a moment and then said, "A lot of work."

I thought about that response for a long time. He's right, of course. It takes a lot of work to design a show, build a stage, load it in, load it out, entertain a crowd, drive all night and do it again. It takes a whole lot of work to put together a band, record songs, make beats, craft melodies and write lyrics. And it takes an almost impossible amount of work to build a following, create demand and cultivate an audience that genuinely cares about what you're doing. A great concert is the explosive flashpoint of years and years of unseen toil, sacrifice and dedication.

If, as "The Boss" says, a lot of work is what it takes to makes a concert great, these are the ones that put in overtime.

#1 Single of the Year:
"Theme from 'A Summer Place'"
Percy Faith

1960

#1 Album of the Year:
The Sound of Music (Soundtrack)
Original Broadway Cast

Muddy Waters
NEWPORT JAZZ FESTIVAL—NEWPORT, RI
JULY 3

THERE'S A RIOT GOIN' ON IN NEWPORT!

It was early in the evening on Saturday, July 2, 1960, and Muddy Waters and his band were about to begin a long, eastbound trek from Chicago to the annual Newport Jazz Festival in Rhode Island. Newport was considered *the* premier live event in the country, so it was worth the grueling 2,000-mile journey, if only for the exposure that such a high-profile gig would bring. They had no idea what was in store for them once they arrived.

A few months earlier, Newport's reputation as a temporary wonderland for jazz and R&B lovers shot through the roof thanks to *Jazz on a Summer's Day*, a documentary that captured a carefully cultivated portion of the 1958 festival. The film's success meant that a greater audience than ever planned to make the sojourn out to the tip of Aquidneck Island to Freebody Park to experience the sights and sounds of Newport. Too many people, as it turned out.

"When the local merchants of Newport saw all these people coming to town coming out of the festival at midnight and 1 o'clock in the morning going back to 1956, they kept their bars open all night long," organizer George Wein told me. "It was like an oasis and we were drawing thousands of people to town that had nothing to do with the festival. That Saturday night, we were sold out, and there were still thousands of people outside trying to get in, but a lot of them were there just to party all night long."

The accepted capacity at the fairgrounds was around 16,500. Between ticket-holders, those who snuck into the park, regular vacationers and party-goers simply out looking for a good time, there were way more people than officials on the sleepy island could have hoped to control. The local police force was bolstered by reinforcements from the State Patrol, but even then, they only numbered around 200 men. The situation quickly grew tense for those in charge.

The trouble started in downtown Newport around 5 p.m., when Muddy was climbing into his car. Two opposing college fraternities went at each other in a turf war. The furor in the city swelled outward and reached the walls of the festival a few hours later. Bottles flew and smashed into the big brick wall that lay at the front of the festival grounds.

Inside the park, fans were mostly oblivious to the mayhem as they watched Ray Charles run through dynamite versions of "Drown in My Own Tears" and "Sticks and Stones." Wein asked Charles and the Oscar Peterson Trio to keep playing, pushing the music well past 2 a.m., to keep those within the park safe from the chaos raging outside. When dawn broke that Sunday morning, 170 people were in police custody. The area surrounding the festival grounds resembled a disaster zone.

This was the scene that greeted Waters and his band as they rolled down the street towards the venue. The group's harmonica player, James Cotton,

SET LIST

I Got My Brand on You
I'm Your Hoochie-Coochie Man
Baby, Please Don't Go
Soon Forgotten
Tiger in Your Tank
Got My Mojo Workin'
Goodbye Newport Blues

was driving and spotted John Lee Hooker standing on a street corner with his guitar on his back. Cotton pulled over to offer Hooker a ride and find out what the hell happened. No one in the car was sure if they even had a gig left to play.

Newport is a town of massive wealth. The millionaires who owned the island's exquisite mansions were appalled by what had transpired the previous evening. An emergency town council meeting was called to shut down the final day of the festival.

Wein made his case to the pissed-off committee that they should keep the music going, at least for the midday blues showcase. "I told them it'd be better to do that than to throw everybody out of town after canceling the evening performances," he explained. The town fathers heard him out and eventually agreed; the evening performances were out, but the blues could continue. "By doing that it really took the edge off the whole situation," Wein said. Waters's 2,000-mile ride wouldn't be a waste of gas after all.

The band takes the stage in the late afternoon without its front man. As the leader of the group, pianist Otis Spann is given an opening slot to run through his own songs before poet Langston Hughes introduces John Lee Hooker.

Beginning his performance with a cover of the B.B. King song "It's My Own Fault," Hooker cuts an entrancing figure. The shifty guitar player has one of the great voices in the whole history of blues genre. It doesn't bowl you over like B.B. King or grate at your eardrums like Howlin' Wolf—at times, it can almost be described as sleepy—but the way it draws you in is borderline magical.

MUSICIANS

Muddy Waters: Lead Vocals/Guitar
Otis Spann: Piano
Pat Hare: Guitar
James Cotton: Harmonica
Andrew Stephens: Bass
Francis Clay: Drums

Around 5:00 p.m. the man of the hour makes his appearance. Muddy shows up clad in a black suit that contrasts gorgeously against the wall of white uniforms worn by the rest of his band. Outdoor festivals are old hat to Waters by now, having revived his career two years earlier, performing in front of several immense, adoring audiences in the U.K. and Europe. He is ready to make an impression.

That this would become one of the defining gigs of Waters's extensive career isn't a foregone conclusion. His days at the cutting edge of what is happening in popular music are well behind him. He's made

The jauntiness in the music causes him to twist and holler with glee.

peace with his new role as an elder statesman of the blues and is more than willing to play to type.

With a Fender Telecaster in hand, the man formerly known as McKinley Morganfield opens his set with an unheard composition titled "I Got My Brand on You" that was written by the prolific Chess in-house producer Willie Dixon. Waters committed the song to tape only month before this show. Its slow tempo keeps most of the crowd glued to their chairs on the lawn in front of him. Waters doesn't sound nervous, but there's the faintest note of trepidation that seeps into his voice as he moves through the track. When it's over, he rolls into the more recognizable hit "(I'm Your) Hoochie-Coochie Man."

Waters's band at Newport isn't the best he's worked with, but they are excellent nonetheless. As a unit, they lock in tight to their front man's rhythm and cadence. They observe and follow along with every movement of his body and every inflection of his voice, standing ready to switch things up or set off into a new direction depending upon his whims. Countless hours in the studio, in small clubs and at overseas festivals have clearly paid off.

The greatest moment of Waters's set and a high-light of his entire career is the song "Got My Mojo Workin'." Recorded three years earlier, on tape it falls just short of the three-minute mark. This afternoon, Waters stretches the song out to seven-plus minutes. "Lay it on me!" he commands his band, and so they do. The jauntiness in the music causes him to twist and holler with glee, driving away any tension that might still linger among the folks spread out in front of him.

Those stuck with the image of Waters as the sul-try, stoic bluesman would be shocked by the exuber-ant presence here. Standing stark still, he recites the chorus repeatedly. Seconds tick by, then minutes. A noticeable current of energy begins coursing through his body. His eyes are shut tight; his hands tremble at his sides.

The song drives forward and Muddy becomes in-creasingly animated. His hips swivel, his fists punch into the air, his cheeks fill with deep breaths and his legs shimmy. When he can't stand in place any lon-ger, he jolts over to the left side of the stage toward Cotton, takes him into his hands and begins to dance. After releasing his harmonica player, he reflexively launches into an animated jitterbug, feet flying in ev-ery direction, before running back to his microphone to sing the remaining choruses. Standing at the front of the stage, he suggestively thrusts his hips in the direction of the crowd.

As the song ends, hundreds of mostly white fans give him an enthusiastic standing ovation. Muddy relishes the moment and then departs behind the curtain. His part is over, but the show isn't done. Mo-ments later Muddy's band emerges once again, but without their leader. Langston Hughes, a member of the Newport Festival Board, wrote a piece titled "Goodbye Newport Blues" to end the set. The only problem is that Muddy is functionally illiterate.

With little time to memorize or learn the new song, he has Spann deliver the final number in his place. The pianist takes hold of the microphone and regales the crowd with a slow-burning elegy to the chaotic weekend. "We were all sitting there crying," Wein remembered. "It was a very moving and historic day. One I'll never forget."

HONORABLE MENTION
Chuck Berry at the Apollo Theater
New York, NY (February 17)

On December 21, 1959, Chuck Berry was arrest-ed in St. Louis for violating the Mann Act, a Jim Crow law that prohibits transporting a woman across state lines for reasons of debauchery or any other immoral purpose. The charges were largely trumped up, but the trial became a media sensation. Very quickly it seemed that the man who all but invented rock 'n' roll might be going away for a very long time. Berry's once-incessant tour schedule all but dried up, except for a reduced-rate residency at the Apollo Theater in Harlem in February. Berry brought along his band (Jasper Thomas on drums, Leroy Davis on the sax and pianist Johnnie Johnson) and spent six nights duck walking, reelin' and rockin' like it was the last time he would ever do it. Early on, Berry learned that Apol-lo audiences were different from almost any other crowd. "If you played anything other than your hits or some hits they all knew, you were in deep trouble," he wrote in his autobiography. Berry stuck with a rep-ertoire that would keep the unabashedly vocal audi-ence cheering, surefire hits like "Johnny B. Goode," "Maybellene," "Roll Over Beethoven," and "Sweet Little Sixteen." The next month, Berry was tried, found guilty and sentenced to five years in prison. He appealed and the term was later reduced to three years, which he began serving in February 1962.

1961

Elvis Presley
BLOCH ARENA—HONOLULU, HI
MARCH 25

ALOHA! THE KING RETURNS

The idea that the biggest pop star in the world would take a couple of years off from his or her career to join the Armed Forces seems unimaginable today. Can you picture Justin Timberlake throwing up a sharp salute in a pressed uniform? Or Taylor Swift, clad in camo fatigues, running through a muddy obstacle course while being screamed at by drill sergeants? No way. Yet that's exactly what happened on March 24, 1958, at Fort Chaffee in Arkansas when Elvis Presley, the "King of Rock 'n' Roll," raised his right hand and enlisted into the United States Army.

It was not a move that Elvis took lightly. Shortly after his induction, he confided to his friend Eddie Fada that he thought his career as an entertainer was "all over." Before Presley took his oath, his wily manager, Colonel Tom Parker, made him a promise: "If you go into the army, stay a good boy and do nothing to embarrass your country, I'll see to it that you come back a bigger star than when you left." The Colonel stuck to his word.

The entire teenage world was fascinated by Presley's turn as a G.I. When he received his duty assignment to join up with the 3rd Armored Division in West Germany, a press corps was called in to keep tabs on his every move. Absence, it seemed, made the clamor for Elvis grow fonder.

On March 2, 1960, after two years of honorable service, Presley left Europe and the life of a soldier behind. At an impromptu press conference in Scotland, he was asked if he was nervous about his prospects for a comeback. "Yes, I am," he admitted. "I mean, I have my doubts. . . . The only thing I can say is that I'm gonna try. I'll be there fighting."

The reception Elvis received back on American soil obliterated any uncertainty he had about his future prospects. The train that took him from New Jersey to Tennessee was mobbed at nearly every stop with fans hoping to catch a glimpse of that famous crooked smile. He hosted another press conference at his home, Graceland, cut into a fan-made cake in the shape of a guitar and smiled for the cameras. Then he started plotting his comeback.

Elvis dove back into his career as an entertainer with gusto, adopting a rigorous schedule filming low-budget films while recording a diverse range of soundtrack and gospel records. In January 1961, he staged a small, private charity benefit show in Memphis for a few local nonprofits, where he was presented with a plaque from RCA for selling over 75 million records worldwide. He took part in another such event in February. It was only when a new call to serve his country arrived that he finally returned to the stage to perform a full set of music in front of a public, paying audience once again.

December 7, 1941, was "a day that will live in infamy," as President Franklin Roosevelt described it. The Japanese Air Force attacked the U.S. naval base at Pearl Harbor, killing 2,403 sailors and airmen and inciting America's entrance into World War II. In the intervening years, the War Memorial Commission had raised funds to erect a monument to those who lost their lives on the battleship U.S.S. Arizona. After fifteen years of efforts, they had accumulated $300,000 but were still $200,000 away from their goal. The 20th anniversary was fast approaching and the prospects of the commission drumming up enough cash to meet their goal in such a short time were grim. Enter Colonel Tom Parker.

Parker's most famous client was set to spend that spring in Hawaii working on his next film project, *Blue Hawaii*. Figuring that he could help raise money and generate positive publicity, Parker put together a benefit concert to help shore up the Arizona's memorial fund. Presley would foot the bill entirely—at least that's what the wily manager told the press. NBC ended up paying $50,000 to produce a television special around the event.

As Parker declared at a press conference, "Everyone's gotta buy a ticket—the governor, Admiral Solomons, Admiral Sides, commissioners, everyone. Even me." The event was a publicity bonanza, and with only around 4,000 seats up for grabs, it was the hottest ticket of 1961.

SET LIST

Heartbreak Hotel

All Shook Up

(Now and Then There's) A Fool Such as I

I've Got a Woman

Love Me

Such a Night

Reconsider Baby

I Need Your Love Tonight

That's All Right

Don't Be Cruel

One Night

Are You Lonesome Tonight?

It's Now or Never

Swing Low, Sweet Chariot

Hound Dog

MUSICIANS

Elvis Presley: Lead Vocals

Scotty Moore: Guitar

Hank Garland: Guitar

DJ Fontana: Drums

Boots Randolph: Saxophone

Floyd Cramer: Piano

Bob Moore: Bass

The Jordanaires Vocal Group

Gordon Stoker

Neal Matthews

Hoyt Hawkins

Ray Walker

Fans spend hours outside the venue, anxiously waiting to be let into the arena. When the gates finally open, they rush through like furies to find their seats. After sitting through several opening acts, the audience loudly cheers when Admiral L. Campbell strides out onto the stage to introduce the man of the hour. Campbell offers a short tribute to the headliner, making sure to highlight his service in the Army.

As soon as the words "Elvis Presley" leave his lips, all decorum and deference go out the window. The audience bursts into a unified, ear-splitting shriek. The volume cranks even higher when the singer saunters out in his trademark gold lamé suit with shiny, sequined lapels. It is the last time he would ever don that spectacular outfit in public.

The band hustles into a tight groove. It's a futile attempt to drown out the frenzied wail of the crowd. Elvis mockingly screams back at them through the microphone, and then, seemingly powerless, he gives in and croons the immortal words "Well, since my baby left me" that open his breakout 1956 hit "Heartbreak Hotel." All hell breaks loose. You can hardly make out the next few lines over the ensuing frenzy.

If there were any concern about whether the Army had tamed the man that television networks once refused to air from the waist down, it's erased in seconds. The hips swivel, the leg shakes, the lip quivers and the eyebrow raises. This is the same loose, uber-sexualized Elvis that captured the hearts and wistful imaginations of teenage girls the world over the previous decade. Gordon Stoker, one of the members of Elvis's backing vocal group, the Jordanaires, later remarked that there was a spontaneity to Elvis's performance that night that "closely resembled a man being let out of jail."

Young women tear at their clothes and hair out of sheer compulsion.

The first song runs so hot that the band blows the electricity in the building, forcing Elvis to vamp for a few moments until they can get the power up and running. Once the juice begins flowing again, "The King" finds his groove and, for the next hour, dazzles the crowd with some of the biggest hits from his impressive back catalog. "All Shook Up," "Are You Lonesome Tonight," "Don't Be Cruel" and his very first single, "That's All Right," to name a few.

The audience eats it up greedily. At times, their fevered howling drowns out both the band and their idol. The spaces in between songs might be even louder than the musical interludes. "For his fans, he has an animal magnetism that communicates itself more strongly than any entertainer we've ever seen or heard," Buck Buchwach wrote in a review for the *Honolulu Advertiser*. "He's much more handsome, much more appealing, much more likeable and a much better entertainer in person … than on records, over TV and in movies."

Undeterred by the sheer mania taking place in front of him, Elvis leans into the maelstrom, whipping the chaos up more and more. The emotional peak comes during the final song of the night, "Hound Dog." Out of nowhere, he sprints from one side of the stage to the other, dipping into a six-foot-long slide on his knees along the way. Any semblance of order is erased as young women tear at their clothes and hair out of sheer compulsion. Then, it's over. He

smiles, he waves and he walks out. Elvis has left the building.

The concert raised $62,000 for the construction of the memorial for the U.S.S. Arizona, which was dedicated on May 30, 1962. Today, if you take the boat ride out to the gleaming white monument seated in the shallow waters of Pearl Harbor, you'll notice a plaque heralding Elvis's role in its construction. For the King of Rock 'n' Roll, there would be more soundtracks, more gospel records and a string of B-movies, but he wouldn't perform in front of a large audience for another seven years.

HONORABLE MENTION
John Coltrane at the Village Vanguard
New York, NY (November 2)

The Village Vanguard in New York City is one of the all-time great venues to catch live jazz. Located off 7th Avenue in Greenwich Village, it's an intimate space, able to hold only 125 people seated around the tables that dot the room. Over time the Vanguard played host to the biggest titans of the genre—Thelonius Monk, Charlie Mingus and Sonny Rollins. Perhaps the best show ever to take place in its hallowed halls came courtesy of legendary saxophonist John Coltrane. In 1961, fresh from a split with Atlantic Records and his former bandleader Miles Davis, Coltrane sought to make his mark by breaking free from some of the genre's more rigid templates. He booked an extended residency at the Vanguard with a newly formed quintet and used them to push the musical envelope. He experimented heavily with modal frameworks, using Indian ragas as a major influence. It was an exciting moment in his career, which was captured for posterity on the live album *Coltrane "Live" at the Village Vanguard.*

#1 Single of the Year:
"Stranger on the Shore"
Mr. Acker Bilk

1962

James Brown
THE APOLLO THEATER—NEW YORK, NY
OCTOBER 24

MR. DYNAMITE'S APOLLO EXPLOSION

As the "Hardest Working Man in Show Business," James Brown set the mold for how a front man should look, sound, act and dance. Many of the greatest performers of all time, like Michael Jackson, Bruce Springsteen, Mick Jagger and Prince, have all cited Brown as a primary influence. But as eye-catching as those figures are in concert, there was no one quite like the "Godfather of Soul."

By 1962, the singer from rural Georgia had racked up a string of number-one hits while earning a reputation as one of the most electrifying entertainers in the world. That success wasn't enough for him though. Brown, craved more, and he instinctively knew how to get it. Banking on his talents as a showman, he pushed King Records label head Syd Nathan to bankroll the recording of a live album. The only problem was that Nathan hated the idea.

Live records didn't sell well, he argued. It was best to stick with the singles. With a firm belief that a live recording would elevate his star to levels he only dreamed of, Brown went around his boss. He funded the project himself with $5,700 he'd saved from a recent run of concerts down South. When the time came to pick the place to record, there was only one option: the Apollo Theater.

Located at 253 West 125th Street in Harlem, the ornate 1,500-seat concert hall was built in 1914. In its first two decades, it operated as a whites-only venue, hosting mostly vaudeville acts. After a brief shutdown during the Great Depression, the Apollo reopened in 1934, serving mainly as a showcase for black artists performing for mostly black audiences. Brown played the Apollo for the first time on April 24, 1959, and it quickly became one of his favorite venues along the National "Chitlin Circuit" of black theaters and juke joints. It was here, during the height of Cuban Missile Crisis, when the fate of the world itself seemed at stake, that Brown staged his masterpiece.

Now, ladies and gentlemen, it's star time. Are you ready for star time?" organist Fats Gonder asks. "Yeah!" the crowd roars, but the introduction is just beginning. The de facto MC runs down a laundry list of his boss's most recognizable hits, each punctuated with an escalating burst of noise from the brass section. "I'll Go Crazy"—boom! "Try Me"—bang! "You've Got the Power"—pow! He exclaims, "Mr. Dynamite! The amazing Mr. 'Please, Please, Please' himself! The star of the show, James Brown and the Famous Flames!"

The words hardly escape Gonder's lips before the band kicks into an up-tempo instrumental marked by a surf-style guitar riff. After giving the band a few moments to vamp and build anticipation, the man of the hour glides out in front of the people, who lose their minds at the mere sight of him. And what a sight he is!

From his hands, to his hips, to his knees and his feet, James Brown is a tornado of movement. Stand-

SET LIST

I'll Go Crazy
Try Me
Think
I Don't Mind
Lost Someone
Please, Please, Please
You've Got the Power
I Found Someone
Why Do You Do Me
I Want You So Bad
I Love You, Yes I Do
Strange Things Happen
Bewildered
Please, Please, Please
Night Train

MUSICIANS

James Brown: Lead Vocals
Bobby Bennett: Vocals
Lloyd Stallworth: Vocals
Bobby Byrd: Vocals
Lewis Hamlin: Musical Director/Trumpet
Mack Johnson: Trumpet
Teddy Washington: Trumpet
Hubert Perry: Bass
Sam Latham: Drums
Clayton Fillyau: Drums
Les Buie: Guitar
Lucas "Fats" Gonder: Organ
Clifford MacMillan: Tenor Saxophone
St. Clair Pickney: Tenor Saxophone
Al "Brisco" Clark: Baritone Saxophone
Dickie Wills: Trombone

ing on one leg, he shimmies over to the microphone, wiggling at the waist the whole way there. He unleashes dance moves that you would swear were impossible until you see him bust them out right here in front of your eyes.

"Hair is the first thing. And teeth the second," Brown once said. "A man got those two things he's got it all." James Brown has it all and then some. His megawatt smile is nearly blinding, and the carefully constructed pompadour that tops his head is the pinnacle of style. He looks good, he feels good and he wants to make sure the audience knows it.

"You know I feel all right," Brown croons into the microphone. "I feel alllllllllllll riiiiiiiiiiight!" he screams. Dispensing with the pleasantries, he gives a quick signal to the band and they begin playing "I'll Go Crazy." From the very first number, even without seeing him move, you get a sense of what makes Brown such an enigmatic presence. The strains of exertion, the wails, the yips, the screams are so alluring and dramatic. His charisma is off the charts. His swagger is undeniable.

Though he would employ an array of different guitarists, bassists, drummers and horn players over the years—Jimi Hendrix and Bootsy Collins being the most notable—there is something special about the Famous Flames as they are arranged on this fateful

night. As great as their collective musical talents are, the true power of the Flames is their almost paranormal ability to follow the direction of Brown as he shakes, shimmies and wails across the stage.

By merely raising his eyebrow, Brown can summon a perfectly timed cymbal crash. With a pained grunt, a sharp burst of saxophone. And with the flick of the wrist, the instant and simultaneous conclusion of all sound behind him. Brown drilled that group like no other bandleader has before or since, and it enabled him to take his audiences to places they'd never been before.

Tonight, the drillmaster has become the drill sergeant. Regular fines that the singer hands out for missed notes or mismatched apparel have been increased from the painful $10 to a crippling $100. Mistakes will not be tolerated. Everyone is on their A-game. The band is in the middle of a weeklong residency at the Apollo, playing five shows a night and perfecting their chemistry with every set. To say that they are sharp is an insult to the adjective.

The syrupy ballad "Try Me" comes next, then "Think," "I Don't Mind," and an extended 10-minute-long version of "Lost Someone." The languid pace of that last number has a cooling effect on the crowd that's shattered the second he transitions into a fierce medley of instantly recognizable songs, beginning with his breakthrough hit, "Please, Please, Please." He can hardly get the first "please" out of his mouth before the audience erupts into a massive, whooping applause that continues unabated for 20 seconds.

From his hands, to his hips, to his knees and his feet, James Brown is a tornado of movement.

For the next six minutes, Brown keeps the energy blazing, playing parts of "You've Got the Power," "I Found Someone," "Why Do You Do Me," "I Want You So Bad," "I Love You, Yes I Do," "Strange Things Happen" and "Bewildered" before circling back to "Please, Please, Please." It's a masterful bit of showmanship.

It's no coincidence that Brown chose to stage this concert on a Wednesday. You'd think a Friday or Saturday would be more ideal, but Wednesday is Amateur Night at the Apollo and it typically draws a far wilder crowd than any other night of the week. Everyone goes nuts as the man onstage pours his blood, sweat and tears into the performance, right down to the little old lady in front who screams out, "Sing it, motherfucker!"

"The audience was with me, screaming and hollering on all the songs," Brown recalled in his autobiography. "I thought, 'Man, this is really going to do it.'"

To close the show, Brown invites everyone to climb aboard his funky "Night Train" and cross between "Miami, Florida, to Atlanta, Georgia." He arrives in New York City, where he asks to be carried home. The song is pure vamp. At this point, Brown, the band and the 1,500 spectators panting down below and up in the balcony are completely spent. They've given everything they've got, and they have nothing left to give. Nearly three minutes in, Brown stops singing altogether, leaving the band to roll on until they close the night out with a final, commingled horn blast.

Brown's gambit paid off. The recording of this show, released as *Live at the Apollo* in 1963, spent 66 weeks on the pop charts, where it topped out at No. 2. It totally changed the trajectory of his career, turning him from a largely black draw into a crossover smash and one of the most popular entertainers in the world. It also helped establish the live album as a viable commercial entity in the music world at large.

HONORABLE MENTION
Ray Charles at the L'Olympia
Paris, France (May 18)

In April 1962, Ray Charles unveiled the greatest studio album of his career, *Modern Sounds in Country and Western Music*. It synthesized elements of rock, jazz, country and grand orchestral music into a document of unparalleled scope and majesty. It was a commercial juggernaut, going gold in the United States and holding down the top spot on the charts for 14 consecutive weeks. Shortly after debuting his masterpiece, Charles took off for a quick tour of Europe, including a four-show residency at the L'Olympia in Paris. The Georgia native brought along an extensive backing band that included a full horn section, as well as his female backup troupe, The Raelettes. At the center of it all was Ray, dancing his fingers across the keys on his grand piano while crooning and wailing through songs off his latest album, like "Bye Bye Love" and "I Can't Stop Loving You," as well as old favorites like "Hit the Road Jack" and "What'd I Say." Some artists might get overwhelmed by the grandeur of such a venue and the overwhelming sound of the band, but not Ray. The highlight of the evening was an extended, jazzy instrumental interlude tucked midway through the set. Just a genius, his piano, a little bass and some light snare work to back him up. The virtuosity is breathtaking, the emotion incredible.

#1 Single of the Year:
"Sugar Shack"
Jimmy Gilmer and the Fireballs

#1 Album of the Year:
West Side Story (Soundtrack)
Various Artists

1963

Sam Cooke
HARLEM SQUARE CLUB—MIAMI, FL
JANUARY 12

SAM GETS COOKIN' IN MIAMI

Sam Cooke was one of the greatest soul singers ever to draw breath. He cut his teeth in the 1950s as a member of the gospel group the Soul Stirrers before breaking out on his own and scoring hits like "You Send Me" and "Chain Gang." His voice, that smoky croon, conveyed a depth of emotion that touched a nerve and resonated with a large swath of the American populace.

Onstage, Cooke adopted a posture similar to Nat King Cole or Perry Como. He spent his evenings in front of crowds either sitting on a stool or standing stark still. He let his voice carry the performance. That all changed in 1962 when he hit the road on a tour of the U.K. with rock 'n' roll's original wild man, Little Richard.

Night after night, Cooke opened the show with his impassioned, pleading songs, and night after night, he was blown offstage by the hurricane that was Richard Penniman. As J.W. Alexander, Cooke's manager, remembered of the headliner, "He came out with a damn chair in his mouth, and he pulled off that robe, and he literally slayed them." Little Richard wailed, convulsed and screamed. He apparently dropped dead in the middle of his show, only to be revived and "awopbabaloobopalopbamboom" some more.

There was nothing wrong with Cooke's set, but Little Richard changed the way he thought about live performance. At Alexander's urging, he decided to modify his style and approach to better grab the audience. Add a little bit of fire, brimstone and sex appeal to the mix.

When he returned to America, Cooke honed in on his new act. In December he set off for a tour that gave him the opportunity to debut his new, wilder, edgier persona. His backing band, the Kingpins, weren't virtuosos, but Cooke wasn't looking for perfection. He wanted a group that could keep it loose and deliver a lot of energy across three sets a night.

The tour began in Texas, where the band picked up saxophone master King Curtis. From there, Cooke and the Kingpins wound their way through the South, arriving at the Harlem Square Club in Miami on January 12, 1963. Harlem Square was a prototypical "Chitlin Circuit" venue. Situated a couple of blocks off I-95 in Overtown, a predominantly black neighborhood north of downtown Miami, it was a regular stop for all the major R&B, soul, jazz and blues acts driving through Florida. It was a cavernous space, like a swanky barn, featuring a large open floor with a balcony dotted with tables for couples to sit at and have a drink while they took in the action down below.

Cooke hosted a preliminary matinee gig in the early evening followed by a second set at 10 pm. Both went over fine, but just before the third performance the feeling in the air shifted. The crowd, filled with cheap beer and stiff liquor, were ready to lose themselves in the music of their idol. No one can remem-

SET LIST

Feel It

Chain Gang

Cupid

It's All Right

(I Love You) For Sentimental Reasons

Twistin' the Night Away

Somebody Have Mercy

Bring It on Home to Me

Nothing Can Change This Love

Having a Party

SIDEBAR: MUSICIANS

Sam Cooke: Lead Vocals

Clifton White: Guitar

Cornell Dupree: Guitar

Jimmy Lewis: Bass

Albert "June" Gardner: Drums

George Stubbs: Piano

King Curtis: Saxophone

Tate Houston: Saxophone

ber why Cooke had picked the Harlem Square Club to record his first live album, but it was a sublime decision. This wasn't just an audience familiar with his music; this was a crowd ready to get down and let it all hang out.

It's already well after midnight, time for the last set of the evening. King Curtis walks out to the microphone: "Right now, ladies and gentlemen, we'd like to get ready to introduce the star of our show. The young man you've all been waiting for, Mister Soul. So what do you say, let's all get together and welcome him to the stand with a great big hand—how about it for Sam Cooke?"

Cooke walks out to a roaring applause. Grabbing the mic from Curtis he takes the temperature of the crowd. "How you doing out there?" The audience claps and cheers loudly in response, but not loud enough. "How you doing out there?" he asks again. The response is a little louder now but still unsatisfactory. "I'll ask you one more time, how you doing out there?" Boom! They scream their heads off. He's got 'em.

"Don't fight it, we're gonna feel it tonight, you understand?" he says. It's not just an intro to the first song, "Feel It," but also a mission statement. Unlike James Brown, who directs nearly every sound and movement on the stage, Cooke likes to let things flow more naturally. He feeds off the energy of both his band and the audience and modifies his tone and tenor accordingly. When he says, "Don't fight it, feel it," it's as much a reminder to himself as it is a command to anyone within earshot.

"Feel It" is more of a vamp-y warm-up than a real song. There aren't many words beyond the title, but it gives Cooke a chance to set the mood. The show begins in earnest with his 1961 hit "Chain Gang," which is delivered with a revelry that belies the song's mournfully deep message. Tonight is not a night for provoking thought. When Cooke asks the crowd to join in with a series of syncopated "oohs" and "ahhs," their enthusiasm draws a big, joyful laugh from the man holding the microphone.

Next comes the excitable ballad "Cupid," which Cooke describes as a "nice little sweet one." That's followed by a one-two punch of "It's All Right" and "Sentimental Reasons." The mood remains light as couples pair up to the sound of Cooke crooning away about forgiveness and everlasting love. Near the end of "Sentimental Reasons" the audience tries to take over for Cooke, belting out every single word of the song's final verse while he wails away over the top.

The energy is ramped up considerably when Cooke introduces "Twistin' the Night Away," with a filthy "one, two, put it anywhere!" Saccharine balladry is replaced with up-tempo jukin' and jivin' driven wild by a spine-busting King Curtis sax solo. Cooke has his foot firmly on the gas pedal and he's pressing down hard. His voice, worn out from the two sets earlier in the evening, is raw and ragged but miraculously precise.

Up in the balcony, Sam's wife, Barbara; his brother, L.C.; and his agent, Jerry Brandt, are sitting at a table watching Cooke do his thing with a mix of concern and amazement. For Barbara, her husband's sexually charged bravado is almost too much and she makes a crack about it to L.C., if only to relieve some of the tension. "Sam was really in his bag, you know," Brandt told biographer Peter Guralnick. "When he was really having fun, he could drive the women into a frenzy; it was almost like he was beating up on them to get an orgasm."

His voice is raw and ragged but miraculously precise.

The highlight of the night is the song "Bring It on Home to Me." For nearly three minutes Cooke teases the crowd with bits and pieces of his signature song "You Send Me." They steadily lose control waiting and waiting and waiting for him to offer a release. When he gives it to them, bursting into the first verse of "Bring It On Home to Me," they explode with jubilation.

Two more songs, "Nothing Can Change This Love" and "Having a Party," follow and then it's all over. Before he leaves, Cooke offers a last bit of advice. "I gotta go, but when you go home, keep having that party," he tells them. "No matter where ya at, remember I told ya, keep having that party. If you're with your loved ones somewhere, keep having that party. If you're feeling good, riding alone with the radio sometime, keep having that party." Cooke takes a final bow while Curtis steps up to the microphone asking for one last round of applause.

As it turned out, Cooke partied a little too hard that night at the Harlem Square Club for his bosses at RCA Records. They had hoped to make a quick buck on the recording of this performance, but when they heard the tapes, they were mortified by the unbridled depravity that their shining soul sensation had exhibited. They locked the tapes in a vault, intent on sealing them away forever. It wasn't until 1985 that the public finally got to hear the recordings.

Cooke wouldn't make it to that date. A little under two years after this singular performance in Miami, he was shot dead by a motel manager in Los Angeles.

HONORABLE MENTION
Nina Simone at Carnegie Hall
New York, NY (April 12)

They called her the "High Priestess of Soul" and for good reason. Nina Simone had an almost shamanic quality about the way she inhabited a stage. Her aura lent incredible depth and gravity to the standards, blues, folk and jazz compositions that she loved to sing. In 1963 she graduated from the basement coffee shops around Greenwich Village to the big time: Carnegie Hall. The chance to become the first black, female classical pianist to play that hallowed venue was a dream she'd held onto since she was a little girl, and through a mix of tenacity and talent, she made it happen. More importantly, she made the most of it. "What makes me the happiest," Simone once said, "is when I'm performing and there are people out there who feel with me and I know I touch them." Opening with a haunting take on Gian Carlo Menotti's "Black Swan" that presaged Jim Morrison's entire career with the Doors, Simone wove together an eclectic set filled out by popular film score pieces like the "Theme from Sayonara," folk standards like "Cotton-Eyed Joe" and original pieces like "If You Knew." To see Simone behind that big shiny grand piano, in her gorgeous white dress and with sequins dotting her eyebrows, bellowing from the depths of her soul, was to witness something truly unforgettable.

1964

Jerry Lee Lewis
THE STAR CLUB—HAMBURG, GERMANY
APRIL 5

STAR TIME

Just six years before he took the stage at the intimate Star Club in the red-light district of Hamburg, Germany, Jerry Lee Lewis was an insurgent teen hero with almost limitless potential. His records sold in the millions. His shows were packed to the rafters. Men wanted to be him and women wanted to . . . well, you know. In terms of popularity there was only one man who could stack up against him and his name was Elvis. Then, just like that, it all blew up in his face.

On December 12, 1957, Lewis, who was 22, tied the knot with his first cousin once removed Myra Gale Brown. It was his third marriage. She was only 13. Around his hometown of Ferriday, Louisiana, it wasn't a shocking development, but to the rest of the world, the union was considered an obscenity.

Shortly after the honeymoon, Jerry Lee took off for a tour of the U.K. and brought his young bride with him. When the couple landed at Heathrow Airport in London, they were met by journalist Ray Berry, to whom Jerry Lee casually revealed that the woman standing next to him was his bride. When the news reached the British public the next day, they reacted violently and called for a cancelation of the tour. Lewis performed just three shows in the U.K. before high-tailing it back to America, where the scandal followed him.

With Elvis off in the Army, it was almost a given that Jerry Lee Lewis would take over as the reigning King of Rock 'n' Roll. That prospect was completely out the window now, and the man many referred to as "The Killer" was left fighting for his professional life. His music was virtually blacklisted from the radio. Even his own label head, Sam Phillips, the iconic president of Sun Records, went behind his back and cut together a fake promo interview to try to explain away the situation. Almost overnight, the demand to see Lewis live dried up, and his take-home plummeted from $10,000 a night to a mere $250.

"People ask me what effect England had on me, and mostly the effect was on Sam Phillips and distribution," Lewis recalled years later. "He just was not puttin' my records out there." Without new music or a promotional push, Lewis's career was left for dead, so he did all that he could do. He kicked out his stool, stood his ground and walloped on his piano like his life depended on it.

In 1963, Jerry Lee returned to London to tape a special titled *Don't Knock the Rock*. The success of that program was the first indication that maybe, if the European audiences hadn't forgiven, they had chosen to forget his prior transgressions. The young crowd went ape for the manic figure hammering away at the piano. At one point, in a fit of unbridled mania, they bum-rushed the stage just to touch him.

As boisterous as that reception was, it was a mere prelude to the sheer explosiveness that took place a week later. After London, Lewis was booked to play the Star Club in Hamburg, Germany. It was

SET LIST

Mean Woman Blues
High School Confidential
Money
Matchbox
What'd I Say
Great Balls of Fire
Good Golly Miss Molly
Your Cheatin' Heart
Hound Dog
Long Tall Sally
Whole Lotta Shakin' Goin' On
Down the Line

the same venue that helped launch the Beatles a little less than a year earlier. He'd performed there once before, around the same time that the Fab Four were cutting their teeth, and apparently enjoyed the experience so much that he hatched a plan with producer Siggi Loch to record a live album. Detractors could say a lot about Jerry Lee Lewis, but the man knew how to deliver the goods before a crowd. Perhaps, he thought, this would be his way of reclaiming his spot at the top.

After an enthusiastic introduction by the German MC, The Killer stalks out of the wings and lets out a playful purr as he seats himself in front of his piano. It's a sound that's as inviting as it is loaded with danger. A twinkling piano roll, then "Mmmmmmmmmmmm got a woman, mean as she can be." The crowd doesn't even let him finish the word "mean" before echoing back the rest of the line: "Sometimes I think she's almost mean as me!"

Jerry Lee is pumping hard on the keys. His pickup band, a British group named the Nashville Teens, is doing all they can to keep up. The Teens' lead guitarist, John Allen, takes a chance on a solo midway through the first song but is overpowered by Lewis's incessant and flamboyant pounding. About two minutes in, he "gets things down real low" while whooping it up with an on-the-beat succession of "uh-huhs" and "yeah-yeahs." He lets loose with a single, long

MUSICIANS

Jerry Lee Lewis: Lead Vocals/Piano
John Allen: Guitar
Pete Shannon Harris: Bass
Barry Jenkins: Drums

"Whooooo!" that sends the crowd into a whistling tizzy. The man up on the stage can only purr and laugh.

"Yeah!" Jerry Lee exclaims at the end of the song. "Thank you! Thank you very much, ladies and gentlemen! I'd like to say it's a pleasure, a great honor to be back at the fabulous, most beautiful, I mean really swingin' Star Club." He gives them a moment to shower him with their adulation before moving on to the next number, "High School Confidential," and by the end of it they're enthusiastically chanting "Jerry! Jerry! Jerry!"

Even though he's aware that the tapes are rolling, Lewis doesn't seem to pay any mind to posterity. Engineers and their levels be damned! He is going to play loud and he is going to bludgeon the paying customers gathered in front of him with his signature brand of flamboyant, nasty rock 'n' roll. Because his energetic wails, percussive stomps and quick jumps move and shake the microphones onstage, the subsequent recording has a visceral raw sound.

In the estimation of Lewis's pre-eminent biographer Nick Tosches, the performance stands as "The perfect suicide-pact marriage between music and methamphetamine, and one of the most overpowering and essential moments in all of rock and roll. A manic paroxysm such as might raise the dead, fell the living, and forever rend the veils of night."

The intensity is incredible. Every song hits a musical climax that seems impossible to top. Then the next song comes and he somehow manages to go harder, faster and fiercer than before. At one point, his stool goes flying across the room with a fierce kick and he hops to his feet, reeling, rocking and moaning all night long. His cover of the Ray Charles classic "What'd I Say" discards all the song's jazzy subtlety and is transformed into a two-part, mile-a-minute ripper. Lewis doesn't sing the song; he hollers it. Then, before you can stop long enough to catch your breath, he digs into his biggest hit of all, "Great Balls of Fire."

He can't stop his fingers from boogie-woogieing all over the keys.

The highlight of the set comes a few songs later when Jerry Lee takes on the immortal Hank Williams tearjerker "Your Cheatin' Heart." In the hands of Lewis, the lovesick ballad becomes a callous, light-hearted rocker. He can't stop his fingers from boogie-woogieing all over the keys. It may be the best example on record of Jerry Lee's singular rock 'n' roll spirit and musical identity. Even a song as staid and true as "Your Cheatin' Heart" bends to the will of his outsized personality. Despair simply doesn't stick to The Killer.

The show ends with an incredible one-two punch of "Whole Lotta Shakin' Goin' On" and "Down the Line." The former is the one time the Nashville Teens measure up to Jerry Lee's musicianship. They finally lock into a groove with their wild and unpredictable bandleader just long enough to deliver an explosion of pure attitude driven home through flaming guitar solos and percussive piano riffs. With a final, boisterous "Yeah!" the concert ends. Jerry Lee thanks the crowd, leaves the stage, and departs for the next gig, in the next town, in the next country.

Live at the Star Club did not become the career-reviving record that Jerry Lee and his label hoped it would be. Due to a bit of legal chicanery, the album wasn't even released in the United States of America until decades later. It stood for years as a highly sought after, lost document that The Killer had left behind in the continent that almost ruined him.

HONORABLE MENTION
B.B. King at the Regal Theater
Chicago, IL (November 21)

Perhaps the highest compliment you can pay to an artist is to say that they are original. B.B. King was an original, maybe not in concept, but certainly in delivery. No one in the history of the blues played guitar quite like B.B. Even working in the well-worn confines of the genre, he managed to create a sound all his own. But for all his tremendous studio singles and albums, his greatest statement as an entertainer came late one night at the Regal Theater in the genre's home metropolis, Chicago. Everything that spoke to his greatness is on display in that performance. The charm, the humility, the emotion, the vibrato, and my God, that voice! Rumbling, deep and wall-shakingly powerful. Opening with "Everyday I Have the Blues," King and his band put together a set touched with class, but uncompromising in feel. The laments are soul-crushing, with "You Done Lost Your Good" and "Please Love Me" being the maybe the most excruciating. You don't need to understand what he's singing to know what he's feeling. "How Blue Can You Get?" Not much bluer than B.B. King did that one wild night in the Windy City.

#1 Single of the Year:
"Wooly Bully"
Sam the Sham & the Pharaohs

1965

#1 Album of the Year:
Mary Poppins (Soundtrack)
Various Artists

The Beatles
SHEA STADIUM—NEW YORK, NY
AUGUST 15

THE FAB FOUR SHEA-K UP NEW YORK

John Lennon, Paul McCartney, George Harrison and Ringo Starr landed together on American shores for the first time on February 7, 1964. Two days later they made their grand debut on *The Ed Sullivan Show*, performing "All My Loving," "She Loves You" and "I Want to Hold Your Hand" in front of an estimated audience of 73 million people. It was a seminal moment in pop culture history: the great cultural awakening of the Baby Boomer generation.

For the Beatles, the rush of fame was instant and overwhelming. This was a band that came up playing for hours and hours in some truly terrible clubs, hopped up on amphetamines in Hamburg, Germany, and their hometown of Liverpool. They were a tight live band and an even tighter brotherhood.

Once they began racking up No. 1 hit after No. 1 hit, legions of kids started turning out to *see* them with little regard to *hearing* them. They screamed, they cried and they threw jelly beans as the "Fab Four" attempted to run through a tight 30-minute set. They did what they could to make themselves heard over the cacophony, but their guitars, drums and voices were no match for the jet-engine torrent of noise blasting back at them from the audience.

The Beatles' first U.S. dates, beginning with a concert at the Washington Coliseum on February 11, 1964, were a little rough around the edges but were nevertheless well received. By the time they set off on a proper tour later that year, they had their act

down. The set list was short, fast and to the point. Get in, play fast, and get out as quick as you can.

They kept things relatively modest during that initial foray into the heart of America, hitting venues like Red Rocks Amphitheater in Colorado, the Cow Palace in San Francisco, and the Hollywood Bowl in Los Angeles. They're all fine venues, but they were woefully inadequate to meet the high demand for tickets. For their next tour through the States, the band would go bigger. Much bigger.

"Shea Stadium was an enormous place," Harrison remembered in *The Beatles Anthology*. "In those days, people were still playing the Astoria Cinema in Finsbury Park. This was the first time that one of those stadiums was used for a rock concert."

Shea Stadium opened for business in 1964. It was an immense, state-of-the-art facility with the capacity to seat around 55,000 people. Promoter Sid Bernstein pegged the home of the New York Mets as the perfect location for the Beatles to kick off their upcoming tour of North America. All he had to do was convince their manager, Brian Epstein.

Epstein heard him out but had legitimate concerns about the band's ability to pack the place. As

Men and women alike pull at their hair and clothes.

SET LIST

Twist and Shout

She's a Woman

I Feel Fine

Dizzy Miss Lizzy

Ticket to Ride

Everybody's Tryin' to Be My Baby

Can't Buy Me Love

Baby's in Black

Act Naturally

A Hard Day's Night

Help!

I'm Down

MUSICIANS

John Lennon: Vocals/Guitar/Piano

Paul McCartney: Vocals/Bass

George Harrison: Vocals/Guitar

Ringo Starr: Drums

popular as the Beatles were, no single act had ever filled that many seats for a concert before. At first, he brushed Bernstein off. It was only after the promoter agreed to sign a contract with a guaranteed sell-out clause that Epstein acquiesced. If the event didn't sell all its tickets, Bernstein would be on the hook to buy the leftovers at around $10 a pop, more than double the highest face-value price.

Some in the band were hesitant to go through with it, but for McCartney, the idea was a no-brainer. "It seemed like millions of people, but we were ready for it," he said. "They obviously felt we were popular enough to fill it." The fact that they were due to receive more than $300,000 for a single night's work helped quell many of their concerns.

After months of anticipation, August 15, 1965, finally arrives. Just as Bernstein promised, Shea Stadium is packed to the rafters with Beatles fanatics excited to see their heroes in person. A small bandstand is erected around second base, and the band's equipment is set up facing home plate. The air around the baseball stadium crackles with electricity.

Off-site, the Beatles load into a helicopter and are flown to the location of the World's Fair in Queens nearby. After landing, they pack into a Wells Fargo armored truck and drive into the venue's basement. "We got changed into our semi-military gear, beige outfits with high collars," McCartney remembered.

"Then, rather nervously, we ran out onto the field."

Ed Sullivan has the honor of introducing the band. Addressing the manic crowd a little after 9 pm, over an hour after the printed start time, the television host attempts to touch the event up with a bit of class. "Honored by their country, decorated by their Queen," he begins. "Here are the Beatles!"

Writing for the *New York Times*, Murray Schumach described the sound that greeted their arrival as "so staggering, so massive, so shrill and sustained that it quickly crossed the line from enthusiasm to hysteria and was soon in the area of the classic Greek meaning of the word pandemonium—the region of all demons."

Men and women alike pull at their hair and clothes. Some dash from their seats and race down the aisles to catch a better glimpse. Some make it out onto the baseball field where they are tackled by police and led away. Some lose consciousness altogether.

The Beatles can only look around in wonder as they gallop out of the dugout. If they feel overwhelmed, they do their best to hide it. They grin like mad and wave happily at the frothing masses.

"Once you go on stage and you know you've filled a place that size, it's magic," McCartney said. "Just walls of people. Half the fun was being involved in this gigantic event ourselves."

After finding their marks, the band launches straightaway into the Lennon-sung "Twist and Shout." The song, already a pretty unhinged rocker, has an extra edge on this occasion. The adrenaline that comes with performing in front of so many people has a physical impact on the group, but none more so than Lennon, who goes wild.

"I feel on that show that John cracked up," Ringo

said. "He went mad! Not mentally ill, but he just got crazy. He was playing the piano with his elbows and it was really strange."

"It was marvelous," Lennon said. "It was the biggest crowd we ever played to anywhere in the world. It was the biggest live show that anybody's ever done, they told us, and it was fantastic. The most exciting we've done . . . the amplification was tremendous."

To help boost the volume coming out of their 100-watt Vox amplifiers, the band's sound is fed into the stadium's PA. By the standards of the mid-1960s it is a state-of-the-art system, and for the first time in ages, they have the decibels to overpower their audience—even an audience as loud as this one. The prospect excites and pushes them as they rip into their standard-length 30-minute show.

Eschewing their early breakthrough hits, the band mostly sticks to songs from its most recent soundtrack albums, *A Hard Day's Night* and *Help!* The title tracks from both records are the second- and third-to-last numbers they play. It's a testament to how far they've come in the last year that, even while omitting record-breaking singles like "She Loves You" and "I Want to Hold Your Hand," the crowd doesn't seem to mind.

During the final song, "I'm Down," Lennon goes totally off the rails behind the keyboard, with Harrison seemingly goading him on from behind. "I was putting my foot on it, and George couldn't play for laughing," he said. "I was doing it for a laugh. The kids didn't know what I was doing."

When the song ends, the band, glazed over in sweat, raise their hands and instruments in triumph. They offer the fans a final salute and make for the exits. A white station wagon quickly escorts them out of the stadium just ahead of the manic flock of people who have jumped onto the field and are chasing them down.

HONORABLE MENTION
The Supremes at the Copacabana
New York, NY (July 29)

Other than the Beatles, no one had more No. 1 hits in 1965 than the Motown trio The Supremes. Diana Ross, Florence Ballard and Mary Wilson took the country by storm with songs like "Come See About Me," "Stop! In the Name of Love," "Back in My Arms Again" and "I Hear a Symphony." The group had crossed over on the radio but had yet to do so on the concert circuit. "Taking them to the Copacabana was a big plan of mine," Motown founder Berry Gordy explained. "We tried to book various supper clubs and they would not use The Supremes. The only way we could break into that circuit was to play the Copa." The trio pulled out all the stops that night at the prestigious New York night club, packing their set with a mix of their own hits, time-honored show tunes like "The Boy From Impanema" and a full medley of Sam Cooke classics. The response was more than they could have hoped for. The Copa crowd loved them, and the show helped paved the way for more soul music acts to grace its hallowed halls in the years to come. "This was the first time we ever signed autographs," Ross remembered in her memoir, *Secrets of a Sparrow*. "I stood there in amazement, holding a piece of paper that someone had asked me to sign, knowing for certain that life had changed."

#1 Single of the Year:
"Ballad of the Green Berets"
S/Sgt. Barry Sadler

#1 Album of the Year:
Whipped Cream & Other Delights
Herb Alpert's Tijuana Brass

Bob Dylan
FREE TRADE HALL—MANCHESTER, ENGLAND
MAY 17

JUDAS!

Few performers ask as much from their audience as Bob Dylan. Whether he's performing a set of Christian music, Sinatra standards, or reimagined classics, you never know what you're going to get from the man. He's not the kind of artist who lives to please the crowd. As an entertainer, he no doubt hopes that the audience will enjoy the show, but the onus is shifted to you, the concertgoer, to keep up with him.

Never was that more evident than in Dylan's most seminal years as a writer and performer: 1965 and 1966. This was the vaunted period when the former folkie "went electric" on albums like *Bringing It All Back Home*, *Highway 61 Revisited* and *Blonde on Blonde* and sent shockwaves through the critical cognoscenti and the culturally aware. Some embraced the change, heralding the amplified sound as the dawn of a new age. Others predicted that it marked the beginning of the end of Dylan's career.

Amongst his biggest acolytes, the electricity now coursing through his new music was a betrayal. They thought they knew who he was—a socially conscious, new-era Woodie Guthrie—and were loath to accept his new persona as a diffident rock star. Either he'd been a fraud then or he was one now.

Dylan premiered his new sound backed by Al Kooper and Mike Bloomfield at the Newport Folk Festival on July 25, 1965, where he played songs like "Maggie's Farm" and "Like a Rolling Stone" from his just released masterpiece *Highway 61 Revisited*. Some in the audience watched passively. Some cheered. Many outright booed him. A mostly apocryphal legend has it that folk singer Pete Seeger almost took an axe to the wires amplifying Dylan's sound on stage.

Outwardly Dylan couldn't care less. "Fuck them… if they think they can keep electricity out of here," he said to event organizer Alan Lomax. In the months to come, Dylan doubled down on that proclamation, taking his new sound to audiences around the U.S., Australia and Europe in the spring of 1966.

To help bring his newer material to life, the singer enlisted a Canadian group named the Hawks and re-christened them The Band. Years later, after emerging from behind Dylan's outsized shadow, The Band would make its own mark on the sound and shape of rock 'n' roll with albums like *Music From Big Pink* and *The Last Waltz*. For now, they remained the anonymous purveyors of his new amplified message.

In the months that followed Dylan's stand at Newport, a mob mentality broke out amidst the crowds that turned out to see him. Now the cool thing to do was to show up to one of his concerts and boo each time he strapped on a Fender Stratocaster. For Dylan, it was one long, masochistic exercise.

The greatest artists don't *need* the public to validate their work, but it sure feels good when people appreciate what you put out into the world. As de-

SET LIST

She Belongs to Me

4th Time Around

Visions of Johanna

It's All Over Now, Baby Blue

Desolation Row

Just Like a Woman

Mr. Tambourine Man

Tell Me, Momma

I Don't Believe You (She Acts Like We Never Have Met)

Baby, Let Me Follow You Down

Just Like Tom Thumb's Blues

Leopard-Skin Pill-Box-Hat

One Too Many Mornings

Ballad of a Thin Man

Like a Rolling Stone

MUSICIANS

Bob Dylan: Vocals/Guitar/Piano/Harmonica

Robbie Robertson: Guitar

Rick Danko: Bass

Richard Manuel: Piano

Garth Hudson: Organ

Mickey Jones: Drums

fiant as he appeared in the press and on stage, the boos wounded Dylan, yet he couldn't bring himself to change course. He had his muse, and he was prepared to follow it to the ends of the earth, even if it meant losing a large portion his fan base.

The ordeal came to a head at the Manchester Free Trade Hall in the U.K. on May 17, 1966. Director D.A. Pennebaker, the documentarian behind *Don't Look Back*, was in the house capturing the performance for his next Dylan-centric film. If he and the singer were hoping for a positive response, they were in for a rude awakening.

The opening portion of the show goes off without a hitch. Dylan enters the dimly lit, cavernous space clad in a sharp, gray jacket, carrying an acoustic guitar and with a harmonica hovering inches from his mouth. The audience applauds gleefully as he runs through gentler fare like "Just Like a Woman," "Visions of Johanna" and the tender "It's All Over Now, Baby Blue." Even the more daring 11-plus-minute opus "Desolation Row" receives a boisterous ovation.

This is their hero, gamely playing to their expectations. They are willing to follow him through more avant-garde forms, so long as he's willing to deliver them within a sonically acceptable framework. The

acoustic guitar is a comfort blanket that Dylan wraps his audience in as he weaves together his sometimes profound, sometimes incongruous strings of words and chord changes. Now he's about to rip it away.

After concluding "Mr. Tambourine Man," Dylan exits the stage. When he returns it's with the dreaded Stratocaster dangling from his chest and with The Band following close behind. The mood in the Hall shifts. Gone is the love between performer and fan. Instead, there's mostly apathy on his end and a growing malevolence on theirs.

Dylan launches into the song "Tell Me, Momma." For the crowd, not only does it carry the strike of being electrified, it's also a song that no one's heard before. "Tell Me, Momma" was played on the road almost exclusively during this period of Dylan's career. It was officially released over thirty years later, when the recording of this show came out in 1998 as part of his officially sanctioned *Bootleg Series*.

Two songs later, during "Baby, Let Me Follow You Down," rebellion foments in the aisles. The hecklers make their presence known, sporadically at first, but with greater fervor as the evening progresses. Dylan does his best to drown them out with sound, while also limiting the time between numbers when their voices can be heard. It's an effective tactic but a losing strategy.

By the time he reaches "Leopard-Skin Pill-Box Hat," the only song in the set from his most recent album, *Blonde on Blonde*, it's clear that he's fighting an uphill battle. The crowd launches into a syncopated handclap meant to disrupt the rhythm of the song. One dissident shouts out a request for a "protest song." Dylan ignores him and soldiers on.

For the penultimate number, Dylan seats himself

behind a piano and plays the acerbic "Ballad of a Thin Man." His voice is filled with bile as he upends "Mr. Jones" and, maybe by proxy, the audience for not recognizing what's happening in front of their very eyes and ears. All apathy has been burned away. Dylan is a vessel brimming with pure, intoxicating fury.

Gone is the love between performer and fan. Instead, there's mostly apathy on his end and a growing malevolence on theirs.

When the song ends, the boo-birds come out in full flight. Then, out of the din, a single voice: "Judas!" The audience laughs at the remark and wildly applauds its sentiment.

With that utterance, Dylan reaches his breaking point. In contrast with the cool persona he'd maintained at Newport and throughout most of this tour, the mask finally slips. "I don't believe you," he snarls. "You're a liar!" He turns to The Band and orders them to "Play it fucking loud!" They respond by launching into a tremendously unhinged, rollicking version of "Like a Rolling Stone."

For the next eight minutes Dylan makes his case in stunning, antagonistic fashion. This is the future, and you can either get with it or be lost to history. "How does it feel / To be on your own?" When the songs ends, he makes a quick turn for the exit. A mixture of applause and jeering follow him on the way out.

Two months later, while riding around his hometown of Woodstock, New York, the singer laid down his Triumph T100 motorcycle in a mysterious accident. To this day, the extent of the injuries from the crash remain unclear, but Dylan used the accident as an excuse to disappear for a while. All tours were canceled, and any recording plans were put on hold.

The revolution would continue, but without its most prominent voice guiding the way.

For over 30 years, the identity of the man who shouted "Judas!" remained lost to history. When he finally broke his silence decades later, Keith Butler revealed just what was going through his mind before the word escaped his lips. "We were just really disappointed," he told MTV. "That wasn't the Bob Dylan we'd been used to listening to. The Dylan we were used to was *The Freewheelin' Bob Dylan.*"

"Can you imagine what it's like as a 20-year-old kid?" Butler asked. "You were just crushed. I was totally embarrassed when he shouted back. I was there with another guy, and that's when we decided to leave."

Even four decades later, the insult continued to burn Dylan, as he told *Rolling Stone*. "If you think you've been called a bad name, try to work your way out from under that," he said. "And for what? For playing an electric guitar? As if that is in some kind of way equitable to betraying our Lord and delivering Him up to be crucified. All those evil motherfuckers can rot in hell."

HONORABLE MENTION

The Rolling Stones, The Yardbirds and Ike &
Tina Turner at the Royal Albert Hall
London, England (September 23)

On September 23, 1966, the Rolling Stones kicked off their only tour of England that year in the fabulous confines of the Royal Albert Hall in London. Before they hit the stage, the ravenous audience was treated to two amazing sets of music. The first came courtesy of the dynamic rhythm and blues duo Ike & Tina Turner, who were riding high off their most recent record, *River Deep – Mountain High*. The second came from a psychedelic blues outfit named the Yardbirds. This gig marked one of only a few occasions that the group boasted a lineup that included future Led Zeppelin founder Jimmy Page and the virtuosic Jeff Beck on dual lead guitar. Though both acts received warm receptions, all bets were off once the Stones appeared. They barely got through their first song "Paint It Black," when their fans went completely out of their heads and rushed the stage. A small riot was eventually put down and the band continued with the show. They spent the next 30 minutes hitting the screaming crowd with the best that they had, hits like "Under My Thumb" and "Get Off of My Cloud" and a cover of Buddy Holly's "Not Fade Away." By the time they got to the last number, "(I Can't Get No) Satisfaction," delirium took hold once again and the Stones had to make a run for it to avoid getting ripped apart by the lust-filled audience.

1967

#1 Album of the Year:
More of the Monkees
The Monkees

Monterey Pop Festival (Jimi Hendrix, The Who, Buffalo Springfield, Ravi Shankar, The Mamas & The Papas and Big Brother and the Holding Company)

MONTEREY COUNTY FAIRGROUNDS—MONTEREY, CA

JUNE 18

LET ME STAND NEXT TO YOUR FIRE

The Monterey Pop Festival in Northern California in 1967 was the perfect hippie-commune-meets-rock-show experience. Sure, Woodstock had the numbers, and the benefit of a Warner Bros.–backed feature film to propagate its outsized legend, but Monterey had better facilities, a better crowd, better vibes, better drugs and better performances. It all started and ended with Jimi Hendrix.

A year before hitting the stage for his career-making gig in Northern California, Hendrix was a veritable nobody playing small clubs around New York City, that is, when he wasn't out on tour backing up the likes of the Isley Brothers and Little Richard. It wasn't until Chas Chandler, bassist for the British Invasion band the Animals, caught him at a gig at the Café Wha in Greenwich Village in 1966 and took him to England that Hendrix began to make a name for himself.

The guitarist hit the ground running in London. After putting together his band The Jimi Hendrix Experience, he hit the road, playing shows on an almost nightly basis. His first album, *Are You Experienced*, dropped on May 12, 1967, and hit No. 2 on the charts in the U.K. In only ten months he'd turned himself into a bona fide star in Europe. Now it was time to wow the people back home. Luckily there was an event just over the horizon that could serve as his breakthrough.

The Monterey Pop Festival was the brainchild of John Phillips of The Mamas & The Papas, record producer Lou Adler and the Beatles publicist Derek Taylor in 1967. At a party, Adler recalled, "Paul McCartney, John and Michelle Phillips, [Mama Cass Elliott] and I were discussing . . . the general perception of rock 'n' roll, and that, while jazz was considered an art form, rock 'n' roll was continually viewed as a fad."

Hoping to change that perception, the group came up with the idea of hosting a multiday festival to highlight the best that the genre had to offer. Adler hunted down investors and opened an office on the Sunset Strip to organize the festival.

"Everyone agreed that the lineup of acts would represent all genres of the immediate past, present and future of contemporary music," Adler said. "For the most part, everyone jumped on pretty quickly, especially the L.A. groups like the Byrds and Buffalo Springfield."

It was McCartney, along with the Rolling Stones' manager, Andrew Loog Oldham, who suggested adding Hendrix to the lineup. The Beatle was particularly taken by the frenzied guitar player, going so far as to write a review of the song "Purple Haze" for the British publication *Melody Maker*, where he called the guitarist, "Fingers Hendrix; an absolute ace on the guitar." With a cosign like that, who could say no?

After a short stay in New York, Hendrix and his entourage hitched a flight to San Francisco, and on Friday, June 16, the first day of the festival, made it

SET LIST

Killing Floor
Foxy Lady
Like a Rolling Stone
Rock Me Baby
Hey Joe
Can You See Me
The Wind Cries Mary
Purple Haze
Wild Thing

MUSICIANS

Jimi Hendrix: Guitar/Vocals
Mitch Mitchell: Drums
Noel Redding: Bass

to the Monterey County Fairgrounds. For the next several days the guitarist hung around the backstage area, dropping acid and mingling with the rock star elite. Meanwhile the crowd out in the field was being treated to an incredible array of performances from artists like Janis Joplin, Buffalo Springfield and Otis Redding.

When the final night arrived, Hendrix got into a dispute with The Who. Neither act wanted to follow the other. Both were aware of the explosive—in The Who's case, sometimes literally explosive—nature of their acts, and each balked at the prospect of having to top the previous set.

"[I was] worried that if Jimi went on before us he might smash his guitar, or set it on fire, or pull off some other stunt that would leave our band looking pathetic," The Who guitarist Pete Townshend wrote in his autobiography. "We didn't even have our Sound City and Marshall stacks because our managers had persuaded us to travel light and cheap. Jimi had imported his, and I knew his sound would be superior."

The matter was settled with a coin toss. Hendrix lost. The Who would go on first, and they made it their mission to do him no favors. The British band blasted through their set with a frenzied energy, ripping through songs like "Summertime Blues" and "A Quick One, While He's Away" before closing with the anthemic "My Generation" and bashing their instruments into kindling. The gauntlet had been thrown down.

Another performer might have been cowed by a spectacle like that, but the stakes were far higher

than just showing up The Who. America itself was on the line. Jimi wasn't about to back down. "For Hendrix, it was a bit strange coming back," his bassist, Noel Redding, said. "He left as an R&B cover guy, and he was coming back with two white guys in a rock band." He had everything to prove, and he knew exactly how to do it.

Brian Jones, guitarist of the Rolling Stones, is given the task of introducing Hendrix to a crowd that is only vaguely aware of his reputation.

"I'd like to introduce you to a very good friend and a fellow countryman of yours," Jones says. "A brilliant performer, the most exciting guitarist I've ever heard: The Jimi Hendrix Experience!"

Hendrix emerges from out of the shadows looking every bit the unpredictable, wild rock star. His hair is puffed up into a wide afro. His tight pants are fire engine red. Up top he's got on a yellow blouse with ruffles running up the middle, around which is cinched a black velvet military vest. You don't have to hear a single note to know that this cat is from a different galaxy altogether.

Over the weekend, Hendrix put to use his skills as a painter to transform his white Stratocaster guitar into a psychedelic frenzy of red flowers and green swirls. The instrument matches the demeanor of the artist wielding it. He picks it up and launches into the first ravaged chords of the immortal blues track "Killing Floor." The intense symbiosis between man and machine is incredible. He makes even the most complex passages seem effortless. The way he carelessly chucks out chords, strings together solos and tosses off riffs is obscene.

With every new song, the audience grows increasingly in awe of Hendrix's abilities and antics. He plays the guitar between his legs. He plays it behind his back. He plays it with his teeth. They've never seen anything like it before. Some are shocked. Others appalled. Most are simply blown away.

Filmmaker D.A. Pennebaker is on the scene, having been tasked with capturing the festival on film, but even he is unprepared for Hendrix. "I was knocked out. I thought, 'This is incredible,'" he told me. "We had a little light on the side of the stage that [folk singer Bob] Neuwirth was in charge of and whenever the red bulb was on that was the song that we would record. We tried to save film as much as possible and there were so many people coming into the concert that we figured we'd shoot one song for each band and then when Hendrix came on . . . we just turned that light on and never turned it off."

"Foxy Lady" gives way to a cover of Bob Dylan's "Like a Rolling Stone." Then comes his first single, "Hey Joe," followed by "Can You See Me" and "The Wind Cries Mary." That last song is the only down moment of the entire show because by this point, Hendrix has knocked his guitar almost completely out of tune with his incendiary soloing.

After a brief tune-up, Hendrix digs into his biggest hit overseas, "Purple Haze." He refuses to give them the song straight, instead transforming it into a wall of grating feedback and warp-speed guitar fills. No one knows what to make of what is going on in front of them, but the best is yet to come.

After "Purple Haze," Hendrix leans into the microphone and addresses the crowd. "I'm going to sacrifice something here that I really love," he says. "Don't think I'm silly doing this, because I don't think I'm losing my mind. This is the only way I could do it."

Stepping back, he slices into the first nasty chords of the Troggs' classic "Wild Thing." He riffs on the garage rock masterpiece for a bit, then turns back toward his stack of amplifiers and grinds his instrument against it in a way that doesn't just suggest sex, it screams it. In the next instant, he drops down to his knees and straddles his Strat, making love to it, while rapidly pulling on the whammy bar. Out in the crowd, hands cover gaping mouths and eyes.

Hendrix dismounts his guitar and darts toward the back of the stage. When he returns, he's carrying a bottle of Ronson lighter fluid. Kneeling once again, he sprays the liquid all over the body of the Stratocaster, bends down to kiss the instrument's neck, strikes a match and drops it.

He bends down to kiss the instrument's neck, strikes a match and drops it.

The flames erupt a foot off the instrument. Hendrix sits there on his knees, coaxing them higher and higher with his twiddling fingers. Grabbing the lighter fluid, he sprays on another coat and watches as his beloved guitar turns into a charred black slab. Suddenly, he leaps to his feet, and with the instrument still engulfed in flames, grabs it by the neck and starts bashing it to the ground repeatedly. With a final savage blow, the body snaps away and falls to the ground. Broken and battered, it continues to emit a ghostly wail.

Hendrix tosses the neck out into the front row along with shards from the body. Mitch Mitchell's drumsticks go sailing into the air shortly thereafter. Just like that, the show's over. Hendrix doesn't even stick around to hear the applause. He simply turns and walks off, a ghostly wail of feedback trailing behind him.

After that singular performance in Monterey, California, Jimi Hendrix didn't just become one of the biggest rock stars on the planet. He laid down a challenge to all the other would-be rockers out there. It wasn't going to cut it anymore just to write good songs and play your instrument well. If you wanted to be a *real* rock star, you had to go further. You had to be daring. You had to be shocking. "Have you ever been experienced?"

HONORABLE MENTION

Aretha Franklin at the Regal Theater
Chicago, IL (October 19)

1967 was the defining year in the life of Detroit soul singer Aretha Franklin. In January, she ditched her longtime label, Columbia, and signed a new deal with Ahmet Ertegun's Atlantic Records. It was the best decision she ever made. Over the next 12 months she experienced a breakthrough the likes of which have hardly been duplicated since. Two of her albums, *I Never Loved a Man the Way I Love You* and *Aretha Arrives* charted in the Top 5 in *Billboard*. Four of her singles went No. 1, including her signature song, "Respect." The Carole King–penned "(You Make Me Feel Like) A Natural Woman" was only blocked from the top spot by James Brown's "Cold Sweat." In October, Aretha and her supernatural voice arrived at the Regal Theater for a three-night residency. She'd performed in the Southside venue numerous times, but this evening was a special night. A local disc jockey named Pervis Spann was on hand with an actual crown, ready to bestow upon her the title "Queen of Soul," a moniker she carried with distinction and grace for the next five decades. "I was floored," she told the *Chicago Tribune*. "It was the last thing I expected when he walked out with that crown and actually put it on my head."

#1 Single of the Year:
"Hey Jude"
The Beatles

1968

#1 Album of the Year:
Are You Experienced
Jimi Hendrix

Cream
THE ROYAL ALBERT HALL—LONDON, ENGLAND
NOVEMBER 26

CREAM'S FAREWELL

Some bands have the stamina and drive to hold it together for decades, carving out a nice career playing the same hits, in front of the same audiences, tour in and tour out. Others blaze hot for a moment and burn out the next. Such was the case of the late-'60s British blues rock supergroup Cream.

Cream was formed in 1966 out of the ashes of the popular London-based blues collectives John Mayall's Bluesbreakers and the Graham Bond Organization. Eric Clapton, Jack Bruce and Ginger Baker chose the name Cream because they considered themselves the cream of the musical crop around England. Egotistical? Sure, but to an extent, valid. When you have swarms of people spray-painting "Clapton is God" all around your backyard, it'd be difficult not to get at least bigheaded.

Though they weren't around for long, Cream made the most of their time together. They released three albums—*Fresh Cream* (1966), *Disraeli Gears* (1967) and *Wheels of Fire* (1968)—and toured constantly. Their unique blend of heavy blues riffs, jazz-inspired drumming and psychedelic wordplay helped create an entirely new sound and dynamic that scores of other bands were quick to adopt. They also helped set the template for the traditional rock 'n' roll power trio.

Both tastemakers in the press and the burgeoning scene of young rock fans adored the group and helped make them one of the most sought-after live entities on the planet. "Touring America is what made Cream as famous as we became," Clapton pointed out in his autobiography. "U.S. audiences really couldn't get enough of us."

The band didn't adhere to any kind of conventional wisdom when it came to playing live. Depending upon the night, songs that were laid down as simple, two-and-a-half–minute blues standards, like "Spoonful," might be stretched out to incredible 15-minute odysseys. The thrill of experiencing that kind of musical mastery and spontaneity led to packed houses nearly everywhere they went.

By 1968, however, Cream was on the verge of an acrimonious end. The same tensions that had driven Baker and Bruce to look for a way out of the Graham Bond Organization had flared up again. In addition, the very thing that helped propel them to the top of the musical hierarchy contributed to their downfall. Clapton explained, "When you are playing night after night on a punishing schedule, often not because you want to, but because you are contractually obligated to, it is only too easy to forget the ideals that brought you together . . . I began to be quite ashamed of being in Cream, because I thought it was a con."

By the fall, they were ready to call it a day. It wouldn't be as easy as going their separate ways, however. They were still on the hook for two more albums and a final tour of America. The three members dutifully fulfilled their responsibilities and tried to get

SET LIST

White Room
Politician
I'm So Glad
Sitting on Top of the World
Crossroads
Toad
Spoonful
Sunshine of Your Love
Steppin' Out

MUSICIANS

Eric Clapton: Guitar/Vocals
Jack Bruce: Bass/Vocals
Ginger Baker: Drums

along as best they could while counting down the days until they could be rid of each other's company.

For their final act, Cream booked a pair of performances at the storied Royal Albert Hall in London. The concerts became the hottest ticket on the planet. The audience was a diverse mix of old fans, the fashion-forward, industry elites and bona fide superstars. It was a show to be *seen at* as much as it was a musical event to witness. The pressure was on to deliver the goods. Cream was uniquely suited to do just that.

After opening sets from the progressive rock band Yes and the Irish blues outfit Taste, Cream is introduced by the popular radio DJ John Peel. They hit the stage in front of a raucous audience and almost immediately launch into the single "White Room." Outside, the scene is pandemonium as ticketless fans pack in tightly against the exterior walls of the domed theater, straining to hear the music within.

The massive response gives the band pause, if only a slight one, about breaking up. "We looked at each other and thought, 'Are we doing the right thing?'" Bruce recalled. "There was a feeling of regret, but nobody was able to step forward and say, 'Oh, let's not do this.'"

The band's first show earlier in the evening had gone fine, but everyone was annoyed that it was cut short so that they could reorganize for the later performance. With nothing to hinder their actions now, the band takes their English worshippers on the ride of a lifetime, pouring every bit of itself into the music.

The sound of both Clapton and Bruce "oohing" out the opening number's wordless intro fills the Hall while Baker pounds out a jaunty martial rhythm behind. The guitarist looks spectacular in his bright orange coat with a Gibson Firebird slung low on his hip. Clapton's face is obscured by a mop of hair as he stares down at his foot, which is rocking back and forth on a wah pedal placed on the ground. In back, Baker cuts his standard, frightening figure while bashing away on his collection of snares and toms. Standing in stark juxtaposition to Clapton's cool aura is Bruce, who seems determined to blow apart the first few rows of fans with his deep, nasal-y voice.

After "White Room," the band shifts into "Politician," a dark track taken from their third album, *Wheels of Fire*. From there they dig deep into a trio of blues covers, "I'm So Glad" by Skip James, "Sitting on Top of the World" by the Mississippi Sheiks and, most thrilling of all, "Crossroads" by Robert Johnson.

Johnson occupies a special place in Clapton's heart. "Crossroads" is one of the few moments where he takes over on lead vocals, becoming the undeniable focal point of the action, rather than the implied one. Clapton's interpretation of the song is far more exhilarating and exciting than the one he delivered on *Wheels of Fire*. Tonight, he sounds like a man unhinged, playing faster and far more furiously than he ever did in the recording studio.

The band is cooking now and ready to take on its dual, over-ten-minutes-long jams for "Toad" and "Spoonful." The former serves as a showcase for Baker to let loose with all the frenetic jazz licks and tom rolls that make him one of the most formidable percussionists in the world. The latter comes off as more of a shootout, with each member of Cream attempting to outshine the others.

The main set ends with the band's biggest and most recognizable hit, "Sunshine of Your Love."

"What if we do 'Sunshine'?" Clapton rhetorically asks. "Does that satisfy anyone?" The crowd roars in the affirmative, and so he chucks out the song's instantly recognizable main riff.

The audience begs for another encore, but there's no going back.

The band tears into "Sunshine of Your Love," with an intensity that probably only comes from the knowledge that it might be your last time performing it together. The 4,500 people in the audience seem fully aware that they are witnessing something special and refuse to wait for the song's end to shower the threesome with overwhelming applause.

When it's over, Cream departs the stage, only to reemerge minutes later to find the audience still screaming and stomping their feet. They reward their enthusiasm with an encore rendition of "Steppin' Out," after which they take their final bow and turn to leave for the last time. Scores of people near the front row rush forward toward the lip of the stage to bombard the three men with confetti. The audience begs for another encore, but there's no going back.

After the show the mood in the dressing room is decidedly somber. "My overwhelming emotion . . . was that we had done the right thing," Clapton said. "At the end of the second show there were no parties, no speeches. We just went our separate ways."

HONORABLE MENTION
Johnny Cash at Folsom State Prison
Folsom, CA (January 13)

Of all the shows included in this book, this is the only one that you may have been glad to have skipped. Johnny Cash is a great performer, but is it worth your freedom to see the man live? Most would say no, but then again, for a performance like the one he gave at the State Prison in Folsom, California, you might at least pause to consider it. At the beginning of 1968, Cash arrived at the maximum-security penitentiary, where he delivered two live sets for the inmates housed there, both of which were recorded for the multiplatinum album *At Folsom Prison*. Cash opened each set with his signature song "Folsom Prison Blues," then regaled the inmates with an eclectic mix of blues, folk and country standards. He didn't preach to them; he didn't talk down to them either. He treated them as people, and they brought out his best side. Near the end, he surprised everyone with a rendition of a song penned by one of the prisoners, Glen Sherely, titled "Greystone Chapel." It was a touching moment, a humanizing one. It showed Johnny's ability to abandon the cloak of superstardom and reach out to the common man. He understood their plight, and they loved him for it.

#1 Single of the Year:
"Sugar Sugar"
The Archies

1969

#1 Album of the Year:
In-A-Gadda-Da-Vida
Iron Butterfly

Woodstock (Jimi Hendrix, Crosby, Stills, Nash & Young, Santana, Richie Havens, Creedence Clearwater Revival, Sly and the Family Stone, Joe Cocker, et al.)
MAX YASGUR'S FARM—BETHEL, NY
AUGUST 15-17

THREE DAYS OF PEACE & MUSIC

The Woodstock Music and Arts Festival remains the definitive, crowning event of the 1960s counterculture movement. Even though a robust crowd of 500,000 people showed up for the four-day event, it seems like half of the early baby boomer population claims that they were there. My father, who was only thirteen years old at the time, swore to his dying day that he was one of the kids that tore down the fence to make it a free event.

I thought he was full of it. But when we made the trek up to Bethel, New York, one summer and walked through that field, the authoritative way in which he pointed things out nearly convinced me that he had seen Joe Cocker, The Who and Jimi Hendrix that fateful August weekend in 1969. Perhaps it was the effect of watching the accompanying film—which hit theaters the following year—that filled his mind with such detailed memories. I just let him have it.

You could fill an entire library with all the books, documentaries and recordings related to Woodstock. If you want to go deep on the subject, check out festival promoter Michael Lang's autobiography, *The Road to Woodstock*, along with *Barefoot in Babylon* by Bob Spitz and *Prisoner of Woodstock* by Dallas Taylor, the drummer for Crosby, Stills, Nash & Young. You should also set aside a day to watch the extended director's cut of *Woodstock: Three Days of Peace & Music*.

I have no intention of rehashing how the festival came together and its impact in these pages. It's been done to *death* from every angle imaginable. I prefer to focus on the actual performances, ranking the Top 10 sets across all four days.

Some of the biggest names that hit the stage at Woodstock didn't make the cut here for one reason or another. It could've been because of stage fright (Janis Joplin, the Jefferson Airplane) or because they blew their minds out with psychedelics and crapped the bed (the Grateful Dead). The performances included below are the ones you couldn't possibly have forgotten, no matter how much brown acid you'd ingested. They're ranked here in descending order, saving the best for last.

10. CANNED HEAT
Saturday: 7:30 pm

Canned Heat was a roots-based rock band from Los Angeles with four modest hit albums to their name. Having performed at the Monterey Pop Festival a couple of years earlier, they thought they knew what they were in for with Woodstock. Just like everyone else who made it out to Max Yasgur's Farm, they were blown away by the size and scope of what greeted them.

Canned Heat was gifted the most conducive set time for their unique brand of country-tinged blues rock music. Playing around sunset on the second day, the five musicians wove together an easy listening playlist that melded perfectly with the cooling summer air and darkening blue sky. Guitarist Harvey Mandel appeared completely at ease while soloing over songs like "Too Many Drivers at the Wheel" and "On the Road Again."

When you think about Canned Heat at Woodstock, you can't help but recall the song "Going Up the Country," which served as the unofficial theme for the documentary film about the festival that hit theaters six months later. The song's bright and cheery vibe matched the feeling that the filmmakers hoped to get across. For the people on the ground, it served as the perfect mood-setter for an epic night of transcendent music to come.

I'm Her Man
Going Up the Country
A Change Is Gonna Come/Leaving This Town
Too Many Drivers at the Wheel
I Know My Baby
Woodstock Boogie
On the Road Again

9. Creedence Clearwater Revival
Sunday: 12:30 am

1969 was a watershed year for Creedence Clearwater Revival. In an unparalleled feat, the California rockers released three timeless albums that year: *Bayou Country*, *Green River* and *Willy and the Poor Boys*. Each one would represent a high point in any rock band's catalog, but it's *Green River*, put out two weeks before Woodstock, that takes the cake. Filled out by songs like "Bad Moon Rising," "Lodi" and the title track, it's the one that best showcases the band's electrifying swampy, blues sound.

The festival organizers were lucky to have an act on the bill that was creatively peaking the way that CCR was at that moment. The only problem was that by the time they hit the stage, most of the audi-

ence had been lulled to sleep by the Grateful Dead's haphazard, stop-and-start set. "I walked up to the mic and said something to the effect of, 'Well, we're havin' a great time up here. Hope you're havin' fun out there!' No response. Dead audience," lead singer John Fogerty remembered in his memoir, *Fortunate Son*.

"Finally, some guy a quarter-mile away in the distant night flicked his lighter, and I heard him say ever so faintly, 'Don't worry about it, John! We're with ya!' So I played the rest of the set for that one guy." As CCR blasted through eleven of their heaviest, most dynamic hits, the audience was roused from its slumber. By the time the final notes of "Susie Q" died away and the band bid them goodnight, the sleeping bags were gone and the audience was back on its feet cheering like mad.

Born on the Bayou
Green River
Ninety-Nine and a Half (Won't Do)
Commotion
Bootleg
Bad Moon Rising
Proud Mary
I Put a Spell on You
Night Time is the Right Time
Keep on Chooglin'
Susie Q

8. Mountain
Saturday: 9:00 pm

The guitar was the weapon of choice for most of the artists at Woodstock, but few wielded it with as much passion or intensity as Leslie West. With his trusted tobacco burst Les Paul Jr. in his meaty hands, West forced the large crowd to notice both him and his band. The six full stacks of 50 watt Sunn amplifiers didn't hurt either. "It was just the biggest, fullest sound, because who could be loud outdoors?" West asked. "You know the sound just goes. But this almost landed. This almost was that loud that I thought, 'Wow! The man upstairs is talking!'"

The only thing that could hope to match the volume and intensity of West's guitar playing was his tremendous voice. His mouth was so large and the sound blasting out of it so forceful that it seemed like the microphone in front of his face was just a prop. Taking it all in was like enduring a category four hurricane.

Mountain made the most of their 60 minutes. When they reached the apocalyptic set-ender "Southbound Train," jaws were left slackened and eardrums ached. You never would have guessed that it was only their third live gig ever.

Blood of the Sun
Stormy Monday
Theme for an Imaginary Western
Long Red
For Yasgur's Farm
Beside the Sea
Waiting to Take You Away
Dreams of Milk and Honey
Blind Man
Dirty Shoes Blues
Southbound Train

7. JOE COCKER
Sunday: 2:00 pm

Joe Cocker's appearance at Woodstock didn't start off as well as he would have liked. "It took about half the set just to get through to everybody, to that kind of consciousness," the gravel-throated British singer told *The Guardian* years later. "You're in a sea of humanity and people aren't necessarily looking to entertain you."

It wasn't for lack of effort that the singer escaped notice at the opening of his set. Cocker raged, kicked and cavorted with terrifying fury, forcing those down below to pay attention. By the sixth song he'd gotten them, and there was no going back. "We did 'Let's Go

Get Stoned' by Ray Charles, which kind of turned everybody around a bit, and we came off looking pretty good that day."

Looking good is an understatement. Cocker and his band were electrifying. Outside of Jimi Hendrix and Sly Stone, no one at the festival came anywhere near as close to cutting as engrossing a figure onstage. His natural gift for singing was undeniable, and when combined with his signature array of spastic movements, bulging eyes and generally crazed demeanor, you simply couldn't tear your eyes off him. Cocker's cover of the Beatles' "With a Little Help from My Friends" ranks as one of the most intense exhibitions of guttural, raw singing as you're ever likely to see or hear again.

Dear Landlord
Something Comin' On
Do I Still Figure in Your Life
Feelin' Alright
Just Like a Woman
Let's Go Get Stoned
I Don't Need a Doctor
I Shall Be Released
Hitchcock Railway
Something to Say
With a Little Help From My Friends

6. RICHIE HAVENS
Friday: 5:00 pm

No one at Woodstock overcame greater odds than Greenwich Village folkie Richie Havens, the man tasked with opening the entire festival. "He was the first act, simply because he and his band were there and ready," organizer Michael Lang explained in his book *The Road to Woodstock*. Though he was reluctant to go on, Havens made the most of his time, performing a tried and true collection of folk classics and Beatles covers.

When he came off the stage, Havens was euphoric. Then they dropped a bomb on him: He had to go on again. The next act wasn't ready and the organizers needed him to kill time. They pleaded until Havens caved, turned around, and picked up his guitar again. He played, and played, and played some more. Then he ran out of songs, and that's when inspiration struck.

"I start strumming my guitar and the word freedom comes out of my mouth as 'FREE-dom, FREE-dom' with a rhythm of its own," he remembered in Lang's book. "I don't know where this is going, but it feels right and somehow I find myself blending it into an old song—'Sometimes I Feel Like a Motherless Child'—a great spiritual my grandmother used to sing to me as a hymn when I was growing up in Brooklyn."

It was one of the defining moments of the weekend, delivered completely off the cuff. One word, over and over: Freedom. Everyone knew what it meant, and everyone felt it in the core of their soul.

The Minstrel from Gault
From the Prison/Get Together
I'm a Stranger Here
High Flying Bird
I Can't Make It Anymore
With a Little Help from My Friends
Handsome Johnny
Strawberry Fields Forever/Hey Jude
Freedom (Motherless Child)

5. Crosby, Stills, Nash & Young
Monday: 3:00 am

Crosby, Stills, Nash & Young put together one of the best sets of music from that entire weekend. It's a feat made even more impressive once you realize that Woodstock was only the second time that they had performed live together. Their first show took place two days earlier in Chicago, in what was more of a glorified rehearsal than a concert. They had released their debut album, *Crosby, Stills & Nash*, three months earlier, and Canadian singer-songwriter Neil Young had only just been brought into the fold.

That said, each member of the group was a seasoned pro and no stranger to big crowds. David Crosby had been in the Byrds. Graham Nash spent years in the Hollies. Both Stephen Stills and Young broke out as the chief songwriters of Buffalo Springfield. Though Woodstock was bigger than anything they'd done before, they were still far more prepared than most artists on the bill.

CSN opened the show sans Y, who was waiting in the wings while his counterparts sat in chairs with acoustic guitars and performed tracks from their debut. Midway through, they swapped out for electric guitars. With Young onstage and the cameras hidden—the mercurial singer didn't want to be filmed—they tore into tremendous renditions of "Wooden Ships," "Long Time Gone" and "Sea of Madness."

"I thought we sounded fabulous," Nash wrote in his memoir, *Wild Tales*. "I was getting higher and higher on that stage. The energy was fierce . . . we killed 'em."

Suite: Judy Blue Eyes
Blackbird
Helplessly Hoping
Guinnevere
Marrakesh Express
4 + 20
Mr. Soul
Wonderin'
You Don't Have to Cry
Pre-Road Downs
Long Time Gone
Bluebird
Sea of Madness
Wooden Ships
Find the Cost of Freedom
49 Bye Byes

4. The Who
Sunday: 5:00 am

Just three months after unveiling its massive,

double-LP rock opera, *Tommy*, The Who was ready to bring it to life in front of the masses at Woodstock. The English group was the perfect example of what a rock band should look like and how it should sound—namely, loud. Guitarist Pete Townshend was the visceral intellectual. Bassist John Entwistle, the quiet thunder. Drummer Keith Moon, the deranged wild man. And lead singer Roger Daltrey, the golden-throated heartthrob.

While their music was as grandiose and bombastic as you could hope for—especially the *Tommy* closer "We're Not Gonna Take It"—the most memorable moment of their set came when Yippie founder and social activist Abbie Hoffman tried to storm the stage and speak out about White Panther party member John Sinclair, who had been sentenced to 10 years in prison for possession of marijuana.

"I think this is a pile of shit while John Sinclair rots in prison," Hoffman began. Before he could finish his screed, Townshend yelled, "Fuck off my fucking stage!" He then chased Hoffman off the stage and swung at him with his guitar. "I can dig it," Townshend deadpanned to the crowd afterwards. Then they played "Amazing Journey."

Heaven and Hell
I Can't Explain
It's a Boy
1921
Amazing Journey
Sparks
Eyesight to the Blind
Christmas
Acid Queen
Pinball Wizard
Do You Think It's Alright?
Fiddle About
There's a Doctor
Go to the Mirror
I'm Free
Tommy's Holiday Camp
We're Not Gonna Take It
See Me, Feel Me

Summertime Blues
Shakin' All Over
My Generation
Naked Eye

3. JIMI HENDRIX
Monday: 9:00 am

How big of a premium do you attach to a single moment? Jimi Hendrix was the unequivocal star of the Woodstock documentary film because of his fiery rendition of the American national anthem. Twisted with feedback and blasted out of stacks of Marshall amplifiers at tinnitus-inducing volume, the song became the great clarion call for a generation fed up with staid traditions and eager to throw a pair of middle fingers in the face of President Nixon's so-called "silent majority."

For those in attendance however, Hendrix's set was almost an anticlimax. The guitarist's manager, Michael Jeffery, was adamant about enforcing a clause in his client's contract that required Hendrix to be the festival's final performer. That meant that he didn't go on until Monday morning, right after the '50 s throwback group Sha Na Na. Only around 25,000 exhausted people stuck around to hear him. The band he assembled for the occasion, Gypsy Sun and Rainbows, didn't help matters. They were bloated, out of sync and out of tune.

Still, this is Jimi Hendrix we're talking about. He's probably the greatest guitar player of all time, and when he left his band behind to essentially play all by himself—like on what was eventually titled "Woodstock Improvisation"—there's hardly anything better. The "Dean of American Rock Critics," Robert Christgau summed it up best when he referred to it as "your basic rock concert as act of flawed genius."

Message to Love
Hear My Train a Comin'
Spanish Castle Magic
Red House

Mastermind
Lover Man
Foxy Lady
Jam Back at the House
Izabella
Gypsy Woman/Aware of Love
Fire
Voodoo Child (Slight Return)
The Star Spangled Banner
Purple Haze
Woodstock Improvisation/Villanova Junction
Hey Joe

2. SANTANA

Saturday: 2:00 pm

Santana wasn't even supposed to be at Woodstock. When they took the stage that Saturday afternoon, their debut album was still months away. Nobody knew who they were. The Latin-blues fusion band was only added to the bill as a favor to super-promoter Bill Graham, whom the organizers had begged to come aboard as a consultant.

Santana was one of Graham's favorite bands. Over the last year, they served as the de facto house band at his venue, the Fillmore West, in San Francisco. If he could get them a bigger platform to gain more exposure, he was more than happy to do so.

Despite the enormity of the event and the high stakes, Santana kept it cool and turned in a career-making performance. Just before they hit the stage, Jerry Garcia offered the group's namesake, Carlos Santana, a tab of mescaline, which he popped into his mouth without question. Moments later the band was whisked onstage, and with their leader blown out of his mind, they launched into the song "Waiting."

The mescaline quickly took a hold of Santana's brain and refused to let go. Hallucinations filled his mind. When he looked down at his guitar he noticed, "It turned into an electric snake, twisting and turning, which meant the strings would go loose if it didn't

stay straight," he wrote in his autobiography *The Universal Tone*. "I kept willing the snake not to move and praying that it stayed in tune."

Carlos kept his snake tamed long enough for the band to reach the highlight of its set, "Soul Sacrifice." The song was an 11-minute epic of bongo drums, incendiary guitar soloing and psychedelic organ play. People looked to one another with astonishment as the band pushed the drama higher and higher. All those in attendance that had never heard of Santana weren't about to forget them any time soon.

Waiting
Evil Ways
You Just Don't Care
Savor
Jingo
Persuasion
Soul Sacrifice
Fried Neckbones and Some Home Fries

1. SLY AND THE FAMILY STONE

Sunday: 3:30 am

The greatest performance at Woodstock didn't come from a rock band. It wasn't a blues, country, folk or psychedelia outfit either. The greatest set came from the Northern California funk collective Sly & The Family Stone. Everything about this performance was perfect, from the time they were slotted to perform, the positive vibes emanating from the crowd and the infectious shot of fun they injected into the festivities.

Sly and the Family Stone rolled onto the stage at the prime moment—late, late in the evening on the second day—and treated all 500,000 hippies to a once-in-a-lifetime outdoor dance party. They came in guns blazing. "Hey, hey, hey," Sly shouted as the horns blasted out the first notes of "M'Lady."

If anyone in the field was hoping to get a little sleep, it wasn't going to happen on Sly's watch. For the next 50 minutes, he and his band turned the rural trappings of the expansive farm into the best dance club in the known world. The front man looked like someone from another planet decked out in his pink shirt, long white-fringed jacket, immaculate afro and oversized sunglasses.

"It was getting kinda cold out," photographer Bob Gruen told me. "People were sort of huddling around these fires. Then when Sly came on, people started jumping around and dancing to the music."

There may have been higher highs across the last four days—Hendrix's "Star Spangled Banner," Richie Havens's "Freedom" and Santana's "Soul Sacrifice"—but nobody came close to sustaining so much explosive energy and verve for as long as Sly and the Family Stone did. Seven songs into the show, Sly screamed out over and over, "I Want to Take You Higher." He really did.

M'Lady
Sing a Simple Song
You Can Make It if You Try
Everyday People
Dance to the Music
Music Lover
I Want to Take You Higher
Love City
Stand!

HONORABLE MENTION
The Beatles
on the Roof of Abbey Road Studios
London, England (January 30)

The other can't-miss concert of 1969 was also a free event. The Beatles were in the middle of filming a documentary about the recording of their album *Let It Be* but were at a loss about how to end it. The idea of staging a concert was floated around, but no one could agree on where to play or when. Then, out of nowhere, someone came up with the idea to bang out a couple of songs on the roof of their recording studio, Abbey Road. "It was good fun, actually," Paul McCartney remembered. "We were playing to virtually nothing—to the sky, which was quite nice. They filmed downstairs in the street—and there were a lot of city gents looking up: 'What's that noise?'" After performing "Get Back" a few times along with "One After 909" and "Don't Let Me Down," the cops showed up and shut them down. The whole thing happened in a flash, and then it was over and, with it, an era.

1970

The Who
THE REFECTORY AT LEEDS UNIVERSITY
LEEDS, ENGLAND
FEBRUARY 14

LIVE AT LEEDS

Following the release of their grand rock opera, *Tommy*, and their appearance at Woodstock in 1969, demand for The Who was at an all-time high. So was the pressure. Less than a year after their most recent release, their record label was strongly encouraging the British rock group, particularly chief songwriter Pete Townshend, to get some new product out into the marketplace. They already had a new single in the can—"The Seeker"— but it wasn't enough. Something more had to be done.

That's when Townshend hit upon an idea: "What about a live album?" The Who is one of the most explosive bands in rock history. Quite literally in some cases, like the time in 1967 when Keith Moon loaded up his bass drum with gunpowder and blew it up on national television, severely damaging his guitarist's hearing in the process. You didn't know what was going to happen at a Who concert. You knew you'd get Roger Daltrey swinging his microphone over his head in 15-foot arcs and Pete Townshend windmilling chords out of his guitar, but outside of that, all bets were off.

"The Who live was not simply music, or 'show,' but something a great deal more than the sum of its obvious parts," critic Greil Marcus wrote in his *Rolling Stone* review of the album *Live at Leeds*. "You understood it viscerally and carried that understanding around like a catchphrase of the shared private mind of a generation."

In the fall of 1969, the band toured the United States, bringing with them a recording engineer tasked with recording their concerts. Any one of them could have made for a fine live album. Unfortunately, when it came time to go through the material, Townshend was horrified to discover that the engineer had failed to take any notes. That meant that the guitarist would have to listen to every minute of every show to pick out what to include on an official release.

"For me to listen to thirty-eight shows would take five days in a studio. Even with notes I would lose track," Townshend wrote in his memoir, *Who I Am*. When the engineer asked what they should do with the material, Townshend was apoplectic: "'Destroy them,' I snapped, and before leaving the room I uttered a warning. 'And if I ever hear a bootleg of any of those tapes I will know where it came from.'"

The Who still needed to turn in a live album, and so a compromise was struck. The band was already scheduled to perform two shows over Valentine's Day weekend at two different universities in the U.K. at Leeds and Hull. They would simply rent a mobile recording apparatus and capture both concerts on tape.

The Refectory at the University in Leeds isn't your typical concert venue. It's a big, long cafeteria illuminated by eight gaudy chandeliers. Nevertheless, in the late '60s and early '70s, it was the go-to place in

SET LIST

Heaven and Hell

I Can't Explain

Fortune Teller

Tattoo

Young Man Blues

Substitute

Happy Jack

I'm a Boy

A Quick One, While He's Away

Overture

It's a Boy

1921

Amazing Journey

Sparks

Eyesight to the Blind

Christmas

The Acid Queen

Pinball Wizard

Do You Think It's Alright

Fiddle About

Tommy Can You Hear Me?

There's a Doctor

Go to the Mirror!

Smash the Mirror

Miracle Cure

Sally Simpson

I'm Free

Tommy's Holiday Camp

We're Not Gonna Take It

Summertime Blues

Shakin' All Over

My Generation

Magic Bus

MUSICIANS

Roger Daltrey: Vocals

Pete Townshend: Guitar/Vocals

John Entwistle: Bass

Keith Moon: Drums

Hell." The blast of volume is tremendous. Taken together, Townshend's Hiwatt-amplified guitar and Keith Moon's massive drum fills are one of the most iconic, earthshaking sounds in rock. To hear it in person is like standing behind the engine of a 747 as it's taking off for flight.

This initial portion of the show features a smattering of covers, new-ish songs and old favorites. During the second half, much as they had done throughout the last year, The Who presents a complete live performance of *Tommy*. It's an all-inclusive way to take in the group's nastier rock 'n' roll proclivities alongside their higher-minded art.

"Heaven and Hell" gives way to one of their earliest singles, "Can't Explain," followed by "Fortune Teller" and "Tattoo." Some of the biggest fireworks of the night come after they burst into the Mose Allison track "Young Man Blues." Townshend tries to explain the group's shared admiration for Allison, referring to him as a "jazz sage," but Moon interrupts as he rambles on and on, demanding that they "Just play the tune!"

Townshend ignores him and keeps talking. Moments later after a little more commentary from Moon, the guitarist gives up and breaks into the song's signature galloping riff. "Young Man Blues" is structured in a start-stop format. It repeatedly hits you with massive tidal waves of sound, followed by moments of hushed silence. A bare-chested Daltrey embodies the persona of an aggrieved youth decrying all the old men who've "got all the money," before Entwistle, Moon and Townshend rush back to the fore with atomic-level force.

The band is focused, and the audience, aware that the tapes are rolling, lose themselves in the music. "University crowds were often irreverent and noisy, but at Leeds they respected the fact that we

the area to catch all the big-time rock 'n' roll bands. Whenever Led Zeppelin or the Rolling Stones roll into town, the students slide away the tables, hang a big white sheet near the back and set up a temporary stage.

The Who makes an entrance on this cold, blustery evening to a boisterous round of applause. They open with an unreleased song titled "Heaven and

were recording, and behaved very well," Townshend remembered. "The sound in the hall was good too. I played more carefully than usual and tried to avoid the careless bum notes that often occurred because I was trying to play and jump around at the same time."

The jam wears on and on, well past the 15-minute mark, morphing into a searing wall of sound.

A little under a half-hour after they started, The Who shifts into *Tommy*. The suite of songs is stripped of much of their studio sheen. Instead The Who shoots for passion, rawness and realism, hitting all three marks perfectly. "Pinball Wizard," the tale of a "deaf, dumb, and blind kid" who "sure plays a mean pinball," is cranked up and blasted open. The same could be said for "Sparks," "The Acid Queen" and "I'm Free."

They finish *Tommy* with a powerful, emotionally charged rendition of the album's closing track, "We're Not Gonna Take It." The Who then races through two more covers—"Summertime Blues" by Eddie Cochran and "Spoonful" by Willie Dixon—before saluting the crowd and departing the stage.

The audience demands more, and after a few tense moments The Who reemerges to deliver an over-the-top medley centered on their biggest hit of all, "My Generation." The jam wears on and on, well past the 15-minute mark, morphing into a searing wall of sound. Townshend steps out front, mixing power chords with dive bombs and heavy riffs with high-pitched wails of feedback that overwhelm all sound in the room.

When it's over, the guitarist thanks the crowd and introduces the final song of the night, "Magic Bus." It takes a lot to top the energy of "My Generation," but

they give it a valiant effort, especially Daltrey, who shows off his significant harmonica chops. About four minutes in, the band abandons any semblance of structure and begins to improvise. This lasts for another four minutes until they bring the night to a close with a cacophonous dual-guitar and drum assault.

Everyone in the band knew that they'd captured the magic in the air that night, but they were still taken aback when *Live at Leeds* hit shelves three months later. The album climbed its way into the top 10 on charts around the world. It was eventually certified double-platinum.

"We'd thought of it as an interim record, as padding designed to quiet Decca and appease our fans. But this album vaulted us to yet another level," Townshend said. In his contemporary review for the *New York Times*, Nik Cohn called it "the best live rock album ever made." Decades later, the assertion still rings true.

HONORABLE MENTION

Elton John at the Troubadour
Hollywood, CA (August 25)

Elton John's first concerts in America were some of the most highly anticipated small club gigs in music history. His self-titled second album—technically his first in the U.S.—made a deep impression across the pond, steadily climbing up the charts before topping out at No. 4. Amongst the audience that night at the Troubadour in Los Angeles, waiting to see Elton's big live debut, were some of the biggest names in the business: Quincy Jones, Neil Diamond, Mike Love from the Beach Boys and Leon Russell, to name a few. At the prescribed time, the man of the hour took the stage by himself. He sat down at his piano and started playing his breakout hit, "Your Song." Midway through, Dee Murray came out and began playing bass. He was followed on the next song, "Bad Side of the Moon," by Nigel Olsson on drums. That night amongst the Hollywood glitterati, Elton turned in the performance of a lifetime, mesmerizing the audience, who couldn't believe how well the voice and piano they heard on the record translated in person. In his review the next day, Robert Hilburn of the *Los Angeles Times* wrote, "Tuesday night at the Troubadour was just the beginning. He's going to be one of rock's biggest and most important stars." Boy, did he nail that prediction!

#1 Single of the Year:
"Joy to the World"
Three Dog Night

#1 Album of the Year:
Jesus Christ Superstar (Soundtrack)
Various Artists

1971

The Allman Brothers Band
THE FILLMORE EAST—NEW YORK, NY
JUNE 27

AN ORAL HISTORY

On March 11, 1971, the Allman Brothers Band took the stage at concert promoter Bill Graham's vaunted Fillmore East theater to perform the first in a series of shows that have gone down as some of the most celebrated in rock history. They weren't even supposed to be the headliners for this residency. In the days leading up to the gigs, the posters Graham printed up read, "Johnny Winter and Elvin Bishop Group. Extra Added Attraction: Allman Brothers." After the scorching performance that the Allmans turned in on opening night, Graham flipped the order for the coming shows.

Over three evenings spread across six different sets of music, the Allman Brothers Band blitzed the New York audience with some of the nastiest, most powerful Southern rock that anyone had ever heard this far north of the Mason-Dixon. Undeterred by bomb threats that almost nixed one show and a disastrous experiment with a patchwork horn section, the band expanded their songs to their absolute limits, redefining what it meant to jam onstage. The nearly 23-minute version of their song "Whipping Post," which they used to close out the final night on March 13, is arguably the high-water mark of their career.

Three months later, on June 27, they returned to the Fillmore East under a completely different set of circumstances. Due to the increasingly high cost of booking acts and staging shows, mixed with a gen-eral sense of burnout, Graham decided to close its doors forever. "With the emergence of the Wood-stock philosophy in 1969, the world was told how big rock 'n' roll really was and by 1971, the managers, the tax consultants and the advisers made life very difficult," he explained to *Bay Area Magazine*. "The pressures came from all sides, and of course, it was augmented by the fact that I was flying 3,000 miles back and forth between the Fillmores East [in New York City] and West [in San Francisco]."

Remembering the magic of their last run on his stage, the promoter handpicked the Allman Brothers Band to give his beloved concert hall a final, proper sendoff. After a marathon night of music kicked off by blues legend Albert King and followed by sets from J. Geils Band, Edgar Winter's White Trash, Mountain, The Beach Boys and Country Joe McDonald, the Allman Brothers took the stage in the wee hours of the morning.

They ended up playing well until dawn that last evening. When it was over, a great church of rock, soul, jazz and blues went with it. Three months after that, Duane Allman died in a motorcycle accident in Macon, Georgia, and an even more important force was lost forever.

To tell the tale of the Allmans' run at the Fillmore East, I asked the people up on that stage to explain how those shows came together and why they've endured in the minds and hearts of so many rock fans.

SET LIST

Statesboro Blues
Don't Keep Me Wonderin'
Done Somebody Wrong
One Way Out
In Memory of Elizabeth Reed
Midnight Rider
Hot 'Lanta
Whipping Post
You Don't Love Me
Mountain Jam

Gregg Allman (Allman Brothers Band lead singer/keyboardist): Bill Graham was the most assertive person I've ever met. He was a straight shooter, a no-bullshit kind of guy. You always knew where you stood with Bill, man. He pulled no punches, but as tough as he was, he was always very fair.

Dickey Betts (Allman Brothers Band guitarist): He was a great guy. You know, either you hated Bill or you loved him and I was one of the latter. He was one of the cornerstones of getting our band going.

Butch Trucks (Allman Brothers Band drummer): When I met Bill Graham for the first time it was when I showed up for that closing night and walked across the stage. [He] saw me and came running. Up until that time I had never met him. He was always just this voice you heard on the other side of the room chewing somebody's ass out who screwed up the night before. Anyway, he came running across the stage and grabbed me by the neck, and he was a large, strong man, and he said, "I can't thank you enough for last night." And he went on and on and on, but in a nutshell he said, "It makes all the years of bullshit that I've had to put up with worthwhile."

Allman: The Fillmore was originally an old Yiddish theater built back in the '20s, and it had a great vibe to it, man. The acoustics were nearly perfect in there. It had nice sightlines for the fans, and I think it held about 2,000 people or so, which was just right. The Fillmore East became a regular stop for us, man.

Betts: It was a great sounding room. It was fun to play. Then you had a guy like Bill Graham that made sure that the PA system was set up correctly. It wasn't too loud, it wasn't too soft and everyone in the room could hear and see.

Trucks: Every time you went in there it just sounded so goddamn good and the audiences were just so in tune with what's going on.

Allman: Bill wouldn't pay you as much as some other promoters, but Bill would take a chance on people, and if you were good enough, he'd invite you back time and again, so we never worried about what he paid us.

Betts: [He] presented the show in a very sophisticated way, in a way that many people weren't used to seeing a rock 'n' roll show done. He took a lot of cues from Broadway, I guess, like rolling drum sets on risers and rollers and setting them up on the sides. He could change bands very quickly. He had his light show and it was very state of the art back then and he would get the old urban and Delta Blues players and educate the audience to what they meant to rock 'n' roll.

Allman: My brother had always believed a live album was what the Brothers needed to do, and the record company finally agreed with him. The Fillmore was just the logical choice. I don't think we even discussed another venue.

Trucks: That was one of the first places that the audience really got it. You know why we were able to record *At Fillmore East*? We actually weren't the headliner that weekend. You go back and look; we were the special guests for Johnny Winter. But after we played our first set on Thursday night, half the audience got up and walked out. Steve Paul, who was

MUSICIANS

Gregg Allman: Vocals/Organ/Piano

Duane Allman: Guitar

Dickey Betts: Guitar

Butch Trucks: Drums

Jai Johanny Johanson (AKA Jaimoe): Drums

Berry Oakley: Bass

Johnny Winter's manager, said, "Well, I guess Johnny is gonna be opening for the Allman Brothers from now on because we can't have that happen again." If that hadn't happened, we absolutely wouldn't have had all that time to do all the stretching out that led to *At Fillmore East*. We only had 90 minutes and had some songs that lasted longer than that!

Betts: It became obvious that we were a great band live. We could really play and the record people came up with the idea that "Man, these guys need to be caught in the act." We had a great situation, you know, we had [producer] Tom Dowd and Johnny Sandlin that came in and recorded those shows and they did a great job of it, of course.

Trucks: We learned very early on that playing music is a very selfish thing. We're up there playing for ourselves first and foremost. If I'm not getting myself off, how can I expect anyone else to get off on it? I start with myself then move out to the guys in the band and then we start communicating; we kick it into overdrive and go into places that we can't go by ourselves.

Allman: We just played and played, one gig after another. You've got to remember that we spent 300 days on the road in 1970. I mean, we were never home. All we did was play, man.

Betts: Duane was a very, very wise man for 22, 23 years old. It was really easy to talk sense with him about what we were trying to do. Let's say we were riding from Georgia down to Florida where our folks lived and stuff, and we'd be drinking a little bit and having these long conversations about things like the Zen aspect of it all. Finding that innocence of mind, or what athletes call "getting in the zone." You just get free and let things happen rather than make things happen.

> # We got into a jam, I think it was "Mountain Jam," that lasted for four straight hours.

Allman: My brother, he was the bandleader on stage. He'd count it off to start a song, and we would end it when he raised his hand, but in between, the band just let itself go wherever the music would take us.

Trucks: For my entire career, from the moment Duane Allman reached inside me, flicked the switch and turned me on, to this day, I've always locked on whoever is playing lead whether it was Duane, if it was Dickey, if it was Gregg or if it was Barry Oakley. Quite often, I will see something they're doing, even if I can't hear it. I'm so comfortable in just feeling Jaimoe [the drummer] that I don't have to listen to 'em. He's just there. So if someone plays a lick or goes somewhere, I'm right on their ass and it's my job to stay on their ass and push them to higher places. I think it's how I got the name "The Freight Train."

Betts: It would switch from one guy to the other as the song evolved. We didn't have anybody we took cues from. We just followed each other. [Barry] Oakley was great if a song was starting to lag. He would start really pumping on the bass to pull us into another direction. At the same time, I would do that, too, start a riff or something that would kind of pick it up and make it sound good in a certain situation. Duane did the same thing.

Allman: My brother made up the set list, and it didn't change very much from night to night. He liked it that way. We'd swap out a song or two, but we pretty much kept the same songs. The thing was, we'd never play them the same way twice.

Betts: We just played whatever came up. Somebody would say, "Let's play 'One Way Out' or something." Okay. Well, except for "Whipping Post," which we usually saved for the end of the show because it was such a slammer. "In Memory of Elizabeth Reed," we'd put that near the end of the show.

Trucks: In those days when we climbed into those songs, that's all there was. It's never been like that since. I mean, I've been able to get into the moment for brief times many, many times since then, but not for those long extended jams like on "Whipping Post," for instance, where once the song started, you climbed in and there was no tomorrow, no yesterday, you were just totally in the moment from the time it started to the time it ended. On every song on that album, that's what was happening. We were just at the peak of reaching the point where we knew each other well enough, we knew the material well enough, to where we didn't have to think about it and could let it all flow so naturally. We knew what each other was going to do, *yet* we were constantly wide open to letting it go and taking a dive and seeing what would happen.

Trucks: When you listen to Dickey's solo on "Whipping Post" he just lets everything go. We're just doodling around, letting him go and then all of a sudden he starts playing this melody, "duh-duh-duh-duh-dow-dow-duh-duh-dow-duh-duh-dow-duh," and you can hear Barry and Gregg and Duane all feeling around for where this chord progression is because we'd never done this before. By about the second or third progression through, Barry and Duane had locked into what the chord progression was and then Dickey really laid into it and it just fucking took off. Then when we came roaring back in with the "Whip-

ping Post" theme again, the place just exploded. We had just paid a visit to a place we'd never been before.

Allman: Bill Graham's introduction when he said, "We're going to finish it off with the best of them all, the Allman Brothers," that is something I'll always remember.

Betts: That was a special show. We played until daylight that morning. I remember it was dark in there and when they opened the door the sun about knocked us down. We didn't realize we had played until seven, eight o'clock in the morning. Bill Graham just let us rattle and nobody said, "We gotta cut the time." It was just a really free kind of thing. All of our performances at the Fillmore were special. For us, just because they had tape rolling in a truck outside, it really didn't affect us that much. We didn't play for the tape, we played for the people.

Trucks: We played for roughly seven straight hours with everything we had. We played a three-hour set and then came back out. The feeling from the audience, not necessarily the volume, but the feeling was just so overwhelming that I just started crying. Then we got into a jam, I think it was "Mountain Jam," that lasted for four straight hours. Nonstop. And when we finished there was no applause whatsoever. The place was deathly quiet. Someone got up and opened the doors, the sun came pouring in and you could see this whole audience with a big shit-eating grin on their face, nobody moving until finally they got up and started quietly leaving the place. I remember Duane walking in front of me, dragging his guitar while I was just sitting there completely burned and he said, "Damn, it's just like leaving church." To this day, I meet people who say they were there, and I can tell if they were just by the look in their eye.

HONORABLE MENTION

The Soul to Soul Concert
Black Star Square Accra, Ghana (March 6)

On March 6, 1957, Ghana declared itself a free
and independent nation. In the mid-1960s, the poet
Maya Angelou, who was living in Ghana, suggested
to the country's president that Ghana hold an annual
celebration and invite prominent African-American
artists to take part. Officials eventually warmed up to
the idea, especially after seeing the success of James
Brown's mega-concert in Nigeria in 1970. Most, if
not all, of the major black American musicians were
invited, with Ike & Tina Turner, The Staples Singers,
Roberta Flack, the Voices of East Harlem, Santana, Les McCann & Eddie Harris and Wilson Pickett
all making the journey. The concert lasted 14 hours
and ended around 7 a.m. The big-name American
acts performed alongside Ghanaian artists, creating
an unprecedented cultural exchange. Of all the acts
on the bill, Pickett garnered the biggest response of
the day. In Ghana, the Stax singer was a peerless superstar, widely referred to as "Soul Brother No. 2."
(Brown was "Soul Brother No. 1.") The fans nearly
stormed the stage as he sweated it out through a
scorching take on the song "In the Midnight Hour."
As *New York Times* critic Howard Thompson wrote
in his review of the documentary of the concert, "In
Soul to Soul black isn't merely beautiful. It's unsur-
passable."

1972

The Rolling Stones
with Stevie Wonder
MADISON SQUARE GARDEN—NEW YORK, NY
JULY 26

S.T.P. IN N.Y.C.

1972 was the year that the Rolling Stones became, as they loudly proclaimed on tour, the "Greatest Rock 'N' Roll Band in the World!" Following the violent disaster of their Hell's Angels–policed Altamont mega-festival outside of San Francisco on December 6, 1969—where three people were killed in accidents and another, Meredith Hunter, was murdered—the Stones disappeared for a while. They went into exile, both real and imagined. Exile from the tax man in England that gazed hungrily on their collected bank accounts and exile as culture warriors—street fighting men—dedicated to the fanciful belief that they could change the world.

The Stones didn't sit idle in their time out of from the spotlight. They locked themselves away in the sweaty, dank basement of Keith Richards's mansion in Nellcôte, France, for months on end and came out with their magnum opus: *Exile on Main Street*. It was a double-album, 18 tracks total, that recounted the near-entire history of blues, country, soul and rock 'n' roll in the grittiest, most exhilarating way imaginable. Released on May 12, 1972, it sold nearly a million copies in its first week alone.

When plotting their upcoming tour of the United States, the band was intent on making a different impression than they had on their previous jaunt. These shows were going to produce some of the most in-demand tickets of all time, and the Stones and their handlers wanted to be professionals about it. They would do their best to mitigate the violence and mania that seemed to follow their every stop on their last tour, while moving through the country with a degree of style and class that rivaled any visiting foreign dignitary that the U.S. had ever hosted.

Everything about the outing was over the top. The Stones surrounded themselves with the beautiful and the important—Truman Capote, Hugh Hefner, Zsa Zsa Gabor, Woody Allen and Bob Dylan. They heavily courted the press. They blew their minds out with weed, cocaine and tequila, all while staging some of the most incredible sets of live rock music ever seen.

Over 500,000 people mailed in postcards for the mere chance to buy a pass to one of the four shows at Madison Square Garden. Purchases were limited to two per customer at a sticker price of $6.50, but the market was soon flooded with scalped passes that were being hawked at $50 or more.

After months of anticipation, the S.T.P. tour—which, depending on who you asked, either stood for the synthetic hallucinogenic of the same name or simply the Stones Tour Party—kicked off in Vancouver on June 3, 1972. The band and its managers picked this far-flung locale to start their summer swing so that they could knock off the rust before taking their show to more media-saturated markets in San Francisco and Los Angeles. The gig went well. The stop in Seattle went better, and by the time they

MUSICIANS

Mick Jagger: Vocals
Keith Richards: Guitar
Mick Taylor: Guitar
Charlie Watts: Drums
Bill Wyman: Bass
Bobby Keys: Saxophone

SET LIST

Brown Sugar
Bitch
Rocks Off
Gimme Shelter
Happy
Tumbling Dice
Love in Vain
Sweet Virginia
You Can't Always Get What You Want
All Down the Line
Midnight Rambler
Bye Bye Johnny
Rip This Joint
Jumpin' Jack Flash
Street Fighting Man
Uptight (Everything's Alright)
(I Can't Get No) Satisfaction

made it to the Winterland Ballroom in the "City by the Bay," they were cooking.

Over the next two months, the Rolling Stones and their coterie of crew members and hangers-on crisscrossed North America. At each stop along the way, the local citizenry paused their lives long enough to gawk at, rejoice in or denounce the "event of the year." In Chicago, the band stayed at Hugh Hefner's Playboy Mansion when they couldn't get secure enough hotel rooms elsewhere. In Houston and Fort Worth, Texas, they brought out a Hollywood film crew to capture the show for posterity. Eventually, that footage would get chopped up and released as *Ladies and Gentlemen: The Rolling Stones*.

A separate, more illicit documentary was also in the works that captured the band's candid offstage exploits. That film, titled *Cocksucker Blues*, was produced by Stones manager Marshall Chess and directed by Robert Frank. Though it would never receive an official release, if you search down some of the darker corners of the Internet, it's not too hard to find. Viewer discretion is advised.

"New York is New York is New York," famed concert promoter Bill Graham explained to author Robert Greenfield, who tagged along for most of the tour and penned the book *A Journey Through America with the Rolling Stones*. "'Til you do it there, it hasn't happened. They could have sold the Garden out for a year. They are the biggest draw in the history of mankind. Only one other guy ever came close—Gandhi."

New York was ready for the Stones, and the Stones were more than ready to take a bite out of the Big Apple. The band's four shows spread over three nights at Madison Square Garden were the unquestioned highlights of the tour, with the final night

pegged as the can't-miss gig. Everyone wanted in on the action.

The scene backstage before the last show is a madhouse. Television host Dick Cavett is on hand to interview Mick Jagger and the rest of the band for an hour-long special. This famous face and that famous face drift in and out of view hoping to get a coveted moment of personal time with someone in the band before they make their way out in front of the masses. Few are successful. Makeup is applied, last-minute documents are signed and the tequila sunrises flow like water.

Before the Stones can take the stage at MSG, the audience is treated to a searing set of music from the opening act, Stevie Wonder, who is just then promoting his latest album, *Music of My Mind* while on the verge of putting out an even greater work, *Talking Book*. It was a huge coup for the headliners to get the Motown piano virtuoso at this precise moment. His single "Superstition" is one of the biggest songs of 1972, well on its way to claiming the top spot on the charts a few months down the road.

Stevie is the perfect foil for the Stones. He isn't

going to compete with them on their terms like another white blues-based rock band like Humble Pie or the Allman Brothers might. He's a different thing entirely. His stage show, while rapturous, is centered on his superb musicianship, his incredible songwriting and his own joyful persona.

A little under an hour after Wonder leaves, the Stones make their grand entrance and launch into "Brown Sugar." Jagger appears dazzling in his sleeveless white jumpsuit, dotted with big sparkling

> **They had eight Super Troopers at the back of the stage shining into this Mylar mirror, shining back onto the band. It was the brightest show I've ever seen.**

sequins, and a long red sash tethered at the waist. A single, large aquamarine jewel is glued to the center of his forehead. His main foil and "Glimmer Twin" Keith Richards, ever the rock 'n' roll pirate, is decked out in black leather pants and a flowing, white blouse, which is left unbuttoned to reveal his gleaming white, sweat-glazed chest.

Jagger eats up most of the attention, hopping across the stage, preening like a prized turkey. His arms flail all around, pointing in multiple directions one moment and enticing the crowd to clap along in the next. "Gold coast slave ship bound for cotton fields / Sold in the market down in New Orleans." The subject matter is chilling, but the thousands singing along sound positively ebullient shouting back each word at their puffy-lipped Messiah.

The pace picks up even more on the next song, "Bitch," which is played at a far faster clip than the recorded version. By the time they get to "Gimme Shelter" they're locked in. The shot of adrenaline that comes from getting smacked in the face by 18,000 people simultaneously has worn off, and the Stones settle into their regular groove.

"They had a unique lighting system that they invented," photographer Bob Gruen told me. The rig was designed by Woodstock MC Chip Monck, who installed a 40-foot by 8-foot array of mirrors near the top of the front of the stage. It was set at a 45-degree angle and had lights shined into it and reflected back onto the band.

Gruen explained, "Up until then in arenas, you had a large spotlight called a Super Trooper, this big carbon arc light up around the rafters in the arena shining down on the stage. They had eight Super Troopers at the back of the stage shining into this Mylar mirror, shining back onto the band. It was the brightest show I've ever seen."

The Stones hit their marks with precision. Keith sounds appropriately cheery during his turn on the microphone for "Happy." Charlie Watts keeps the party chugging along, crashing cymbals and kicking the hell out of his bass drum on "Bye Bye Johnny." Mick Taylor sounds like a man possessed during his regular extended solo on "Midnight Rambler," proving that he is the best pure musician in the band.

Still, it's Jagger that the fans have come to see, and he doesn't disappoint. The singer remains the ultimate icon of style and panache. Even with all the obvious effort and energy he expends on stage, he does so in a way that screams cool. When they reach the final song of the main set, "Street Fighting Man," he's flinging blood red rose petals over the heads of those screaming their vocal cords to shreds in the front row.

The night isn't quite over yet. A few moments pass and the band reemerges for a rare encore with Stevie Wonder in tow to perform the latter's hit "Uptight (Everything's Alright)." As that song comes to an end, Richards kicks into the instantly recognizable riff to "Satisfaction," and he and the rest of the band take flight.

The performance is breathtaking. Bobby Keys's sax mingles with Wonder's backing band, transforming the straight-ahead rocker into a full, swinging soul sensation. Jagger is giving everything he's got left in the tank, pushing his voice harder and harder, straining to be heard above the cacophony.

As the last notes of their biggest hit ping across the cavernous walls of the basketball arena, a giant, burning cake is brought onto the stage to commemorate Jagger's 29th birthday. The crowd is enticed to sing "Happy Birthday." Somewhere, someone picks up a pie and a full-on food fight takes place in front of thousands of fans. Only Watts seems to be off-limits from the chaos. Once the supply of pies runs out, Mick jumps forward to give the crowd a salute and then he and the rest of the band depart for the last time.

A few hours later, the Stones and their crew, along with a host of the well-to-do, find themselves at the St. Regis Hotel to take part in a final party hosted by Atlantic Records head Ahmet Ertegun. In jarring contrast to the friendly atmosphere inside the Garden, the mood here is almost somber. Everyone in the band are all physically and emotionally spent. The party wraps sometime around dawn and they all scatter to the wind.

HONORABLE MENTION

Marvin Gaye at the Kennedy Center Washington D.C. (May 1)

By the time he arrived onstage at the Kennedy Center in 1972, it had been roughly four years since Marvin Gaye had performed live before a paying audience. A lot had changed in his life—some good, a lot of it bad. Tammi Terrell, his regular singing partner, died of a brain tumor in 1970. Shortly after that, he became locked in a battle with his boss, Motown label president Berry Gordy, over creative control of his next record, *What's Going On*. The fight took a lot out of him, but Gaye prevailed in the end, producing one of the most celebrated albums of all time; a record that captured the feeling of that tumultuous era in stunning fashion. Now, Gaye was set to return to his hometown to deliver a blowout show of epic proportions. Though he was nervous about the prospect—"Until the last few minutes, I wasn't going to go," he told his biographer, David Ritz—Gaye didn't let the crowd down. He opened the show with a 13-minute medley of his earliest hits before moving into his more contemporary *What's Going On* material. Besides being an incredible performance, the concert had a healing effect on Gaye's wounded psyche. "I understood that I'd been punishing myself by staying away so long," he explained. "I'd been denying self-love, and that's one of the most foolish things a man can do."

#1 Single of the Year:
"Tie a Yellow Ribbon 'Round the
Ole Oak Tree"
Tony Orlando & Dawn

1973

David Bowie
THE HAMMERSMITH ODEON—LONDON, ENGLAND
JULY 3

FAREWELL ZIGGY STARDUST

Of all the shows on this tour, this particular show will remain with us the longest because, not only is it the last show of the tour, but it's the last show we'll ever do."

The audience at the Hammersmith Odeon unleashes a single, commingled gasp of horror. Surely the man onstage is joking. For the last year David Bowie, personified by his alter ego Ziggy Stardust, appeared like a Technicolor vision of rock 'n' roll's future. Now he was going to disappear? It didn't any make sense.

Only Bowie, his manager and his main musical foil, his guitar player Mick Ronson, were aware of his plans to bow out tonight. The enigmatic singer had kept his wife, the rest of his band and the world at large totally in the dark. "We were just thinking, 'Is it the truth or another one of his stories?'" drummer Mick "Woody" Woodmansey told *NME*.

It wasn't a story. He was dead serious. This would be the last time that Ziggy would ever play guitar.

Bowie adopted many personas throughout his decades-long career—The Thin White Duke, Aladdin Sane and Jareth the Goblin King, to name a few—but Ziggy Stardust was his most indelible. Ziggy touched down for the first time on June 16, 1972, in conjunction with the release of Bowie's fifth record, *The Rise and Fall of Ziggy Stardust and the Spiders from Mars*. It wasn't quite a concept album, but in broad strokes, it relayed the story of an extraterrestrial rock 'n' roller

who arrived on Earth to relay a message of hope in the planet's five remaining years before the apocalypse wiped everyone out.

Bowie as Ziggy, a visage of red hair, ornate jumpsuits and caked-on makeup, touched a nerve in the counterculture. Over the next year, the singer catapulted in status from a nominal one-hit wonder (1969's "Space Oddity") to a bona fide rock sensation. Fans copied his look, followed his every movement and worshipped him as the pinnacle of a new Glam era.

The pressure took a toll. In the years leading up to his big breakthrough, Bowie had tried out several desperate gambits in the pursuit of fame. Now that he finally reached his goal, the unforeseen trappings overwhelmed him. "There were times, frankly, when I could have told the audience to do anything," he said in 1974. "That's frightening." The Starman needed a break.

There was more to his decision to retire than exhaustion. Bowie's manager, Tony Defries, had convinced his client's label, RCA, to underwrite his two previous tours of the United States, but for the coming run his company MainMan would be on the hook for the entire bill. He didn't have the funds to make it happen. Rather than hitting the road with a stripped-down presentation that would have severely impacted Bowie's over-the-top, larger-than-life image, he convinced him to "retire" and pick up the pieces later.

SET LIST

Hang On to Yourself

Ziggy Stardust

Watch That Man

Wild Eyed Boy From Freecloud

All the Young Dudes

Oh! You Pretty Things

Moonage Daydream

Changes

Space Oddity

My Death

Cracked Actor

Time

The Width of a Circle

Let's Spend The Night Together

Suffragette City

White Light/White Heat

Jean Genie

Around and Around

Rock 'N' Roll Suicide

Why let a bit of financial chicanery stand in the way of a grand, theatrical moment? Bowie agreed.

High above Queen Caroline Street, the marquee of the Hammersmith Odeon reads: "From 8 pm We're All Working Together with David Bowie." Down below, the children of Ziggy Stardust—decked out in a host of eye-catching garments and with lightning bolts painted on their faces and hair puffed up and sprayed into impressive towers of style—shuffle *en masse* into the building and take their seats.

The lights go out and the crowd goes wild. Instead of Ziggy, a fellow named Mike Garson walks onstage, plops down behind a piano and runs through a ten-minute medley of Bowie's songs. Call it an appetizer, a prelude of what's to come.

When Garson finishes, an announcer takes his place. The audience breaks into a steady handclap as he begins to speak. "Ladies and gentlemen, straight from his fantastically successful world tour, including the United States of America, Japan, now his home country, for the last time, David Bowie!"

MUSICIANS

David Bowie: Vocals/Guitar

Mick Ronson: Vocals/Guitar

John Hutchinson: Guitar

Trevor Bolder: Bass

Mick "Woody" Woodmansey: Drums

Ken Fordham: Saxophone and Flute

Brian Wilshaw: Saxophone and Flute

Mike Garson: Piano/Organ/Mellotron

Geoffrey MacCormack: Backing Vocals

Bowie and the Spiders from Mars step out onto into the limelight and are blasted by a wave of applause. Apparently, the crowd doesn't register that "last time" part in the introduction as abnormal. The band wastes little time before launching into the vintage rocker "Hang On to Yourself." Bowie looks as dynamic and impressive as ever. His red hair is teased to perfection. His multicolored eyes are ringed by thick black mascara, and his body is encased in a gorgeous silvery-blue and red jumpsuit. Peak glam.

The energy in the room is electric as the first song explodes out of the amplifiers. Bowie sings his lines at a rapid-fire clip, trying to keep up with the Spiders playing behind him. "Come on, come on / We've really got a good thing goin' on," Bowie declares over and over.

At song's end, Bowie cedes the spotlight to Ronson, who unleashes a monstrous solo from his faded gold Gibson Les Paul. As the guitarist finishes, two stagehands rush out to tear away Bowie's costume, revealing a silver kimono-like ensemble. He stands there for a moment letting the audience drink it all in then steps to the microphone to sing the first "Oh, yeah" from "Ziggy Stardust."

Bowie understands spectacle in a way that most artists don't. In a lot of ways, he pioneered the idea of a concert as more than just an opportunity to hear your favorite songs performed live. He brings a sense of theater to his live shows, wowing crowds sonically and visually.

D.A. Pennebaker, the documentarian behind films like the Bob Dylan portrait *Don't Look Back* and the *Monterey Pop Festival*, told me that he thought Bowie had "written songs almost for this kind of performance. It wasn't that he was writing just to get a song into the songbook. He saw the whole thing as a staged event."

His multicolored eyes are ringed by thick black mascara, and his body is encased in a gorgeous silvery-blue and red jumpsuit. Peak glam.

The night wears on and Ziggy Stardust and the Spiders from Mars play their parts like their lives depend on it. Bowie is the consummate front man. It's almost impossible not to fall in love with him as he winks and blows kisses at the audience in between his lines on "Moonage Daydream."

In the middle of that song, while the band marks time, Bowie departs for a quick costume change backstage. When he comes back, he picks up an acoustic guitar and digs into two of his most popular singles, "Changes" and "Space Oddity." The audience is rapturous in its praise. Bowie responds to their affection by offering another inkling that something about this show is dramatically different.

"This is a quiet song," he says while introducing "My Death." "This is something that we used to do a long, long, long, long, time ago, and we thought, as it is the last show, we'd like to do it tonight." Maybe it's because it's the final show of the tour that the audience still can't comprehend the gravity of what Bowie is saying.

Near the end of the main set, Bowie busts out a cover of the Rolling Stones' "Let's Spend the Night Together" before slipping into his hit song "Suffragette City." He closes the set with the Velvet Underground's "White Light/White Heat," and for the encore he invites the virtuosic former Yardbird Jeff Beck

to trade licks and solos with Ronson during "Jean Genie" and the Beatles' "Love Me Do."

After Beck departs, Ziggy and the Spiders break out into "Around and Around." Before playing the last song, Bowie addresses the crowd again and drops the hammer. "Not only is it the last show of the tour but it's the last show we'll ever do."

The crowd is stunned. It can't be true! They loudly protest, but Bowie is committed. "Thank you," he says. He takes a bow and the band strikes up "Rock 'N' Roll Suicide."

Arriving at the emotional "Give me your hands" coda, Bowie jumps down to the front of the stage, taking hold of all the outstretched arms that are thrust in his direction and grabbing onto him for dear life. He finally tears himself away, races back to the microphone, thanks the crowd and takes a bow. As he's leaving, Bowie is rushed by a fan who leaps onstage to give him a parting hug. He remains all smiles as the fan is wrestled off him. "I love you," he says, and then fades away into the darkness.

The party after the show is outrageous. As Bowie's wife, Angela, remembered, "David posed for photos with Ringo Starr and chatted with Mick [Jagger]. Lou Reed invited us to his next recording session, Bianca [Jagger] and I danced together to 'Honky Tonk Women' and one woman exposed her breasts to Barbra Streisand, or so I heard. We didn't leave for our hotel on Hyde Park until 5:30 A.M."

The next day, Bowie was already thinking about his next move. His next film project. His next album. The next version of his personality that he would present to the world.

HONORABLE MENTION

Van Morrison at the Rainbow Theater
London, England (July 24)

Van Morrison was always a reliable live act, going back to his days as the front man of Them in the mid-1960s. The Irishman took his performance chops to new heights in 1973 when he hit the road backed by one of the most incredible musical outfits ever assembled: The Caledonia Soul Orchestra. They were an 11-piece band made up of drums, guitar, piano, trumpet and saxophone players and a four-person string section. Each stop of the three-month tour was dynamite, but this gig at the Rainbow, which was simulcast on BBC, finds Morrison at his peak. Throughout a 15-song set list that married his past and his future, Van pours every ounce of sweat and energy he has into this performance. He pays homage to the blues masters with electric covers of Willie Dixon's "I Just Want to Make Love to You" and Sonny Boy Williamson's "Take Your Hand Out of My Pocket." He airs out choice material like "Caravan," "Domino," "Moondance" and an incredibly raucous "Wild Night." He ends with the greatest garage rock anthem, an atomic-force rendition of "Gloria." Afterward he cries out, "It's too late to stop now!" and stalks off the stage like a prizefighter.

1974

Crosby, Stills, Nash & Young
SEATTLE CENTER COLISEUM—SEATTLE, WA
JULY 9

CSNY MEET THEIR DOOM

There had never been a concert tour as massive as the one that David Crosby, Stephen Stills, Graham Nash and Neil Young were about to embark upon. There had been major festivals like Woodstock and Isle of Wight that brought hundreds of thousands of people together to see a diverse lineup. The Beatles and Led Zeppelin had sold out huge baseball stadiums on single occasions, but for one band to accomplish that feat night after night seemed crazy. With unheard of sums of money being thrown at them, CSNY gave it a shot.

The years leading up to this tour had been great for the members of Crosby, Stills & Nash. Their first eponymous album (1969) brought them wide acclaim, with many heralding the trio as America's answer to the Beatles. Following the success of that record, they brought Canadian singer, and Stills' former Buffalo Springfield bandmate Neil Young into the fold to shore up their live sound and beef up their recorded output. They issued an even better studio album, *Déjà Vu* (1970), followed by a terrific live album, *Four Way Street* (1971), that was recorded at the Fillmore East.

With success came tension. Things reached a boiling point around 1971. The four men decided to go their separate ways and work on solo albums and different collaborative projects. Nash put out the solo album *Songs for Beginners*. Crosby worked through his grief over the death of his girlfriend, Christine Hinton, on *If Only I Could Remember My Name*. Stills released two self-titled solo albums and put together a new band named Manassas. Young unveiled the only No. 1 album of his career, *Harvest*, before releasing a live album, *Time Fades Away*, and a boozy sendup to his departed friend Bruce Berry, *Tonight's the Night*.

The foursome reconvened to write new music in 1973, but the sessions were almost doomed from the start. "The music was jelling; it just didn't sustain itself. The time wasn't really right," Stills told journalist Cameron Crowe. "We played each other a lot of our new songs and gave each other our opinions. Basically, we set the groundwork for this summer when we'll be recording a new CSNY album and doing a tour of ballparks and speedways."

The album never happened, but a summer run through North America was already well in the works. "As far as this tour, we did one for the art and the music, one for the chicks. This one's for cash," Stills said.

To handle the logistics of this unprecedented venture, the band's manager, Elliot Roberts, reached out to live music impresario Bill Graham, who had just completed a nationwide arena run with Bob Dylan and The Band. "It was the first pure stadium production tour and . . . Bill was the best production-oriented guy," Roberts said. "He already had FM Productions and he had his own shop for building sets. There had been other tours with outdoor shows, but none that was *all* stadiums. It was real big and we wanted

SET LIST

Love the One You're With

Wooden Ships

Immigration Man

Cowgirl in the Sand

Change Partners

Traces

Grave Concern

Black Queen

Almost Cut My Hair

Ohio

Suite: Judy Blue Eyes

Helplessly Hoping

Blackbird

Human Highway

Prison Song

As I Come of Age

Carry Me

For Free

Guinnevere

Southbound Train

Another Sleep Song

Our House

4 + 20

Know You Got to Run

You Can't Catch Me

Word Game

Love Art Blues

Long May You Run

A Man Needs a Maid

Don't Be Denied

First Things First

Déjà Vu

My Angel

Pre-Roads Down

My Favorite Changes

Long Time Gone

Revolution Blues

Pushed It Over the End

Carry On

What Are Their Names

Chicago

MUSICIANS

Neil Young: Vocals/Guitar/Piano

Stephen Stills: Vocals/Guitar/Piano

David Crosby: Vocals/Guitar

Graham Nash: Vocals/Guitar/Piano

Tim Drummond: Bass

Russ Kunkel: Drums

Jo La La: Percussion

to make sure that the production values would be the best."

Graham was maybe the only person in the world who could manage a project of this scale and turn a profit. The sets were designed from scratch and shipped from town to town in a fleet of six 30-foot-long tractor-trailers. Along with the band and its entourage, 18 crewmembers were hired to set up and run the show. Graham modified, expanded and re-used the speaker setup that Dylan had lugged around the country, saving a couple of bucks along the way.

After going back and forth with numerous promoters and municipalities, CSNY were on the hook for 31 concerts in 24 cities spread over two months. Even with such a heavy slate, Crosby remained optimistic. "There's no chance of this thing turning sour," he said. "Everybody confronts everyone else, face-to-face and nose-to-nose, about everything. We're totally out front with each other. It's the only way we can function. . . . There's no pussy-footing around going on." How wrong he was.

The first show is set to kick off at the Seattle Center Coliseum in a couple of hours. The band flew in for the gig earlier that day, checked into the local Hilton and traded old war stories at the hotel's rooftop restaurant. The weather is gloomy, cold and grey, about as far from the warmth of Laurel Canyon as one could imagine, but the mood is upbeat, if not cut with nervous tension.

At 9:00 pm the band hits the stage opening with "Love the One You're With" from Stephen Stills's 1970 self-titled solo record. Buoyed by the joyful energy from the crowd, CSNY run through the next nine songs with infectious energy and verve. Just as Crosby said, there's a convivial feeling between everyone onstage. As they finish one song, someone steps to the microphone with a big grin on his face to tell the audience who wrote it, then the author gives the crowd a friendly wave or a slightly embarrassed smile.

The show is constructed so that the band plays a set of electric songs, takes a break and comes back out with acoustic guitars for about an hour. After that, they'd whip through a few solo stints, before throwing the Fenders and Gibsons back on and plugging in for the finale.

Neil was the greatest. He'd just pull one out of his ass or his hat and the rest of them would grab and hang on.

After "Love the One You're With," they move into "Wooden Ships" from their debut record, before breaking into Nash's "Immigration Man," Young's "Cowgirl in the Sand" and an especially electrifying rendition of Crosby's "Almost Cut My Hair." The exhilarating opening set closes with an apoplectic take on the Kent State massacre protest song "Ohio." The way Crosby frantically asks, "How many more?" and "Why?" over and over again sends chills up people's spines.

Reemerging a few minutes later, they kick into the multipart *Crosby, Stills & Nash* opening track "Suite: Judy Blue Eyes." The weeks of rehearsal at Young's Broken Arrow Ranch before the tour are clearly paying off. As a band, they've never sounded tighter or more in sync with one another. The power of their collective harmonization is staggering. "Helplessly Hoping" and "Carry Me" are fine examples of the seamless way that Nash and Crosby in particular

are able to weave their voices together to create a sound unlike anything else in rock.

The peak example of this magical fusion is the ancient-sounding ballad "Guinnevere." It's almost impossible to discern where one singer's voice ends and the other's begins, as they pour their souls into the song's beautiful, profound, haunting melody.

After some reshuffling, all four members re-emerge to jam on the Spanish-flavored "Déjà Vu." Crosby opens the song with a full minute of scatting while the other three men groove in the background. The intro goes on and on until they all step up to the microphone blast out the opening lines in perfect unison, "If I had ever been here before I would probably know just what to do / Don't you!" The band kicks into a higher gear during the initial verses before settling back down to allow Stills and Young to take alternating languid guitar solos. The expansive, dynamic arrangement is repeated on the songs "Long Time Gone," "Carry Me" and the set-closer, "Chicago."

Crosby, Stills Nash, & Young perform 40 songs total in Seattle, ending the show sometime after 1:30 am. Alongside their well-known material, they slip in nine different tracks that haven't been released to the public yet. "We had a shitload of songs," bassist Tim Drummond said. "Neil was the greatest. He'd just pull one out of his ass or his hat and the rest of them would grab and hang on. That's what made it so fresh and exciting."

In an interview with the *Los Angeles Times* a week after the show, Crosby recalled, "Seattle was really good. The feeling in the band is better than I've ever seen it, even better than when we started the first time. We're all older and we've had a lot of corners knocked off. We've all been hit in the face with a couple of pies from life. Everybody seems to have more of a sense of each other's worth. There's a lot of respect and what seems to me to be a very sincere, genuine try to work together."

In the days that followed this transcendent kick-off concert, the band continued to perform at an exceedingly high level in front of increasingly larger audiences. As the tour wore on, a lot of the bloom would go off the Seattle rose. From the outside looking in, their chemistry and camaraderie never appeared tighter, but the band was slowly coming apart at the seams. The expectations to perform for so many people put everyone on edge. That feeling wasn't helped by the readily available cocaine that was a fixture in their private planes and dressing rooms.

"We actually had a guy that was employed just to provide us with cocaine," Nash recalled in his memoir, *Wild Tales*. "We needed an incredible amount of energy to pull off that tour and I'm sure it helped in a way, but it is a very subtly destructive drug and there was a lot of it around. We were rock and roll stars at the height of our power and the height of our commerciality and the height of our ability to put asses on seats. We had it all. And sometimes you need to break that tension. Drugs and women were a part of that entire process."

While Crosby, Stills and Nash took to flying from gig to gig in a state-of-the-art (and expensive) Learjet, Young crossed the country in a GMC mobile home that he nicknamed "Mobil-Obil" with his son, Zeke; his romantic partner, actress Carrie Snodgrass; his friends David Cline and James Mazzeo and his dog Art. As the weeks wore on, the distance between Young and the other three men grew wider.

"Playing venues that big created a sort of circus atmosphere," drummer Russ Kunkel said. "There were just so many people. You have to remember, it wasn't just CSNY. There were opening acts like Joni Mitchell, Santana, the Beach Boys, The Band. It was an amazing bill."

Circus might be the operative word to describe the tour, though Crosby had another one: "Doom." "People have said to me, 'How can you call it the Doom Tour if it was so good?'" he said. "I was talking about stuff outside the music when I labeled it that." The environment turned toxic, and by the end, it was all they could do just to make it to the stage each night.

When the Doom Tour finally ended in front of 90,000 people at Wembley Stadium in London, all four men were burned out and sick of one another. The performance was well received by the U.K. music press, but almost the minute after it ended, all four guys took off for supposedly greener pastures. Crosby, Stills, Nash & Young wouldn't play together in front of a paying audience for another decade.

HONORABLE MENTION
The Stooges at the Michigan Palace
Detroit, MI (February 9)

Throughout the early '70s, there wasn't a more dangerous or unpredictable band in America than the Stooges. Led by the inimitable Iggy Pop, the Detroit-area rockers were all about shock and awe. They practically invented punk rock. By 1974, just a year after releasing its seminal album *Raw Power*, the band was set to call it a day. They wouldn't go gentle into that good night and booked one, last desperate gig at the Michigan Palace. Following an opening set from a then-unknown group named Aerosmith, the Stooges hit the stage with blood on their mind. Throughout the show the Stooges dodged a hailstorm of bottles and cans. Not one to back down from a fight, the group's wiry front man gave it right back while pouring everything he had into songs like "Gimme Danger" and "Rich Bitch." A short while after their main set ended, the Stooges reemerged to perform an obscene encore of the Kingsmen classic "Louie, Louie." When it was over, Iggy had a message for the unruly audience. "You nearly killed me, but you missed again," he sneered. "You better keep trying next week."

1975

Led Zeppelin
EARL'S COURT—LONDON, ENGLAND
MAY 25

ZEPPELIN HOLDS COURT

No band codified what it meant to be rock stars more than Led Zeppelin. While the critical elite scratched their heads trying to understand the appeal of this proto-metal, blues-rock foursome, the kids understood just fine. Their brand of rock 'n' roll—filled with charging riffs, atomic drumming and uber-sexualized, darkly whimsical lyrics delivered at piercing volumes—provided a near-perfect soundtrack for the angst-riddled, adolescent experience.

1975 was the peak moment of the band's career. They may have hit creatively higher highs earlier in the decade with the release of their untitled fourth album, but they were never more culturally or commercially vibrant than they were that year. In 1975, the band released its sixth record, a double-LP titled *Physical Graffiti*, which shot to the top of the charts, dragging the group's entire catalog back into the Top 200.

Shortly before its release, Led Zeppelin announced a full-scale tour of North America, set to kick off on January 18 in Bloomington, Minnesota. The demand for tickets was incredible, with fans camping out overnight in front of box offices. Zeppelin rewarded their tenacity with a run unlike anything anyone had ever seen.

"The records were just a starting point," bassist John Paul Jones once explained. "The most important thing was always the stage show. . . . At our worst we were still better than most. At our best we could just wipe the floor with the lot of them."

Zeppelin's not-to-be-fucked-with mountain of a manager, Peter Grant, negotiated a deal with Concerts West to promote the band's tour and spared little expense in putting together their stage show. There would be enhanced sound, lasers, ornate costumes and pyro. At the end of every gig, a giant lighting rig at the back of the stage would blast forth the band's name in untold amounts of mega-wattage. They would overwhelm your eyes as well as your ears.

Behind the scenes, things were even more over the top. The group was ensconced in the finest hotels—most notably the Continental Hyatt House or, as it was otherwise known, the Riot House, just off the Sunset Strip in L.A.—and traveled between gigs in a private 720B passenger jet named The Starship. Drugs, drink and willing groupies were everywhere.

"Looking back on it, this tour's been a flash," singer Robert Plant told a young Cameron Crowe, who was profiling the band for *Rolling Stone*. "Really fast. Very poetic, too. Lots of battles and conquests, back dropped by the din of the hordes. Aside from the fact that it's been our most successful tour on every level, I just found myself having a great time all the way through." The great times weren't over yet.

In addition to being the greatest year of their career, 1975 was also the year that Led Zeppelin ran up against a problem unique to British rock 'n' roll bands: They made way too much money. For the

SET LIST

Rock and Roll

Sick Again

Over the Hills and Far Away

In My Time of Dying

The Song Remains the Same

Rain Song

Kashmir

No Quarter

Tangerine

Going to California

That's the Way

Bron-Y-Aur Stomp

Trampled Underfoot

Moby Dick

Dazed and Confused

Stairway to Heaven

Whole Lotta Love

Black Dog

Heartbreaker

Communication Breakdown

MUSICIANS

Robert Plant: Vocals

Jimmy Page: Guitar

John Paul Jones: Bass/Keyboards

John Bonham: Drums

highest earners in the U.K., taxes could reach as high as 90 percent of earned income. That meant that almost all the money Zeppelin had pulled in from their highly lucrative tour of the U.S., their millions in album sales and their fresh deal with Atlantic Records could be scooped up by the treasury and thrown into the general fund.

The Rolling Stones, Rod Stewart and David Bowie had all found themselves in a similar position and come to the same conclusion: We love you, Your Majesty, but we ain't paying. They all picked up sticks and cleared out for different corners of the world, where the British Treasury secretary couldn't lay claim to their hard-earned gains. Led Zeppelin was set to follow their lead.

To take some of the sting out of their departure, the band announced a three-night residency at the new Earl's Court Exhibition Centre just outside of London. Due to "Demand unprecedented in the history of rock music," as the promoter Mel Bush put it, two additional nights were added to the slate. "Mel told me that we had enough ticket applications to have done ten shows," Grant later boasted.

These weren't going to be stripped-down, peeled-back affairs. Zeppelin wanted to give the U.K. its best and had their American tour stage rig shipped over piece by piece. They even set up gigantic projection screens so that those in the cheap seats could get an up-close look at the band in all its glory.

The price tag for this mini-residency was astronomical, but the band didn't care. "We were so determined to do the same sort of show and more than what we'd been doing in America that in the end we came out of it with just a few hundred pounds," Page said. "It didn't matter because the vibe was so electrifying." Their goal was simple: to put on a spectacle the likes of which had never been seen before in the United Kingdom.

The lights in the vast arena go down and the popular English deejay Alan "Fluff" Freeman, strides onto the stage. It's the final night of Zeppelin's residency, and everyone in Earls Court is a mess of nervous anticipation.

"Good evening, music lovers," he begins. "What I want to know is . . . listen . . . are you ready?" The unseen mass roars back at him with ear-piercing affirmation.

"I wanna tell you something. We are here tonight because you and I have great taste. That is for sure! Wanna hear it? Music lovers, ladies and gentlemen, here is Led Zeppelin!"

Out of the darkness, Jimmy Page strolls over to his amp and plugs in his trusted 1959 sunburst Gibson Les Paul, giving it a few whacks to test the sound. Robert Plant, clad in a pair of the tightest jeans any man has ever worn, is all smiles as he waves to the crowd. In the back, John Paul Jones fiddles with the knobs on his bass. Suddenly the crash of John Bonham's cymbals breaks through the applause, beginning the show.

Led Zeppelin's final night at Earl's Court kicks off much in the same way as the band's run through America had a couple of months back, with a raucous take on its fourth album standout, "Rock and Roll." The mood is celebratory, particularly for Page, who struts across the stage with his low-slung guitar practically crashing into his knees. The energy remains explosive as they tackle the next song, "Sick Again."

"Good evening, and welcome to the last concert in England for a considerable time," Plant says after the opening numbers. "*Quelle dommage, quelle dommage.* [What a pity, what a pity.] But on the other hand, who knows? There's always the 1980s." The crowd loudly boos the singer's joke, but he laughs and keeps talking.

Bonham is bashing away on his kit with the force of a Mack truck slamming into a brick wall at 80 MPH.

"What we intend to do tonight is to take you through some of the colors of . . ." Plant pauses to reconsider his train of thought. "If you regard music as being a prism . . . we've explored the prism and we've developed music along patterns of color. Some light, some dark, and this is how it all starts: with a dream, over the hills."

The spotlight turns to Page, catching him just as he flutters out the opening notes of "Over the Hills and Far Away." The audience cheers in recognition of the melody, but they are swiftly overpowered by the full force of the band as they break into the second verse. From there they shift into "In My Time of Dying," "The Song Remains the Same," "Rain Song" and the heavy, Moroccan-flavored sixth album standout

"Kashmir."

All three of the musicians receive an extended solo turn in the spotlight to show off their considerable talents. Bonham proves why he's considered by many to be the greatest drummer of all time with his twenty-minute solo on "Moby Dick." Jones, bathed in a soft, blue light, brings out the dry ice and intricate mellotron melodies for an extended version of "No Quarter," which closes with a cloud of soap bubbles fluttering over the crowd.

Page feeds into his image as a master of the dark arts, drawing out sinister screeching noises from his guitar with a violin bow on "Dazed and Confused." Plant happily assumes his role as the charming MC, working the crowd over in between numbers, telling jokes about his favorite soccer team the Wolverhampton Wolves, cracking wise about the band's ongoing tax issues and singing snippets of the Dave Clark Five and Scott MacKenzie.

The biggest difference between this show and the American concerts is an acoustic mini-concert placed in the middle of the set. It's something that they hadn't done since their 1972 tour of the U.S. For about 30 minutes, Zeppelin ditches the mega–rock star posturing, diving headlong into more sensitive material like "Going to California" and "That's the Way." Page has always been fond of describing the band's aesthetic as a mix of light and shade. This is the best way to showcase that dichotomy.

The main set ends with an exquisite performance of the band's biggest song: "Stairway to Heaven." Plant introduces the bombastic ballad with a loving allusion to his young daughter Carmen, before ceding the spotlight to Page and Jones, who open it up on guitar and keyboards. The massive arena goes dark as the two men begin the song's ancient, tender intro. Page looks like the ultimate guitar god, with his mighty double-neck Gibson EDS-1275 clattering about his waist.

Plant sings the initial verses with stunning grace, "There's a lady who's sure . . ." Around the four-minute mark, Bonham explodes into view with a few whacks on his snare and tom-tom. Two minutes later,

Page lifts his mighty instrument high up into the air, signaling the beginning of his immortal solo. When they slam into the song's sweltering final moments, a palpable sense of wonder fills the air.

Plant belts out the song's coda with fury: "As we wind on down the road!" Jones is totally locked in, playing that rock solid underlying riff. Bonham is bashing away on his kit with the force of a Mack truck slamming into a brick wall at 80 MPH. All eyes are on Page, his body glistening with sweat, as he pours every ounce of emotion that he has into the song's final, climactic notes.

When it's over the audience, already on its feet, explodes in applause. Above them, the spotlights hone in on a large mirror ball dangling from the center of the stadium, reflecting sharp beams of light back into their eyes. Never again would Led Zeppelin reach such a tremendous emotional and musical high.

The band makes for the wings after "Stairway," only to reemerge for an encore suite of "Whole Lotta Love," "Black Dog" and "Heartbreaker." The band is having just as much fun as the audience and seems just as loath for the evening to end.

Before parting for the final time Plant takes one more shot at the British government. "You'll see gentlemen with white shirts passing a hat around because the equipment and [Chancellor of the Exchequer] Dennis [Healey] cost us so much. We got no bread to fly out of the country! So if you see a hat come round, please put bread in it. Somebody's gonna make some money somewhere!" Then they bust out a furious rendition of one of their earliest hits, "Communication Breakdown."

Backstage it's all smiles as they bask in the glow of the greatest moment of their professional lives. It's late in the evening when they all hop into limos and take off for their respective homes. Thence, a dark, tragedy-riddled future.

HONORABLE MENTION
Bob Marley and Stevie Wonder at the National Stadium Kingston, Jamaica (October 4)

The Wonder Dream concert was a benefit gig organized by Stevie Wonder in 1975 in Kingston, Jamaica, to raise funds for that country's Institute for the Blind. Stevie was a massive star by this point, and in the midst of putting together what would become his greatest album, *Songs in the Key of Life*, but his popularity on the small Caribbean Island country paled in comparison to that of his opening act, Bob Marley. For this special show, Marley pulled out all the stops and reassembled his band the Wailers for the first time since 1973. This show was also the last time they would ever perform together. When the day came, the reggae superstar summoned forth all the passion and energy he could muster, while working his way through an exciting collection of deep cuts and early classics like "One Love" and "No Woman No Cry." The high drama reached its apex hours later when Wonder brought Marley back out at the end of his set to duet on their biggest hits, "I Shot the Sheriff" and "Superstition." The show was a rare opportunity to catch two of the biggest stars of their respective genres at their absolute peak.

#1 Single of the Year:
"Silly Love Songs"
Paul McCartney

#1 Album of the Year:
Frampton Comes Alive
Peter Frampton

1976

The Band with Bob Dylan, Neil Young, Emmylou Harris, Van Morrison, Ronnie Hawkins, Joni Mitchell, Muddy Waters, Eric Clapton, et al.
THE WINTERLAND BALLROOM—SAN FRANCISCO, CA
NOVEMBER 25

THE LAST WALTZ

By 1976, The Band had reached the end of the line. They backed up Bob Dylan on his self-flagellating electrified tours of the mid-1960s, wrote and recorded with him in seclusion on the fabled *Basement Tapes* and released seminal albums under their own name. Few artists had made as great an impact on rock music across the last decade. Now they were ready to walk away.

"One night in 1976, I spoke to the guys about the possibility of bringing this phase of our journey to a conclusion," guitarist Robbie Robertson wrote in his autobiography. "At every concert we played, packs of destructive influences showed up like they were in the business of helping you drown. Somewhere along the way we had lost our unity and our passion to reach higher. Self-destructiveness had become the power that ruled us."

The Band, specifically Robertson, wanted to branch out and do something different. Rather than just putting out a press release announcing their breakup or simply fading away, they had a far grander idea: one last star-studded concert. They invited the biggest names in the music business to share the stage with them as they aired out their history for an especially lucky group of fans.

"It was gonna be the concert of the century, maybe the show to end the whole so-called rock era. That's what they told me, anyway," drummer Levon Helm wrote in his memoir.

San Francisco was the kingdom of concert impresario Bill Graham, and it only made sense to bring him on to organize and stage the event at his ornate, 5,000-seat Winterland Ballroom venue. Graham was the kind of guy who went all out. From the chandeliers taken from *Gone with the Wind* and the elegant backdrop borrowed from the San Francisco Opera House's production of *La Traviata* to the gigantic Thanksgiving dinner served just prior to show time, no detail was too small to escape his notice.

The guest list remained hidden from the concertgoers that managed to score one of the highly priced, highly coveted $25 tickets. The names that Robertson called in represented a veritable "who's who" of the last quarter-century of popular music: Eric Clapton, Joni Mitchell, Stephen Stills, Muddy Waters, Ringo Starr, Ronnie Wood, Neil Young, Van Morrison, and the Staples Sisters, to name a few. Then there was the guest of honor: Bob Dylan.

If this was going to be the "concert of the century," Robertson wanted someone there to document it. He put a call in to a hot, up-and-coming director named Martin Scorsese, who agreed to film the entire thing as a documentary.

It's early in the evening on Thanksgiving Day. The doors to the Winterland fling open, and thousands of people who've been waiting patiently in their finest eveningwear begin to stream inside. After mak-

SET LIST

Up on Cripple Creek

The Shape I'm In

Life Is a Carnival

The W.S. Walcott Medicine Show

Georgia on My Mind

Who Do You Love?

Ophelia

King Harvest (Has Surely Come)

Rag Mama Rag

This Wheel's on Fire

The Night They Drove Old Dixie Down

Stage Fright

Mystery Train

Such a Night

Down South in New Orleans

All Our Past Times

Further on Up the Road

Helpless

Mannish Boy

Four Strong Winds

Coyote

Shadows and Light

Furry Sings the Blues

Dry Your Eyes

Tura Lura Lural (That's an Irish Lullaby)

Caravan

Caldonia

The Genetic Method

Chest Fever

Acadian Driftwood

Evangeline

The Weight

Baby, Let Me Follow You Down

Hazel

I Don't Believe You (She Acts Like We Never Have Met)

Forever Young

Baby, Let Me Follow You Down

I Shall Be Released

Don't Do It

ing it through the door, their ears are greeted by the dulcet strains of the 45-piece Berkeley Promenade

MUSICIANS

Rick Danko: Vocals/Bass/Fiddle

Levon Helm: Vocals/Drums/Mandolin

Robbie Robertson: Vocals/Guitar/Piano

Richard Manuel: Vocals/Piano/Organ/Drums/Clavinet

Garth Hudson: Organ/Piano/Accordion/Saxophone

Orchestra. Long tables covered in white cloth are set up throughout the large ballroom, and waiters in tuxedo T-shirts mill about delivering food and re-filling glasses. Professional dancers sweep around the floor, taking people by the hand and engaging in impromptu waltzes.

After several hours of eating and dancing, the last table is cleared, folded and put away. The lights go down, and The Band takes the stage around 9:00 pm. They open with one of their most recognized and beloved songs, "Up on Cripple Creek," with Helm singing and pounding away behind his drum kit. The band's sound is filled out by a full horn section led by acclaimed New Orleans jazz wizard Allen Toussaint.

The Band holds the stage down by itself for the first hour, taking the audience on a sonic journey through some of their most beloved material, including "This Wheel's on Fire," "The Night They Drove Old Dixie Down" and "Stage Fright." They depart for a brief intermission, leaving the audience to speculate about what guest might show up in the next set. Never in their wildest dreams could they imagine what they were in for.

When The Band reemerges it's with their original leader from back when they tooled around Canada as the Hawks, Ronnie Hawkins. Together, they launch into the Bo Diddley song "Who Do You Love?" which stokes a lot of old memories. "In the middle of one of my solos, Ronnie took off his hat and fanned my fingers like the guitar was going to catch fire," Robertson said. "Just as he had done back when I was 17."

After Hawkins's guest spot, New Orleans piano man Dr. John makes his way out for "Such a Night" and "Down South in New Orleans," followed by Paul Butterfield for "Mystery Train" and then Muddy Waters for "Caledonia" and "Mannish Boy." Everyone in the room is floored as superstar after superstar shows up, plays their part and then gives way to someone else even more mind-blowing.

After Muddy "King of the Chicago Blues" Waters leaves, Eric "King of the British Blues" Clapton takes his place to play "All Our Past Times" and "Farther Up the Road." The homage to The Band's bluesy roots is followed up by a tribute to their Canadian ones. Neil Young is brought out and launches into Ian & Sylvia's "Four Strong Winds" before segueing into his ode to that "town in North Ontario" where he grew up, "Helpless."

Young, who strums and sings oblivious to the great gob of cocaine sticking out of his nose—Scorsese managed to obscure the offending narcotic in the film—eventually cedes the stage to the other great Canadian singer-songwriter in the building that night, Joni Mitchell. She takes the lead on three songs, "Shadows and Light," "Furry Sings the Blues" and "Dry Your Eyes."

The most entertaining moment of the night comes courtesy of the finicky Irish singer Van Morrison. Van the Man had apparently shown up to rehearsals looking something like a 1930s private detective in a long trench coat and a hat. When the night of the show arrives, he emerges without any introduction in a tight, garish, maroon leisure suit dotted with sparkling sequins. The costume combines the worst fashion sensibilities of the 1970s in one horrendous ensemble.

Van is here to kick things up several notches, quite literally as it turns out. As he pours himself into the music, his legs fly off into the air. His voice is deep and nasally but imbued with fire as he roars over one of his most cherished songs, "Caravan." He dances and shakes all around the front of the stage, adding physical exclamations to specific moments of music transcendence. The Band is still playing when he abruptly says "Thank you," drops the microphone and walks off.

Van is a tough act to top, but The Band still has an ace up its sleeve. Nearly four hours after the show

THE GUESTS

Bob Dylan

Neil Young

Paul Butterfield

Eric Clapton

Neil Diamond

Dr. John

Emmylou Harris

Ronnie Hawkins

Joni Mitchell

Van Morrison

Pinetop Perkins

Carl Radle

Cleotha Staples

Mavis Staples

"Pops" Staples

Yvonne Staples

Ringo Starr

Stephen Stills

Muddy Waters

Ronnie Wood

began, they kick into a four-song run that culminates with their most enduring hit, "The Weight." It's as fitting a denouement as you could hope for, except there is still more to come.

"We'd like to bring on one more very good friend of ours . . . Bob Dylan" Robertson says. The man who put them on the map strolls out of the shadows. The audience bursts into a loud round of applause at the appearance of the disheveled figure in the leather jacket, plaid shirt and outlandish, floppy white hat.

Dylan doesn't say a word until The Band begins playing "Baby, Let Me Follow You Down," when he asks the song's opening question, "Can I come home with you?" His voice sounds especially engaged and full of passion. Over the next several minutes, they shift into "Hazel," "I Don't Believe You (She Acts Like We Have Never Met)" and "Forever Young" before finally returning to "Baby, Let Me Follow You Down." The night ends with The Band, Dylan and most of the night's guest stars, including Ron Wood and Ringo Starr, taking the stage for an incredible rendition on the final track from their first album, "I Shall Be Released."

Everyone seems reluctant to go. Some of the performers stick around, taking up an informal jam. "Levon and Ringo weren't going anywhere yet. They kicked into a feel-good beat, and I put my guitar back on," Robertson said. "Eric, Ronnie, Neil and Butterfield all started trading licks. Dr. John took over at the

Superstar after superstar shows up, plays their part and then gives way to someone else even more mind-blowing.

piano. Rick, Garth and I continued our duties as hosts and let the good times roll."

The jam ends and they depart once again. The party is already underway backstage when Graham bursts in to tell them that the audience refuses to exit. He begs them to go back on for one last encore. The members of The Band look to one another, consider the prospect and eventually agree. "It was one of those nights, and no one wanted to let go," Helm said.

The return of The Band is met with an almost deafening applause. Helm counts them in, "One. Two. Three. Uh!" and they blast into a cover of Marvin Gaye's "Don't Do It." The incredible amount of star power they gathered transformed this show into a once-in-a-lifetime affair, but here was an important reminder of who and what this was all about. For their last act, The Band stands tall as brothers, playing in the imitable style that endeared them to fans around the world.

"At the end of the last chorus, there were only the five of us in the world. No audience. No celebration. Nobody. Just the sound of The Band ringing in my ears," Robertson said. Keyboardist Richard Manuel is the one who makes the end official. "Thank you, good night," he says with a wave. "Good-bye."

HONORABLE MENTION

Sex Pistols at the Lesser Free Trade Hall
Manchester, England (June 4)

The Sex Pistols were only about a year old when they stormed the stage at the Lesser Free Trade Hall in Manchester on June 4, 1976, and still more than a year away from releasing their era-defining masterpiece, *Never Mind the Bollocks*. Only 35 to 40 people made it out to the venue that fateful evening, but what the audience lacked in size, they more than made up for in musical excellence. A very young Steven Morrissey of the Smiths was in attendance, as was Ian Curtis, Bernard Sumner and Peter Hook of Joy Division, Mark E. Smith of The Fall and Howard Devoto and Pete Shelley from the Buzzcocks. "They say everyone who was at those gigs went out and formed a band," lead singer John Lydon said. "But that wasn't our plan, or our fault!" The Sex Pistols played thirteen songs that fateful evening, mostly covers, including "Substitute" by The Who, "What'cha Gonna Do About It" by the Small Faces and "No Fun" by the Stooges, which they ran through twice. While they may not have the material, they more than make up for it with aggressive attitude and unbridled intensity. "They are not the saviors of culture, but the destruction of it—which suits me quite perfectly," Morrissey wrote in his autobiography. "I find my freedom only in the liberating shouts of others as they sing themselves into view. Nothing is ever enough, and I want my turn."

#1 Single of the Year:
"Tonight's The Night (Gonna Be Alright)"
Rod Stewart

1977

#1 Album of the Year:
Rumours
Fleetwood Mac

The Ramones
THE RAINBOW THEATRE—LONDON, ENGLAND
DECEMBER 31

ROCKET TO THE RAINBOW

New York punk progenitors the Ramones were consummate road warriors. Across the 22 years they held it together, the band managed to play a staggering 2,263 shows. From dingy clubs in New York to ornate theaters in Europe and large outdoor festivals in South America, there wasn't a stage in the world that the Ramones wouldn't happily burn to the ground.

With the release of their self-titled debut album in 1976, the Ramones effectively invented punk rock. Though earlier groups like the Stooges, the New York Dolls and the Velvet Underground paved the way, it was the Ramones that codified what it meant for music to be punk: simple, fast and loud.

As ferocious as they were on record, it was on the stage that the full power of the band was realized. The experience of hearing Dee Dee fire out that "1-2-3-4!" count into the next song, watching Johnny brutalize the strings of a Gibson Les Paul Jr., peering up at Joey and trying to make out the contours of his face through that large mop of hair and feeling the kick of Tommy's drum wallop you in the chest was life-altering.

1977 was the Ramones' peak as a band. They put out two albums that year, the superb *Leave Home* and the sublime *Rocket to Russia*. As the punk scene expanded, they got better bookings around the U.S., but it was in the U.K. where they enjoyed their most devoted, vocal fan base. Their debut record hit No.

1 on that country's import charts, an incredible feat when you consider that it hadn't even cracked into the Top 100 in the good ol' U.S. of A.

John Giddings, a booking agent in London, remembered, "Everyone was talking about the Ramones. They were the Gods from America. They already started it. The [Sex] Pistols were quite good, but none of them could play like the Ramones."

Underneath the admiration was a love-hate relationship between the band and the English press. "[They] treated us like clowns," Dee Dee wrote in his memoir, *Lobotomy*. "At first, we went on the defensive and acted tough. Then, we stopped caring."

Adding to the New Yorker's ambivalence about Great Britain—beyond that country's lack of readily available ice to cool their beverages—was a nasty habit that many of the young punkers had adopted.

"English audiences liked to spit at us," Dee Dee said. "It's an insult to the band," Johnny added in his autobiography, *Commando*. "If they do something to anyone in the band, they're doing it to the whole band. In England, it was twenty kids spitting. It would ruin the show for me because I wouldn't move to the front because I didn't want to get spit on. I'd look into the lights and try to dodge it if I could."

Despite all that, they kept coming back. Even with the condescending writers and the loogey-hawking fans, the U.K. gave them the greatest opportunity to perform in some of the best venues in front of some

SET LIST

Rockaway Beach

Teenage Lobotomy

Blitzkrieg Bop

I Wanna Be Well

Glad to See You Go

Gimme Gimme Shock Treatment

You're Gonna Kill That Girl

I Don't Care

Sheena Is a Punk Rocker

Havana Affair

Commando

Here Today, Gone Tomorrow

Surfin' Bird

Cretin Hop

Listen to My Heart

California Sun

I Don't Wanna Walk Around with You

Pinhead

Do You Wanna Dance?

Chain Saw

Today Your Love, Tomorrow the World

Now I Wanna Be a Good Boy

Judy Is a Punk

Suzy Is a Headbanger

Let's Dance

Oh Oh I Love Her So

Now I Wanna Sniff Some Glue

We're a Happy Family

MUSICIANS

Joey Ramone: Vocals

Johnny Ramone: Guitar

Dee Dee Ramone: Bass

Tommy Ramone: Drums

es in to hitch a ride with the zealous British audience. The roughly 3,000 fans press hard up against the front of the stage, fists pumping in the air as the Ramones hammer them with as much wattage as they can push through the speakers. It's New Year's Eve after all, and everyone is in the mood to celebrate.

"Everything was going right for that show," the Ramones road manager Monte Melnick told me. "The lights were great, the sound was great, they played the songs terrifically, the crowd was amazing; everything clicked. For the original four, that was their best show: Johnny, Joey, Dee Dee and Tommy."

"Rockaway Beach" turns into "Teenage Lobotomy" before segueing into their all-time greatest song. "It's good to be back in England, and it's good to see all of all you again," Joey says. "Take it Dee Dee." The bass player counts off and the band explodes into the infectious, anthem "Blitzkrieg Bop."

Sid Vicious corners Dee Dee and tells him repeatedly how much he loves his work.

Joey breaks out into the song's catchy "Hey-ho / Let's go" refrain, which the audience echoes back at the band at twice the volume. On the left side of the stage and on the right, both Johnny and Dee Dee jump, dance and bang their heads with fervor. In the back, Tommy bashes away at his kit with an undefinable coolness, while upfront Joey's leg twitches and shakes in place as he sings his lines. The kids are losing their minds, pulsating to the backbeat.

"Blitzkrieg Bop" comes to a climatic finish. The Ramones hardly give the audience time to lavish

of the biggest, most boisterous audiences around. VFWs across the U.S. remained their bread and butter for years to come, but something special happened when they crossed the Atlantic.

Following short opening sets from the Rezillos and Generation X, the Ramones storm the stage of the nearly 50-year-old converted movie house and ready themselves for the coming assault. Johnny blasts out a chord on his guitar as Joey steps up to make his introduction. "Hey, we're the Ramones! This one's called 'Rockaway Beach!'"

Dee Dee counts off "1-2-3-4!" and the band rush-

them with applause before moving on to the next number, "Glad to See You Go," and the one after that, "Gimme Gimme Shock Treatment," and the one after that "You're Gonna Kill That Girl." Over the next 45 minutes, they pack in an incredible 20 more songs.

Even at that breakneck pace, the energy in the room hardly falters. The band slams the crowd with one genre-defining number after another—songs like "Sheena Is a Punk Rocker," "Commando" and "Pinhead." Joey keeps stage banter to a minimum. There's an allusion to some chicken vindaloo that made him sick, but that's about it. There's no time to talk when you gotta rock. The show ends a little after midnight with "We're a Happy Family."

"We'd like to thank y'all for coming," Joey exclaims. "Good night!" After exiting the stage, the band is met by none other than a beaming Elton John, decked out in motorcycle leather and excited to tell them how great they were. Elsewhere, Sid Vicious corners Dee Dee and tells him repeatedly how much he loves his work.

With over 2,000 shows to choose from, it's almost impossible to pick what represents the best concert that the Ramones ever performed. If you had to, this one gig at the Rainbow in 1977 is a good choice. "I think our peak, our greatest moment, is that New Year's Eve show of 1977 into 1978," Johnny Ramone said. "I think that's our greatest moment as a band."

HONORABLE MENTION

KISS at the Forum
Inglewood, CA (April 2)

KISS was one of the most innovate live music entertainers of all time. A KISS concert wasn't merely an event where you'd go to hear your favorite band blast your face off at hazardous volume. It was a real *show*. It was four guys from New York, faces slathered in black and white Kabuki makeup, wearing foot-high platform boots, spewing blood from their mouths and fire from their guitars. It was part rock 'n' roll, part science fiction movie come to life. It's no coincidence that it was a live record titled *Alive!* (1975) that broke KISS through to the mainstream. Two years later, they had their act down and were pushing the concert medium into uncharted territories. As they loudly proclaimed before the show began, "You wanted the best? You've got the best!" This gig, the last of three nights that they performed at the Forum outside of Los Angeles, is maybe *the* best they ever performed. "Kiss mixed demonic makeup, fire-spitting antics and flashy stage effects for some sideshow hokum that would have made even P. T. Barnum take note," *L.A. Times* writer Robert Hilburn noted in his review. "The concert is like an extension of the barroom scene from *Star Wars*." Kicking off with "I Stole Your Love," KISS puts on a clinic of overblown theatrics and virulent, gaudy rock 'n' roll that culminated with a dramatic loud/quiet/ loud encore of "Detroit Rock City," "Beth" and "Black Diamond." The recording of this show made up the bulk of *Alive II*, one of their all-time bestselling records.

1978

Bruce Springsteen
THE CAPITOL THEATRE—PASSAIC, NJ
SEPTEMBER 19

DARKNESS ON THE EDGE OF JERSEY

Throughout the latter half of the 20th century and well into the 21st, Bruce Springsteen has reigned as one of the most exhilarating rock 'n' roll performers on the planet. Nearly every time the Boss hits the stage he stirs up a passion in his audience that turns fans into believers and believers into acolytes. He makes it his mission every night to take the crowd of people gathered before him to places that they've never been before. He rarely ever fails.

1978 was peak live Springsteen. That year he released his edgy, angst-riddled fourth album, *Darkness on the Edge of Town*. Filled out by songs like "Adam Raised a Cain," "Streets of Fire" and "Prove It All Night," it was an internal examination of his personal shift from innocence to experience. If on his earlier albums he contemplated busting out of the confines of his familiar life as a New Jersey artist with dreams left unfulfilled, *Darkness* was Springsteen coming to terms with the aftermath of grasping the brass ring.

There was another element fueling Springsteen during this tremendous run. It had been three years since he'd put out his breakthrough record, *Born to Run*. Three years of hype, three years of lawsuits and three years of people loudly wondering if he had only been a flash in the pan. "With the burden of proving I wasn't a has-been at twenty-eight, I headed out on the road performing long, sweat-drenched rock shows featuring the new album," he wrote in his autobiography.

Though much had changed in his life, the one constant was his faithful backing group, the E Street Band. If anything, the marathon of dates on the road supporting *Born to Run*, along with the interminable hours spent in the studio heightened their musical chemistry to near telepathic levels. E Street was a motley crew filled with a lot of outsized personality, but Springsteen needed them, leaned on them—sometimes literally—and they never let him down.

"Show after show we drove hard, expanding our new songs to their limits until they hit home, until the audience recognized them as their own," he said. "The live power, the strength, of the E Street Band proved invaluable and night after night, we sent our listeners away, back to the recorded versions of this music, newly able to hear their beauty and restrained power."

The Darkness Tour kicked off at Shea's Performing Arts Center in Buffalo, New York, on May 23, 1978. *Rolling Stone* editor Dave Marsh was there and wrote, "The show took the idea of a rock and roll concert into a place of self-revelation and communal ecstasy." He added, "Bruce seemed desperately joyous at the chance for physical release. The audience near mass delirium."

That same communal release was enjoyed by hundreds of thousands of people that turned out to one of the 115 gigs across the United States and

SET LIST

Badlands
Streets of Fire
Spirit in the Night
Darkness on the Edge of Town
Independence Day
The Promised Land
Prove It All Night
Racing in the Street
Thunder Road
Meeting Across the River
Jungleland
Kitty's Back
Fire
Candy's Room
Because the Night
Point Blank
Not Fade Away
She's the One
Backstreets
Rosalita (Come Out Tonight)
4th of July, Asbury Park (Sandy)
Born to Run
Tenth Avenue Freeze-Out
Detroit Medley
Raise Your Hand

MUSICIANS

Guitar/Vocals: Bruce Springsteen
Saxophone: Clarence Clemons
Lead Guitar: Steven Van Zandt
Drums: Max Weinberg
Piano: "Professor" Roy Bittan
Organ: Danny Federici
Bass Guitar: Gary Tallent

Canada over the next eight months. Even hardened critics were turned into fawning worshipers by the exuberant musical marathons that Springsteen and the E Street Band staged night after night.

"I realized the faith I was beginning to put in Springsteen the December day in 1978 that I drove 400 miles to Tucson, Arizona, to see him in concert," veteran *L.A. Times* music critic Robert Hilburn wrote. "Seeing Springsteen push himself so hard on stage and listening to the eloquence of his songs made me forget about doubts and think about my own dreams again."

How do you choose a single show to highlight from a list of 115 of the greatest nights of live rock 'n' roll ever performed? It's a tall order. Amongst his most ardent fans, the ones that have seen him

100 times and more, there's hardly a more divisive question than "What's the best *Darkness* show?"

Some say it's the August 9 gig at the Agora Ballroom in Cleveland, Ohio. The citizens of the "Believeland" love their rock stars almost as much as they love their possibly cursed sports teams and were eager to give the Boss a great response. Springsteen and his band basked in the glow of that love, turning in a three-hour performance marked with an electrifying, communal spirit. One of the biggest Boss fans I know refers to this gig as "The night rock attained perfection."

Others point to the show near the end of the tour on December 15 at Bill Graham's Winterland Ballroom in San Francisco. It was one of the last performances ever hosted at the old skating rink, and Springsteen made it a night to remember. "Tonight you're gonna hear [the] concert of your life," he promised early in the gig, a promise that remained unbroken. The show was another three-hour tour de force, featuring a mishmash of *Darkness* songs, earlier hits, covers of classic songs by artists like Bo Diddley and Mitch Ryder and unreleased material like *The River* opening track "The Ties That Bind."

More than a few fans would roll their eyes at both of those selections, opting for something a little cozier, like his July 7 blowout at the Roxy in Hollywood. Just two days after tearing it down at the Forum in Inglewood, Springsteen surprised his So-Cal fans with a super intimate gig at a small club on the Sunset Strip. The streets outside were flooded with fans who couldn't score a ticket but craved to be close to the action. "I want to thank you's for coming down," Springsteen said to the fortunate few who made it into the gig. "I wasn't trying to turn this into no private party 'cause I don't play no parties anymore, except my own. So gimme a little slapback on this microphone . . . we're gonna do some rock 'n' roll for you!" He proceeded to blast them away with an exuberant, high-drama set of music. At one point he sang while being carried around on the shoulders of the "Big Man," saxophonist Clarence Clemons.

They'd all be wrong, of course. The best show from that vaunted run took place an hour away from Springsteen's hometown on September 19 in Passaic, New Jersey. It wasn't just the greatest show of the 1978 tour or the greatest show of Springsteen's entire career. This one night at the Capitol Theater stands as one of the greatest presentations of live rock 'n' roll of all time.

Hey, New Jersey, can you hear me?" Springsteen asks. The Garden State crowd cheers wildly. They can hear him just fine. With a wide smile on his face Bruce counts, "1-2-3!" and behind him, the E Street Band blasts into the galloping show opener, "Badlands." The audience loses their ever-loving minds at the first sound of "Professor" Roy Bittan's instantly identifiable, twinkling piano riff.

Springsteen looks like he's trying to class things up a bit these days, eschewing his earlier, signature leather jacket and floppy hat ensemble for a dark sport coat and a white button-up shirt left open at the top. The rest of the band appears equally dapper, with the "Big Man" perhaps the best dressed in his three-button suit.

The first number ends and they immediately slide into "Streets of Fire," which gives the bandleader a moment to show exactly what he can do with his trusty Fender Telecaster/Esquire hybrid. When the moment for his solo arrives, Springsteen drops almost to his knees and rips into the instrument. A hurricane of notes explodes out of the amplifier, bringing wide smiles and hearty cheers.

The next song, "Spirit in the Night," gives Clemons the opportunity to counter the Boss's musical virtuosity. After the song's second chorus, Springsteen

calls out, "Big Man, if you will." With that, the 6'5" former offensive lineman jumps into the audience and lets loose with a powerful sax solo. Springsteen dives right in after him. The crowd engulfs the two men, latching hard onto the singer, with women clamoring tightly around his neck and planting kisses on his face. He breaks free from them long enough for someone to lift him back onto the stage, where he belts out the final, mournful verse.

A single wail from his guitar that sounds like a thousand chainsaws chewing through the trunk of a 300-foot-tall Sequoia

The men of E Street fervently race through the next three songs until reaching the peak moment of the show. Most performers might save the emotional apex for the end of the main set or the encore. Bruce Springsteen is not most performers.

"Prove It All Night" opens with an original light piano piece courtesy of Bittan. It sets the mood and lulls the audience into a moment of quiet reflection. A moment later, Springsteen breaks the spell with a single wail from his guitar that sounds like a thousand chainsaws chewing through the trunk of a 300-foot-tall Sequoia. For the next two minutes the front man takes center stage with one of the nastiest, grittiest guitar solos you've ever heard, fleshed out with numerous dive bombs, warp-speed pull-offs and waves of feedback.

When he reaches the end of his opening guitar-gasm, the rest of the band slams into the song like a Mack Truck doing 60 mph through a cement wall. Springsteen stands there with his arm raised and one finger pointing toward the ceiling. Then he walks to microphone and starts to sing. "I've been working real hard trying to get my hands clean."

Midway through, Springsteen steps to the front again to show off some more six-string acrobatics. The exertion is plain to see on his face, which is scrunched into a pained expression. His exposed biceps bulge and the sweat pours down his chest.

"You gotta prove it all night," Springsteen screams at song's end. The crowd chants "Bruuuuuuuuce" in appreciation. There's still so much more to go. For the next two-and-a-half hours, Springsteen alternates emotional gut-wrenchers like "Racing in the Streets," "Jungleland," "Because the Night" and "Thunder Road" with ass-shaking party anthems like "Kitty's Back," "Rosalita (Come Out Tonight)," "Backstreets" and "Born to Run." It's a lifetime of feelings and experiences packed into a single set of music.

"The energy is what I take away from most of it," David Reiss, a then-20-year-old fan told me about witnessing this gig. "Back then in '78 when I would go to concerts, I was always afraid that the person whose recordings I had fallen in love with would be a tremendous disappointment when I saw them live. Springsteen was the opposite. Just phenomenal. Every aspect of the concert."

The night closes out with a joyous rendition of the soulful Eddie Floyd hit "Raise Your Hand." Springsteen uses the song to close out most of his shows during the 1978 tour. "Are you talking to me?" he asks the crowd. "Well, I'm talking to you in Boston, in Providence, in Worchester, in Hartford, in New York, in Philadelphia, in Baltimore, in Washington D.C., in New Jersey!" When he finally mentions his home state, the Jersey crowd goes wild.

The last song ends a couple of minutes later. The audience, wide-eyed and beaming, shuffles out the doors of the Capitol Theater into the chilly evening air. Springsteen and the band retire backstage to laugh and joke and prepare to repeat the act the next night. And the night after that. And the night after that.

HONORABLE MENTION
Cheap Trick at Budokan Hall
Tokyo, Japan (April 28)

It's a rare occasion that a single concert can break open an entire career. It's not impossible, but extremely unlikely. The most notable example might be the case of Cheap Trick and its performance at the Budokan in 1978. Through a weird confluence of events, the band from Rockford, Illinois, were bigger stars in the Japan than they were in their own backyard. Their song "I Want You to Want Me" was a No. 1 hit in the Far East country, and demand for tickets in Tokyo was off the charts. Their Japanese fans were ready to flip out for their joyful, explosive brand of rock 'n' roll. Fortunately, someone was rolling the tape that night. The show was released as *Cheap Trick at Budokan* the following year in the U.S., where it cracked into the Top 5 on the Billboard 200. The songs had always been good, they just needed that extra bit of energy and enthusiasm that only the live experience can bring to get people to pay attention.

1979

Van Halen
THE CALIFFORNIA WORLD MUSIC FESTIVAL
MEMORIAL COLISEUM—LOS ANGELES, CA
APRIL 8

CALIFFORNIA JAM

Van Halen's one-night stand at the CaliFFornia World Music Festival in 1979 reigns as one of the most over-the-top events in rock history. That's without even mentioning what happened onstage. Though they had only "made it" the year before, following the release of their self-titled debut album, Van Halen had spent the last several years plugging away in the San Gabriel Valley as a beer-swilling, cop-enraging, backyard party band. They were four guys who knew how to have a good time and delighted in pushing the envelope.

Van Halen was the co-headliner for the festival's second day alongside an on-the-edge-of-disintegrating Aerosmith. From the second they arrived at the Memorial Coliseum, they did just about everything they could do to attract attention. The band, their crew and their coterie of hangers-on—about 300 people—rolled up to the venue in a fleet of 16 white stretch limousines. Backstage, a pair of little people acted as the band's "security team," but their chief responsibility was to fetch lead singer David Lee Roth more beer whenever his cup ran low.

Rocking the faces off tens of thousands of adoring fans wasn't the only thing they had on their agenda that day. To while away the hours before they hit the stage, Van Halen concocted a prank to play on Aerosmith. They parked a yellow Volkswagen Bug in front of the Coliseum and periodically had someone make an announcement to the crowd asking for "someone in the Aerosmith organization to please move their car."

Meanwhile, Van Halen had already rented a World War II–era Sherman tank from a Hollywood entertainment company with the intention of running over "Aerosmith's Bug." As Roth explained, "The theory being that after all of these announcements throughout the day and the night, the lights would go down, they'd go, 'Ladies and gentlemen . . . da-da-da . . . Van Halen,' the spotlights would hit us and the tank would come out from under a cover on that landing, run right over the Volkswagen and we'd pop out of the tank and run down the stairs to the stage."

Aerosmith found out and put the kibosh on Van Halen's plan. "We discovered several days before the show that Aerosmith had been put wise to our little scheme and had found some stock footage of airplanes blowing up tanks, and that's what they were going to show when they came on after us," Roth said. "We decided that because Aerosmith had a little trump card that we weren't going to do the tank trick, so we never ran over the Volkswagen, we just ran down the stairs. We didn't want to be one-upped on our one-upmanship, you know?"

With their plan to sabotage the Aerosmith's set thwarted, Van Halen were going to do something even better. They were going to blow the headliners completely off the stage.

SET LIST

Light Up The Sky
Somebody Get Me a Doctor
Drum Solo
Runnin' with the Devil
Beautiful Girls
On Fire
Bass Solo
You're No Good
Feel Your Love Tonight
Outta Love Again
Ain't Talkin' 'Bout Love
Eruption/Spanish Fly
You Really Got Me
Bottoms Up!

MUSICIANS

David Lee Roth: Vocals
Eddie Van Halen: Guitar
Alex Van Halen: Drums
Michael Anthony: Bass

Van Halen is introduced to the large crowd by the festival's MCs, the stoner comedy duo Cheech & Chong. At the mention of their name, the band shoots down the stairs just as the sun begins to sink below the lip of the Coliseum. Without wasting a second they launch into the hard-charging track "Light Up the Sky" from their new album, *Van Halen II*. Roth is quite a sight decked out in electric yellow lyrca pants and an unbuttoned rainbow striped shirt. Next to him, Eddie Van Halen is beaming as he rips into his self-modified red and white "Frankenstrat" guitar.

"Los Angeles!" Roth screams when the song ends. "We got a bunch of new ones for ya, baby!" Alex Van Halen taps in a soft four-count on his cowbell and the band blasts into another *Van Halen II* cut, "Somebody Get Me a Doctor." From there they go back in time, pulling out their first album single, "Runnin' with the Devil," before hitting the crowd with their latest hit, "Dance the Night Away."

Unlike many of their '70s rock contemporaries who rely on hundred-thousand–watt lighting rigs, pyrotechnics and lasers to make an impression, at this point in their career all Van Halen needs to keep the audience's attention is their outsized charisma and significant musical chops. The massive stage set-ups—no brown M&MS please!— would come in time. But at this moment Eddie's incredible fretboard gymnastics, Michael Anthony's nimble harmonies, Alex's frenetic double-bass footwork and Roth's midair splits and ear-piercing wails are more than enough to keep the crowd enthralled.

Amongst the 65,000 people in the audience that night was future Guns N' Roses guitarist Slash, and the dizzying display made a lasting impression. "I subconsciously knew then that rock 'n' roll was entering into a new era as a result of this great new band. They were really powerful and alive, and there was a palpable rush of excitement the moment they hit the stage," he remembered. "It was loud and aggressive, melodic, rhythmic, and fluid, with a boatload of charisma and showmanship on top of all that. That first experience seeing [Eddie] play has stuck with me to this day."

Roth has a clear read on this audience and takes special delight in toying with them throughout the show. "There seems to be a lot of concern, especially about this show with all of the kids doing drugsssssss," he deadpans during a breakdown in the middle of "Ain't Talking 'Bout Love." The crowd cheers wildly. "And I don't know, but I heard there's a rumor that a lot of people do sex after they do the drugs." The crowd cheers even more wildly. "So what I wanna do is take my own, personal Van Halen survey. So I wanna ask ya: Who likes to get high around here?!" The crowd explodes, affirming *en masse* their love of narcotics and all the accompanying side effects. Roth beams like the Cheshire cat.

After this comedic interlude, the band breaks back into "Ain't Talking 'Bout Love." At the behest of the lead singer, the Coliseum turns into a galaxy of upraised lighters while Van Halen brings the song to its "Hey, hey, hey" conclusion. Then comes the moment that everyone has been waiting for. A spotlight shifts over to Eddie as he pings out the first harmonic notes to his extended guitar solo "Eruption."

For five full minutes, the smiley-faced virtuoso shows all that he can do in a volcanic display of mind-blowing musical wizardry. The notes pour out of his stack of Marshall amplifiers faster than the mind's ability to fully digest them. Then he shifts into the warp-speed second half of the song, the part where he abandons his pick altogether and starts tapping the notes out on the fretboard of his instrument. It's all everyone can do to keep their jaws from hitting the floor.

> ## The night ends with gobs of chocolate cake flying through the air and copious amounts of cheap beer disappearing down their throats.

The second Eddie finishes his solo, the band dives headfirst into its first-ever single, a cover of the Kinks' classic "You Really Got Me." The cheering shakes the walls of the Coliseum to their foundation. When the song ends, the band departs and the audience spends the next several minutes begging for an encore. When Van Halen emerges to perform "Bottoms Up!" the scream of appreciation is deafening. "I got to tell ya," Roth says to the crowd, "L.A., you are, and you always will be, the fucking greatest!"

A little over an hour after they started, Van Halen waves goodbye and retreats backstage, where their parents are all waiting for them in their dressing room. But if you thought that the presence of maternal and fraternal authority might curb their bad behavior, think again. The night ends just as chaotically as the day began, with gobs of chocolate cake flying through the air and copious amounts of cheap beer disappearing down their throats.

HONORABLE MENTION
Concert for The People of Kampuchea at The Hammersmith Odeon
London, England (December 26-29)

Most people are aware of George Harrison's Concert for Bangladesh at Madison Square Garden in 1971, which featured performances by Bob Dylan and Eric Clapton. It was one of the first all-star benefit gigs. Fewer people are aware of this four-night run presented by Paul McCartney to raise funds for the people of Cambodia. While Macca didn't break new ground, he arguably put together a better bill. The first night featured Queen, who delivered a massive 28-song tour de force that ended with a one-two punch of "We Will Rock You" and "We Are the Champions." The next night was headlined by The Clash, who had just put out their seminal album *London Calling* less than two weeks earlier. The Pretenders and The Who held it down on the third night. For the final evening, McCartney mounted the stage with his band Wings for what turned out to be their final performance ever. He closed the run joined by 30 other English musicians for a collaboration he called a Rockestra, playing "Let It Be" and "Lucille."

#1 Single of the Year:
"Call Me"
Blondie

#1 Album of the Year:
The Wall
Pink Floyd

1980

Pink Floyd
LOS ANGELES MEMORIAL SPORTS ARENA
LOS ANGELES, CA
FEBRUARY 7

L.A. MASONRY

On July 6, 1977, Pink Floyd performed the final date of their In the Flesh World Tour at Olympic Stadium in Montreal. It was their 55th show in just under six months, a grueling schedule that left them worn out. They didn't phone the gig in by any means, but it was apparent that they were eager to finish up and head home. The only problem was the crowd that night was behaving rudely, talking during the quieter parts of the show and setting off firecrackers.

Bassist Roger Waters tried to begin the song "Pigs on the Wing Part 2" multiple times, but he was repeatedly interrupted by small explosions. Finally, he had enough. "For fuck's sake, stop lettin' off fireworks and shouting and screaming, I'm trying to sing the song!" he roared.

The 80,000-person crowd shouted back, but Waters wasn't finished. "I mean, I don't care . . . if you don't want to hear it, you know, fuck you. I'm sure there's a lot of people here who *do* want to hear it. So why don't you just be quiet? If you want to let your fireworks off go outside and let them off there, and if you want to shout and holler, go and do it out there. I'm trying to sing a song that some people want to listen to. *I* want to listen to it."

A little later, just as Waters was about to break into "Pig (Three Different Ones)," anger welled up inside his chest. He couldn't take it anymore. He drew his head back and spit at some fans in the front row. The show continued, but the incident left him shaken

and scarred. That moment was the catalyst for him to create the great work of his life and career: *The Wall*.

"*The Wall*," Waters reflected years later, "grew out of an alienation from certain sections of our audience that I'd felt at one stage of my career. It's also about the alienation I felt at the loss of my father—who was killed during World War II. In fact, seen as a broader canvas, about alienation in general."

Pink Floyd's eleventh album hit the shelves on November 30, 1979, and flew up the charts. It claimed the top spot in January 1980 and held onto that position for a staggering 15 consecutive weeks. Listeners loved the breathtaking scope of the double-LP rock opera. Songs like "Hey You," "Comfortably Numb" and "Another Brick in the Wall (Part II)" became FM radio fixtures for decades to come. "Another Brick in the Wall (Part II)" was the only Pink Floyd single ever to hit No. 1.

While waiting for the album's release, Waters spent a considerable amount of time thinking about how to put together a show that properly—and spectacularly—conveyed its themes and central story. Then he had it. During the show, as the band played the new material, stagehands would slowly, steadily build a wall between them and their audience.

"I don't think anybody had any conception of what was going on in Roger's mind," sound crew chief Robbie Williams said, "and when we first heard that he wanted to build this wall with the band per-

SET LIST

In the Flesh?
The Thin Ice
Another Brick in the Wall (Pt. 1)
The Happiest Days of Our Lives
Another Brick in the Wall (Pt. 2)
Mother
Goodbye Blue Sky
Empty Spaces
What Shall We Do Now?
Young Lust
One of My Turns
Don't Leave Me Now
Another Brick in the Wall (Pt. 3)
The Last Few Bricks
Goodbye Cruel World
Hey You
Is There Anybody Out There?
Nobody Home
Vera
Bring the Boys Back Home
Comfortably Numb
The Show Must Go On
In the Flesh
Run Like Hell
Waiting for the Worms
Stop
The Trial
Outside the Wall

MUSICIANS

Roger Waters: Vocals/Bass/Guitar
David Gilmour: Guitar/Mandolin
Nick Mason: Drums/Guitar
Richard Wright: Piano/Keyboards/Accordion

There was one drawback to all that spectacle. Because of all the moving parts and intricate choreography, *The Wall* couldn't tour in the traditional sense. Instead of hitting multiple cities like Cleveland, Philadelphia, Chicago or San Francisco, Pink Floyd held extended residencies in big arenas in the largest metropolitan markets in the world. They began with seven nights in Los Angeles, followed by five nights in New York, six nights in London, eight nights in Germany and a final five nights back in London.

The show reportedly cost the band around $1.5 million before they even made it out in front of a paying audience. "It was absurdly expensive," drummer Nick Mason said. "It couldn't possibly travel because of the sheer expense of getting this thing to move. It was miles ahead of anything that had been done in rock 'n 'roll and the amount of effort that went into every single detail was unheard of. It was very fucking difficult to do but we had some very good people on board who made it happen."

forming behind it, we all said, 'You've got to be fucking mad!' We thought the audience would storm the stage and that the poor guys at front of house were going to get killed. Fortunately, it didn't turn out that way!"

Immense, inflatable characters would be introduced during the show, as would a series of animated projections. It would be the most forward-thinking, visually stunning rock show anyone had ever attempted. As the *New York Times* predicted, "*The Wall* show will be the touchstone against which all future rock spectacles must be measured." That statement is as true today as it was in 1980.

Local DJ Cynthia Fox is still onstage giving her intro when the first booming notes of *The Wall's* opening track, "In the Flesh?" comes avalanching out of the massive 45,000-watt P.A. system. An explosion of fireworks goes off, a curtain is pulled back and the members of Pink Floyd come into view. The audience goes wild, but there's a problem. A Roman candle has set fire to the curtain.

Because of the intense, hours-long rehearsals, where Waters repeatedly called for things to be stopped, the guys manning the board blow him off. They assume he's either crying wolf or playing to the crowd. As the flames grow higher and smoke begins to fill the arena, they cut the sound.

"Eventually I looked up and saw one of the riggers, a guy called Rocky, leap about six feet through the air, with no safety harness or anything on him, from one drape to another," Waters remembered. "He had a fire extinguisher in one hand and he was trying to put the thing out . . . then lumps of burning drape the size of tennis balls started hitting the stage all around us and the auditorium was beginning to fill up with smoke."

A gigantic plane swoops down out of the rafters and crash-lands behind the band with an incredible explosion.

After a short delay, "In the Flesh?" kicks in again, and Pink Floyd takes 15,000 fans on a sonically exhilarating and visually stunning journey through the darkest corners of Waters's mind. As the opening number ends, a gigantic plane swoops down out of the rafters and crash-lands behind the band with an incredible explosion. It's the first of many stunning visual effects to come.

For the next hour or so, Pink Floyd runs through the first and second sides of their most ambitious work as giant inflatable monsters stalk the stage and roadies stack up dozens of white cardboard bricks. With every song, "Another Brick in the Wall (Part 2)," "Goodbye Blue Sky," "Young Lust" and "Mother," their construction goes higher and higher. The sound in the arena is spectacular. The band has a state-of-the-art quadrophonic speaker system that allows it to play different noises in different places throughout the venue.

The last song of the record's first half, "Goodbye Cruel World," concludes with Waters alone singing into a handheld microphone in the last empty space available. He bids the crowd goodbye, and the final brick is put into place. *The Wall* is complete. The implied separation between artist and audience is physically manifest in the starkest and most imposing way.

While impressive, performing an album in sequential order in such a well-choreographed manner has its drawbacks, chief among them the lack of spontaneous moments of unplanned musical inspiration. For guitarist David Gilmour, the tradeoff is worth it.

"For me, *The Wall* show was terrific fun," he said. "I had to take on the role of music director and deal with a lot of musical details on stage so that Roger didn't have to think about that. It was really tough at first. Later on it got a little easier, once we all got into it." He added, "I had to transmit with very primitive equipment to all the delay lines onstage. Very tricky. Except for the 'Comfortably Numb' solo, there were virtually no moments where I could say, 'Forget everything. Just play.'"

Following a brief 20-minute intermission, the second act begins with a poignant performance of the melancholy "Hey You." It's the moment when the album's protagonist realizes that secluding himself behind a wall isn't a great idea and makes a futile attempt to reconnect with the world. Gilmour's soaring, fearsome solo drives the desperation home.

The band members are intermittently seen through "windows" in the massive wall, depicted in little tableaus. Eventually they make their way out front and dive into the album's second half with gusto. The emotional high point of the night comes courtesy of Gilmour, who performs his iconic solo to "Comfortably Numb" from the top of the wall. After that, they sprint through songs like "Run Like Hell" and "Waiting for the Worms" until they reach the denouement, "The Trial."

A stunning, cartoonish visual is projected onto the Wall. All the people that the protagonist has ever mistreated—his teacher, his wife, his mother—are allowed their chance to speak and then the Judge passes down the sentence. The Wall must come down. A spine-tingling refrain breaks out overhead. "Tear down the Wall! Tear down the Wall!" A slow rumble vibrates throughout the arena. One brick falls. Then another, and another. Then it all comes crashing down.

Waters sings the final track, "Outside the Wall," while a melancholy mandolin is strummed behind him. "It's not easy," he admits. "Banging your heart against some mad bugger's wall."

HONORABLE MENTION
AC/DC at the Gaumont Theatre
Southampton, England (January 27)

No one could have known that this gig, the final date of AC/DC's Highway to Hell Tour, would be lead singer Bon Scott's last performance. A little over two weeks after they bid their *adieus*, the enigmatic front man died in his car outside a London club named the Music Machine following a night of heavy drinking. The tragedy has given this show an added weight of poignancy, but even divorced from subsequent events, it's an incredible gig. The band was firing on all cylinders, riding high on the success of its most recent album. Angus Young, the diminutive lead guitarist, clad in his schoolboy outfit, was in fiery form, blasting the paint off the walls with his incendiary solos on songs like "T.N.T.," "Whole Lotta Rosie" and "High Voltage." His energy was matched by Scott, who tore into each number with his signature, nasal wail. There are a lot of what-ifs in the AC/DC story, especially after the rest of the band carried on with new lead singer Brian Johnson and scored the biggest commercial success of their career with *Back in Black*. For many Scott enthusiasts, this gig was the band at its apex. It's a look toward what their future could have been, free from tragedy and filled with possibility.

1981

The Clash
BOND CASINO—NEW YORK, NY
MAY 28

THE CLASH BOND IN TIMES SQUARE

Die-hard fans know that The Clash is "The Only Band That Matters." Even though that moniker started out as a marketing gimmick, by the summer of 1981 it might as well have been true. No band on the planet rocked harder or mattered more than Joe Strummer and company. The proof is in the band's extended residency at Bond's Casino in the heart of Times Square through the Spring of 1981.

A few months earlier, on December 12, 1980, the band unveiled a gargantuan, 36-song, triple-LP, *Sandinista!* Its title referred to the Sandinista National Liberation Front, a socialist group that overthrew the Somoza Dynasty in Nicaragua in 1979. The music was a politically charged mix of funk grooves, calypso rhythms, disco beats, rock riffs and reggae stomps. *Sandinista!* was met with generally positive reviews, but it has since been heralded as a masterpiece, second in critical esteem only to the band's breakthrough third album, *London Calling.*

Around the same time The Clash dropped *Sandinista!,* they brought their original manager, Bernie Rhodes, back into the fold. Singer/guitarist Joe Strummer was particularly unhappy with the direction The Clash's career was headed in and threatened to quit unless the rest of the band agreed to the change in leadership. One of Rhodes's first acts was a masterstroke of publicity-garnering gamesmanship.

"Bernie came back on the scene because people thought that we'd gotten out of control," lead guitarist Mick Jones said. "The first thing he wanted to do was book us for seven nights in New York."

It started out as seven—eight, actually—nights. What Rhodes wanted was a full-scale tour of the U.S., but The Clash's record company refused to cover the up-front costs. A residency in a single city was the best they could hope for, and where better than the Big Apple? Rhodes eschewed some of the more established venues in the City and booked the band in a recently converted department store named Bonds Casino, which had a capacity of around 1,750 people. The demand for tickets was off the charts, and in the lead-up to the gigs, The Clash sold almost double the venue's capacity on a nightly basis.

The first show went down on May 28 and was packed to the rafters. The fire marshal was notified, and the next night, only the first 1,750 ticketholders could enter. A near riot broke out in the streets, started by those who had camped out for tickets and were now turned away. Fortunately, order was restored before the whole thing turned violent.

The May 30 performance was canceled and the rest of the engagement was thrown into jeopardy. The crisis was averted when the band agreed to perform an extra slate of shows for all the fans that were left out. The Clash would now take the stage at Bonds a staggering 17 times. For far less money and for way more effort, they performed for nearly as many people in three weeks as could fit into Madison Square

SET LIST

London Calling
Safe European Home
(White Man) in Hammersmith Palais
Train in Vain
Lightning Strikes (Not Once but Twice)
Junco Partner
The Guns of Brixton
Complete Control
Ivan Meets G.I. Joe
The Call Up
The Leader
Charlie Don't Surf
The Magnificent Seven
Wrong 'Em Boyo
Bankrobber
Somebody Got Murdered
Career Opportunities
Clampdown
One More Time
Brand New Cadillac
Janie Jones
Armagideon Time
Washington Bullets
Police and Thieves
I'm So Bored with the U.S.A.

MUSICIANS

Joe Strummer: Vocals/Guitar
Mick Jones: Guitar
Paul Simonon: Bass
Topper Headon: Drums

Garden in a single night. Total punk rock.

The residency turned into a full-fledged media event, especially after the near-riot and the canceled performance. Celebrities of all stripes flocked both to the band's Gramercy Park Hotel and to Bonds to see The Clash and to be seen with them. The band even filmed a small cameo in the Martin Scorsese film *King of Comedy* while in town. All the notoriety wouldn't have mattered for anything if The Clash didn't deliver, and did they ever! Across 17 different nights, they set a new bar for rock 'n' roll in all its loud, sweaty, violent and rapturous glory.

To start off their shows at Bonds, The Clash enlisted a diverse range of opening acts. Before you could see the acclaimed English punkers, you were treated to sets by the likes of the Dead Kennedys, The Fall, Lee "Scratch" Perry and Bad Brains. For this first night, The Clash brought in Grandmaster Flash and the Furious Five. The Bronx rap pioneers hit the stage with good intentions, but are viciously booed by the rock-loving crowd. When the group tries to engage the audience in their typical call-and-response on the song "Beat Street," instead of shouting "Say Ho!" the audience defiantly chants back, "Fuck you!"

A short while after Melle Mel and The Kidd Creole packed up their turntables, The Clash storms the stage and is met with a loud, gracious cheer. "Good evening," Strummer says. He looks around the room and then starts stabbing out the E minor chord intro to "London Calling." The heat in the intimate space is sweltering. The humidity rises from the crowd like a dense fog. The sweat is pouring down the walls.

"It was an unusual room," photographer Bob Gruen told me. "It wasn't like the Beacon Theater or Irving Plaza. It was a big square room with a linoleum floor on the second floor of this building on 42nd Street."

The earlier caustic atmosphere is transformed in the presence of The Clash. The show feels like a tightly packed party among like-minded friends. This is especially true when the band busts out the extremely danceable single "Train in Vain" four songs into the set. The 3,000-plus people gathered together jump, shout and whistle as Strummer shimmies and waves his arms while repeatedly asking them to "stand by me."

The band crisscrosses through their discography, paying special attention to include selections from *Sandinista!*, songs like "Ivan Meets G.I. Joe," "One More Time," "The Leader" and "Washington Bullets." There are several fan favorites thrown in like "Brand New Cadillac," "The Guns of Brixto" and "Wrong

'Em Boyo." They even bust out "This Is Radio Clash," which won't be officially released for several more months.

The humidity rises from the crowd like a dense fog. The sweat is pouring down the walls.

The Clash sweats it out onstage for well over an hour, pouring every ounce of energy they have into their 19-song set. Strummer feeds off the fury of the spastic crowd, whipping himself into a tornado of passion and fury. His worn-down Fender Telecaster bounces precariously around his hips as he grabs the microphone by both hands and lets loose with all the volume his vocal cords can propel out his throat.

As *New York Times* reviewer Stephen Holden observed during this show, "the quartet translates into thunderous rock, the violent enthusiasm of a revolutionary street gang. If Mr. Strummer's singing is the rude voice of the mob, Topper Headon's powerful drumming drives their apocalyptic war cries with an ominous jack-booted determination." Holden added that the band "demonstrated that fervent, critical adulation and some commercial success haven't diluted their intransigence."

The main set closes with a 'roided out version of "Clampdown." The Clash disappears for a few moments then returns to play another seven songs. The crowd eats it up, cheering and singing with all they've got. By the time they reach the last number, "I'm So Bored with the U.S.A." it's clear that the men onstage are anything but.

The Clash's run at Bonds is a clear demarcation point in their history. Before it, they were essentially a critically adored buzz band with a respectable amount of commercial success and cultural relevance. In its wake, they became superstars. Roughly 18 months after this gig, they'd be playing just before The Who in front of 55,000 people at Shea Stadium.

HONORABLE MENTION

Rick James at Long Beach Arena
Long Beach, CA (July 30)

Rick James was one of pop music's true wild men. He was a guy who liked to have a good time and wasn't afraid to get into a little bit of trouble. In 1981, everything came together for him. After more than a decade of toiling in near obscurity, James scored the biggest hit of his career with the album *Street Songs*. Audiences went crazy for turbo-charged funk hits like "Superfreak" and "Give It to Me Baby." The subsequent tour sold out almost instantly. "Even in a place like Memphis scalpers were making a fortune off our shows," James recalled in his memoir, *Glow*. Already an eccentric, high-energy entertainer, James took things to another planet for his show at the Long Beach Arena. The crowd flipped for the *Street Songs* material, but it was the song "Mary Jane" that provided the explosive climax. Stretched out to more than 10 minutes, James described the ode to marijuana as "the tune where I stood before twenty-foot joints made out of papier-mâché with smoke coming out the tips. I'd always fire up. So did the rest of the crowd. It was our big bonding moment." James didn't even sing most of the song. The audience took care of those duties with the braided funkmaster acting as their cheerleader. "Shit, goddamn, get off your ass and jam," he implored. They were only too willing to oblige.

1982

Ozzy Osbourne
VETERANS MEMORIAL AUDITORIUM—DES MOINES, IA
JANUARY 20

THE BAT INCIDENT

A few days into 1982, 17-year-old Mark Neal's little brother brought a curious pet home from school. It was a bat. The loud, flapping creature didn't last long in the company of the Neals and died shortly thereafter. The brothers were faced with several options about what to do with the remains of the departed mammal. They could have buried it or thrown it away, but rather than go with any of those sane, level-headed approaches, the teenager's friends convinced them otherwise.

Neal had tickets to see metal legend Ozzy Osbourne. Why not bring the deceased bat along for the gig? The former Black Sabbath front man was renowned for his depraved antics, both onstage and off. The year before in March, he bit the heads off two living doves during a record sales convention in California. Surely, he would welcome a bat carcass!

"I just remember this PR woman going on and on at me," Osbourne recalled of the dove incident. "In the end, I said, 'Do you like animals?' Then I pulled out one of these doves and bit its fucking head off. Just to shut her up. Then I did it again with the next dove, spitting the head out on the table, and [the woman] fell on the floor screaming. That's when they threw me out. They said I'd never work for CBS again."

On January 20, Neal sealed the bat inside a plastic bag, tucked it into one of his jacket pockets and made his way out to the Veteran's Memorial Auditorium in Des Moines. Little did he realize that he was about to create one of the greatest legends in rock history.

The lights go out in the large, barn-like building. 5,000 screaming metal fans rise to their feet, as a canned rendition of "Diary of a Madman" plays overhead. The music reaches a crescendo. Just then, Ozzy spins into view seated in a large gothic throne at the top of a staircase that's built into the set. Everyone goes into convulsions as the Ozzman descends carrying a large, silver, gleaming cross.

He reaches the bottom, throws down the cross and manically cries out, "Let the madness begin!" Suddenly Tommy Aldridge's drum set wheels into view at the landing of the staircase and he starts beating out the intro of "Over the Mountain." A pair of iron gates lift from two different castle-like towers located stage right and stage left, releasing guitarist Randy Rhoads and bass player Rudy Sarzo. High up in one of the towers, a hooded Don Airey ominously pumps away on the organ.

This show is just like every other on the tour, filled with over-the-top theatrics—at one point they "hang" a little person named Ronnie—and musical virtuosity on the part of Rhoads. The former Quiet Riot guitar player helped Ozzy spark his fledgling solo career following his dismissal from Black Sabbath. "You should have heard him play, man," Ozzy recalled of the first time he heard Rhoads perform. "I almost cried, he was so good."

SET LIST

Diary of a Madman
Over the Mountain
Mr. Crowley
Crazy Train
Revelation (Mother Earth)
Steal Away (The Night)
Suicide Solution
Goodbye to Romance
I Don't Know
No Bone Movies
Believer
Flying High Again
Iron Man
Children of the Grave
Paranoid

As flashy as Rhoads's dynamic guitar solos are—and his spot just after "Suicide Solution" is unbelievable—it's hard to tear your eyes off Ozzy. Decked out in a blue chain-mail cat suit with a matching codpiece, metal's greatest front man demands your attention.

The band runs through the prime material from Osbourne's two solo albums, songs like "Mr. Crowley," "Crazy Train" and "Flying High Again," before segueing into his best known Black Sabbath material at the end of the gig. Everyone goes wild when Rhoads digs into that first, elongated, terrifying chord of "Iron Man," and the energy level stays high throughout "Children of the Grave." Amongst the crowd, Mark Neal finally works up the nerve to do what he came to do. He removes the baggie from his coat, drops the bat into his hand, reaches back and chucks it in a high arc toward the stage. It lands with a thud. Mission accomplished!

Ozzy notices the dark object flying through the air and walks over to see what it is. "Obviously a toy," he remembered thinking in his autobiography. "I held it up to the lights and bared my teeth while Randy played one of his solos. The crowd went mental. Then I did what I always did when we got a rubber toy on stage: chomp."

MUSICIANS

Ozzy Osbourne: Vocals
Randy Rhoads: Guitar
Rudy Sarzo: Bass
Don Airey: Keyboards
Tommy Aldridge: Drums

Ozzy knows something is wrong, the second the oozing, putrefied skull touches his tongue. "My mouth was instantly full of this warm, gloopy liquid, with the worst aftertaste you could ever imagine. I could feel it staining my teeth and running down my chin."

Ever the showman, and despite the bat blood swishing around inside of his mouth, Ozzy finishes out the gig with a fearsome take on "Paranoid." Afterward he is rushed to the emergency room where, he receives the first of a series of intensely painful rabies shots, courtesy of "a syringe the size of a grenade launcher," as he put it.

> *My mouth was instantly full of this warm, gloopy liquid, with the worst aftertaste you could ever imagine.*

The news of Ozzy's bat encounter spread quickly. The media sensationalizes the episode so that the bat was supposedly alive before Ozzy ripped its head off, then he intentionally poured the blood down his throat. The singer became public enemy No. 1. The ASPCA sent people to monitor his shows. Due to the heat they were taking from parental groups and local politicians, several promotors canceled upcoming gigs. "The fans didn't help, either," he said. "After they heard about the bat, they started bringing even crazier stuff to the gigs. Going on stage was like being at a butchers' convention."

The ordeal quickly spun out into one of the greatest legendary tales in the annals of rock 'n' roll. "It really freaked me out," Neal admitted in the days after the gig. For the next several decades, Ozzy could hardly get through an interview without someone asking him about the incident.

Sadly, the episode with the bat wasn't the most consequential event on that tour. Two months after that fateful night in Des Moines, the band found itself stuck in Leesburg, Florida, en route to a show in Orlando. Andrew Ayock, the bus driver, offered to take Rhoads and his hairdresser out for a flight in one of the property's Beechcraft Bonanza F35 airplanes. The inexperienced Ayock clipped the bus with one of the plane's wings, causing the aircraft to spin out and crash into the ground, killing everyone on board.

For Ozzy, the loss of Rhoads was something that he never quite got over. "It took me a very long time to get over his death," he later said. "Randy gave me a purpose. He gave me hope."

HONORABLE MENTION
Genesis at the National Bowl
Milton Keynes, England (October 2)

In 1982, pop singer Peter Gabriel staged a mega-concert in the U.K. named WOMAD (World of Music, Arts and Dance). Thanks to poor planning, the event was a financial disaster. "The debts were more than I could ever hope to sort out personally," Gabriel recalled. To settle up, he did something he thought he'd never have to do in his lifetime: reunite with his old band, Genesis. Gabriel had left the group in 1975. In that seven-year span apart, both entities had grown in stature and acclaim—the former through four critically acclaimed solo albums and the latter with a collection of platinum-selling releases featuring drummer Phil Collins on lead vocals. On the night of the show—they were billed as Six of the Best instead of Genesis—it started pissing down rain, but none of the 47,000 people in the crowd gave a damn. Gabriel emerged from a coffin that had been placed onstage and for the next two hours, he and Genesis dove headlong into some of their earliest, most beloved material, songs like "The Lamb Lies Down on Broadway," "Supper's Ready" and "Back in N.Y.C." As a special surprise, former guitarist Steve Hackett made a grand entrance to play on the encore performance of "I Know What I Like in Your Wardrobe" and "The Knife." This single show remains the final time that Gabriel and Genesis played together.

1983

U2
RED ROCKS AMPHITHEATRE—MORRISON, CO
JUNE 5

BLOOD RED TRIUMPH

Everything was on the line. Every dime they had, every dream yet to be realized—everything hinged on this one gig at the breathtaking Red Rocks Amphitheatre just outside of Denver, Colorado. And it was all about to be washed away.

U2 discovered the incredible natural beauty of Red Rocks during a swing through the Rocky Mountain state while on the Boy Tour in 1981. A promoter named Chuck Morris took them up into the hills and showed them around. They were all awed by the place. "From the moment we saw it, we were thinking, 'Some day we will play here,'" bassist Adam Clayton recalled.

As U2 was gearing up for a U.S. tour to promote *War* in 1983, their manager, Paul McGuinness, began planning a live concert film. The enterprise would cost about $250,000, which was no small potatoes. With only about $30,000 on hand, U2 turned to promoter Barry Fey and their label, Island Records, to pitch in the rest. Fey, who promoted the band in the Southwestern U.S., suggested that filming take place at Red Rocks.

"Only in America would you find this beautiful place at the top of the mountain where you could put on rock concerts," U2 drummer Larry Mullen Jr. remembered in the band-authored biography *U2 by U2*. "There was a lot of money riding on this. . . . everything that was in the bank basically. We felt we were well organized, camera crews set up all over the

gig. We had brought extra lighting equipment from Hollywood, searchlights, all kinds of stuff. Then on the day it started to rain."

Rain is an understatement. Lightning blazed across the sky and flash flood warnings went out across the region as a torrent of water fell from above. A massive amount of electricity was needed to power and capture their performance, and every inch of water threw the prospects of their performance further into doubt. Serious discussions took place between the members of U2, their manager and the promoter. It seemed like they were going to have to pull the plug, but they couldn't bring themselves to make the call.

"Our concert promoter was going on the radio saying, 'The gig is canceled; we'll reschedule for another time,' but that really wasn't an option," Clayton said. "We didn't have the money to reschedule it—this was a one-shot for us."

Even though opening acts the Alarms and the Divinyls backed out, U2 went against their promoter. Lead singer Bono hopped on the phone and pleaded over the radio for people to come to Red Rocks, even though he still wasn't sure if there would be a gig to play when they got there. Over 4,000 people braved the elements on *the off chance* that U2 would make it to the stage. As the gates opened, assigned seating was thrown out the window and the show became general admission.

SET LIST

Out of Control

Twilight

An Cat Dubh

Into the Heart

Surrender

Two Hearts Beat as One

Seconds

Sunday Bloody Sunday

The Cry

The Electric Co.

I Fall Down

October

New Year's Day

I Threw A Brick Through a Window

A Day Without Me

Gloria

Party Girl

11 O'Clock Tick Tock

I Will Follow

40

MUSICIANS

Bono: Vocals

The Edge: Guitar

Adam Clayton: Bass

Larry Mullen Jr.: Drums

Two hours before U2 went on, the downpour relented. An omnipresent mist filled the air—cold, but bearable. U2 was ready for their moment. The show would go on.

Bob Dylan did it. They made a movie. They called it *Hard Rain*, and that's what you got right here," Fey exclaims to the audience, while bundled up in a puffy green jacket. "Thanks for bearing with us. God bless you. Ladies and gentlemen please, a warm Red Rocks welcome, from Dublin, Ireland, U2!"

The band's name echoes around the rocks as the band gallops to their instruments. Down in front, the crowd surges forward as one, fighting to get as close as they can to the lip of the stage. Clayton starts plucking away at a single bass note.

"Good evening!" Bono yells while running to the front of the stage. "Here we go!"

The first song of the night is "Out of Control," taken from their debut album, *Boy*. Despite the cold, the band are scantily clad in their finest, over-the-

top '80s apparel. Bono and guitarist The Edge forego sleeves altogether. You can see the white puffs of steam pour out of their mouths as their warm breath hits the frigid air.

"It was freezing cold," Bono later recalled. "Edge was finding it hard to play guitar because his hands were frozen stiff."

Despite the adverse elements, U2 soldiers on. They pour their hearts into dynamic, shimmering takes on "An Cat Dubh," "Into the Heart," "Surrender" and "Seconds" before reaching their most recent single, "Sunday Bloody Sunday." As the song whips along, the sky above turns black and fills with even more mist. Large torches on either side of the stage rage with fire. The harsh elements provide a poignant backdrop to the band's militaristic anthem about 13 unarmed civil rights demonstrators, gunned down by British paratroopers in Northern Ireland. Bono drives the message home when he marches out just after The Edge's solo and plants a giant white flag at the front of the stage.

"It became such a symbol for us," The Edge said about the dramatic gesture. "But the thing is, it's something we took from our audience; it isn't something Bono went out to do intentionally. Lots of people would bring flags and banners to the shows, and Bono just went with it."

The moment feels impossible to top, but Bono does his damndest two songs later, when he climbs the scaffolding of the stage during "The Electric Co." It's a risky move considering all the exposed wiring and slick rain covering the set. He gets the rise out of the audience that he's looking for while giving the director another iconic flourish for the film.

"What audiences learned from engaging with U2 in concert is that it is essential to care," journalist Anthony DeCurtis wrote in the liner notes to the official live album release, *Under a Blood Red Sky*. "One of the band's great strengths is its willingness to provoke, and no one could leave one of the band's shows without feeling energized, exercised and ready to tangle with the world to whatever end."

The hits keep coming: "New Year's Day," "I Will Follow" and "October." What the crowd lacks in numbers they make up for in enthusiasm. They hang onto every word coming out of Bono's mouth and roar with delight at every musical divergence. By the time U2 finishes the last song of the night, "40," they unknowingly miss their cue.

"At the end of the concerts on the War Tour . . . there was this phenomenon of people singing the refrain from '40,' 'How long to sing this song. How long to sing this song,'" Bono explained. "But no one was singing it that night."

As the song whips along, the sky above turns black and fills with even more mist.

Jumping into action, the band's tour manager, Dennis Sheehan, grabs a microphone and sings the line himself just out of view from the audience, which entices them to join along. It's a contrived bit of theater, but it looks and sounds great in the film. "What I really love about rock 'n' roll [is] the spontaneity and the spirit of it," Bono said. "But I also love the strategy, the illusion, the smoke and mirrors, the shamanistic aspects. It's just such a big bag of motivations and you end up with magic."

U2's performance at Red Rocks had a far greater impact than they could have imagined. It bolstered their reputation as one of the most vital live rock bands going. It exposed them to a much wider audience in the U.S. It also helped them convince visionary musician Brian Eno to produce their next record, *The Unforgettable Fire*. Eno and U2 went on to have a long, fruitful relationship, creating some of the most well-regarded records of the next 15 years. It's hard

to imagine any of it happening if not for that one transcendent night in the mountains of Colorado.

HONORABLE MENTION
The Police at Shea Stadium
Queens, NY (August 18)

The Police's one-night stand at Shea Stadium was their crowning achievement as a band, as well as the harbinger of their disintegration. In June, the New Wave rockers unveiled their greatest, most commercially successful album to date, *Synchronicity*. Filled out by hits like "Every Breath You Take," "Wrapped Around Your Finger" and "King of Pain," the record hit No. 1 in the U.S. and sold millions of copies worldwide. A gigantic world tour was booked, the centerpiece of which was this show at Shea Stadium on August 18. After opening sets from Joan Jett & the Blackhearts and R.E.M., the Police took over the baseball park and kicked off its set with the songs "Synchronicity I" and "Synchronicity II." As Jon Pareles noted in his review in the *New York Times*, "What makes the Police stand out among performing bands is that it never bothers to imitate its records." Adding, "So it goes to the other extreme, revamping every song in a gleeful whirl of improvisation." For two hours, the Police dove headlong into its catalog, packing the set with an array of deep cuts and fan favorites. They left it all out on the field that night, and it doomed them. "That was the point where I realized that it can't get any better than this . . . this was Everest," Sting explained. "I made the decision on stage [at Shea] that this is where this thing stops."

1984

The Replacements
FIRST AVENUE—MINNEAPOLIS, MN
DECEMBER 26

THE SHIT HITS THE FANS

The biggest thrill of catching The Replacements live during their mid-1980s heyday was the feeling that truly anything could happen. The Mats, as the group's fans called them, were one of the most unpredictable bands in the history of rock 'n' roll. Going into a show, you had no idea whether you were going to witness the kind of performance that could change your life or an utter, disgusting train wreck.

The band formed in 1980 in the suburban Minneapolis basement of guitarist Bob and bassist Tommy Stinson. They called themselves Dogbreath before changing their name to the Impediments shortly after singer and rhythm guitarist Paul Westerberg came aboard. After getting banned by a few venues around town for their wild behavior, they changed their name again in the hopes of booking more gigs. Thus, The Replacements.

By 1984, they hit their stride, writing and recording the material that would comprise the greatest record of their career, *Let It Be*. As Westerberg recalled, the album's name was "our way of saying that nothing is sacred. That the Beatles were just a fine rock and roll band. We were seriously gonna call the next record *Let It Bleed*."

The Replacements were road warriors who booked tours and played shows across the country. It was a grind, but it was the only way that the band could sustain itself. After every show, they would pile into roadie Tom Carlson's ramshackle van, load up on booze, make the drive, play another gig, drink more, pass out, rinse and repeat. It was constant, low-rent Bacchanalia on the tightest budget. At times, they even set fire to their cash per diem just for kicks.

Once, in the summer of 1983, they booked a high-profile eight-date run with a very buzzy Athens, Georgia, rock group named R.E.M. It didn't go well. The R.E.M. crowds were baffled by The Replacements and viciously heckled them. Rather than stand for the abuse, the opening act antagonized back until they were nearly run off the stage.

As their renown grew, so too did their need to subvert their own chances at success and acceptance. Typically, this urge manifested itself in front of paying audiences and at the worst possible times. One of the most infamous shows they ever played took place at CBGB in New York City on December 9, 1984. The band was billed as Gary & The Boners for the evening. A gaggle of big label record executives turned out to see them perform and talk was in the air about a big-money contract. Rather than try to impress the "suits," the band took a dive, performing one of the most horrible sets of music it could.

"Last night [at CBGB] was a classic example," Westerberg explained to RJ Smith of the *Village Voice* in the aftermath. "We went up there, we did what we wanted to do, and they [the record industry] wanted us to play our best songs as best we could. And we didn't feel like it. And so they figure, 'They're a small-

SET LIST

I'm in Trouble
Favorite Thing
Color Me Impressed
Nowhere Is My Home
I Will Dare
Can't Hardly Wait
Sixteen Blue
Lookin' for Ya
Takin' a Ride
Willpower
Hay Day
Baby Strange
Take Me Down to the Hospital
Johnny's Gonna Die
Black Diamond
Tommy Gets His Tonsils Out
Bang A Gong (Get It On)
Unsatisfied
Gary's Got a Boner
Answering Machine
God Damn Job
Hitchin' a Ride
Do the Clam
Yeah Yeah
Easier Said Than Done
If I Only Had a Brain

MUSICIANS

Paul Westerberg: Vocals/Guitar
Bob Stinson: Guitar
Tommy Stinson: Bass
Chris Mars: Drums

any night of the week. On December 26, the day after Christmas, 1,500 fans braved the Minnesota winter to catch the Mats do their thing. The band rewarded them for their efforts.

"I knew that we had to make them remember us somehow," Westerberg said. "If we played on a Tuesday night, on Wednesday afternoon you don't see your friend and say, 'Man, did you hear The Replacements last night?' It's like, 'Did you *see* The Replacements?!' It became a visual thing more and more."

The Mats cut a striking figure onstage this evening. Westerberg walks out in front of the adoring crowd clad in a Stroh Brewing Company T-shirt, while Tommy Stinson goes the more formal route with his signature spiked-out hair and button-down shirt. His brother Bob is patently loony tunes, wearing fishnet stockings, a pork pie hat and a tutu.

Bob Stinson is the crazed, wild heart of The Replacements. He's an unhinged guy both onstage and off, and his appearance tonight mirrors the way he lives his life—brimming with absurdity, marred by excess. His guitar playing is as manic as his personality. You never could tell in which direction one of his volcanic solos might blow.

"Minneapolis audiences are mighty reserved, and learning to command an audience in a place where people are notorious for being quiet will either make you a wallflower, quiet artist, or it will make you really boisterous, aggressive, or flamboyant," Westerberg said. "It's a cold place to live in more ways than one."

If the crowd comes in icy, The Replacements are determined to turn up the heat. The band kicks off the show with an incendiary version of its song "I'm in Trouble" from its debut album before moving into an impressively straight take on the more recent track "Favorite Thing." It's clear that this is not one of the band's

time bunch of amateurs.' That's one way to look at it, and that's partly true. But I think it's also the spirit that makes rock exciting and immediate."

If the CBGB show was one of the deepest valleys of their career, then The Replacements' concert back home in the familiar confines of the First Avenue club in Minneapolis a couple of weeks later was a heady peak. Throughout the '80s, First Avenue was a prime enclave of cool. Another Minneapolis native, Prince, was known to take the room over for impromptu shows, eventually commandeering the space for a full month to film a good portion of *Purple Rain*.

While The Replacements didn't have the same national recognition as Prince, in their hometown, they could pack them in as tight as "The Purple One"

so-called "pussy sets"—its intentional dive concerts.

Feeling at ease in front of a familiar audience, only four songs into the show they bust out an as-yet-unrecorded number, "Nowhere Is My Home." The Mats commit the track to tape a few months later with Big Star front man Alex Chilton producing in a session that would yield both "Left of the Dial" and "Can't Hardly Wait" as well. The latter song made it into the set list later in the evening.

Bob is patently loony tunes, wearing fishnet stockings, a pork pie hat and a tutu.

"Nowhere Is My Home" goes over fine, but the energy onstage cranks into a high gear when they shift into their biggest "hit" at the time, the *Let It Be* opener "I Will Dare." From there the set weaves in and out of the band's standard pool of original songs and classic rock favorites, including an impressive run-through of T-Rex's glam rock masterpiece "Bang a Gong (Get it On)."

Of course, it wouldn't be a Mats gig without a few duds thrown into the mix. "Sixteen Blue" can best be described as "loose," with Westerberg missing more than a few lines and generally singing behind the rest of the band. The next song, "Lookin' for Ya," is equally ragtag. They eventually regain their footing with an explosive rendition of "Takin' a Ride" that finds Bob Stinson doing all he can to push as much volume out of his white Gibson SG as possible.

The high-water mark of the show arrives 18 songs into the set with "Unsatisfied." The touching song is given even more emotional heft when Westerberg falls apart screaming "I'm so, I'm so . . . unsatisfiiiiiied!" repeatedly to an empathetic audience that sings the refrain right back to him. Bob Stinson adorns the tune with a surprisingly tasteful solo until, in classic Mats fashion, the whole thing goes over a cliff and Tommy is left playing a bass lick alone, by himself.

An hour and a half after it began, the concert closes out in characteristically irreverent fashion, with roadie Bill Sullivan jumping in from the wings to warble out an untethered, bluesy version of the *Wizard of Oz* classic "If I Only Had a Brain."

Across their career, The Replacements performed a handful of better shows than this one and a bevy of ones far worse. Coming just two months after the release of the band's masterpiece, in front of a truly adoring home crowd, while on the cusp of signing a major label deal, this one-night stand at First Avenue might just be its most indelible.

HONORABLE MENTION
The Jacksons at Texas Stadium
Irving, TX (January 20)

After releasing his music industry–saving sixth album, *Thriller*, instead of hitting the road by himself, Michael Jackson opted to tour North America's finest football and baseball stadiums alongside the rest of his family. For 55 nights, Michael sang and moonwalked beside his brothers Tito, Jermaine, Randy, Marlon and Jackie in an extraordinary, over-the-top production they called the Victory Tour. The set list each night was comprised of hits from *Thriller* along with songs from Michael's *Off the Wall* and Jacksons material from *Destiny* and *Triumph*. Oddly enough, nothing from the actual *Victory* album nor the "Thriller" single made the cut. The stage set-up was incredible. Weighing in at well over 300 tons, it included a state-of-the-art light display and elevating platform. For this one show at Texas Stadium, Michael Jackson unveiled a major surprise. When time came to perform his No. 1 hit song "Beat It," a smiling Eddie Van Halen strolled out and regaled the crowd with a live approximation of his immortal guitar solo. Though the tour was the highest grossing in history up to that point, raking in a staggering $171 million, backstage squabbles amongst the brothers left a bad taste in everyone's mouth. A planned European leg was scrapped as Michael began distancing himself from the rest of his family.

1985

#1 Album of the Year:
Born in the U.S.A.
Bruce Springsteen

Prince
THE FORUM—INGLEWOOD, CA
FEBRUARY 23

PURPLE STORM AT THE FORUM

It's a testament to Prince's nearly unmatched powers as a live entertainer that a quarter of this book could have been dedicated to any number of concerts he staged over the years. Whether it was his birthday show at First Avenue in Minneapolis in 1984, his deliriously excellent late night after-show performance at the small Trojan Horse Club in The Hague in 1988 or his final concert in 2016 at the Fox Theatre in Atlanta during his sparse *Piano & Microphone* tour, Prince had a natural gift for staging epic musical showcases. At the crossroads between musical genius, expert showmanship, boundless energy, sexual magnetism and unbridled charisma stood Prince Rogers Nelson.

Many people argue that 1984 was the greatest year in pop music. Given the sheer number of seminal albums that came out, it's not an argument without merit. Bruce Springsteen's *Born in the U.S.A.* hit the shelves that year. So did Madonna's *Like a Virgin*, Tina Turner's *Private Dancer*, Van Halen's *1984* and U2's *Unforgettable Fire*. Bon Jovi made their debut with their self-titled release. So did Run D.M.C. So did the Red Hot Chili Peppers. And yet, there was one album that loomed larger than everything else: Prince's *Purple Rain*.

When *Purple Rain* the film debuted in July 1984, it was an instant hit, overtaking *Ghostbusters* to become the No. 1 film in America. The soundtrack made an even greater impact, spending 24 consecu-

tive weeks at the top of the *Billboard* album charts. It spawned four Top 10 singles: "I Would Die 4 U," "Purple Rain," "When Doves Cry" and "Let's Go Crazy." The latter two were No. 1 hits.

Suddenly Prince was everywhere. For kids, teenagers and twenty-somethings coming up in the buttoned-up Ronald Reagan era, Prince was a godsend. He was everything you could wish for in a rock star. He was hyper-sexualized, at times pornographic, like on his ode to female masturbation, "Darling Nikki." He was perverse and dangerous, a mesmerizing enigma. He was also a superb musician, adept on multiple instruments but one of the greatest ever to pick up an electric guitar.

Prince kicked off his *Purple Rain* tour on November 4, 1984, at the Joe Louis Arena in Detroit. The supersized jaunt ran for five months, concluding at the Orange Bowl—redubbed the "Purple Bowl"—in Miami on April 7, 1985. Supporting Prince onstage was the same band that he used in the film and the recording studio to create his greatest work. He called them The Revolution.

Demand for tickets was off the charts. Prince booked multi-night stands in the country's biggest markets. Six nights at the Cow Palace in San Francisco. Five nights at the Omni in Atlanta. Six nights at the Nassau Coliseum on Long Island. And five nights at the Rosemont Horizon just outside of Chicago. While there's hardly such a thing as a "bad"

SET LIST

Controversy

Let's Go Crazy

Delirious

1999

Little Red Corvette

Take Me With U (When You Were Mine)

4 The Tears In Your Eyes

Yankee Doodle

A Case Of You

Free

Raspberry Beret

Do Me, Baby

Irresistible Bitch

Temptation

Let's Pretend We're Married

International Lover

God

Computer Blue

Darling Nikki

The Beautiful Ones

When Doves Cry

I Would Die 4 U

Baby I'm a Star (Medley)

Ice Cream Castles

Bodyheat

Partyup

America

Purple Rain

MUSICIANS

Prince: Vocals/Guitar

Wendy Melvoin: Guitar

Brown Mark: Bass

Lisa Coleman: Keyboards

Matt "Doctor" Fink: Keyboards

Bobby Z.: Drums

Prince show, some have that little extra something that sets them apart. The run near his hometown at the Saint Paul Civic Center was certainly special, as was the massive tour closer in Miami. But if you could go back in time and attend any single show from that tour, you'd have to pick his final performance of a six-night run at the Forum just outside of Los Angeles on February 23, 1985. The show itself was predictably grandiose, culminating in one of the most incredible live pop music moments of the entire decade.

Unlike nearly every other stop along the *Purple Rain* tour, the February 23 concert begins with a preliminary performance of the 1981 song "Controversy," with Prince's figure left obscured in the darkness. It's a delightful tease designed to get the crowd going. Moments later, the steady hum of a synthesizer crackles through the air.

Suddenly a voice like that of God booms out through the speakers. "Hello, Los Angeles. My name is Prince, and I have come to play with you." A light purple glow emanates from a stage now completely shrouded in a thick fog of smoke. The crowd erupts in a scream before the voice returns: "Dearly beloved, we are gathered here today to get through this thing called life.'"

Prince levitates from under the stage, while keeping pace with the iconic opening monologue of "Let's Go Crazy." He keeps talking while a drum kicks to life providing a steady back beat. Suddenly there's a spotlight, and Wendy Melvoin steps forward playing the song's opening chords on guitar while Prince dances next to her in the vague darkness. When he arrives at the final line of the spoken-word intro, "Go Crazy!" the crowd responds by doing just that.

In a flash the lights go up and there's Prince in all his violet-tinged glory, shuffling in sync with the rest of the Revolution as they dance and gyrate around the stage. A thousand rays of tiny light reflect off the obscene amounts of sequins and jewelry dangling from the members of the band. The man of the hour is even more dazzling as he sings, dances and rips off some of the most incredible, nonchalant guitar lines that any human being has ever produced.

A few minutes in, the song devolves into a tornado of swirling synth noises and dies out. The crowd tries to catch its breath, but Prince isn't about to give them the luxury of oxygen. Instead he counts in "1-2-

3!" before shrieking like a banshee and hitting them with "Delirious." From there, the title track to *1999* followed by his mega-hit "Little Red Corvette." All of this happens in just under 18 minutes. There is still over an hour and forty-five to go.

It's one of the most star-packed, mind-bending musical interactions of the 1980s.

"Take Me With U" comes next, followed by a live rarity, the song "4 The Tears In Your Eyes," which won't see a proper release until two months after this show. Prince was asked by Michael Jackson and Quincy Jones to participate in the star-studded collective USA For Africa for the charity track "We Are the World." He declined but gave them "4 The Tears in Your Eyes," which was included on the *We Are the World* album instead. It's basically a re-telling of the story of Jesus Christ. He rarely performed it in front of a crowd again.

The night wears on and the hits keep coming, but Prince is saving his best for last. By the time the 18th song in the set rolls around, he starts playing the bulk of his best material from *Purple Rain*. "Computer Blue" bleeds into "Darling Nikki," which is followed by stunning versions of both "The Beautiful Ones" and "When Doves Cry." "I Would Die 4 U" gets a sped-up, almost perfunctory airing, and then the shirt comes off and the real craziness begins.

A programmed drum machine cracks to life—boom, chuck, boom, chuck, boom, chuck—that signals the beginning of "Baby, I'm A Star." Prince is a ball of pure energy, whipping through the song with a frenzy. Four minutes and twenty seconds later, the song ends, or at least, it's supposed to end, but the Purple One has only begun.

"Aww, we in L.A.," the singer says with a smirk. "I can see y'all ain't gonna be satisfied until we get sleazy off in this mug!"

The screaming shakes the Forum to its foundation. "Good gawd!" Prince exclaims.

The song starts up again with even more intensity than before. Prince calls out for Sheila E., who suddenly appears and unleashes a savage drum solo. Then, boom! Everything comes to a screeching halt. Prince starts singing a near-acapella rendition of "Ice Cream Castles," a song that he wrote for his on-screen nemesis, Morris Day and The Time.

The only other sound in the arena besides his voice is the faint chuck of a guitar. Prince finishes the first verse, then casually looks over his shoulder and asks, "Bruce, you wanna play something?" At that invitation, Bruce Springsteen, the Boss himself, steps out of the shadows to take a nasty, funky, blues guitar solo. If that weren't enough, off to the side of the stage the ultimate "Material Girl" Madonna is dancing away. It's one of the most star-packed, mind-bending musical interactions of the 1980s. The crowd doesn't know how to respond. They've nearly been stunned into silence.

For the next few minutes Prince passes around solos between members of the Revolution, each musician getting their chance to show what they can do. The man at the center of it all seems completely at ease, dashing off instructions like "Eric, blow your horn!" or "Everybody stop on the one!" Or "Gimme a B flat!" To the crowd he says, "You can join in if you want, we're just jamming."

Suddenly, the medley takes a new form as Prince and the band slip into the track "Partyup" from his third album, *Dirty Mind*. They keep it loose, mostly jamming on the chorus while the Purple One commands the crowd to sing back the song's refrain, "Party up / Go to party up" over and over and over. Then bam! Another stop. Prince announces, "We got to get outta here, y'all." The crowd loudly protests, but he just turns around, looks to his band and says, "We back in D." Together, they slide into "Baby I'm a Star" once again. "We love you, goodnight!"

The show ain't over yet. Prince and the Revolution reemerge a few moments later to play a 15-minute version of a new song named "America" that would be released as part of the album *Around the World in a Day* two months later. It's a bold move for an encore, but the crowd seems grateful just to be back in his presence.

After finishing "America," they depart again, only to return one last time for a breathtaking rendition of "Purple Rain." The sound of the very first chord sends all 17,000 people into pandemonium. Hundreds of disposable Bic lighters flick to life and are raised into the air as everyone joins in on the song's "who-hoo-hoo-hoo" coda, which Prince has repurposed as the intro.

This extended opening goes on for almost nine minutes, punctuated in the middle by a one-of-a-kind Prince guitar solo. Just as he's about to lose them, he breaks the trance and opens his mouth to promise that he "Never meant to cause you any sorrow" and that he "Never mean to cause you any pain."

They hang on his every word, echoing it back at double the volume. By the second chorus, he just gives it to them. The audience is rapturous as they sing the title over and over again. When the song ends Prince steps to the microphone. "Los Angeles!

> *This extended opening goes on for almost nine minutes, punctuated in the middle by a one-of-a-kind Prince guitar solo.*

We had a good time, didn't we?" he asks. Of course they did, and they roar back to let him know. "We don't know how much time we've got left on this earth. Try and love one another. We can do it. Thank you so very much. Goodnight. May you live to see the dawn."

HONORABLE MENTION

**Live Aid at Wembley Stadium
London, England
and John F. Kennedy Stadium
Philadelphia, PA (July 13)**

While there had been megastar-filled benefit concerts prior to Live Aid, the intercontinental event took things to a level never seen before and hardly matched since. Billed as a "Global Jukebox," Live Aid was the brainchild of Boomtown Rats front man Bob Geldof. He had the idea following the charity single "Do They Know It's Christmas?" which benefited famine victims in Ethiopia. Geldof booked massive outdoor stadiums in the U.S. and the U.K. and filled them with as many of his famous friends as he could track down. While some turned in less than stellar performances—like the reformed Led Zeppelin with Phil Collins on drums; Paul McCartney, who had some sound issues; and Bob Dylan, who was panned for suggesting that some of the money go to farmers in the U.S.—many acts elevated themselves to new levels of fame and acclaim. Queen turned in the greatest set, with U2 a close second. David Bowie was fantastic, as were Elvis Costello, Black Sabbath (with Ozzy Osbourne back on the microphone), Tom Petty, and Mick Jagger with Tina Turner. Live Aid set the template for numerous high-profile benefit gigs in the decades to come.

1986

Queen
WEMBLEY STADIUM—LONDON, ENGLAND
JULY 12

QUEEN ROCKS WEMBLEY

When you hear the name Wembley Stadium, two things inevitably spring to mind: soccer and the glam rock band Queen. Few artists are more synonymous with a venue than the popular British group and the massive London football pitch. Sure, there are the Beatles and the Cavern Club, the Ramones and CBGB and Guns N' Roses and the Roxy, but those are all relatively small clubs that each group played many, many times early in their careers. It says something about the size and scope of Queen that they are most readily identified with a 72,000-seat open-air facility.

Queen performed at Wembley for the first time during the Live Aid mega-concert on July 13, 1985. The event featured a bill as stacked as any ever assembled: Led Zeppelin, U2, David Bowie, Bob Dylan, Elton John, Elvis Costello, Paul McCartney, Sting, The Who, Black Sabbath, the Beach Boys, Neil Young, Tom Petty, Eric Clapton, etc. After the night ended, all anyone could talk about was Queen.

In just six songs spread across 21 minutes, Queen put on a clinic on how to capture the imaginations of a large crowd and blow their minds apart. They completely stole the show. "That was entirely down to Freddie," guitarist Brian May said. "The rest of us played OK, but Freddie was out there and took it to another level."

You can easily make the claim that Freddie Mercury was the greatest front man that has ever lived.

"The best virtuoso rock 'n' roll singer of all time," Roger Daltrey said. "A man of the theater and someone who constantly transformed himself. In short: a genius," Lady Gaga proclaimed. David Bowie, who knew a thing or two about theatrics, stated, "Of all the more theatrical rock performers, Freddie took it further than the rest."

Mercury had it all: style, panache, wit, a love of entertaining, a personality that filled the room and a voice like no other. Everything that made him great was on high display during that Live Aid show—from the dramatic opening of "Bohemian Rhapsody" when he was seated behind a grand piano to the way he sashayed across the stage with his sawed-off mic stand to the famous "Note Heard Round the World" improvisation after "Radio Ga Ga," Mercury came, he saw and he conquered.

A few months after Live Aid, Queen decamped to Switzerland and Munich to work on *A Kind of Magic*. Though the press didn't love the record—*Rolling Stone* called it "heavy plastic"—it sold well, hitting No. 1 in the U.K.

With a new album to promote, Queen announced a 26-date run through Europe. The centerpiece of the tour was two back-to-back shows at the scene of their greatest triumph, Wembley Stadium. They knew that the audience waiting for them was expecting something special, and Queen was eager to give it to them.

SET LIST

One Vision

Tie Your Mother Down

In The Lap of the Gods . . . Revisited

Seven Seas of Rhye

Tear It Up

A Kind of Magic

Under Pressure

Another One Bites The Dust

Who Wants to Live Forever

I Want to Break Free

Impromptu

Now I'm Here

Love of My Life

Is This the World We Created

(You're So Square) Baby I Don't Care

Hello Mary Lou

Tutti Fruitti

Gimme Some Lovin'

Bohemian Rhapsody

Hammer to Fall

Crazy Little Thing Called Love

Big Spender

Radio Ga Ga

We Will Rock You

Friends Will Be Friends

We Are the Champions

God Save the Queen

MUSICIANS

Freddie Mercury: Vocals/Piano

Brian May: Guitar

John Deacon: Bass

Roger Taylor: Drums

A thick fog of smoke obscures the massive array of lights and Vox guitar amplifiers piled up around the stage. The crowd titters with anticipation while a solitary synth note hangs in the air. Suddenly, the sound of a guitar comes crashing through the array of speakers dangling from the massive scaffolding structures. Brian May, clutching his homemade "Red Special," emerges from the white cloud. Seconds later, Freddie Mercury glides out toward the front decked out all in white except for the yellow mustard–colored jacket clinging tightly to his shoulders.

"Hey, everybody," he says as the band kicks into the lead single from its latest album, "One Vision." Behind him, May and bassist John Deacon are both decked out in near-matching white jackets with white pants. Roger Taylor is hammering away on the drums in the back in a simple, striped long-sleeve shirt.

Mercury has never met an audience he couldn't overwhelm with his incredible talent and charming personality, but for this show, Queen went to great lengths to make it easier for him to project. The band commissioned one of the biggest stages ever constructed: 160 feet wide and 52 feet tall. It was flanked by two elevated runways that were 40 feet in length. The production was so heavy that the production crew was forced to bore deep down into the concrete foundation of the stadium to properly support it all.

Above the stage, the band is broadcast in startling detail thanks to one of the first jumbotrons used at a rock concert. The 20-foot x 30-foot video screen is large enough that even those in the nosebleed section can see the veins popping out of Mercury's neck as he unleashes the full fury of his octave-shifting voice through the half-million–watt, 180-speaker sound system.

"One Vision" becomes "Tie Your Mother Down." Just ten minutes into the show, Mercury calls out "Give it to 'em," and a blast of pyro erupts from the stage, leaving everyone wide-eyed.

"Hello again, my beauties," Mercury says.

"Hello!" they scream.

"Wanna fool around?" a smirking Mercury asks before taking a swig out of an immense plastic cup filled with beer.

The front man wails away on the opening line to "In the Lap of the Gods . . . Revisited." Queen runs through another two songs before reaching the title track of A Kind of Magic, when the stage really comes to life. A multicolored array of light flashes in every direction, as two oversized blow-up figures—meant to resemble the ones seen on the album's cover—inflate on either side of the stage. One bounces lazily into the audience while the other lifts off high into the air.

The visual spectacle is overshadowed by an auditory one once the song ends. Mercury reprises his "Note Heard Round the World" operatic vocal exercises from Live Aid. The crowd echoes back nearly every warble with glee. He closes it out with an endearing smile and a loving "Fuck you," and then he points over to Rourke as he begins thumbing out the opening bassline to "Under Pressure."

> ## Even those in the nosebleed section can see the veins popping out of Mercury's neck as he unleashes the full fury of his octave-shifting voice.

From there they bust out "Another One Bites the Dust," and Freddie, drenched in sweat, ditches the jacket. The songs keep coming: "Who Wants to Live Forever," "I Want to Break Free" and "Tutti Frutti." A light rain starts to fall on the massive audience, but no one seems to care. Queen is just getting warmed up.

Day turns to evening, and evening slips into night. There are wardrobe changes, an acoustic set and a melodramatic rendition of "Bohemian Rhapsody" that turns into a breathtaking 72,000-person sing-along. Mercury straps on a Fender Telecaster to play "Crazy Little Thing Called Love" before bringing it home with a set-ending performance of "Radio Ga Ga."

The lights lay low as the audience pleads for more. A single spotlight shines down on Roger Taylor. He raises his drumsticks high into the air and sends them crashing down into his toms and snare. *Boom,*

boom, bap. Boom, boom, bap. Boom, boom, bap.

Mercury comes rushing out of the shadows wearing a resplendent white jacket with red trim that's left open to expose his hairy, sweat-soaked chest. Behind him, a long train of white satin whips in the breeze. He marches in time to the beat, finally raising the microphone to his lips and singing "Buddy you're a boy, make a big noise/Playing in the street gonna be a big man someday!"

He doesn't even get to the chorus of "We Will Rock You." The crowd takes it away from him, singing the name of the song repeatedly with glee. When it's over, Queen makes the curious decision to slip into one of their newer selections, "Friends Will Be Friends," before closing it all out with a triumphant "We Are the Champions."

The band is still playing when Mercury rushes backstage, reemerging moments later with an immense, regal crown atop his head and a long, red cape draped around his shoulders. "Thank you, beautiful people," he says while raising his crown in the air. "Goodnight and God bless you." A prerecorded version of "God Save the Queen" bursts through the speakers as the band waves *adieu.*

Less than a month after this performance, Queen ended their Magic Tour with a final concert at Knebworth House. That show was the last time they ever performed live with their iconic front man. Not very long after that, around Easter in 1987, Mercury discovered that he'd tested positive for the AIDS virus. The singer kept the diagnosis quiet until the day before he died on November 22, 1991.

"The Wembley concerts in 1986 were the pinnacle for us," Brian May said on reflection. "We were at our height, band-wise, and Freddie had developed this phenomenal way of dealing with stadium audiences. Being back home in London playing two sell-out nights was such a big, big occasion for us."

HONORABLE MENTION

The Smiths at Brixton Academy
London, England (December 12)

On December 12, 1986, the British indie pop group The Smiths shared the stage together for the final time at an anti-apartheid gig at the Brixton Academy. Over the last three years, few groups had elicited a higher level of rank devotion in the U.K., but the effort was draining. "There was no one around us to suggest that we disappear somewhere to rest," front man Morrissey said in his autobiography. "The split is our final loss of innocence." Even if they were coming apart at the seams, you wouldn't know it from their performance in Brixton. The Smiths are completely on top of their game, especially guitarist Johnny Marr, who is still feeling the effects of a car accident that forced this gig to get pushed back a month. Morrissey stalks the stage like a wounded animal, pouring his heart out over songs like "Bigmouth Strikes Again," "The Queen Is Dead," their first-ever single "Hand in Glove" and, for the only time live, "Shoplifters of the World Unite" and "Some Girls Are Bigger Than Others." In a prophetic twist, the singer closes the show by telling the crowd, "I'll probably never see you again." Seven months later, it was officially over.

1987

Guns N' Roses
PERKINS PALACE—PASADENA, CA
DECEMBER 30

PASADENA PARADISE

1987 belonged to Guns N' Roses. That year, the L.A. quintet rose from the muck and grime of the burgeoning hair-metal scene centered around the Sunset Strip, dropped their seminal debut album and brought the music world to its sha-na-na-na-na-knees. They were a caustic combination: the manic, unhinged energy of singer Axl Rose, the powerful dual guitar attack of Slash and Izzy Stradlin, the punk-inspired rhythms of bassist Duff McKagan and the in-your-face drumming of Steven Adler. There was no one else as exciting, as enticing or as dangerous.

"In that period of the band's career . . . nobody fucking rocked with as much purpose and sneer or with the same level of recklessness and bad intentions," McKagan wrote in his memoir, *It's So Easy and Other Lies*. "We were just firing on all cylinders."

After ending 1986 with a New Year's Eve show at the Glamour in Hollywood, the band hunkered down to put together its first full-length record, *Appetite for Destruction*. With a budget of $370,000, Guns took their time recording and perfecting the 12 songs that would make up the final track list. The process was marked with moments of inspiration, frustration and unprecedented hedonism, like the time when Rose had sex with Adler's girlfriend in a vocal booth to add the moans of carnal ecstasy heard during the breakdown on "Rocket Queen."

Appetite sold more than 30 million copies worldwide. Shortly after they finished creating it, the band hit the road, alternating between headlining tours of clubs and theaters and extensive runs as the opening act for The Cult, Mötley Crüe and Alice Cooper. Their reputation for onstage pyrotechnics and offstage hedonism was bolstered along the way.

To close out their year of triumph, the band booked a four-night residency at a converted 70-year-old movie house named Perkins Palace in Pasadena. Opened as the Raymond Theater in 1922, the building was sold in 1978 and started hosting live music events shortly thereafter. It was showcased in the films *This Is Spinal Tap*, *The Bodyguard* and *The Decline of Western Civilization Part II: The Metal Years.*

He drops into a crouched position and spins in circles like a tornado while the notes come raging out of the large stack of Marshall amplifiers behind him.

The guys in Guns were all looking forward to the Perkins gigs, but just a few weeks before making it back to L.A., disaster struck. Adler was out drinking

SET LIST

It's So Easy
Move to the City
Mr. Brownstone
Out Ta Get Me
Sweet Child O' Mine
Used to Love Her
My Michelle
Rocket Queen
Knockin' on Heaven's Door
Welcome to the Jungle
You're Crazy
Nighttrain
Paradise City
Patience
Mama Kin

MUSICIANS

Axl Rose: Vocals
Slash: Guitar
Izzy Stradlin: Rhythm Guitar
Duff McKagan: Bass
Fred Coury: Drums

at a bar, tossing back kamikaze shots like they were going out of style. "I got terminally shit-faced and became pretty damn obnoxious," he recalled in his memoir.

Eventually, his behavior got him tossed, but rather than accept his dismissal and drink somewhere else, Adler fought back, punching the metal casing on the club's front door and breaking the little finger on his right hand. When they found out about their drummer's injury, the band looked for a replacement. Fred Coury from the metal band Cinderella was brought in at the last minute and joined Guns N' Roses out on the road for the final three dates of their run through the Midwest, before ending the year in Pasadena.

"The Perkins Palace shows were some of the best shows we'd ever done," Slash declared in his autobiography. It was, he said, "a homecoming, friendly crowd the likes of which we'd never seen."

The group's shows in Pasadena on December 26, 27 and 28 were great, but everyone knew that the final night was the one you couldn't miss. As a minor consolation to all the fans who couldn't make it, KNAC-FM broadcast the concert live to the rest of the city.

The lights go out in the old theater. Amid the darkness, Guns N' Roses amble out of the back and over to their instruments. Given the cue, McKagan starts thumbing out a riff on his heavy bass strings, rattling the ribcages of the fans banging their heads near the front of the stage. Fred Coury joins him with a spitfire snare roll before the rest of the band comes to life and kicks into the first song of the night, "It's So Easy." Axl Rose takes hold of the microphone, his face obscured by dark sunglasses and a bandana wrapped tightly around his head.

"It's so easy / when everybody's tryin' to please me, baby!" he sings. Rose's hips move in a distinctive swivel motion, like a charmed snake. To his right, Izzy Stradlin is ripping out the chords of the song, his body flailing to the rhythm. Slash remains largely in the shadows until it's time to take his solo, when he steps out into the front and lets loose with a brain-warping lead. He drops into a crouched position and spins in circles like a tornado while the notes come raging out of the large stack of Marshall amplifiers behind him.

The song ends and the band immediately take off into "Move to the City" from their 1986 EP *Live ?!*@ Like a Suicide.* When they finish, Axl grabs hold of the microphone and addresses the crowd for the first time. He talks about friends he's known who've entered $15,000 rehab centers two or three times and cautions the shrieking audience to "use your head and keep your ass alive."

"You're the only one who's really gonna look out for your own ass," he says. "I've seen a couple friends come and go and I don't wanna see it happen no more, so you be careful when you're dancing with 'Mr. Brownstone.'" The words barely escape his lips, and Slash is already gliding up his fretboard to kick-start the group's cautionary tale of heroin addiction. "I used to do a little but a little wouldn't do/ so the little got more and more," Axl warns.

"Out Ta Get Me" comes next, preluded by a rambling intro by Axl about a fight he got into with a singer he won't name at the Cathouse the night before. Then it's time for "Sweet Child O' Mine," which the front man dedicates to "my friend Erin," his former lover and the song's inspiration. The band's biggest hit won't be released as a single for another eight months, but already the crowd reception is astounding when Slash picks out the graceful intro.

Heads bang and fists fly into the air as the guys in Guns chug through the verses. By the time they reach the "Where do we go now?" breakdown, the entire floor is a swirling mosh pit of crowd surfers and colliding bodies. Slash leans back and lets the notes scream out of his Les Paul during the final, high-pitched solo.

After that transcendent high, Guns N' Roses head into the gutter, busting out their ode to revenge murder, "Used to Love Her"; a send-up to cocaine, "My Michelle"; the song "Rocket Queen," which Axl dedicates "to every girl that doesn't mind the cold, she's gonna show off what she's got." After that, a cover of the Bob Dylan classic "Knockin' on Heaven's Door," during which the audience raises their lighters. Security tries to discourage the impromptu pyrotechnics until Axl warns them, "Don't hassle them for the lighters."

After the Dylan track, Axl brings out Steven Adler, who appears wearing a cast around his bum hand. He explains the reason for his absence and introduces his replacement Fred Coury as a "highly satanic motherfucker from hell," then grabs a tambourine to join along with his band as they kick into the first *Appetite* single. "Welcome to the fucking jungle, baby," Axl rasps. Slash unleashes the song's instantly identifiable descending guitar riff and the audience roars with deafening recognition.

The next 40 minutes of the show roar past. The band brings the main set to an end with the infectious, sing-along–inducing "Paradise City." When Guns N' Roses come back out for the encore, the grateful audience explodes, then settles back down as Guns slip into a song written by Izzy named "Patience." The whistling ballad won't receive an official release until nearly a full year later, on the EP *G N' R Lies*.

"You like Aerosmith?" Axl asks when "Patience" ends. "You wanna talk to your fucking mother right now?" The crowd seems open to a discussion, and for the final song of the night, Guns N' Roses rip into their high-octane cover of "Mama Kin" that's featured prominently on *Live ?!*@ Like a Suicide*.

"Thank you!" Axl screams over the final wallops of Coury's tom-toms. "Good! Fucking! Night!"

HONORABLE MENTION
Def Jam '87 at Madison Square Garden
New York, NY (September 3)

In 1987, the greatest collection of artists from "The Golden Age of Rap" came together for a run of dates through America dubbed the Def Jam '87 Tour. It was a stacked bill from top to bottom, anchored by legendary talents like LL Cool J, Public Enemy, KRS-One and Eric B. & Rakim. On September 3, the tour landed back home in the birthplace of rap, New York City, for a blowout show at Madison Square Garden. KRS-One was still hurting from the death of his Boogie Down Productions partner Scott La Rock just a week before, but as *New York Times* writer Robert Palmer noted, "The rhymes came whiplashing out, the voice was strong and supple, and the energy was unrelenting." Public Enemy suffered for trying to get the crowd involved and spent most of their set chatting instead of rapping, but Eric B. & Rakim brought precision and style to the songs from their most recent release, *Paid in Full*. As the headliner, it was the kid from Queens, LL Cool J, who stole the show. "LL Cool J is an especially absorbed performer," Palmer noted. "His wit and verbal inventiveness, the way his raps dance and jab and feint over the heavy rhythms . . . make him an impressive talent. And the young women swoon for him the way they did for rhythm and blues and rock-and-roll stars several generations ago." What can you say? The ladies love cool James.

1988

Michael Jackson
WEMBLEY STADIUM—LONDON, ENGLAND
JULY 16

THE KING OF POP GOES BAD

In 1987, Michael Jackson set off on his first world tour as a solo artist. He loudly proclaimed that it would be his final live run ever, a clever bit of marketing designed to stir up demand for tickets. Not that he needed it. Jackson was far and away the biggest musical star of the 1980s. The "King of Pop" earned his title five years earlier when he unleashed his sixth album, *Thriller*, which quickly became the best-selling record in history.

On August 31, 1987, Jackson dropped the long-awaited follow-up album, *Bad*. His seventh solo record topped the charts for six weeks, eventually selling 32 million copies worldwide. It yielded a record-breaking five number-one singles: "I Just Can't Stop Loving You," "Man in the Mirror," "Dirty Diana," "The Way You Make Me Feel" and "Bad."

A month before *Bad* hit the shelves, Jackson's manager, Frank DiLeo, announced that a full world tour would kick off in September in Japan, after which it would crisscross North America and Europe. Jackson would perform 127 concerts, spread across 15 countries to an audience of 4.4 million people. At its conclusion, he was awarded a Guinness World Record for the largest-grossing tour of all time: $125 million.

In his typical fashion, Jackson was meticulous in preparation. He spent months assembling the band, the dancers and the stage, then spent many more months rehearsing and putting it all together. The stage featured 700 lights along with 100 speakers, 40 lasers and two 24-foot x 18-foot projection screens. Spectacle was Michael Jackson's bread and butter, and he was going to lay it on thick.

Many people were needed to support such a massive endeavor. "Swarming about this backstage area are members of the 45-strong production crew, who have brought raw materials of the show in 22 trucks, and worked nonstop for 38 hours to assemble them," writer Frank Noyer observed during the tour's kickoff show on September 28 at Korakuen Stadium in Tokyo. "There are another 28 people in what is designated 'the band crew,' 11 of them actual performers. A further 20 individuals comprise Michael Jackson's official entourage. . . . There are two personal chefs to oversee Michael's vegetarian diet. There is longstanding personal bodyguard Billy Bray. Also in attendance are attorneys, accountants and publicity personnel." Jackson chartered a separate plane specifically for his chimpanzee, Bubbles.

After closing out his run through Japan and the U.S., Jackson landed in Rome for back-to-back shows at the Stadio Flaminio on May 23 and 24, then spent the next four months traversing Europe. The highlight was seven sold-out performances at London's Wembley Stadium. The first five took place between July 14 and 23, with additional dates on August 26 and 27.

More than half a million Londoners turned out to see the "King of Pop" Moonwalk his way into the his-

SET LIST

Wanna Be Startin' Somethin'

This Place Hotel

Another Part of Me

I Just Can't Stop Loving You

She's Out of My Life

I Want You Back/The Love You Save/I'll Be There

Rock with You

Human Nature

Smooth Criminal

Dirty Diana

Thriller

Bad Groove

Workin' Day and Night

Beat It

Billie Jean

Bad

The Way You Make Me Feel

Man in the Mirror

tory books. Each concert was an extravaganza that no one inside the massive soccer stadium could ever forget, but the highlight came on the evening of July 16.

That particular show got a late start, but for a very important reason. Jackson was held up while meeting with Prince Charles and Princess Diana to present them with a $50,000 donation to the Prince's Trust.

"I wrote a song called 'Dirty Diana.' It was about a certain kind of girls that hang around concerts or clubs, you know, they call them groupies. I took it out of the show in honor of Her Royal Highness," Jackson later told Barbara Walters. "She took me away and she said, 'Are you going to do "Dirty Diana"?' So I said, 'No, I took it out of the show because of you.' She said, 'No! I want you to do it!'" Needless to say, the song made it back into the set list.

After what seems like a lifetime of waiting, the lights go down and the large screen at the back of the stage comes to life. An animated version of Jackson's iconic Florsheim shoes walks across until they stand up straight, adopting one of the singer's most recognized poses. Waves of controlled guitar feedback scream out of the speakers. Fans are blinded by the long row of bright lights.

The guitar eventually fades, giving way to a single, glistening keyboard note. The lights slowly dim to reveal the man of the hour standing stark still in front of a microphone with two pairs of dancers on either side. The crowd goes berserk. Jackson looks out of this world in his bedazzled black jacket, which he's left open to reveal a silver long-sleeve shirt and championship-sized silver belt.

A drumbeat kicks in and he strolls toward the front, then engages in a bit of choreographed grinding alongside his dancers. Horns blast. He does his patented twirl, leg kick and point to the sky, then peels off back to the microphone. "Ooh!" he squeals then rips into "Wanna Be Startin' Somethin'."

You see the way Michael's singing that song—he's not of this world.

The man is a dancing tornado. The classic moves—the crotch grabs, the finger snaps, the hip thrusts, the foot swivels, the "Hee-Hee's"—explode out of his body. Another blast of horns leaves Jackson standing as still as a mannequin on top of a lighted platform with a wind machine whipping his curly black locks away from his face, until the beat kicks in, bringing him back to life. His backup singers croon their "mamase mamasa mamakusa" lines over and over, giving Jackson a moment to scat and spin until the song ends in a final burst of light.

Jackson sings and dances his way through the next number, "This Place Hotel," and then addresses the audience for the first time. "Hello, London!" he screams. "And welcome to our royal guests," he adds. The crowd roars and Jackson counts in the next song, "Another Part of Me." That's followed by "I Just Can't Stop Loving You," for which he duets with a then-unknown Sheryl Crow, who is one of the backup singers.

"I didn't even own a passport when I landed the job," she later told the *Daily Mail*. "Walking out in front of full stadiums every night was exhilarating enough. To be performing alongside Jackson was something else altogether. Seeing him dance a few feet away from me was an otherworldly experience."

After serenading a fan on "She's Out of My Life" and running through a medley of Jackson 5 classics, he starts churning through some of his biggest hits, songs like "Rock with You," "Beat It," "Smooth Criminal" and "Thriller." The last two are presented much like they appear in the music video, with Jackson wearing a sharp white zoot suit for the former and the iconic red leather jacket for the latter. For "Billie Jean" he busts out the single white sequined glove to approximate his iconic 1983 performance at the Motown 25 show.

"As the costume changes came and went and the stage and lighting effects grew more audacious, he took control with a performance of matchless virtuosity," John Peel wrote in his review for *The Observer*. "Making much of stagecraft learned, surely, from James Brown . . . Jackson led his dancers, singers and musicians, all fearsomely well-drilled and rakishly handsome, through less a sequence of songs, more a series of scenes, the whole resembling some futuristic, technological pantomime."

"Who's Bad?" The question flashes continuously in giant letters on the video screen hanging above the stage. When the darkness lifts, Jackson is standing there shuffling to the beat of the title track from his latest record. It's the last song of the main set, and he's giving it everything he's got—high-energy kicks, moonwalks and one final, gleeful "Heh-heh."

Reemerging moments later for the encore, you can feel a different tone in the air. Jackson runs through "The Way You Make Me Feel" and completely pours his heart out on "Man in the Mirror." The emotions are overwhelming. Near the final chorus, he spins out and drops down to his knees, pleading with everyone to "Make the change." He then rais-

es his arms straight out in a Christ pose, allowing the audience's love to wash over him as the lights fade to black.

"If you look at that performance, he's somewhere else," director Spike Lee observed. "That's one of the great performances ever. You see the way Michael's singing that song—he's not of this world. He's somewhere else."

HONORABLE MENTION
Depeche Mode at the Rose Bowl
Pasadena, CA (June 18)

On June 18, 1988, Depeche Mode's eight-month, 101-date Music for the Masses Tour came to an end in front of 65,000 adoring fans. It was by far the biggest gig the English synthpop group had ever played. Led by enigmatic front man Dave Gahan, Depeche Mode put together a two-hour long extravaganza of light and sound featuring tracks like "Everything Counts," "Behind the Wheel" and "Just Can't Get Enough." The show was shot by director D.A. Pennebaker, who counts the subsequent film, *101*, among his all-time favorites. "The thing I noticed was that the whole audience was so tuned into this underground movement that was going on there," he told me. "At the end, during 'Never Let Me Down Again' when [Gahan] goes up and starts waving his arms and the audience picks it up is just so fantastic. When I think about it, it gives me chills."

1989

N.W.A
CELEBRITY THEATER—ANAHEIM, CA
MARCH 23

FUCK THA POLICE

Back in their late '80s heyday, N.W.A were billed as "The World's Most Dangerous Group." The Compton rap outfit drew widespread critical recognition and political condemnation for shining a spotlight on the harsh reality of what life was really like as an underprivileged black youth in America. They had the nerve to inject that view into the minds and ears of a mostly white youth audience. They were dangerous because they had the balls to stand up and loudly say, "Fuck Tha Police," even after the FBI warned them not to.

N.W.A were five badasses: Eazy E, Dr. Dre, Ice Cube, DJ Yella and MC Ren. Following the release of their debut album, *Straight Outta Compton*, on August 8, 1988, the group was branded as a subversive band of vulgar agitators by the powers that be. When the U.S. government put "Parental Advisory" labels on albums with coarse language, violent imagery and sexually suggestive themes, *Straight Outta Compton* was one of the first to get the sticker.

As the adage goes, any press is good press, and the notoriety helped boost album sales to a level that no one could have anticipated. The gangsta rap outfit became one of the most inexplicable crossover acts in pop music history. Everyone from Sinéad O'Connor to Axl Rose loudly endorsed their sound, their words and their outlaw image. As a result, for the first time, the geographic center of rap shifted from its birthplace in New York City to the fringes of Los Angeles.

A little over six months after releasing their debut, N.W.A faced the biggest drawback to their newfound infamy: a scarcity of venues that would allow them to perform. A few months back, they'd co-headlined the Bring the Noise Tour with Public Enemy, but as they began plotting their own headlining dates, they found it tough to find places to play. Whether it was fear from the promoters about the kind of audience they would draw or pressure from local authorities who didn't want them in their neighborhoods, N.W.A—and their fans—were getting the shaft.

On March 23, 1989, the group locked down a show 20 miles or so from Compton at the Celebrity Theater in the predominantly white So-Cal city of Anaheim, opening for Ice T. No one knew what would happen, but that was half the thrill. "My mom would tell me, 'Don't you go near that show,'" a 15-year-old attendee named Jason Crouch told the *Los Angeles Times*. "There could be a riot . . . maybe even people with machine guns!'"

For all y'all niggas that don't know the time, yo Dre, gimme a funky ass bassline," Ice Cube demands after introducing N.W.A on the stage. Given his cue, the Doctor pushes play on the group's second single, "Gangsta Gangsta," and the audience goes nuts.

Cube wears his signature, menacing scowl that lets you know he's not the kind of guy you want to mess with. The 19-year-old MC stalks the stage like

SET LIST

Gangsta Gangsta

I Ain't Tha 1

Fuck Tha Police

Dopeman

Boyz-N-The-Hood

2 Hard Mutha's

Still Talkin'

Eazy-er Said Than Dunn

Radio

We Want Eazy

MUSICIANS

Eazy E: Vocals

Ice Cube: Vocals

MC Ren: Vocals

Dr. Dre: DJ

DJ Yella: DJ

This could be the moment where it's all going to go to hell—where N.W.A's vivid depictions of violence and anti-authoritarianism cause those in the room to get carried away. Cube calls for Dre to stop the music and steps up to squash it. "If (you) want to fight, come up here on stage," he says. "This ain't [the movie] *Colors*. You didn't come to see a fight. You came to see a concert."

The skirmish is quelled by the venue security and the show rolls on. The band continues "Dopeman," bringing onstage a young woman named Lisa whom the audience loudly boos. "Since the crowd don't like you," Ren says, playing to their spite, "Tell this dirty bitch what she needs." "You need a nigga with money so you get a dopeman," Cube loudly responds. The audience bursts out laughing, then loudly joins in for the chorus.

So this is what I want all of y'all to do. I want y'all to say 'Fuck tha police!'"

a caged lion warning those down in front that he "Never should have been let out the penitentiary," because "I'm a crazy motherfucker from around the way."

The atmosphere in the air is electric, but also filled with tension. There are 50 security guards, more than enough it would seem, to keep the crowd of 2,500 people in check. Before fans could enter the theater, they had to pass through a metal detector and receive a pat down. Machine guns, hats, bandanas and any gang colors are strictly prohibited.

The band quickly runs through "I Ain't Tha 1" before getting to the moment everyone showed up to see. "Check this out, Anaheim, before we came up here, they didn't want us to do this show because they said Eazy E and N.W.A promote gang violence and drugs," MC Ren says. "The police won't let us do no more concerts at the sports arena. We can't do no more concerts in Long Beach. This the only place they'll let us do it," Ice Cube adds. "What that means is niggas can't be fucking up. You gotta kick it together, cos this is the only place we can party within the city . . . y'all with that?"

The crowd is down and shouts to let N.W.A know. "So this is what I want all of y'all to do. I want y'all to say 'Fuck tha police!'" The audience repeats the phrase twice and then N.W.A kick into the most incendiary song off their debut. Despite Cube's preface, the audience gets a little rowdy, and by the time they end the track and shift into "Dopeman," a full-on fight breaks out.

When the song finishes, the MCs break into a "this side of the room" vs. "that side of the room" volume contest before Ren starts singing "Where is Eazy, where is Eazy" to the tune of "Frère Jacques." When the man in the dark shades and black baseball hat emerges and sings back "Here I come, here I come," the audience loses it. The beat shifts and Eazy E breaks into the opening verse of his signature song, "Boyz-N-The-Hood."

After that, N.W.A run through "2 Hard Mutha's" and "Still Talkin'" before ceding the limelight to Eazy for a medley of "Eazy-er Said Than Dunn," "Radio" and "We Want Eazy." Before they could complete that song, another fight breaks out in the lobby and spills out into the streets. A dozen police cruisers are dispatched to the area to restore order, but by the time they get there, the perpetrators have split. N.W.A are already gone too. No arrests are made.

HONORABLE MENTION
Metallica at the Seattle Center Coliseum
Seattle, WA (August 29)

Metallica has performed dozens of epic gigs across their decades-long career—the 1991 Monsters of Rock gig outside of Moscow jumps to mind—but this show at the Seattle Center Coliseum might be their best. Hitting the road to support their latest album, *...And Justice For All*, the Bay Area metal masters summoned forth a set brimming with raw, caustic fury. Across more than two hours, they treat the Pacific Northwest audience to some of the hardest-hitting headbangers they have at their disposal. It's hard to pick a peak moment. The renditions of "One," and "Fade to Black" are incredible, but the real highlight is the song "Harvester of Sorrow," which puts the studio rendition to shame. Metallica's Seattle performance was filmed and recorded for posterity and later released as part of the box set *Live Shit: Binge & Purge*, which has been certified 15x platinum.

#1 Single of the Year:
"Hold On"
Wilson Phillips

1990

#1 Album of the Year:
Rhythm Nation 1814
Janet Jackson

Madonna
STADIO FLAMINIO—ROME, ITALY
JULY 10

BLOND AMBITION

Beyond her obvious musical talent, the one element that has catapulted Madonna into the pop music stratosphere is her instinct to provoke. Whether it's making out with Britney Spears and Christina Aguilera during an award show, releasing a coffee table book filled with erotic photography or threatening to blow up the White House the day after President Donald Trump assumed office, she has an innate sense for what actions will attract the largest number of eyeballs. In 1990, she may have bitten off more than she could chew when she went toe to toe with Pope John Paul II.

The trouble began a year earlier after Madonna released the music video for "Like a Prayer." It depicted several highly controversial scenes, like Madonna dancing in front of a field of burning crosses, receiving the stigmata and kissing a black saint, presumably Jesus. It ruffled a lot of feathers.

Religious and conservative groups the world over quickly denounced Madonna. Pepsi, which had just inked a $5 million—dollar sponsorship deal with her, was pressured to pull a two-minute spot they had filmed with the singer titled "Make a Wish." So eager was the soda company to extract themselves from the controversy that they allowed her to keep the money after tearing up the contract.

The big boom came when the Pope went public, issuing a statement calling for all Catholics to avoid going to Madonna's concerts while also seeking to ban her from performing at any venues in Italy. Rather than stifle the singer's fortunes however, the controversy drove up both her popularity and the demand to see her live. *Like a Prayer* went No. 1 on the *Billboard* charts, a position it held for six consecutive weeks. It ended up selling around 15 million copies worldwide.

Near the end of the year, she announced her next world tour, dubbed Blond Ambition. The run of dates began on April 13, 1990, in Japan and lasted for four months, during which she performed 57 different shows. In defiance of His Holiness, Madonna booked three concerts in Italy: two in Rome and one in Turin.

On July 2, Madonna landed at the Ciampino Airport in Rome, where she was instantly mobbed by a throng of paparazzi. Rather than run, she stood her ground and addressed the Church that condemned her.

"My show is not a conventional rock show, but a theatrical representation of my music," she said. "Like theater, it asks questions, provokes thoughts and takes you on an emotional journey portraying good and bad, light and dark, joy and sorrow, redemption and salvation. I do not endorse a way of life, but describe one, and the audience is left to make its own decisions and judgements. This is what I consider freedom of speech, freedom of expression and freedom of thought. To prevent me from performing my show, you, the Catholic Church, are say-

ः

SET LIST

Express Yourself
Open Your Heart
Causing a Commotion
Where's the Party
Like a Virgin
Like a Prayer
Live to Tell
Oh Father
Papa Don't Preach
Sooner or Later
Hanky Panky
Now I'm Following You
Material Girl
Cherish
Into the Groove
Vogue
Holiday
Keep It Together

ing that you do not believe in these freedoms."

It was an explosive statement. Even more so coming from someone raised Catholic. Madonna ultimately canceled her second planned performance in Rome because of low ticket sales, no doubt influenced by the Pope's decree, but the show on July 10 was still a go and she wasn't about to make any compromises.

Plumes of white smoke fill the stadium. A pulsating beat pumps through the speakers as seven male dancers engage in elaborate choreography on the stage. Behind them, a hydraulic platform churns to life, elevating the star of the show into view. The crowd goes wild.

"Ciao, Roma! Ciao, Italia!" a beaming Madonna announces. The singer looks very stylish in a ripped black pantsuit with short, curled hair and a gold monocle dangling from her neck. Madonna asks the crowd in their native tongue, do you believe in love? "*Credi nell'amore*? Well then, I got something to say about it and it goes something like this!" It's the prelude to the first song of the night, "Express Yourself."

Madonna does a quick spin, kicks her legs into the air and busts out a series of robotic dance moves as the music blasts out of the mountain of speakers. The "Material Girl" saunters down the stairs to the floor of the stage, striking a pose every so often that sends the audience into a tizzy. When she reaches the bottom, she slowly tears away her jacket to reveal her now-iconic crème-colored corset with the pointy, conical breasts, designed by Jean Paul Gaultier. Then she breaks into a routine featuring a gratuitous amount of crotch-grabbing and dry-humping.

Just like every other stop on the tour, this show is broken up into four different sections. The first is devoted to upbeat dance tunes like "Where's the Party" and features a set design mirroring the aesthetic of the 1927 Fritz Lang film *Metropolis*. The second set deals with religious themes and iconography. The third relates to her recent involvement in the *Dick Tracy* film. The final section is dedicated to some of her biggest hits like "Vogue" and "Into the Groove."

The Pepsi money has been put to good use. The show is a tremendous spectacle featuring several different backdrops, costume changes and special

> *The "Material Girl" saunters down the stairs to the floor of the stage, striking a pose every so often that sends the audience into a tizzy.*

effects. As *L.A. Times* writer Robert Hilburn observed when he viewed the performance a few months earlier, "Madonna's approach offers the kind of dazzle—a flashy set, colorful costumes and a cadre of dancers—that is sometimes used to cover up artistic weaknesses. But Madonna—blessed with a marvelous sense of performance—commands the stage as fully when she is surrounded by dancers as when she is sitting alone on a chair."

The second act, the religious portion of the show, is the one that causes the most nervous tension backstage, but you would never know it looking at Madonna in front of the crowd. Beginning with a down-tempo, Arab music–tinged version of "Like a Virgin," Madonna re-enacts the scene that nearly got her arrested in Toronto. She simulates masturbation on a plush red bed surrounded by two male dancers who run their hands up and down her torso.

The graphic scene becomes frenzied and then stops on a dime as the lights go down and a curtain rises in the back to reveal a five-tiered votive candle rack, flickering with dozens of points of soft red light. Under the cover of darkness, Madonna is wrapped into a black, hooded robe and a large gold crucifix is ceremoniously placed around her neck. She writhes on the ground as an industrial drumbeat clinks and clanks overhead.

The sound shifts and Madonna sits up on her knees. "Life is a mystery/Everyone must stand alone." The crowd explodes at the recognition of the opening words to "Like a Prayer." She rises to her feet and the beat changes again. The performance is perfectly timed feat of choreography. Dancers clad all in black run into view, shuffling from side to side with Madonna guiding their movements. She sings half of the second verse while flat on her back and raised into the air by one of her dancers, underneath an ornate metal cross.

Midway through, the somber aura is replaced by a joyful, almost revivalist spirit, more reminiscent of the Baptist school of religion than the classic traditions of the Church located five miles down the road. The joy on the stage is mirrored by the audience who is only too happy to clap and dance along.

After "Like a Prayer," she slips into a straightforward take on the ballad "Live to Tell," before the lights drop out again and dramatic keyboard progressions ring out through the speakers. When the spotlight rediscovers her, Madonna is seen kneeling before an altar. A few beats later, she slowly rises and walks over to the skyward crucifix. She reenacts

a mystic, Stevie Nicks–style spin and begins singing "Oh Father." This portion of the show concludes with "Papa Don't Preach." Madonna races off the stage, leaving her dancers to regale the crowd with some high-performance ballet while she changes into her next costume.

Almost an hour and a half after it began, the show closes with an encore performance of her first hit single, "Holiday," followed by one of her more recent ones, "Keep It Together," with a small bit of

She writhes on the ground as an industrial drumbeat clinks and clanks overhead.

"Family Affair" by Sly and the Family Stone thrown in for good measure. As the concert closes, Madonna is all smiles. Decked out in a black, strapped one-piece outfit, she hugs her dancers and crew as she bids the Italian crowd a warm goodnight.

In the face of extreme pressure and high stakes, Madonna adopted the Julius Caeser approach. *Veni Vidi Vici*. She came, she saw, she conquered. That being said, if you thought Madonna's battle with the Catholic Church ended in 1990, you are sorely mistaken. Sixteen years later, the singer returned once again to Rome to perform another concert, where she staged a mock crucifixion. "This concert is a blasphemous challenge to the faith and a profanation of the cross," Cardinal Ersilio Tonino said in anticipation of the act. "She should be excommunicated."

Not one to back down because of a threat, Madonna's show went on as planned, crucifixion and all.

HONORABLE MENTION

Janet Jackson at the Great Western Forum
Inglewood, CA (April 20)

Despite releasing her debut record in 1982, Janet Jackson underwent her first major world tour as a solo artist eight years later. She couldn't have picked a more opportune time. The 23-year-old notched the most commercially successful album of that year, *Janet Jackson's Rhythm Nation 1814*, a record that melded new jack swing with shiny pop elements and icy industrial tones. This show, which took place the same day she received her star on the Hollywood Walk of Fame, was the first of seven she would perform at the Great Western Forum in 1990. That's an incredible feat for any artist and an unprecedented accomplishment for a female one. Jackson set out to prove that her brother Michael wasn't the only one in the family who could blow away a crowd. At a reported cost of $2 million, she put together a show filled with dancers, lights, pyrotechnics and illusory magic. All that spectacle wouldn't have meant anything if not for the songs, and Jackson delivered a set bursting with hits. Opening with "Control," she delighted the L.A. crowd with recognizable bangers like "Nasty," "What Have You Done for Me Lately," "Escapade" and "Black Cat." The live show rookie came through, and as Chris Willman wrote in the *L.A. Times*, "She's able to provide more pure entertainment value for your dollar than just about any elder on the market."

#1 Single of the Year:
"(Everything I Do) I Do It for You"
Bryan Adams

1991

#1 Album of the Year:
Mariah Carey
Mariah Carey

Jane's Addiction, Siouxsie & The Banshees, Living Colour, Nine Inch Nails, Ice T & Body Count, Butthole Surfers and Rollins Band
IRVINE MEADOWS—IRVINE, CA
JULY 23

JANE'S FAREWELL LOLLAPALOOZA

This is it, homeboys. Youth revolution!" screams Jane's Addiction front man Perry Farrell. It's the second evening of the band's three-night residency just outside its hometown of Los Angeles. This is no ordinary tour, however. Lollapalooza is a package program with six (and sometimes seven) acts, criss-crossing the country and bringing the alternative and the underground to the masses. "A portable Wood-stock for the black-lipstick-and-nose-ring set," as *Rolling Stone* writer David Fricke called it.

Lollapalooza was a simple concept that became a cultural phenomenon. Farrell came up with the idea after his band canceled a headlining performance at the Reading Festival in the U.K., because the singer blew out his voice at a club gig the night before. Some members of Jane's Addiction stuck around Reading, hanging out with the other bands and the fans, and they fell in love with the vibe. Jane's was on the cusp of calling it quits and wanted to go out in style with a tour that mirrored the vibe and feel of Reading and the other popular outdoor festivals around Europe.

"If I'm going to do something of that size, I want to surround myself with other great bands and great things on the grounds—food, books, art—to make it worth the money," Farrell told *Rolling Stone*. "I'm very proud of my band. I think we're great. But I don't think it's worth twenty-five bucks to see a flyspeck."

The band, along with agent Marc Geiger and manager Ted Gardner, spent ten months plotting out the tour. No detail was too small to escape their attention, from assembling the talent and picking the poster artwork to arranging for a large supply of free condoms to be passed out. They booked 26 shows, mostly in outdoor amphitheaters across the United States. The name of the tour popped into Farrell's head after watching an episode of *The Three Stooges*. "The definition of 'lollapalooza' was something or someone great and/or wonderful," he explained to *Spin*.

Putting together the lineup was stunningly straightforward. "The first bill was decided by Jane's Addiction and myself in London at the hotel," Geiger told me. "We literally went around the room. I came up with the format and said, 'Here's what we can do. Everybody gets to pick a band.' Dave [Navarro] picked Siouxsie [& The Banshees], Perry picked Ice-T, Eric [Avery] picked Butthole Surfers, Stephen [Perkins] picked Rollins and I picked Nine Inch Nails and Pixies. They ended up turning it down, which created the spot for Living Colour."

Package tours weren't a new concept in America. Artists had been boarding buses and hitting the road together since Dick Clark's Caravan of Stars in the 1950s and earlier. More contemporary examples included the Monsters of Rock Tour in 1988 that featured Van Halen, Scorpions and Metallica. More than pioneering anything, Lollapalooza represented a breakthrough moment for a new generation of music

SET LIST

Up the Beach

Whores

Standing in the Shower . . . Thinking

Ain't No Right

Three Days

Been Caught Stealing

Don't Call Me Nigger, Whitey

1%

Ted, Just Admit It . . .

Then She Did . . .

Mountain Song

Stop!

Ocean Size

Classic Girl

fans. "This is a pioneer tour," Ice-T told *Rolling Stone.* "All the groups in their own way have pioneered a certain form of music."

The second day of Lollapalooza at the Irvine Meadows Amphitheatre starts in much the same way that the first had. As opposed to the kickoff show in Arizona that had been an overheated, emotional train wreck, these gigs were a stunning success. "Irvine was the first real show they didn't blow up," Geiger remembered. "The first show in Phoenix blew up because of problems with the stage and then Jane's got into a fight. Irvine was our first glimpse of fires on the lawns and people dancing in the fires and jumping through them. It was pretty interesting."

The Rollins Band opens the festival around 2 p.m. Former Black Flag singer Henry Rollins rages away on songs like "Obscene," shirtless and in just his black skivvies, before ceding the stage to another indelible front man, Gibby Haynes, and his band, Butthole Surfers. It's a caustic way to kick off your day, with both acts turning in savage 45-minute sets. Next up, Ice-T and Body Count take over, bringing their aggressive, anti-authoritarian gangsta rap to the surf-bros and stoners splayed out before them.

At 5 p.m., Nine Inch Nails storm the stage, practically stealing the show with their angst-ridden,

synth-fueled songs. Trent Reznor and company look like no else on the bill with their short hair and tattered black clothes, screaming out in full fury the music from their debut album, *Pretty Hate Machine.* "I feel like everyone's got a semi-positive vibe, and we're the negative antichrist onstage," Reznor explained to *Rolling Stone.* Their vibe strikes a chord with the young crowd. Nine Inch Nails are the only act able to match the headliner's T-shirt sales numbers.

An hour later, it's Living Colour's turn in the spotlight and they go into full-on guitar hero mode, with Vernon Reid laying it on thick over songs like "Funny Vibe" and "Cult of Personality." For the penultimate performance of the evening, Siouxie and the Banshees offer up a set brimming with elemental gothic pop. Singer Siouxsie Sioux has a bewitching presence and casts her spell over the rapt crowd while singing about things like a fear of the unknown and a banana split lady named "Christine."

Just after 9 p.m., Jane's Addiction walks out in front of the grateful crowd. They begin their set in the most apropos way imaginable: playing track one, side one, of their first album, "Up the Beach." It's difficult to feel nostalgic about something that's only three years old, but the selection is a reminder of what this tour is all about. They're no longer interested in looking forward together.

Jane's has long had a penchant for absurd, dramatic garb, and they don't disappoint. As Fricke recalled, "With his closely cropped hair, oversize red woolen suit and jittery, stick-figure dancing, Farrell looks even more extreme and dangerous than when he had braids and wore an S&M bodysuit—like a psycho-ward cross between Mr. Natural and Groucho Marx."

The band pours its heart out for the next hour and a half as the audience whoop, holler and bang their heads. Songs like "Whores," "Ocean Size" and "Three Days" garner enthusiastic waves of applause. Midway through, guitarist Dave Navarro gets the opportunity to stretch his fingers and kick in his wah pedal on "Mountain Song."

The most exhilarating moment of the show comes as the band slides into a cover of the Sly and the Family Stone deep cut "Don't Call Me Nigger, Whitey." Out of the wings comes Ice-T, who walks up to Farrell and caustically recites the song's title directly into his face. The singer steps back aghast, then sings "Don't call me whitey, nigger." Eyes go wide around the amphitheater as the word leaves Farrell's lips. Ice-T takes off his sunglasses and glares at him while Navarro's ghastly guitar fills soundtrack the tension. They repeat their repartee, this time with added emphasis on their insults. Farrell screams his obscenity, and the dual sound of Jane's Addiction and Body Count explodes to life behind the singers.

All the weird ones got together, painted their faces, slam-danced in fields and made memories that lasted a lifetime.

"They didn't know the song," Geiger remembered of the crowd's reaction. "The hip-hop community hadn't crossed over so people didn't understand it. There was a certain amount of edgy, racist calling out. It was exciting."

The air is filled with the manic frenzy of savage drumming and ferocious guitar soloing. Farrell and Ice-T stalk around each other until midway through, when they both step to their microphones. The Jane's Addiction front man shouts, "I'm proud to be a," while T adds, "Say it loud!" It's as close to a chorus as they get before resuming their adversarial roles. When the song breaks down again, they take each other in their arms and waltz around the stage.

"Peace!" Farrell shouts. Both men wave to the crowd, and Jane's Addiction resumes their regularly scheduled programming.

"This is it, homeboys. Youth revolution!" Farrell says at the beginning of the last song of the night.

"Last chance. Let's get on with it!" On cue, the mosh pit in front of the stage rages to life, looking like a scene out of Pandemonium. When the chaos reaches its apex, Farrell dives in to dance and shove along with them. It takes security a while to extract him from the scrum, and when he resumes his place onstage, he and the rest of the band finish the song and bid the crowd adieu. There's another insurrection to prepare for the following night.

Lollapalooza was a beautiful event where all the weird ones got together, painted their faces, slam-danced in fields and made memories that lasted a lifetime. As Simon Reynolds wrote in the *New York Times* that year, "Lollapalooza seems to be a conscious attempt to re-invoke the '60s sense of rock as counterculture, in defiance of today's perception of rock as leisure industry." He added, "Lollapalooza is a boon for the twentysomething generation, a happening that may instill pride in teenagers who have grown up under the shadow of rock's mythic past."

Of course, Lollapalooza's subversive spirit couldn't possibly endure. The necessary corporate elements eventually forced the carefully curated touring rendition of the festival to transform into a standalone, four-day behemoth held annually in Chicago's Grant Park. "In America, or any consumer-driven society, anything that stands still long enough turns into a demographic and is marketed to," Rollins explained to *Spin*. "I can only speak for the first Lollapalooza, but I think it was very innocent. There's no way the subsequent ones weren't, in some way, calculated."

You can be cynical about such things, or you can choose to appreciate the moment of purity for the short time it lasts. As Farrell sang in that last song in Irvine that night, "Classic Girl," "They may say those were the days/But in a way, you know for us, these are the days."

HONORABLE MENTION
The International Pop Underground Convention
Olympia, WA (August 20-25)

If Lollapalooza represented the alternative to the mainstream, then this event in Olympia was the alternative to the alternative. Organized by K Records founder and Beat Happening front man Calvin Johnson, the convention hosted fifty different bands spread across multiple venues around Olympia, with most of the bigger names playing the Capitol Theater. Pop Underground is the key phrase here, and Johnson put together a lineup that included some of the best bands from that world, like Fugazi, the Melvins and Built to Spill. The first night was dubbed *Love Rock Revolution Girl Style Now* but has come to be known as "Girl Night" for all the tremendous, female punk bands like L7 and Bikini Kill that took the stage. "It showed that the ideas of how things could be aren't so utopian," Johnson told the *Seattle Weekly*. "It's not 'could be.' It was. It is."

#1 Single of the Year:
"End of the Road"
Boyz II Men

#1 Album of the Year:
Ropin' the Wind
Garth Brooks

1992

Nirvana
READING FESTIVAL—READING, ENGLAND
AUGUST 30

WITH THE LIGHTS OUT

Would they, or wouldn't they? That was the question running through the minds of the 60,000 people standing out in the expansive, muddy bog that had been transformed into the Reading Festival grounds. After months of anticipation, Nirvana, the biggest rock band in the world, was set to take the stage . . . or maybe they weren't. No one knew.

1992 should have been the greatest year of front man Kurt Cobain's young life. His band's second full-length album, *Nevermind*, was burning up the charts. He had just married the lead singer of Hole, Courtney Love, on a beach in Hawaii, and the pair was expecting their first child. Yet things were about to take a very dark turn.

As much as he craved the spotlight, Cobain was ill-equipped to deal with it. To help cope with the anxiety and pressure he was feeling because of his newfound superstardom, he turned to heroin. Whispers about the singer's addiction bubbled up in the press, but the real trouble had landed weeks earlier when a profile of him and Courtney was published by *Vanity Fair*. The piece was titled "Strange Love" and was written by Lynn Hirschberg. She sought to find out whether "the pair were the grunge John and Yoko? Or the next Sid and Nancy?"

The biggest revelation, and the one that caused the greatest uproar, was that Love was supposedly shooting heroin while pregnant with their child, Frances. Cobain and Love fiercely denied the accusation.

Based on the claims made in the *Vanity Fair* piece, shortly after Love gave birth, Seattle child welfare services took custody of Frances for four weeks. It was only after Cobain and Love submitted to multiple urine tests and made regular visits with a social worker over many months that they could regain full custody of their daughter.

Things weren't going so great inside of Nirvana either. A spring tour of the United States had been canceled. They picked up again in June for a short run through Europe before Love's health complications forced them back off the road. With the all the drama, rumors and speculation swirling around Cobain's personal and professional relationships, many were left to wonder. . . was this it for Nirvana?

The chaos of the last few months is at the forefront of everyone's mind as they wait for the band to make its grand entrance. The crowd has already enjoyed an incredible weekend of music courtesy of Mudhoney, Beastie Boys, the Melvins, Public Enemy, Nick Cave, Smashing Pumpkins and more, but it's Nirvana that they want to see. All they know is what they've read in the newspapers, tabloids and rock magazines. Kurt is said to be a shell of his former self. A hopeless junkie, in and out of hospitals, practically on death's door.

Moments later, Krist Novoselic and Dave Grohl walk out onto the stage. The crowd impulsively

SET LIST

Breed
Drain You
Aneurysm
School
Sliver
In Bloom
Come as You Are
Lithium
About a Girl
Tourettes
Polly
Lounge Act
Smells Like Teen Spirit
On a Plain
Negative Creep
Been a Son
All Apologies
Blew
Dumb
Stay Away
Spank Thru
Love Buzz
The Money Will Roll Right In
D-7
Territorial Pissings

MUSICIANS

Kurt Cobain: Vocals/Guitar
Dave Grohl: Drums
Krist Novoselic: Bass

es out of his chair and grabs hold of the microphone. He stands there for a long while letting the suspense build until opening his mouth and sarcastically crooning, "Some say loooooooove / It is a river. . ." He trails off and then he collapses onto his back. He lies there motionless for a few seconds while Grohl taps out a beat on his drum kit.

Out amongst the crowd, people nervously laugh. It feels like a put-on, but is it? Suddenly, Cobain springs back to his feet, turns around and straps on a tobacco sunburst Fender Jaguar. He doesn't say a thing as he adjusts the height of the mic stand and kicks on one of his guitar pedals. A horrible noise of feedback breaks out, which Kurt manipulates on his fretboard, sending the awful sounds rocketing up into the air and shooting back down again.

His guitar is his weapon, and he uses it to battle back against all the criticism, all the harassment, the never-ending churn of rumor.

The tension reaches its boiling point, then finally Cobain turns the awful, frantic sounds into the first chords of the song "Breed." The crowd bursts into a triumphant cheer. The lights dance frantically across the stage, creating a stultifying strobe effect. From the back, the drummer from the band Bivouc, Antony Hodgkinson, hops onto the stage and starts doing a weird, one-man slam dance with himself.

The song's first "I don't care" stanza hurtles out of Cobain's mouth five times in a row. Three words

cheers, but Cobain's absence is discouraging. Suddenly, a figure with long blonde hair in a hospital gown is rolled out by the rock critic Everett True.

"The lights. That's all I can remember," True wrote in his biography of the band. "You can't see a single face. The crowd is invisible, and all that you feel is this incredible euphoric roar that increases every step you make towards the microphone."

Novoselic steps forward and says to all those invisible faces that the moment is "too painful." Then turning to Cobain, who is now parked just to his right, he says, "You're gonna make it, man," before leaning down and offering his hand. Turning back to the crowd Novoselic proclaims, "With the support of his friends and family, he's gonna make it!"

The bassist wanders away while Cobain shakily ris-

repeated over and over again, practically the clarion call for the disaffected Generation X. Any doubts about whether Kurt could "go on" are erased in that instant.

There's something special about watching someone perform when they have something to prove. Much has been made of athletes who cultivate a chip on their shoulder to push themselves to greater heights. While it feels odd to compare Cobain, the definitive slacker, to the jocks that he no doubt grew up hating, at Reading he carries an edge that belies his typical "don't give a shit" posture. His guitar is his weapon, and he uses it to battle back against all the criticism, all the harassment, the never-ending churn of rumor that has plagued him for the last few months.

"I really thought, 'This will be a disaster, this will be the end of our career for sure,'" Grohl later admitted. "Kurt had been in and out of rehab, communication in the band was beginning to be strained. Kurt was living in L.A. Krist and I were in Seattle. People weren't even sure if we were going to show up. We rehearsed once, the night before, and it wasn't good."

Aside from that one shaky rehearsal, it had been two full months since the band had played together, not that you could tell. Grohl is as bombastic as ever, bashing the hell out of his drums. The real focal point of course is Kurt, and he plays his part with an unexpected degree of humor and intensity.

Thirteen songs in and Nirvana prepares to launch into the single that everyone's been waiting to hear: "Smells Like Teen Spirit." In typical Cobain fashion, he refuses to play it straight. He teases the audience, stringing together that famous four-chord progression, while perverting its form, shifting instead to a ragged cover of Boston's "More Than a Feeling." Cobain doesn't even sing the song. With a goofy grin plastered across his face, he watches and listens to Grohl and Novoselic sloppily double-track each other instead.

The mosh pit in front of the stage rages on unabated. As Michael Azerrad reported in *Rolling Stone*, "The madly pogoing crowd was so tightly packed that its body heat generated huge billows of steam, like a human forest fire."

A few lines pass and the ruse falls apart. The band kicks into the proper arrangement, and the crowd goes wild. It's not a technically great performance, but the pure joy flowing between the three guys onstage as they tear into their biggest hit for the 1,000th time is palpable. Cobain attempts to pick out the first two clean, chorus-painted notes, which ring out after the main, fuzz-driven riff, but he misses. His fingers are about two keys away from the right place on the fretboard. Rather than jump ship, he goes with it, playing purposefully wrong notes to cover up for his mistake. It's all Novoselic can do to keep from bursting out laughing.

After the final "denial" echoes over the heads of the diehards, the band takes a momentary pause before picking up again with "On a Plain," which is followed by "Negative Creep" and "Been a Son." When they reach "All Apologies," Cobain steps up and dedicates the song to his 12-day-old daughter along with his wife.

Addressing the audience directly for the first time about the monkey attached to his back, he says, "There's been some pretty extreme things written about us. Especially my wife, and she thinks everybody hates her now. So um . . . this is being recorded, so I want you to give her a message and say, 'Courtney, we love you.' Okay, ready? On the count of three. One, two three . . ."

The crowd jumps in before Cobain can even join along with them, shouting as one, "COURTNEY, WE LOVE YOU!"

"Thanks," Cobain says with a shy but appreciative smile.

The main set concludes about an hour after it began with "Blew." The fans clamor for an encore, and after a few tense moments, Cobain and company return to give them one. They don't just hit the crowd with one or two more songs either. Nirvana sticks around for another half-hour, running through seven more songs. Most of them are older Sub Pop–era cuts like "Love Buzz" and "Spank Thru." They end the show properly with "Territorial Pissings" off *Nevermind*. Over the course of the night, they play every track from that album, apart from the ghostly "Something in the Way."

As the show ends, the band goes into full-on destruction mode. Novoselic repeatedly throws his bass 10 and 15 feet up into the air. Sometimes he catches it, and sometimes he doesn't. Grohl kicks over his drum kit off the riser and starts tossing cymbals around the stage like Frisbees. Cobain calmly walks over to his stack of Marshall amps and knocks them on their backs while continuing to manipulate sound out of his blood-stained Fender Stratocaster.

He sits on the cabinets for a moment, creating this piercing, discordant wall of sound with bits of the "Star Spangled Banner" mixed in, before jumping down into the pit in front of the stage, handing the guitar off to a cluster of hands reaching out from the front row and walking off. The MC's voice cracks to life to thank everyone for coming out and bids them all goodnight.

"They had something to prove and they wanted to prove it," Nirvana road manager Alex MacLeod recalled. "They wanted to stand up, in front of all these people who were saying, 'It's over, he's a fuck-up, he's useless,' and say to them, 'Fuck you. It's not over.'"

Honorable Mention
R.E.M. at the 40 Watt Club
Athens, GA (November 19)

In 1991, alt-rockers R.E.M. released the best-selling album of their career, *Out of Time*. That was followed the next year by *Automatic For the People*, their second best-selling album and maybe their finest overall. Combined, both records sold around 30 million copies worldwide. R.E.M. had never been more popular, and yet, outside of a short promo tour of Europe, they mostly stayed off the road. As guitarist Peter Buck told *Spin*, "I hate to sound like the Band with *The Last Waltz*, but we basically spent the last ten years on the road. It's time to get away from it." One of the only shows they played during this time took place in their hometown of Athens, Georgia. It was a benefit gig for the environmental activist group Greenpeace. In front of just 600 people, one of the biggest bands in the world turned in a scorching 80-minute set comprised mainly of material from their most recent album. As a reviewer for the *Atlanta Journal Constitution* noted, "The group gathered steam and wrapped up the show with loose-limbed versions of Iggy Pop's 'Funtime' and their first recording, 'Radio Free Europe'. . . . Somewhere in the back in the dark, a blond woman, alleged to be Kim Basinger, swayed."

1993

Big Daddy Kane, Notorious B.I.G. and Tupac Shakur
MADISON SQUARE GARDEN—NEW YORK, NY
OCTOBER 24

EAST VS. WEST

In the years before they became mortal enemies, Christopher Wallace (a.k.a. The Notrorious B.I.G.) and Tupac Shakur were good friends. They truly enjoyed each other's company—kicking back, smoking weed and sipping Hennessey. When Biggie would fly out to L.A. he sometimes crashed on Pac's couch. When Pac came to New York, he'd typically swing by Brooklyn to talk shit and shoot dice.

In 1993 Biggie was still a year away from releasing his career-making debut, *Ready to Die*, whereas Tupac was already one of the biggest stars in the music world. In February, he released his second album, *Strictly 4 My N.I.G.G.A.Z...*, which went platinum. He had a new movie out that year, *Poetic Justice*, and was then cast to appear as the prime bad guy Birdie in *Above the Rim*. They weren't yet on equal footing, but the superstar was quick to recognize the talent of the young up-and-comer and was eager to help him along. "I trained the nigga, he used to be under me like my lieutenant," Tupac later said.

The good feelings came to an end on November 30, 1994, when Tupac arrived at Quad Recording Studios in New York, where he was shot by three assailants in army fatigues who beat him and robbed him of his jewelry. The L.A. rapper played dead waiting for them to leave and then made his way over to an elevator. He rode it up to the recording studio, where he was met by Biggie and his label boss, Puff Daddy. For whatever reason—blood loss, shock or the THC coursing through his veins—Pac didn't like the way the group looked at him. "It was like they were mad at me," he later explained.

Tupac eventually recovered from his attack, but in the back of his mind, he couldn't shake the feeling that Biggie and Puff were in on it. The seeds were sown for an epic East Coast vs. West Coast beef that would end with both men shot and killed: Pac on September 7, 1996, in Las Vegas and Biggie six months later, on March 9, 1997, in Los Angeles.

Tupac and Biggie didn't have that many opportunities to collaborate before their friendship turned sour. The most notable occasion took place on October 24, 1993, as part of a package show at Madison Square Garden in the middle of a set by the legendary MC Big Daddy Kane. Neither man was supposed to take the stage that night. Biggie was a guest of the DJ Mister Cee and happened to bring Tupac along with him. Everyone was hanging out backstage and it suddenly occurred to Kane to ask if either man wanted to take a turn on the mic during his set. Surprisingly, they both agreed.

Biggie went first after a turn from Scoob and Shyheim the Rugged Child. He got a monstrous ovation right off the top by shouting out Brooklyn and then bragged about his arsenal and lyrical acumen. "I give MCs the runs drippin' when I throw my clip in / The AK, I slay from far away." Pac answered with a similar set of themes: "No matter how you try, niggas never die / We just retaliate with hate, then we multiply."

Mister Cee recorded the entire show thanks to the guy manning the mixing desk, who chose to look the other way. The tape he made has become one of the greatest artifacts in rap history. Here's the story of how it all went down from the two men who made it happen.

Not only was Brooklyn in the house, but hip-hop was in the house.

Mister Cee: It was October of 1993 and it was the Budweiser Superfest at Madison Square Garden. Big Daddy Kane was on the show; I think Patti LaBelle was on the show . . . I know we was the only hip-hop act on the show. They only gave us 15 minutes to perform.

Big Daddy Kane: I believe that it was me, MC Lyte, Patti LaBelle, LaVert, I think BBD [Bell Biv DeVoe] and Sylk. It was hip-hop and R&B together and it was something real new in the whole touring scene, but it meshed. We had great chemistry and we were having fun on the road. With me, I tried to put together a show that could cover all dimensions because at the same time I had Shyheim the Rugged Child from the Wu-Tang Clan out on the road with me. We did all that, made it entertaining, brought out special guests and all that. Then with that particular night, we ended up having Pac and Biggie in the same building to spit bars over a drum break.

MC: I invited Biggie to the show that night because [he] was a huge Big Daddy Kane fan. A lot of people don't know that. Biggie was still on the bubble of being the Biggie we all know and love now. At that time, the only record that was out by Biggie was "Party & Bullshit" and a Mary J. Blige remix of "Real Love."

BDK: That was the first night I met Biggie. Mister Cee told me that Biggie wanted to come to the show. I was like, "Cool, cool, cool, yeah. No problem. Ain't nothing but love." Then he said, "Yeah, but Tupac is in town filming a movie and he wants to know if it's okay if he brings Pac with him?" At that time, Pac was real hot as an MC and stuff and my mentality as an MC was like, "Oh . . . Pac wanna come?" So I'm like, "Yeah, yeah, yeah, bring him too. Matter of fact, see if they wanna get onstage!" Now I'm in that battle frame of mind like, this is the hot dude right now. So Big and Pac and a couple of the other people came and we was backstage talking, chopping it up, and I said, "Y'all wanna come onstage and spit something?"

MC: Kane was backstage in the dressing room cooking up with the artists a freestyle session. The minute he started thinking along those lines of wanting to do that, I went to the soundboard guy in the middle of the arena and asked him, "Can I tape our show." The sound guy gave me a real hard time because it was against union rules to record a show without permission, so I begged him and he finally gave me the okay, like, "Nah, you're good just as long as we don't get caught."

BDK: With the Biggie and Pac thing it was a situation where Pac was a superstar. He was in New York filming *Above the Rim*. He's that dude and the very last person you'd expect to see come on the stage. Big at that time may have had "Party & Bullshit" but I don't think he even had "Juicy" yet. It was the type of thing that Biggie was like the local hero and then they heard Pac's name and went bananas! I mean, they went bananas. They screamed, I brought him onstage, dropped the beat and everybody rhymed.

MC: 45 King did a remix of "Spread Love" by Take 6 and at the end of "Spread Love" there's a beat that runs, and that's what I used for the freestyle.

BDK: Tupac, his rhyming style is one that carries a message and he'll drop some jewels on you to let you know that he understands your pain in the hood, so for what we were getting into, I don't think that's what he was really prepared for as an MC. Big on the other hand he was ready. I loved the rhyme that Big said. He was breaking down the guns that he got; he was ready and he said a lot.

MC: When Biggie came on and was like, "Where Brooklyn at?" and remember, this is the Budweiser Superfest, this is an older generation, people who came to see the R&B acts, but Brooklyn was still there. For Biggie to come onto the stage with that chant, aw man, you had to be there! It just set the whole tone to let it be known that not only was Brooklyn in the house, but hip-hop was in the house. You know, you had Big Daddy Kane who's the Brooklyn hip-hop legend and you had Biggie who was the up-and-coming Brooklyn cat and then this is our first show at the Garden. It made a deep statement, like, we're here.

BDK: They both meant so much to the '90s and to have it where they were friends, and they were sharing the stage having fun I thought it was beautiful. The fact that neither one of them is here anymore, I'm glad that I was part of that night and made it possible.

MC: We were just trying to fit in a small, 15-minute show and give everybody some love. Hindsight's 20/20. You look at it now and think, "Wow, three of the greatest rappers of all time, all on the same stage at Madison Square Garden, at an R&B show putting on one of the greatest freestyle performances ever." We were just doing our thing. We didn't know that that segment of the show was going to be so well known and world renowned as it is now.

HONORABLE MENTION
Whitney Houston at Radio City Music Hall
New York, NY (July 20)

The Mount Rushmore of iconic divas would be woefully incomplete without Whitney Houston. In 1993 she reached the peak of her success following the release of the film *The Bodyguard*. The soundtrack included her immortal, bombastic cover of the Dolly Parton song "I Will Always Love You." On July 20, her star touched down at Radio City Music Hall, where she kicked off a five-night residency. Though she could have packed arenas by now, Houston opted to perform in theaters because of the better acoustics and more intimate feel. In that first show, she didn't banter and she didn't dance. Whitney just sang with all the force and precision that God granted her. It was more than enough. As Stephen Holden wrote in the *New York Times*, "The high point of the show was a too-brief medley of theater songs that fused 'I Loves You Porgy' and 'Porgy, I's Your Woman Now,' with 'And I Am Telling You I'm Not Going,' as it offered a tantalizing glimpse of what Ms. Houston might have been were she not trapped in the gilded cage of pop mega-stardom and its limiting commercial formulas."

1994

Nine Inch Nails
WINSTON FARM—SAUGERTIES, NY
AUGUST 13

MUDSTOCK

The vibe of the 1994 rendition of Woodstock couldn't have been more different from the original incarnation. The ethos of peace and love that permeated that fateful weekend in 1969 had given way to heavy doses of corporate branding and predatory capitalism. Where once Wavy Gravy and his Hog Farm stood amongst the people dishing out bowls full of free oatmeal, this new festival was brought to you by Pepsi and Häagen-Dazs.

If you wanted to attend Woodstock '94, it was going to cost you a hefty $135. Too much? You could order the Pay-Per-View and enjoy it from the comfort of your couch for a mere $49 instead! And to prevent a repeat of the famous gate-crashing scene that helped bankrupt the original event, the organizers set up nine miles of chain link fence. Once you made it on site, you had to pass through a metal detector. No outside food or beverages were allowed. No exceptions.

When *Rolling Stone* asked why he agreed to end Nine Inch Nails' Self Destruct Tour at Woodstock '94, front man Trent Reznor provided a characteristically droll response. "The money, to be quite frank," he said. "It's basically to offset the cost of the tour we're doing right now." PolyGram, the company financing the festival, had put up $50 million and the organizers in charge weren't shy about busting out the checkbook to get the acts they wanted.

"We were reluctant to do it for two reasons," Nine Inch Nails' booking agent, Gerry Gerrard, told me. "One, we were headlining our own tour where you're in control; it's your own sound and your own lights. We also knew from Lollapalooza that to be lower on a bill means you don't get your production and you don't get a sound check. We resisted for a long time." In the end, the money and the chance for exposure were just too good to pass up. "It was a very good offer, maybe double what the band was getting in general."

Woodstock '94 was made up of one of the most diverse, antithetical lineups ever assembled for one musical event. Artists who were present for the original festival (like Santana, Joe Cocker and Crosby, Stills & Nash) commingled with classic rock contemporaries (like Bob Dylan, the Allman Brothers Band and Traffic) as well as new acts (like Green Day, Rollins Band and the Red Hot Chili Peppers) who'd been in diapers or just beyond when the first Woodstock went down.

To be honest, Woodstock '94 needed bands like Arrested Development, Metallica and Salt-N-Pepa in the lineup. When you look back at the original Woodstock, it's insane how young and vital so many of the acts were. For instance, it was only Mountain's third live show ever. Crosby, Stills, Nash & Young's second. For Woodstock '94 to succeed and carry into the future, the organizers had to incorporate a youthful element. Across all three days, nobody got the kids more amped than Nine Inch Nails.

SET LIST

Terrible Lie

Sin

March of the Pigs

Something I Can Never Have

Closer

Reptile

Wish

Suck

Burn

The Only Time

Down in It

Dead Souls

Help Me I Am in Hell

Happiness in Slavery

Head Like a Hole

The crowd is growing restless as they wait for Nine Inch Nails to follow Crosby, Stills & Nash's set on the North Stage. It's the early evening of the festival's second day and anticipation is high. "Let's just take one step back so folks can breathe," an announcer requests moments before the band hits the stage. There's a little movement, but the audience still presses hard up front to get a close look at Reznor and company.

A few seconds later, Calvert DeForest (aka Bud Melman of David Letterman fame) comes out to make the introduction: "Ladies and gentlemen, punch your balls off and please welcome Nine Inch Nails!"

The lights go out and a menacing synth line crackles to life through the speakers. A soft yellow glow emanates from the stage in a slow strobe effect, blurred out by waves of smoke. The tone of the sounds, fleshed out with a fuzz-drenched guitar melody speeds up and slows down with little rhyme or reason.

Out of the darkness, Reznor crawls into view on his hands and knees, stands up and enacts a Christ pose. The masses down below cheer wildly. He grabs a hold of the microphone and along with the rest of the band shouts "Hey God!" to kick off the first song, "Terrible Lie."

As the stage becomes more illuminated, you can't help but notice that the band members are caked from head to toe in mud. Though it's stopped now, rain had been a near constant presence, turning the fields of Winston Farm into a bog. The next day, Green Day would engage the crowd in a mud fight that gets out of hand, leaving bassist Mike Dirnt with two of his front teeth smashed out.

"On the way to the stage there was a little accident," Reznor later told MTV. "It turned into kind of a mud wrestling thing that escalated to a full scale mud riot." When pressed further he revealed, "I accidently tripped [keyboardist] Danny [Lohner] and pushed his face into the mud and then he retaliated by body slamming me."

That's only part of the story, the part that's gone down in legend. Nine Inch Nails made a conscious choice to douse themselves in mud. "Trent came up with the idea," Gerry Gerrard said. "The fight was spontaneous, but the idea in Trent's mind was to be one with the audience. The fact that it looked terrifying was just a big bonus."

The band members are caked from head to toe in mud.

Reznor's instincts are spot on. He and his band present a powerful, terrifying visage. Combined with the incredible intensity of the music and with Reznor screaming his lungs to shreds, it made for one of the signature images from the alt-rock decade.

"Terrible Lie" is a pretty aggressive place to begin the show—"I feel my hatred grow all the more extreme"—but the mayhem gets cranked even higher on the next songs, "Sin" and then "March of the Pigs." The audience embraces the mania. A sweltering mosh pit breaks out down below as body surfers glide around overhead. As the show wears on, the gravity of the entire festival seems to move toward the stage. Soon, Nine Inch Nails have amassed one of the largest crowds of the entire weekend.

After running through "Something I Can Never Have" the band breaks into its big hit song "Closer." It's a raunchy, uber-sexualized swank track wherein Reznor repeatedly declares that he wants to "fuck you like an animal," because "you get me closer to God." The thousands and thousands of kids in the audience delight at screaming back the explicit chorus.

"When we said we'd do this fucking thing . . . I was kinda worried that it would suck," Reznor admitted before playing Nine Inch Nails' 1989 single "Down in It." "But I think it's turned out to be a pretty cool thing." He then coughs, wipes some mud out of his eye and says, "Plus, I got the chance to say the word 'fuck' on Pay-Per-View. Fuck!"

A cover of the Joy Division classic "Dead Souls" is followed by the unsettling "Help Me I'm in Hell." From there they break out into the shriek-filled "Happiness in Slavery." When the song ends, Reznor picks up his microphone stand and smashes it into the vast array of keyboards and amplifiers arranged on the stage. Their set finishes with a bracing rendition of the *Pretty Hate Machine* single "Head Like a Hole." In a final wanton act of destruction, Reznor whips his guitar off his chest, hurls it high into the air and walks off before it even hits the ground. Show's over.

"That was the day that music switched from Heavy Metal to Alternative," Gerrard said. "Nine Inch Nails went from playing theaters to playing Madison Square Garden in months. They went from having sold 250,000 records to 4 million within months. It was all because of that show."

HONORABLE MENTION
Lollapalooza '94 at The Gorge
George, WA (August 31)

Nirvana was supposed to headline Lollapalooza 1994, but because of lead singer Kurt Cobain's suicide, the whole tour was thrown into disarray. Undeterred, event organizers put together a slate of bands at the peak of their artistic powers, offering an unparalleled 10-hour–long musical extravaganza. At the top of the bill was Smashing Pumpkins, who were then riding a massive wave of popularity due to their critically acclaimed album *Siamese Dream*. Bay Area punks Green Day were enjoying their own breakout moment after releasing the eventually diamond-certified *Dookie*. Beastie Boys, A Tribe Called Quest and the Pharcyde represented hip-hop. For those looking for something more eclectic, there were George Clinton and the P-Funk All-Stars, Stereolab, L7 and Nick Cave and the Bad Seeds. It was impossible to escape the "What if?" shadow that Cobain's death cast upon the show, especially three hours away from his Seattle home. Still, you could hardly find a better venue than The Gorge. The expansive vistas of the Columbia River Valley provided a stunning visual backdrop for the lucky thousands splayed out on the grass, taking in some of the most vital musicians of the mid '90s.

#1 Single of the Year:
"Gangsta's Paradise"
Coolio (Featuring L.V.)

1995

#1 Album of the Year:
Cracked Rear View
Hootie & The Blowfish

Pearl Jam
SOLDIER FIELD—CHICAGO, IL
JULY 11

RAGING AGAINST A MACHINE

Few bands seemed as vital or intense in the early-to-mid 1990s as Pearl Jam. They released three albums that went platinum multiple times over: *Ten*, *Vs.* and *Vitalogy*. Their live shows, with lead singer Eddie Vedder dangling precariously from large scaffolding structures, became the stuff of legend. Things couldn't have been better.

Then, just like their idol Neil Young did in the early '70s, when they reached the pinnacle of their success, Pearl Jam drove straight into the ditch. They took on the mammoth concert industry itself. More specifically, they took on the corporation that lorded over it: Ticketmaster.

In June 1991, Ticketmaster purchased its biggest competitor, Ticketron, essentially creating a monopoly in the marketplace. If you wanted to see a band, the odds were damn good that you had to go through Ticketmaster to secure your seat. This didn't sit well with Pearl Jam, who called foul on the company's capricious service fees. Pearl Jam wanted to charge their fans less money to come out and see them, no more than $20. Ticketmaster stood square in the path of allowing that to happen so in May 1994, the band filed a grievance with the Justice Department.

Two months later, bassist Jeff Ament and guitarist Stone Gossard went before Congress to argue their case. "Pearl Jam believes that if Ticketmaster is unable or unwilling to provide the level of service that Pearl Jam believes is appropriate for the distribution of tickets to Pearl Jam concerts, then we should have the option to make arrangements to distribute tickets to our concerts through other means," they said in a prepared statement. "That freedom of choice—a basic principle of competition in this country—does not effectively exist in the music industry today."

The band put their money and their reputation on the line. They announced that they would do their best to circumvent Ticketmaster by playing offbeat venues outside their purview, like the Empire Polo Fields in Indio, California, which later became the host site for Coachella. "We were so hardheaded about the 1995 tour," Ament told *Spin* years later. "Had to prove we could tour on our own, and it pretty much killed us, killed our career. Building shows from the ground up, a venue everywhere we went."

Going a step further in his puritanical pursuit of the rock 'n' roll ideal, Vedder traveled to shows in a van, separate from the rest of the group. "It worked for a while," he said to *Spin*. "And then I just got too fuckin' tired." The ramshackle nature of the tour took a heavy physical toll on everyone. Vedder contracted food poisoning right before a major concert in Golden Gate Park, and the band canceled six of the final dates of the tour, leaving just a show at Summerfest in Milwaukee and a blowout at Soldier Field in Chicago on the docket.

The man tasked with setting up the final gig, JAM Productions vice president Andy Cirzan, had a hell

SET LIST

Release

Go

Last Exit

Spin the Black Circle

Tremor Christ

Corduroy

Whipping

I Got Id

Dissident

Even Flow

Deep

Jeremy

Glorified G

Daughter

Animal

Habit

Lukin

Not for You

Elderly Woman Behind the Counter

Immortality

Alive

Porch

Everyday People

Let My Love Open the Door

Better Man

Rearviewmirror

Black

Blood

Yellow Ledbetter

MUSICIANS

Eddie Vedder: Vocals/Guitar

Mike McCready: Lead Guitar

Stone Gossard: Rhythm Guitar

Jeff Ament: Bass

Jack Irons: Drums

you do a test run on a new system," Cirzan said.

Six days before they hit the stage in Chicago, the band had the rug pulled out from under it when the Justice Department closed its investigation into Ticketmaster. "My understanding is that the division found that there were new enterprises coming into the arena and based on that evidence," Attorney General Janet Reno said, "we do not have a basis for proceeding."

"They booked this show long before thinking 'Okay, we're fighting this fight, we're gonna continue.' Then they heard the news that they had basically done all of this for nothing," *Chicago Tribune* music critic Greg Kot told me. "There was a real sense that this band wasn't going to continue much longer. People were coming to that show thinking it could be the last show."

Despite the defeat, despite all the rumors swirling around about their impending demise, the mood within the band was relatively upbeat. "It seemed like a really positive vibe," Cirzan said. "They seemed almost relieved and excited that they were getting to do a big show in a city that's very important to them. And for the audience, I don't think people could have been more excited to be at a rock show."

A swirling mass of crowd surfers, head bangers and slam dancers.

of a time getting it off the ground. "I had a relationship with Ticketmaster too. You could not get around them at the time," he told me. "I was someone actively involved in negotiating out the idea that we're not going to play Soldier Field unless the band can use their own ticketing system."

The two sides played chicken with one another for quite some time. At one point Pearl Jam pulled the plug on the show before eventually reaching an agreement: the band could proceed using its own ticketing system. "It worked well for a leap of faith because let me tell you, a 50,000-seater is not how

Pearl Jam arrives at Soldier Field two days after the Grateful Dead played their final concert ever with Jerry Garcia in the same stadium. "I don't think we should play another note until we thank the Grateful Dead for letting us use their stage," Vedder announces midway through the set. "They left it for us . . . there are still joints left on it from Saturday. So, we think it's only right that we play as long as they do."

After opening the show with "Release" from its debut album, *Ten*, the band runs through six high-octane songs in a little over 20 minutes, with hardly a break in between. The audience doesn't get so much as a "How ya doin?" until after a blistering rendition of "Corduroy." There's a discernable edge to the performance that permeates the songs. They clearly have something to prove.

For nearly three hours Pearl Jam turns the home of the Chicago Bears into a swirling mass of crowd surfers, head bangers and slam dancers. The incredible energy amongst the fans is mirrored onstage, where it seems like Vedder's head is going to pop off as he screams out the lyrics to songs like "Spin the Black Circle," "Tremor Christ" and "Even Flow."

"There was a lot of heart in that band," Kot said. "These days, Vedder is a relatively static stage presence, but back then there was electricity flowing through his body. He was constantly on the move, stalking the stage; hungry for connection with the audience that went deeper than I'm playing the song for the millionth time. There was a sense of 'I'm reliving this and I need you guys to be with me.'"

During his introduction to the acerbic *Fuck you!—*filled track "Not for You," an astounding 20 songs into the show, Vedder finally addresses the elephant in the room. Using the Bears and Soldier Field as an example, the singer recalls that while growing up just outside Chicago, he and his family never came to a game because they couldn't afford tickets. After the song finishes, he continues with his train of thought while the crowd breaks out into an impromptu chant of "Ticketmaster sucks!"

"It's up to you guys. We tried our bit," Vedder says. "I hate to think that's the way of the future where corporate giants . . . I don't know. Some of them just can't be toppled, I guess. . . . Aw, God, now you got me all fucking depressed thinking about that

shit. The whole band was over that whole fucking thing and we were just moving on. We didn't get a lot of support from other bands on that thing. There was a few but most of them were scared of getting in the ring. But I gotta say, it seemed like a lot of people were behind us, and for that we appreciate it."

The most dramatic moment of the night comes during Mike McCready's mournful solo on "Immortality." Just as he's ripping into his Fender Telecaster, a lightning storm breaks out just over the horizon. Streams of bright white electricity flash and dance across the sky as the guitarist pours out his soul one note at a time. It was as if God was lending them the perfect backdrop.

"It was surreal," Kot recalled. "As a writer, you live for these metaphorical things, you know the cloud hanging over the band. It was kind of fitting."

That might been the perfect finale, but there was still a lot more to get through, like the cover of Sly & The Family Stone's "Everyday People" along with incredible takes on "Better Man," "Rearviewmirror" and "Black." During the last song, "Blood," Vedder picks up his mic stand like a battle-axe and smashes it repeatedly into his guitar, turning the instrument into a neat pile of kindling. Moments later, they reappear to end the night properly with an encore performance of "Yellow Ledbetter."

Over the last three hours, and for nearly a year, Pearl Jam had given everything they had. The fight is now over. The battle won, the war lost.

HONORABLE MENTION

Selena at the Astrodome
Houston, TX (February 26)

On February 26, 1995, 65,000 people descended on the Astrodome in Houston to see the "Queen of Tejano Music" blow them away with her singular mix of Spanish- and English-language hits. Incredibly, it was the singer's third time performing at the massive baseball stadium and she treated the place like she owned it. Opening the show with a medley of disco hits, Selena put together a set list dominated by her most popular Spanish material like "Amor Prohibido," "Bidi Bidi Bom Bom" and "No Me Queda Más." Sadly, this blowout gig turned out to be Selena's final public performance. A little over a month later, she was shot and killed by Yolanda Saldívar, the founder of her fan club, at a Days Inn Motel in Corpus Christi, Texas.

1996

Oasis
KNEBWORTH PARK—KNEBWORTH, ENGLAND
AUGUST 11

KNEBWORTH SUPERNOVA

Some bands are just born to perform in front of tens of thousands of screaming people. Britpop rockers Oasis was one of those bands. With egos almost as big as the hooks in their many anthemic hits, brothers Liam and Noel Gallgagher seemed completely at home bashing away for the true fanatics in massive outdoor football stadiums. They were volatile and aggrandizing to the point of ridicule, but always compelling.

"People will never, ever, ever forget the way you made them feel," Noel told the filmmakers behind the documentary *Oasis: Supersonic*. "There's a chemistry between the band and the audience. There's something magnetic drawing the two to each other. The love and the vibe and the passion and the rage and the joy that comes from the crowd, if anything that's what Oasis was."

1996 was an interesting time in the landscape of rock and pop. After the rise and fall of the Seattle-based grunge and alternative bands, the eyes and ears of the world gravitated to England, where a rash of new acts raced to fill the void. Anglophilia spread like wildfire. It seemed that any band with an airbrushed Union Jack over their kick drum could sell a half-million copies of their next record. Bands like Blur, Suede, Pulp and the Verve became platinum sensations in the U.S.

Oasis was popular the world over, but they were nearly gods in the English Isles. In October 1995, they released their second album, *(What's the Story) Morning Glory*, which dominated the charts in the U.K. with an authority that hadn't been felt in years. Led by generational singles like "Wonderwall," "Champagne Supernova" and "Don't Look Back in Anger," the record was eventually certified 14x platinum in their native country.

A month after dropping *Morning Glory*, Oasis staged two sold-out shows at Earl's Court in London for 40,000 screaming fans. Five months later, after crisscrossing the Atlantic a few times, they played a pair of homecoming concerts at the immense soccer stadium Maine Road, home to the band's favorite team, Manchester City. It would have been a career-defining performance for the young Mancunians if not for the event their management had lined up next.

"Somebody suggested the next thing we should do be these things at Knebworth," Noel said. "Somebody's only got to whisper in my ear, 'Oh, these are the biggest gigs of all time,' and I go, well, yes, that's me. You just sold it to me, thank you very much."

Across two nights, the band performed for a quarter of a million people. Even then, the demand for tickets far outstripped the supply. Somewhere around 2.5 million people, nearly 5 percent of the population of the United Kingdom, signed up for the chance to purchase one of the coveted passes. Not bad for a group that had been discovered three years earlier playing King Tut's Wah Wah Hut in Glasgow,

SET LIST

Columbia
Acquiesce
Supersonic
Hello
Some Might Say
Roll with It
Slide Away
Morning Glory
Round Are Way
Cigarettes & Alcohol
Whatever
All the Young Dudes
Cast No Shadow
Wonderwall
The Masterplan
Don't Look Back in Anger
My Big Mouth
It's Getting Better (Man!!)
Live Forever
Champagne Supernova
I Am the Walrus

MUSICIANS

Liam Gallagher: Vocals
Noel Gallagher: Guitar/Vocals
Paul "Bonehead" Arthurs: Rhythm Guitar
Paul "Guigsy" McGuigan: Bass
Alan White: Drums

remembered in the *Queitus*. "You could tell this because, when Noel Gallager wandered in, he was instantly mobbed by autograph-seekers. Within this moderately-exclusive marquee, there was a separate VIP quadrant. This roped-off corner was soon besieged by people who all stood there staring at Kate Moss and Patsy Palmer."

After a day filled with music from the Chemical Brothers, the Charlatans, Prodigy, and the Manic Street Preachers, Oasis takes the stage just as the sun sets over the heads of the 125,000 people gathered before them. The second their five idols come into view, the crowd lets out an earthshaking roar. The band stands near the front of the stage drinking it all in then walks over to their instruments.

"This is history! Right here, right now, this is history!" Noel declares.

"I thought it was Knebworth," Liam counters.

"Good evening, planet Earth," Noel says.

"Columbia," Liam responds, announcing the title of the first song of the night.

Noel picks out the song's languid intro while Liam stalks the stage in circles, banging away on a tambourine. When the moment arrives, he steps forward and starts singing into the microphone, "There we were, now here we are / All this confusion, nothing's the same to me." You can hardly see his face behind a pair of large black sunglasses and a Johnny Ramone–style bob. His voice is half bleat/half siren, wholly distinct and incredibly alluring.

"Acquiesce" comes next, followed by "Supersonic," "Hello," "Some Might Say," "Roll with It" and "Slide Away." A lot of bands might be overwhelmed by the enormity of an event like this, but Oasis appears remarkably comfortable and totally locked

Scotland. It's an especially galling feat once you realize that tickets went on sale on FA Cup Final Day, which featured a match between two of the most popular teams in the competition, Liverpool and the Manchester United.

The enormity of what they were about to do didn't hit the band until they flew above the massive crowd in helicopters. "It landed behind the stage but we were like: 'Let's just do a once round and take it all in,'" recalled rhythm guitarist Paul "Bonehead" Arthurs. "I'll never forget it."

"It felt fucking biblical," Liam said. "It was a miracle that we got there. It was everything and more than I asked for. You felt untouchable, man. Supersonic even."

Backstage the scene was pure pandemonium. Legend has it that 7,000 people were added to the guest list, a figure that seems impossible but isn't entirely crazy. "The music-industry types were diluted by numerous family and friends," Roy Wilkinson

in. Even the new songs performed near the end of the show, "My Big Mouth" and "It's Getting Better (Man!!)," are performed with verve and are received well by the adoring mass.

Always the coolest motherfucker in any room he walks into, Liam somehow seems both awed and above it all. "I've clipped my toenails for this," he drolly reveals. Noel is more intense and a little more uptight, until he remembers that the show is being broadcast live across the country. "This is going out live to 300,000 people, so I just have to say . . . fuck, shit, cunt, tit, bum," he exclaims.

About 30 minutes in, Oasis kicks into "Morning

My idea was Knebworth today, the Moon tomorrow.

Glory" and the place explodes. The audience sings nearly every word of the verses, and each time the chorus comes, the multitudes nearly swallow Liam's voice while Noel adds his own "Wellllllll" undertones. The sing-alongs are repeated on "Wonderwall," "Don't Look Back in Anger" and the set-closer, "Live Forever."

After a short leave of absence, the band reappears with a special guest for an encore. "What's this man doing here?" Noel asks while John Squire of the Stone Roses walks out. "Champagne Supernova," he announces, leading Liam to ask the immortal question, "How many special people change?" The crowd goes out of its mind. Midway through, Noel and Squire trade incendiary solos while Liam strolls around the stage throwing up covert middle fingers to the cameras.

As the song ends, the beat slows to a crawl until all sound dies away. Both brothers step to their microphones to thank the crowd. "We'll do it again some time, yeah?" Noel says. The band close out the concert of their lives by paying homage to their biggest influence, the Beatles, with a cover of "I Am the Walrus." It ends with an explosion of fireworks across the sky.

Oasis's stint at Knebworth was the high-water mark that the band and the entire Britpop movement were never able to top. "I remember sitting there, at Knebworth, in the backstage area, and someone saying, 'Well, what now?' And I was like, 'I couldn't tell ya,'" Noel admitted to *Uncut*. "That was how I felt for a good couple of years afterwards. I really suffered. It's like, what do you do when you've done everything? You kind of sink into boredom. Kind of directionless."

Liam was more defiant about the experience. "Me personally, at that time, it was like right, we're doing Knebworth, fuckin' hell, well, what's next?" he said. "My idea was Knebworth today, the Moon tomorrow."

HONORABLE MENTION

Smashing Pumpkins at Brixton Academy
London, England (May 15)

On October 24, 1995, the Chicago rockers Smashing Pumpkins unveiled their magnum opus, a sprawling, two-hour double-album titled *Mellon Collie and the Infinite Sadness*. Piggybacking off the success of their previous effort, *Siamese Dream*, the Pumpkins were widely considered to be the new torchbearers of the burgeoning alt-rock movement. Shortly after dropping *Mellon Collie*, the Billy Corgan–led outfit hit the road in America before crossing over into Europe and playing this gig in London on May 15. It was an incredibly expansive show lasting three hours across two sets of music—the first acoustic, the second electric—and ending with three different encores. Nearly every hit and fan favorite was included into the set list, songs like "Disarm," "1979," "Today," "Bullet with Butterfly Wings" and "Mayonaise." Corgan was rocking his iconic shaved head and "Zero" T-shirt look, which, reviewer Ryan Gilbey wrote in the *Independent*, "even without the guitars that sounded like chainsaws . . . told you it was time to rock." Just two months after this show, touring keyboardist Jonathan Melvoin and drummer Jimmy Chamberlin both overdosed on heroin in New York City. Chamberlin was revived, arrested for drug possession and later kicked out of the band. Melvoin died.

#1 Single of the Year:
"Candle in the Wind 1997"/"Something About the Way You Look Tonight"
Elton John

1997

#1 Album of the Year:
Spice
Spice Girls

Radiohead
GLASTONBURY—PILTON, ENGLAND
JUNE 28

MESMERIZING THE MASSES

The Glastonbury Festival is one of the most important live music events in the world. Held in the English countryside, it's a special occasion where superstars cement their legacies and up-and-comers strive to break through to a large and influential audience. It's a place where anything can happen.

Founded on September 18, 1970, Glastonbury became the forerunner to many of the modern music festivals staged across Europe and North America today. It takes place nearly every year at Worthy Farm in Pilton, a two-and-a-half-hour drive west of London. Entry into the first festival cost £1 and came with free milk from the farm. 1,500 people showed up to be entertained by the likes of Marc Bolan, Quintessence and Al Stewart. The most distinctive feature of the event was the giant pyramid-shaped stage. Though Glastonbury has changed greatly, the Pyramid Stage has remained, albeit with massive technical upgrades.

Today, Glastonbury is a five-day musical megalopolis and the largest greenfield festival in the world. 175,000 people regularly make the journey out to its fertile fields to take in an eclectic collection of rock, pop, hip-hop, punk, country, R&B and EDM acts. It's a place to see and be seen. As the memories of its contemporaries—Woodstock, Monterey Pop, Altamont and the Isle of Wight—fade, Glastonbury endures.

The festival has hosted a wide array of incredible and iconic performances over the last several decades. The Smiths in 1984 spring to mind, as do The Cure in 1986, Orbital in 1994 and Pulp in 1995. More recent examples include David Bowie in 2000, Jay Z in 2008, Beyoncé in 2011, Dolly Parton in 2014 and Kanye West in 2015. Of all the fantastic performances at Worthy Farm over the years, perhaps the greatest took place in 1997, when Radiohead came, saw and creeped everyone out.

A month prior to their headlining set at Glastonbury, the band unveiled the greatest artistic statement of its career. *OK Computer* marked a significant departure from the group's first two alt-rock–informed records, *Pablo Honey* and *The Bends*. *OK Computer* is icy and atmospheric, chock full of big ideas; disparate, grating noises; and elegant, affecting vocal passages from singer Thom Yorke.

Spin described it as "a DIY electronica album made with guitars," while *Rolling Stone* called it a "stunning art-rock tour de force." In his review for *MOJO*, famed music journalist Nick Kent predicted, "In 20 years' time I'm betting *OK Computer* will be seen as the key record of 1997, the one to take rock forward instead of artfully revamping images and song-structures from an earlier era." Talk about a called shot!

"For us, this gig means a fucking lot," Yorke admitted to the gigantic audience during the band's Glastonbury encore. He wasn't lying. That summer, as Oasis dithered, snorted mountains of coke and

SET LIST

Lucky

My Iron Lung

Airbag

Planet Telex

Exit Music (For a Film)

The Bends

(Nice Dream)

Paranoid Android

Karma Police

Creep

Climbing Up the Walls

No Surprises

Talk Show Host

Bones

Just

Fake Plastic Trees

You

The Tourist

High and Dry

Street Spirit (Fade Out)

MUSICIANS

Thom Yorke: Vocals/Guitar

Jonny Greenwood: Guitar/Keyboard/Synth

Colin Greenwood: Bass

Ed O'Brien: Guitar/Percussion

Philip Selway: Drums

wiped any semblance of bass from their next record, Radiohead overtook their place as the next big thing in rock. Glastonbury wasn't necessarily a make-or-break event for them, but it was an important one. It was a milestone event. It was the moment they stepped into the spotlight and planted their flag for a new generation of paranoid androids. It meant a fucking lot.

The lights go out, turning the vast, muddy field into a gaping black void. The enormous Pyramid Stage emits a soft yellow glow as the members of Radiohead glide into view. Yorke is clad in a brown leather jacket and button-down shirt and has his hair buzzed short. He straps on a black Fender Jazzmaster and strums out the eerie opening chords to the most down-trodden song from their latest record, "Lucky." Lighters flick to life amongst the crowd, illuminating the field below as they sway back and forth.

"Pull me ooooooouuuuut of the aircrash!" Yorke pleads as the band explodes to life behind him. Jon-ny Greenwood kicks into a restrained, melodic guitar solo, offering a tasteful counterpoint to the bombastic rhythm. "We are standing on the edge," Yorke warns at the end of the first chorus.

"Lucky" isn't the most obvious way to start off a concert. Most bands want to punch the audience in the face from the opening bell, grab their attention and hold on to it as best they can. Radiohead take a different tack. They aim to mesmerize. They want to suck you in before they blast you into the stratosphere.

"They took the stage at a moment when the festival had become an exercise in grimly *telling* yourself you were having fun," *MOJO* writer Paul Trynka recalled. "Within seconds, it became obvious that something special was happening. All the songs which might seem to flirt dangerously with prog on record seemed transformed: introverted, me-against-the-world diatribes turned into expansive, joyful anthems."

"My Iron Lung" comes next, followed by "Airbag," "Planet Telex" and "Exit Music (For a Film)." Things are going well, but this year's Glastonbury is the one of the most rain-soaked in memory. As the band digs into its set, the skies open once again and the rain comes pouring down. The added moisture wreaks havoc on the sound equipment, especially the monitors. Ever the professionals, they band plays through the obstacles.

Just before kicking into "Paranoid Android," Yorke has a request. "Andy," he says, addressing an unseen crew member. "Can you turn on the lights so we can see the people? We haven't seen them yet." Andy obliges and the mud-caked visage of tens of thousands of people screaming their heads off comes into focus.

"There were 40,000 people up the hill, holding lighters and fires burning, and tents pitched, and I don't think I've ever felt like that in my entire life," Yorke told *Melody Maker* afterwards. "It wasn't a human feeling; it was something else entirely."

The symmetry of Yorke crooning the dramatic line "Rain down, rain down / Come on, rain down on

> # They aim to mesmerize. They want to suck you in before they blast you into the stratosphere.

me" as water falls from the sky is almost too perfect. You can't plan a moment like this. The serendipity is overwhelming.

When it's over, the crowd cheers wildly. Yorke turns his back on them, picks up a black acoustic guitar, counts "1-2-3" and starts playing "Karma Police." Though the song has only been out for a month, the entire crowd appears familiar with the words. They relish belting them out, especially Yorke's anguished plea, "For a minute there I lost myself / I lost my-seeeeeeeeelf."

One sing-along is replaced by another as the band slips into perhaps its most recognizable song, "Creep." Though they grew reluctant to perform it live in the years to come—and Yorke seems to disdain the karaoke classic—they check their misgivings at the door this evening. It's a special night . . . so fucking special.

The main set comes to an end a little over an hour after it began with "Fake Plastic Trees." When Radiohead returns for the encore, Yorke demands that the two lights shining into his face be turned off. "Now! And for the rest of the show," he commands, "I want to see them."

The techs comply and Radiohead kicks into a parting coda comprised of "You," "The Tourist," "High and Dry" and "Street Spirit (Fade Out)." When it's over, Yorke thanks the audience and wishes them a great weekend. The cheering nearly drowns him out as he sways with his guitar around his hips, drink-

ing in the adoration.

"Just after Radiohead went offstage I bumped into a friend I'd been trying to find for hours," Trynka remembered. "We were both in some kind of altered state; all we could say was 'Did you see *that*?'" Glastonbury organizer Michael Eavis was even more succinct: "It was the most inspiring festival gig in 30 years."

HONORABLE MENTION
Wu-Tang Clan and Rage Against the Machine at Continental Airlines Arena East Rutherford, NJ (August 20)

1997 was a good year for both the politically aware rap-rockers Rage Against the Machine and Staten Island's own boom-bap samurais, the Wu-Tang Clan. The former was riding high off the release of their multiplatinum album *Evil Empire*. The latter released the follow-up to their breakout debut, a sprawling, 111-minute double disc titled *Wu-Tang Forever*. The idea to join forces seemed like a no-brainer, and so a six-week, 30-city program was booked. Unfortunately, they never made it to the end. The Wu bailed long before the last show of the tour following several no-shows from some of their nine members and an enticing opportunity to perform at Hot 97's annual Summer Jam. For those lucky enough to catch one of the earlier dates before the Clan bounced, there was hardly a better live show that year. This gig in New Jersey was perhaps the high-water mark, finding Rage at their politically provocative best, including a 15-minute tirade by De la Rocha about police brutality. For their part, the Wu-Tang Clan wove together tracks from their debut and *Forever* as well as solo material from GZA's *Liquid Swords*, Ol' Dirty Bastard's *Return to the 36 Chambers* and Ghostface Killah's *Ironman*. The highlight of the night came during Rage's encore, when Wu-Tang's RZA came out to trade rhymes alongside the band on "Freedom."

1998

Elliott Smith
LARGO—LOS ANGELES, CA
APRIL 11

LANDING AT LARGO

There's something special about seeing art created in an intimate environment. It's exhilarating to witness the exertion on a musician's face as they struggle with their instrument. To make eye contact with them as they pour their souls out into a microphone, becoming overwhelmed with an unshakable feeling that each word coming out of their mouth is meant specifically for you.

Few musicians have adopted a style more conducive to this kind of performance than indie rock hero Elliott Smith. Few institutions fostered that kind of environment better than the Largo in Los Angeles. Put the two of them together and you have a recipe for an unparalleled musical experience.

Owned by Mark Flanagan, Largo was a 100-seat club and one of the hottest incubators of live music in L.A. from the late 1990s through the mid-2000s. Powerful members of the music industry hobnobbed with regular folks, equally in search of a night of musical transcendence. While artists and audiences alike loved the cozy, familiar environment and low-set stage, its initial popularity can be chalked up to one man, a musical wizard named John Brion.

Shortly after gaining full control over Largo around 1996, Flanagan reached out to Brion to offer him a weekly residency. While Brion was a respected session musician, producer and arranger, he was relatively unknown to the public and balked at the suggestion. "He said, 'I want you to play Friday nights here,'" Brion told *Off Camera* host Sam Jones. "I said, 'You shouldn't give me that night, that's gonna be your best night for people drinking and making money and I want this thing to be a success. I'll open for people on Mondays and Tuesdays.'"

Flanagan was insistent, and after a bit of back and forth, Brion agreed to appear on Friday nights. With an emphasis on improvisation, the multi-instrumentalist stretched out songs into places that dazzled the small crowds gathered to see him play. Largo quickly became an "It" place to see and be seen in Los Angeles. It didn't take long until getting a ticket became next to impossible.

Beyond showcasing his own music, Brion regularly sat in at the club with a wide range of guest artists. Aimee Mann and Fiona Apple were frequent collaborators. In 1997, another name was added to the list, a singer-songwriter from Portland, Oregon, named Elliott Smith.

Smith was an indie rock darling and pop music savant who mined the depths of his own depression and self-doubt and channeled those feelings into music. The songs he wrote were some of the most beautiful, melodic explorations of the darker side of the human condition that have ever been committed to tape. He released his first album, *Roman Candle*, in 1994 as a side project from his group Heatmiser. A self-titled album came the next year, followed by the tremendous *Either/Or* in 1997.

SET LIST

Tomorrow Tomorrow

Between the Bars

Waltz #2 (XO)

Division Day

Angeles

Clementine

St. Ides Heaven

Oh Well, Okay

Say Yes

Some Song

Rose Parade

No Name #3

Coming Up Roses

Alameda

Clouds

Southern Belle

Jealous Guy

The Biggest Lie

Needle in the Hay

Pictures of Me

All My Rowdy Friends

Lost Highway

No Name #1

Alphabet Town

Thirteen

Brion met Elliott for the first time at one of Smith's shows at another LA venue, Spaceland. "It was some musical blind date set up by Mary Lou Lord," Brion told photographer Autumn De Wilde. After an awkward introduction, Brion and Smith started playing together and then everything clicked. "We were pretty much close from that second on," he said.

Smith didn't need bombast to capture people's attention. Armed with just his acoustic guitar and his voice—a wispy, pained warble—he had a way of filling up a room with his presence. "People would get really quiet for him," Jackpot! Recording Studio owner and *New Moon* producer Larry Crane told me. "The intensity of his performances really captured people's attention."

In 1998, Smith was the victim of mainstream recognition when his song "Miss Misery," which was included in the film *Good Will Hunting*, was nominated for an Academy Award. On March 23, after much handwringing and cajoling, he arrived at the Shrine Auditorium and performed the song in a white suit before the Hollywood glitterati. He didn't win, but he gave a powerful performance that stuck in people's minds. It became a defining moment in his career.

Three weeks later, on April 11, Elliott came to Largo and put together a performance just as stunning. There was no white suit this time—he was more of a jeans and T-shirt guy—and no fancy orchestra to lend gravitas to his seemingly simple songs. There was just a man, a guitar and his friend Jon to accompany him. That's all he needed.

My fucking stress is over from this moment onwards," Flanagan says as he introduces the evening's headliner. "We're shutting the door and it's just us and Elliott."

Smith ambles out to a rowdy applause from the crowd. He doesn't say a word but begins to play a song they've never heard before, "Tomorrow Tomorrow" from his not-yet-released album *XO*. He gets about two minutes in until he loses his way during the solo and then, with a sigh, aborts it altogether.

"How do you like me now?" he nervously jokes. "C'mon man, it's too serious." The audience laughs as he begins to play something they definitively do know, the *Either/Or* standout "Between the Bars." In typical Smith fashion, there are multiple ways to read this song. One view is that it's an entreaty from the bottle, begging to be sipped. Another view is that it's an anguished plea for companionship. Either interpretation is devastating, and as Elliott sings a heaviness settles over the room.

Another unreleased song, "Waltz #2 (XO)," comes next. It's one of his best: a tale about a night of karaoke gone wrong, performed in that signature 3/4 beat. Even though the audience isn't familiar with it, they fervently applaud when he finishes and moves onto "Division Day." The songs come and go quickly. It seems that tonight, the typically quiet and reserved

Elliott is eager to please. "Wanna hear a fast song or a slow song?" he asks the small crowd. "Angeles!" a woman shouts, and he obliges her request after finding a capo for his guitar.

> # An expression of childlike innocence that cleanses the palette from the tapestry of darkness he wove together.

The powerful intimacy in the room can't be overstated. It's one of Largo's charms. In between songs, the sounds of clinking glasses fill the air, as do calls for different songs that the patrons hope to hear, including a curious request for "anything off *Mic City Sons*," his final album with Heatmiser. Sometimes Elliott acknowledges them, and sometimes he doesn't.

Halfway through the show, he begins playing "Coming Up Roses" before catching himself. "Oh, wait, I need Jon," he says. Brion rushes to the stage and takes his place behind a marimba, adding twinkling grace notes to the ballad. He remains in place for the next number, "Alamada," before taking a seat back in the audience.

A few songs later, Elliott asks, "Is Jon here?"

"I'm listening," he shouts from out in the crowd.

"Come play," Elliott implores.

"Goddamnit," he exclaims in mock indignation while marching up to the stage. "It took me the whole last song to find a seat."

Brion pulls up a stool at the upright piano and plays along with Smith on a cover of John Lennon's "Jealous Guy." A few numbers later, he's called on again when Smith launches into "Pictures of Me."

After running through a cover of the Quasi song "Clouds," the crowd bombard Elliott with requests. One woman pleads for people to "leave him alone." He asks, "How about we take a smoke break?" which gets a big laugh, but then he leaves. Returning a few minutes later, Smith plays the semiautobiographical "Southern Belle."

Lighter moments—like his cover of Hank Williams Jr.'s party anthem "All My Rowdy Friends" and the elder Hank's classic "Lost Highway"—are mixed with extreme darkness. Those songs include "Needle in the Hay," his ode to heroin addiction, and "Alphabet Town," which is about a couple simply going through the motions of their relationship.

"Thanks a lot, you guys," Elliott says to the audience before playing his last song, a cover of "Thirteen" by Big Star. It's a tender way to end the show. An expression of childlike innocence that cleanses the palette from the tapestry of darkness he wove together across the last 90 minutes.

"Love you," someone shouts as he places his guitar back in the stand and leaves the stage.

A few months after this gig, Elliott released *XO*, then hit the road for an extensive tour of the U.S. with the two-piece band Quasi backing him up. "That was my favorite tour that I ever did with him," Quasi bassist Sam Coomes told me. "Kinda was all downhill from there."

As the years wore on, Elliott's struggles with depression and drug dependency worsened. His physical appearance deteriorated. His live shows often devolved into shambolic meanderings of half-finished songs and forgotten words. On October 21, 2003, after an argument with his girlfriend, he stabbed himself in the chest, twice, ending his life.

Largo remained on Fairfax Avenue until 2008, fostering the careers of Tenacious D., Robyn Hitchcock and Eels, as well as the Western half of the alt-comedy movement, before moving to its present location up the street. You can still catch Jon Brion performing there once a month, if you can luck into a ticket.

HONORABLE MENTION

Marilyn Manson at the Roy Wilkins Auditorium
St. Paul, MN (October 31)

Two years after releasing his career-making album, *Antichrist Superstar*, in the fall of 1998, shock rock master Marilyn Manson unleashed his platinum-selling follow-up, *Mechanical Animals*. A full supporting tour kicked off in Lawrence, Kansas, on October 25, but if there was ever a time that you'd want see Manson in all his horrifying glory, it'd have to be Halloween. Luckily for the people of the Twin Cities, he had a gig scheduled that night at Roy Wilkins Auditorium. Nothing about the presentation was subtle. From Manson's black and blue, alien-chic outfit to the gigantic stilts he wore while singing "Mechanical Animals" and the sign that flashed the word "DRUGS," the show was designed to shock and overwhelm. The mosh pit raced in circles as the man onstage spit water over their heads while screaming his way through "The Dope Show" and "The Beautiful People." There was supposed to be a second encore after a cover of the Eurythmics' "Sweet Dreams (Are Made of This)," but Manson missed a step while walking back to the stage and knocked himself unconscious, bringing the concert to a close a few minutes early. Rock 'n' fucking roll.

1999

Rage Against the Machine, Tool, Beck, Morrissey, The Chemical Brothers, Perry Farrell, Pavement, et al.
EMPIRE POLO FIELDS—INDIO, CA
OCTOBER 8-9

COACHELLA IS BORN

Heading into the summer of 1999, Woodstock '99 was viewed by many as *the* can't-miss musical event of the year. Staged at Griffiss Air Force Base in Rome, New York, the four-day festival was stacked from top to bottom with some of the biggest names in the industry: Sheryl Crow, Metallica, Kid Rock, Elvis Costello, Willie Nelson, Creed, Megadeth, Red Hot Chili Peppers, Muse, etc. Hopes were high that this gig would be a defining moment of the era. In almost every way imaginable, it turned into a complete disaster.

Woodstock '99 was marred by 100-degree temperatures, exorbitant concession prices, a mile-long walk between stages on a scalding-hot tarmac, a lack of proper security, multiple sexual assaults and a full-on bonfire and riot during Red Hot Chili Peppers' cover of Jimi Hendrix's "Fire." 44 people were arrested, 700 came down with heat exhaustion and the Woodstock name was forever tarnished in the eyes of the public.

If Woodstock '99 was "The Day the Music Died," as the *San Francisco Chronicle* proclaimed, then the seeds of the festival industry's renaissance were sown 3,000 miles away just a few months later at an event called The Coachella Valley Music and Arts Festival. The two-day festival was the brainchild of Paul Tollett, CEO of the promotions company Goldenvoice. The promoter came up through the Southern California music scene, booking mostly punk rock shows in smaller venues.

As the years wore on, so did his ambition. The only problem was that Goldenvoice didn't have many concrete assets. Then, the idea struck. Instead of finding investors and shelling out exorbitant sums on an outdoor amphitheater, they went all in on an annual music festival. "We had nothing going," he admitted. "We had a lot of relationships and our wits, but on that level, it was just, there's a field everywhere, just find it and put some creativity into it."

The field Tollett picked for Coachella was chosen several years earlier. During Pearl Jam's infamous fight with Ticketmaster over their pricing models in the early '90s the band tried to forego venues under the ticketing company's purview. That led them to Goldenvoice, which helped them secure the Empire Polo Club in Indio, California, a small town adjacent to Palm Springs. The concert, staged on November 5, 1993, was a stunning success. It drew 25,000 fans from across the region and proved the site's viability as a venue for large-scale live music events.

"[We] looked at a bunch of different places. But then we thought 'Why not go back out there?'" Tollett told *Billboard*. "Even before we looked at it, it hit us. We wanted it to be far. So you surrender. So you can't leave your house and see a couple bands and be back home that night. We want you to go out there, get tired and curse the show by Sunday afternoon. That sunset, and that whole feeling of Coachella hits you."

SELECTED COACHELLA LINEUP

Rage Against the Machine

Tool

Beck

Morrissey

The Chemical Brothers

Perry Farrell

Pavement

Ben Harper & The Innocent Criminals

Moby

DJ Shadow

Modest Mouse

At the Drive-In

Super Furry Animals

A Perfect Circle

Gil Scott Heron

Kool Keith

While plotting out what Coachella would become, Tollett looked at a wide array of multiday festivals taking place around Europe. "[I] went to Glastonbury and that was eye-opening when I saw that. No finer event to this day," he said.

He also drew inspiration from the Golden State's history as a festival incubator. "California has always had incredible festivals," he declared. "Monterey Pop Festival being maybe the first rock one out there, you know, US Festival, Cal Jams through the Seventies. These were probably the seeds to what we were doing and then Lollapalooza came in '91 in the amphitheaters and that was cool."

The lineup for Coachella was incredibly diverse. At the top of the bill were a variety of alternative and indie rock acts like Tool, Rage Against the Machine, Beck, Pavement, Perry Farrell and Morrissey. The down card was filled out by established and up-and-coming electronic artists like the Chemical Brothers, Moby, DJ Shadow and A-Trak. Though they probably could have sold more tickets with Korn or Kid Rock topping the marquee, Tollett and company were banking on the idea that people would make the drive out to the desert for the sheer quality of the lineup from top to bottom.

Tickets cost $50 per day, and sales were solid, with the first day selling around 17,000 tickets. The second day did a little bit better, with 20,000 sold. Still, it was far short of the 35,000 per day cap that Goldenvoice had put in place. That was bad news for the company but great news for the many fans who had ample space to wander around and discover new music.

The So-Cal sun isn't doing anyone any favors and the heat climbs into the triple digits, but the palm trees and the three covered dance tents provide enough shade. When the sun sets around 6 pm, the weather turns nearly perfect. The clear sky above is filled with stars.

The first day is marked by a wealth of fantastic and exciting EDM acts. As Steven Mirkin noted in his review for *Rolling Stone*, "Saturday night at Coachella announced that electronic dance music has moved fully into the mainstream. As the sun went down, the glow sticks rose and electronic music swept the festival, with the big beat imperatives of the Chemical Brothers on the main stage, Underworld slamming away on the second stage and DJ Rap working the turntable in the largest of the three rave tents."

This is the first time that the Chemical Brothers play Coachella, but far from the last. The British electronic music duo will grace the festival another five times in the years to come. That's an impressive tally, but it falls well short of Perry Farrell, one of the main-stage acts, who will perform at Coachella every year for the next decade in one capacity or another. For this performance, the shirtless Jane's Addiction front man turns in a stellar set replete with exotic dancers and world music–infused pop/rock.

Topping the bill this evening is Beck, who is a month away from releasing his next album, *Midnite Vultures*. Decked out in fringe, Beck is, in *Los Angeles Times* reviewer Robert Hilburn's estimation, the "evening's high point," delivering a high-energy performance filled with hits like "Where It's At" and "Loser." "Morrissey, on the other hand, was, well, Morrissey,"

Hilburn wrote about the one-time lead singer of the Smiths. "Treating his loyal fans to another serving of his usual music hall pathos."

While the next day is brimming with talent from opening bell to closing note, most people are here to see the two headlining acts: Rage Against the Machine and Tool. The former is less than a month away

Tollett and company were banking on the idea that people would make the drive out to the desert for the sheer quality of the lineup.

from unveiling its multiplatinum album *The Battle of Los Angeles*. Even though front man Zach de la Rocha is battling laryngitis, Rage turns in a savage two-hour showcase that sends the audience into a frenzy of moshing. Things almost get out of control during "Guerrilla Radio," when the folks up front nearly break through the barricade, but order is quickly restored.

After Rage departs, Tool brings the festival to its noisy, angst-ridden conclusion. Four songs into their set, the industrial prog-rockers offer one of the biggest surprises of the weekend when they bust out a cover of the Peach song "Spasm" with Buzz Osbourne of the Melvins joining in on guitar. Osbourne comes out again five songs later with another Peach cover, "You Lied."

A bald, Speedo-clad Maynard James Keenan stalks the stage with microphone in hand, crooning his lines, while drummer Danny Carey puts on a percussive clinic behind him. Tool finishes two hours after they began with "Jerk Off." The stage is swathed in eerie blue light as the band brings its haunting and abrasive set-closing song to an end.

As great of a success as Coachella was for the fans, it was a financial disaster for the organizers. Because of the tremendous losses, Tollett's plans for future festivals were thrown into serious doubt. Thankfully, bands like Tool, Rage Against the Machine and Beck agreed to defer their payments to prevent Goldenvoice from going belly up.

"We paid our bills late," Tollet told *Billboard*. "If one agent had turned on us, we would been out of business. They let us pay some talent three, four, five months later. The staff back then was just so into Goldenvoice and Coachella that they rolled with any bumps. They would deal with anything."

Coachella took a year off in 2000 and came back again in 2001 with a reunited Jane's Addiction topping the bill. To pay their outstanding bills and continue the festival, Tollett and his business partner sold Goldenvoice to AEG that year. "Owning it, not owning it—thing is, I still get to do the shows and I'm happy," Tollett said. In the years since that first show in 1999, Coachella has become the highest-grossing and most-impactful live music event every year in North America. It's an industry juggernaut, a must-see event.

"We just wanted to do something different," Tollett said. "We weren't thinking business necessarily. Like, there's business to it, but it's almost like you're trying to impress your friends and your staff, which is one and the same."

HONORABLE MENTION

Lauryn Hill at the New Jersey Performing Arts Center Newark, NJ (April 1)

In 1997, the esteemed hip-hop trio Fugees decided to go their separate ways. Pras Michel started working on movie soundtracks. Wyclef Jean jumped into several different projects, eventually attempting to run for president of Haiti. Meanwhile, Lauryn Hill slid into a solo career, spending hours and hours in her attic studio while pregnant with her first child and writing one of the greatest albums of all time. *The Miseducation of Lauryn Hill* is a sprawling, personal masterpiece that fuses a multitude of genres—rap, hip-hop, rock, soul, R&B, jazz and pop—into one incredible document. It spent three weeks at the top of the *Billboard* album charts, while spawning the No. 1 single "Doo Wop (That Thing)." Shortly after the album came out, Hill embarked on a two-month run of dates through America with OutKast supporting. On April 1, the tour hit her home state, where she put together a mesmerizing 90-minute performance of material from her most recent release, beloved Fugees tracks and incredible covers like Bob Marley's "Redemption Song." There was dancing, singing and a ten-minute musical battle between her live band and a hip-hop DJ. As Robert Hilburn observed in the *L.A. Times*, "Hill didn't just live up to the enormous expectation level surrounding her these days; she far exceeded it, in what may be the most accomplished tour ever by a hip-hop artist."

#1 Single of the Year:
"Breathe"
Faith Hill

#1 Album of the Year:
No Strings Attached
NSYNC

2000

OutKast
THE HOUSE OF BLUES—LOS ANGELES, CA
OCTOBER 26

OUTKAST STANK UP THE SUNSET

With all due respect to Eric B. & Rakim, Clipse, EPMD, Mobb Deep, Run the Jewels, Gang Starr, and DJ Jazzy Jeff and the Fresh Prince, the greatest rap duo of all time is OutKast. Representing the "Dirty South," André "André 3000" Benjamin (a.k.a. Possum Aloysuis Jenkins, a.k.a. Dookie Blossum Gain the 3rd) and Antwan "Big Boi" Patton Sr. (better known as Big Boi, a.k.a. Daddy Fat Sax, a.k.a. Lucious Leftfoot) hit the scene in 1994 with their debut album, *Southernplayalisticadillacmuzik*. The Atlanta duo spent the next dozen years making some of the most exciting, genre-bending, commercially successful music in rap.

OutKast sold millions and millions of records. They introduced new acts onto the scene like Goodie Mob, CeeLo Green, Killer Mike, and Janelle Monáe. They almost single-handedly broke the iron grip that the East Coast and the West Coast had on the rap game throughout the 1990s and put Atlanta on the map as a new Mecca of the genre. Besides Lauryn Hill, they are the only rap act ever to take home the Album of the Year prize at the Grammys, which they did in in 2004 for *Speakerboxxx/The Love Below*, the best-selling rap album of all time.

What set OutKast apart from everyone else was the interesting and engrossing way that André 3000 and Big Boi swapped stories and blended voices across a wide palette of sonic backdrops and irresistible hooks. In this corner, you had the spitfire, mile-a-minute delivery of Big, and in the opposing corner, the syrupy, precise and high-minded flows of Dré. They were so different yet so in sync with one another. As a listener, you couldn't help but get drawn in as they rapped about Cadillacs, women, weed, Atlanta, the world at large and the universe beyond.

OutKast reached the peak of creative powers around 2000 with their fourth album, *Stankonia*. Released on Halloween, it's a 24-track masterpiece that combines elements of funk, rock, jazz, gospel, soul and modern rave into one explosive package. "Hip-hop was at a point where everything was kind of laid back and smooth," André told *Spin*. "I wanted something that sounded a little more urgent and fierce."

That feeling of ferocity and urgency wasn't confined to the recording studio. Onstage, Big and Three Stacks are two of the most exhilarating performers on the planet, willing to let it all hang out as they bob and weave around one another. To help promote *Stankonia*, OutKast hit a few smaller venues around the country and played some of the new material alongside older favorites for a few hundred diehards. That's how they ended up at the House of Blues in Los Angeles just five days before their new record came out. There was hardly a hotter ticket anywhere in the world.

Y'all ready for OutKast? Make some goddamn noise!" DJ Swift, the man behind the turntables,

SET LIST

Gasoline Dreams

ATLiens

So Fresh, So Clean

Spottieottiedopealicious

Skew It on the Bar-B

Elevators (Me & You)

Da Art of Storytelling Pt. 1

Spaghetti Junction

Humble Mumble

Ms. Jackson

Red Velvet

Gangsta Shit

Rosa Parks

Bombs Over Baghdad

Call Before I Come

is on the microphone getting the lucky fans assembled on the floor and in the balconies of the garish, Sunset Strip venue turned the hell up. It's not a tough task. Everyone in the place is primed and ready to go off.

Swift gets the cue that the duo is ready and pushes play on a recording of André 3000's voice. "Live, from the center of the earth," he intones in an icy, digitally enhanced monotone. It's the intro track from their upcoming album, which defines *Stankonia* as "a place from which all funky things come."

"D.F. (Interlude)" hits, and OutKast makes their grand entrance. Strolling out into view, Big and André appear as opposites in style. The former is rocking a New York Mets baseball jersey with a thick gold chain swinging around his neck, while the latter, according to *L.A. Times* writer Marc Weingarten, is decked out in a "ghetto-fabulous, flamboyantly foppish getup [that] suggested a refugee from either Parliament-Funkadelic or H.R. Pufnstuf."

"Yeah!" Big shouts. Behind him Swift drops the needle on one of the most incendiary songs they have at their disposal, "Gasoline Dreams." A wah-wah guitar kicks in, providing the bedrock for André to go all the way in on his "Alright, alright, alright" intro and opening verse. Big is hyping him up on the side, inter-

mittently punctuating his abrasive flow before taking over himself on "ATLiens" a few minutes later.

The crowd is going nuts. Up in the balconies the ladies are swaying to the beat, while down below fellas are fervently bouncing their hands in the air. Some know the words of both songs well enough that they succeed in keeping up with the frenetic pace of the two men onstage. Most simply hop in to shout out the choruses.

Both men coast through the verses, hardly skipping a word on the 153-beat-per-minute rager.

"Los Angeles, California, how y'all feeling this evening?" André asks. The audience screams back, letting him know they are feeling fine indeed. "We got a new album coming out on Tuesday called *Stankonia*," Big declares. "We came here tonight to give you a little bit of the new album, a little bit of that *Southernplayalisticadillacmuzik*, a little bit of that *ATLiens* and a little bit of that *Aquemini*. Right now, we gonna go off into some of that new shit. This one right here's called 'So Fresh, So Clean.'"

The beat drops and the pair take off once again. In addition to their DJ, OutKast has brought along two different guitar players and a trio of backup singers. As Dré and Big spit bars throughout the night, the sound of the interlocking guitars and the choral voices behind them lend a depth to the music that is sometimes lacking from live rap performances. They sound especially nice on "So Fresh, So Clean."

Just as Big Boi promised, OutKast treats the Hollywood crowd to a showcase of some of the best material from their first three albums as well as the hotly anticipated one to come. "Elevators (Me & You)" from *ATLiens* bleeds into "Da Art of Storytelling Pt. 1" from *Aquemini*, which gives way to their biggest single to date, "Ms. Jackson." A few months later, the song will net them a Grammy for "Best Rap Performance by a Duo or Group," beating out their other *Stankonia*-nominated single "Rosa Parks." That one gets busted out two songs later.

After almost an hour and a half of scorching hits, OutKast prepares to close the night out with a bang. "Right now we gon' speed this motherfucker up," André says before kicking into the last song of the night. "We about to do some real hip-hop on crack!"

The whispered count-in commences and Three Stacks starts rhyming at a mile a minute over the most frenzied OutKast song of them all, "B.O.B.," a.k.a. "Bombs Over Baghdad." He wasn't kidding when he said they were going to speed things up. Watching both men coast through the verses, hardly skipping a word on the 153-beat–per-minute rager is an impressive sight to behold.

Behind them, Swift adds an extra element of mania via some absurd live record scratching. By the time the guitar solo hits, all bets are off. Every time the chorus comes around, the crowd boisterously joins in: "Don't pull that thang out unless you plan to bang/Bombs over Baghdad!"

"And on that note right there, the album will be out on Tuesday," Big reminds them as the song ends. "We'll see y'all at the after-party," Dré chimes in. OutKast hits them with one last track, "Call Before I Come," and then take off for a night no doubt filled with the finest weed and women that Hollywood has to offer.

HONORABLE MENTION
D'Angelo at the House of Blues
Los Angeles, CA (March 1)

In 2000, neo-soul singer D'Angelo dropped *Voodoo*, a nearly 80-minute musical odyssey through some of the most thrilling funk/soul/jazz hybrid sounds ever recorded. D'Angelo hit the road in support of the album, beginning with a five-night residency at the House of Blues in Los Angeles. Despite the venue's relatively intimate confines, the man who critic Robert Christgau once called "R&B Jesus" spared no expense. His band, dubbed the Soultronics and led by Roots drummer Questlove, numbered 13 people. The sound was tremendous. For nearly three hours, D'Angelo put on the kind of high-impact performance that would've made his heroes, Prince and James Brown, very proud. "Two hours into the show, and the roof is on fire," Touré wrote in *Rolling Stone*. "We've gone from smooth soul to rock funk to Pentecostal church, the grooves shifting without a moment's pause in a breathtaking musical assault." The concert ends well past midnight, with D'Angelo still dancing, still singing and still working the crowd, ready to do it all again the next night.

#1 Single of the Year:
"Hanging by a Moment"
Lifehouse

2001

Jay Z
NASSAU VETERANS MEMORIAL COLISEUM
UNIONDALE, NY
JUNE 28

JAY Z ASSUMES THE THRONE

There's a lot of shit going on in rap music, a lot of cats yappin'," Jay Z says. "Y'all know what I do. Your boy handles his business."

With a microphone in his hand and bad intentions on his mind, the Jiggaman stalks across the stage at the annual Summer Jam music festival hosted by the New York radio station Hot 97 like a caged lion, preparing to unleash the most savage diss track in rap history. By the time he's through, he's completely derailed the career of one group and kicked off a feud with another artist that would change the course of music history.

There's a competitive streak at the heart of rap that's unlike anything in any other genre. It's not enough to sell the most records, although that's a major part of it. You have to prove that you're the best on the mic and in the booth. Feuds are common, as major players and up-and-comers alike vie to be the greatest or most impactful lyricist in the game.

Jay Z is no stranger to beefs. As a close friend and high school classmate of the Notorious B.I.G., he's intimately aware of the cataclysmic outcomes such conflicts can carry. But he also knows they're a great way to gain attention and catapult yourself to the top. Just two years earlier, Jay arrived at Summer Jam and took a shot at 50 Cent, rapping, "I'm about a dollar, what the fuck is 50 cents?"

After the Notorious B.I.G. was killed in 1997, there was a huge void left at the top of the New York rap hierarchy and a whole host of artists clamoring to fill it. The most viable candidates were Jay and a rapper from the Queensbridge projects named Nas. At the time, Nas was undoubtedly the more popular of the two. While Jay was riding high on his earthshaking debut, *Reasonable Doubt*, Nas had already logged an all-time classic with *Illmatic* and earned multiplatinum mainstream success with his sophomore work, *It Was Written*.

Nas and Jay Z could best be described as passing acquaintances, obstacles to overcome in their individual pursuit of larger commercial success. They danced around one another, taking gentle jabs. On Nas's 1999 track "We Will Survive," he addressed Biggie while calling out Jay, saying, "These niggas is wrong using your name in vain/And they claim to be New York's King?"

Things really kicked off the next year when Nas took a shot at Jay's friend and label-mate Memphis Bleek on "Nastradamus."Not one to take a slight lying down, Bleek clapped back months later with "My Mind Right," rapping, "Your life a lie, but here's the truth/You ain't hype to die, but you hype to shoot."

At the same time, Jay Z was getting pulled into a feud with another rapper from Queensbridge, Prodigy from Mobb Deep. On his 1998 song "Money, Cash, Hoes," Jay rapped, "It's like New York's been soft ever since Snoop came through and crushed the buildings." Prodigy took exception to the line, arguing that Jay mostly stood on the sidelines during the big East Coast vs. West Coast battle of the mid '90s.

By the time Summer Jam rolled around in 2001, Jay had had enough. He'd let the cats yap for almost two years, and now was the time to end it. Your boy was about to handle his business.

After a full evening packed with short sets from some of the buzziest names in hip-hop—including OutKast, Ludacris, Ja Rule and Destiny's Child—the audience explodes when Jay Z makes his entrance. Decked out in a Latrell Sprewell New York Knicks basketball jersey over a white T-shirt, with a blue do-rag covering his head and a long gold chain dangling from his neck, Hov came to play.

Flanked by Memphis Bleek, Beanie Sigel and a host of friends and accomplices, Jay kicks off a set that's as filled with surprises as it is with crowd-pleasing hits. On "Is That Your Chick," he brings out Missy Elliott to reprise her verse from that song, before delivering a bit of her own smash, "Get Ur Freak On." After that he kicks into "Big Pimpin'," which comes with some live instrumentation courtesy of a violin player named Miri Ben-Ari, which garners a standing ovation.

After letting loose about the yappin' cats, Jay takes aim at his detractors, unveiling a song called "Takeover." The track was produced by a then-unknown Kanye West, who sampled "Five to One" by the Doors and "Sound of da Police" by KRS-One to create a hugely infectious backbeat. Even though Jay doesn't air out the whole thing, the verses he unleashes are devastating.

Setting his sights on Prodigy, Jay goes for the jugular. "You little fuck, I got money stacks bigger than you," he boasts. At the part where Jay calls Prodigy a ballerina, the large screen hanging above the stage is lit up with two gigantic images of a smiling young boy in full dancer's apparel. The caption reads: "Prodigy of Mobb Deep in 1988." The audience roars with laughter.

A few minutes later, "Takeover" ends with a surprising twist, "Ask Nas, he don't want it with Hov,"

SET LIST

Is That Your Chick (Missy Elliott)
Get Ur Freak On (Missy Elliott)
So Wat Cha Sayin' (EPMD)
Big Pimpin'
Best of Me
Takeover
I Want You Back
H to the Izzo

Jay declares. It's a warning shot. The world doesn't know it yet, but there's a third verse to this song that Jay is holding back. In it, he savagely takes down Nas, not only for being phony but also for turning in mediocre albums well past his prime. The line he delivers tonight is just a taste. When it's released weeks later, "Takeover" kicks off one of the greatest feuds in rap history, a battle that rages unabated for four long years.

Jay's not done though. He's got one last special guest left that he wants to bring to the stage. "I know Michael Jackson better come from behind that muthafuckin' curtain," he declares. The audience can't believe what they just heard, but Jackson is nowhere to be seen. The cheers morph into boos as the wait stretches on. "You want me to go back and get him myself?" Jay asks. "Okay, I'mma go get him."

The King of Pop's mere presence is more than enough to ordain Jay Z as the new, reigning King of Rap.

The rapper disappears behind the curtain and when he reemerges, sure enough, there's Michael Jackson, decked out from head to toe in all black. "They had a close-up of him on the screen, and the crowd was in awe of what he looked like close-up," *Video Music Box* host Ralph McDaniels told the *Village*

Voice. "It was scary, but it was exciting."

"Who brings Michael Jackson to a hardcore hip-hop concert?" Hot 97 DJ Enuff asked *Complex*. "It was unheard of. It's like [Jay Z] was at a poker table with the illest hand, and he was bluffing, but once he pulled it out, it was like, oh wow. Everybody now tries to outdo the next person with their celebrity guests during their set. I don't know, though. How do you beat Michael Jackson?"

Jackson didn't sing or dance. The King of Pop's mere presence is more than enough to ordain Jay Z as the new, reigning King of Rap. If you have the power to get Michael Jackson, what can't you do? The two men pose for pictures. Jackson tells the crowd, "I love you all," and then he's gone. Minutes later, Jay rips into his next single "Izzo (H.O.V.A.)" which features a prominent sample of the Jackson 5 hit "I Want You Back." Months later, the song would become his first Top-10 hit.

The fallout from Jay Z's set at Summer Jam was as dramatic as it was consequential. Six months after this gig, Nas, responded to "Takeover" with his own incendiary diss track, "Ether." In it, he accuses Jay of stealing from KRS-One while asking, "How much of Biggie's rhymes gonna come out your fat lips?" Nas was invited to perform at the next Summer Jam in 2002, alongside Mobb Deep, but he bailed on the event after organizers rebuffed his plans to hang Jay Z in effigy.

The two men wouldn't reconcile until a show dubbed "I Declare War" in Philadelphia in 2005, when Jay brought out Nas to rap on the song "Dead Presidents." By that point, there was no longer any question who stood at the top of the New York rap kingdom. Jay Z had assumed the throne.

HONORABLE MENTION
The Concert for New York City at Madison Square Garden
New York, NY (October 20)

The terrorist attacks on September 11 remain one of the darkest chapters in American history. Out of this horrific tragedy, however, the country rallied together in a way that most didn't think possible. American flags adorned nearly every house acros the nation as citizens donated time, money and blood to help their fellow countrymen. Military enlistment soared, and in the entertainment industry, mega-benefits were organized to help the families and rescue efforts. The biggest of these shows took place at Madison Square Garden, a fifteen-minute subway ride away from Ground Zero. Jay Z was there, as were Destiny's Child, Paul McCartney, Billy Joel, The Who, Elton John, Eric Clapton, James Taylor and David Bowie, who opened the show with a cover of the Simon & Garfunkel song "America" before seguing into his own hit "Heroes." It was an emotional evening, with many of the victims' families present to take in the scene. The event raised over $30 million dollars to support the Robin Hood Foundation, which administers a relief fund for disasters in New York City.

#1 Single of the Year:
"How You Remind Me"
Nickelback

2002

#1 Album of the Year:
The Eminem Show
Eminem

The Strokes and The White Stripes
RADIO CITY MUSIC HALL—NEW YORK, NY
AUGUST 15

STROKES OF WHITE

It's very rare that two era-defining bands appear on the same bill while both are at, or very near, their artistic peaks. Such was the case of the White Stripes and the Strokes at Radio City Music Hall in New York City on August 15, 2002. The White Stripes were touring behind their head-turning third album, *White Blood Cell*, while on the verge or putting out their next breakout hit record, *Elephant*. The Strokes had spent the last year galvanizing the New York rock scene and the world at large with their tight, sneering, almost-perfect debut, *Is This It*.

Of course, buzz alone does not a great show make. Both Jack and Meg White as well as Julian Casablancas and Co. tore into the crowd at Radio City that night with a fervor. The White Stripes stomped and raged on cuts like "I Think I Smell a Rat" and "Jack the Ripper" and a cover of Dolly Parton's "Jolene." Despite Casablancas's foot being wrapped in a cast, the Strokes cut a galvanizing presence, exuding dual rays of magnetism and complete cool on "Meet Me in the Bathroom" and "Last Nite." By the time Jack White came back out to guest with the headliners for "New York City Cops," it almost felt like a torch had been passed.

In the months and years that followed, the White Stripes would surpass the Strokes by leaps and bounds in terms of both popularity and commercial appeal. While Julian Casablancas will always remain the definitive New York cool guy front man

for the 2000s, Jack White has gone on to become the de facto guitar hero of the 21st century. Whereas *Is This It* stands as the Strokes' masterpiece, The White Stripes were months away from unleashing *Elephant* and forever altering the playlists of sports stadiums around the world with their anthemic single "Seven Nation Army."

Back in 2001, Kelefa Sanneh, who now writes for the *New Yorker*, covered the show for the *New York Times*. I spoke with him to get his perspective on what made this gig so exceptional, while also gauging its place as one of the defining moments of the early '00s rock revival.

As a resident New Yorker, can you describe what it was like to live through the rise of the Strokes?

I started working full-time for the *New York Times* early that year in 2002, so when the Strokes were coming up in the years before that, I missed all those formative shows. I never saw them at Arlene's Grocery or any of those places. I encountered them just like a regular consumer. When the album [*Is This It*] came out I remember being blown away. Some bands never find a way to translate what they do onto a record, and the Strokes, in retrospect, seem like the opposite of that. They made a record that, to me, was so good that it's almost better than the band.

SET LISTS

THE WHITE STRIPES

When I Hear My Name

I Think I Smell a Rat

Jolene

Dead Leaves and the Dirty Ground

Apple Blossom

Hotel Yorba

Isis

Death Letter

Little Room

The Union Forever

Rated X

Astro

Jack the Ripper

Farmer John

We're Going to Be Friends

Offend in Every Way

Poor Wayfaring Stranger

Cannon

Screwdriver

Boll Weevil

THE STROKES

The Way It Is

Someday

Soma

Meet Me in the Bathroom

The Modern Age

Hard to Explain

Is This It

Take It or Leave It

Between Love & Hate

Trying Your Luck

Last Nite

Alone, Together

You Talk Way Too Much

Barely Legal

New York City Cops (with Jack White)

THE WHITE STRIPES

Jack White: Guitar/Vocals

Meg White: Drums

What do you mean by that?

The first record to me is just kind of perfect, partly because it's a small record. It's short. There's nothing extra in any of the songs. Although at the time, we got it without the "New York City Cops" track, which was pulled from the American edition after 9/11.

What kind of trajectory did it seem like the band was on? Were they still on the way up? Were they bona fide stars?

By the time that show came around it was like they were doing a victory lap. I think at that point "Someday" was out as a single and they were just kind of triumphant. It was a strange moment where you were starting to see a little bit of a gold rush . . . any band that sounded vaguely garage-y playing around New York was starting to get looked at and getting deals. It ended up becoming a curse where everyone was getting compared to everyone else. To me, what I think I remember is that they cast such a long shadow over the city. It got everyone excited to find scrappy guitar bands in New York.

How did Julian Casablancas's injury impact this show? Did it make it any better or worse to see him sing from a bar stool?

I always like the idea that he was, I don't know if I would say subversive, but he definitely upended some notions about what a "punk singer" was supposed to be like. Just because his band would be hammering away, even on the record, he had this kind of languorous sensibility. He always sounded as if he were sitting down. He would almost be crooning. The obvious thing to do with that music would to be more confrontational, to be more throaty, to be jumping up and down and getting in people's faces, and part of what was so charismatic about Julian was there was always this sense with him that you couldn't quite tell if he gave a shit. So seeing him slouched in his chair, annoyed that he had this injury, didn't bother

THE STROKES

Julian Casablancas: Vocals
Nick Valensi: Lead Guitar
Albert Hammond Jr.: Rhythm Guitar
Nickolai Fraiture: Bass
Fabrizio Moretti: Drums

me at all. Bands tour and bands play so many shows; I always enjoy seeing something a little out of the ordinary. I liked the idea that that show was different from so many other Strokes shows because of that.

Heading into this concert, what were your expectations?

To me it was one of those victory lap shows, which I really enjoy. You're getting to the end of the album cycle or you're some of the way into the album cycle. The excitement about this record had been growing. The fan base was still growing. It felt like they were the biggest, best band in the city and then they were going to have this show where they celebrate with their fans. . . . It really felt like a celebration. They were in this big beautiful room, they've achieved more than they thought they probably would, and the room is going to be filled with nothing more than true believers, basically. In retrospect, you can make the case that that was peak Strokes.

Can you juxtapose the statuses of the Strokes and the White Stripes in that moment?

You know, the White Stripes were popular, but they were very much the opening band. It's certainly possible to see [this concert] as a passing of the torch with the White Stripes, and Jack White in particular being bigger, more influential, more a lot of things than the Strokes. People still sing that White Stripes song ["Seven Nation Army"] at every sporting event. Jack White is still pretty synonymous with electric guitar and vinyl, which is a pretty good measure of his influence and the shadow he casts.

The early appeal of the White Stripes was this mystery that they wrapped themselves up in.

They were still sticking to the story that they were brother and sister, for instance. How much did you know about them?

White Blood Cells was out and that's what they were touring on, so I certainly knew the music from that. The Internet wasn't as advanced as it would soon become, so there were these rumors like, "They say they're brother and sister, but they're supposedly divorced." I can't remember if someone had dug up the divorce record by then, but that's what the talk was. It's funny to remember now because Jack White wears dark colors and lives in Nashville and has this furious Johnny Cash kind of thing, but at the time a lot of their iconography was very playful. They dressed like two peppermint candies. There were just two people in the band, which at the time was pretty unusual.

> *It felt like they were the biggest, best band in the city and then they were going to have this show where they celebrate with their fans.*

What was your impression when you saw the White Stripes onstage that night?

I remember being shocked at how raw it was. You know, they're on this huge stage at Radio City Music Hall, which is a place where most of the bands would be professional in a certain way, and they just seemed really unpolished, even compared to the Strokes. You know, Jack White was doing these big squealing guitar riffs. It often seemed as if, even though she was the drummer, Meg White was locking into Jack and that he was setting the rhythms and she was playing along with him, which gave the songs a really herky-jerky feel. The rhythm was never regular. They were always pushing and pulling, and speeding up, and slowing down. There was something really radical about that.

How does this show stack up amongst your more memorable concerts?

There's a lot of things that can go into a show being memorable. There's almost two categories of memorable shows: the ones where something crazy happens, like Courtney Love at Bowery Ballroom where she kept jumping off the stage and it seemed like maybe she was going to get hurt. There was high drama. And then there are big bands in small rooms like Arcade Fire at Mercury Lounge—stuff like that is very memorable. Or shows where it seems like something is happening. I remember seeing a Rilo Kiley show . . . right as they were becoming popular. And it was one of those shows where it seemed like they didn't realize they were popular and that people knew all the words to their songs. I certainly remember this one.

HONORABLE MENTION

Wilco at the Riviera Theatre

Chicago, IL (May 2)

In 2001, Chicago indie-rockers Wilco turned their fourth record, *Yankee Hotel Foxtrot*, in to their record label, Reprise. The powers that be hated it. The suits claimed that they didn't hear a single amongst the tracks and disdained the band's sonically adventurous direction. Reprise rejected the album and released Wilco from their contract. It was a stunning development, eliciting an outpouring of support for the group and an intense backlash against the company. Wilco was ultimately given the rights to *Yankee Hotel Foxtrot* without having to pay fees and shopped around for a new home. Wilco signed a new deal with Nonesuch (which, ironically, was owned by Time Warner, Reprise's parent company), and *Yankee Hotel Foxtrot* was released on April 23, 2002. The album was a critical hit and the band's biggest commercial success. Wilco returned home to Chicago and put together a marathon, three-set performance at the Riviera Theatre. They kicked off the show with the *Yankee Hotel Foxtrot* opening track, "I Am Trying to Break Your Heart." Over the course of the evening they played every song from the album minus "Poor Places." The fans couldn't get enough.

2003

The Dixie Chicks
SHEPHERD'S BUSH EMPIRE—LONDON, ENGLAND
MARCH 10

THE PRESIDENTIAL SALUTE

Twelve words. That's all it took for singer Natalie Maines to nearly destroy the Dixie Chicks' career. Twelve words that don't seem all that incendiary in retrospect, but which landed with the force of an explosion as soon as the news of their existence spread. To an adoring English audience, Maines, a native of the Lone Star State, declared, "We're ashamed that the president of the United States is from Texas."

When she spoke those words in 2003, Maines and her bandmates, Martie Maguire and Emily Robinson, reigned as one of the most commercially powerful and celebrated artistic forces in the music world. They had been certified as the best-selling female group of all time, surpassing titans the Supremes, Destiny's Child and the Spice Girls. Their first two albums, *Wide Open Space* and *Fly*, both went diamond (over 10 million in sales) and then some. The latter was a No. 1 hit, while their most recent effort, 2002's *Home*, made it into the Top-5.

They won *Billboard*'s Country Artist of the Year award in 1999 and 2000. They'd won numerous Academy of Country Music and Country Music Association prizes, a People's Choice Award for Favorite Musical Group and seven Grammys. They sang the American National Anthem at Super Bowl XXXVII that January. There was hardly anyone bigger.

Shortly after *Home* hit the shelves, the Dixie Chicks announced a new Top of the World Tour that would kick off with three promotional shows at Shep-

herd's Bush Empire in London, with the first taking place on March 10. While the band was preparing for that run, the dark cloud of on an impending war with Iraq hung heavy over the world. Three weeks before the Dixie Chicks landed in London, the city took part in the largest anti-war rally in human history. Nearly a million people marched and demonstrated against the war as part of a global protest that took place in 600 cities. Despite their efforts, the bombs began raining down on Baghdad on March 20.

Everyone goes home pleased, totally unaware of the shitstorm headed their way.

Though the crowd is ready to have a good time, lose themselves in the music and dance some of their cares away, the feeling inside the band is less celebratory, especially for Maines. She can't seem to shake the feelings of anger and frustration about the situation in Iraq and the man pushing it forward. But, as they say, the show must go on. At the appropriate time, the lights go out and the Chicks make their way in front of the adoring audience.

The band knows what the crowd wants and is

MUSICIANS

Natalie Maines: Vocals/Guitar
Emily Robinson: Guitar/Banjo/Vocals
Martie Maguire: Fiddle/Mandolin/Vocals
Roscoe Beck: Bass
John Deardrick: Keyboards
John Gardner: Drums
David Grissom: Guitar
Ben Truitt: Mandolin
Robbie Turner: Steel Guitar
John Mock: Pennywhistle/Percussion/Guitar

SET LIST

Lubbock or Leave It
Truth #2
Goodbye Earl
The Long Way Around
Landslide
Everybody Knows
I Like It
Cowboy Take Me Away
Lullaby
White Trash Wedding
Lil' Jack Slade
Not Ready to Make Nice
Easy Silence
Long Time Gone
Some Days You Gotta Dance
So Hard
Top of the World
Wide Open Spaces
Sin Wagon
Travelin' Soldier
Mississippi
Ready to Run

only too eager to oblige with a set dominated by its many hits, songs like "Travelin' Soldier," "Goodbye Earl" and "Longtime Gone." The audience revels in the group's glistening three-layered harmonies, as well as Robinson's pedal steel guitar licks and Maguire's sometimes jaunty, sometimes mournful fiddle fills. Taking the lead on vocals, Maines sounds exquisite, vibrant and powerful belting her way through the band's impressive oeuvre.

Midway through the show, Maines steps forward to air out her true feelings about the impending war. "Just so you know," she says while staring at her fingers lying idle on the neck of her guitar. "We're on the good side with y'all. We do not want this war, this violence." The English crowd cheers the sentiment, but of course, she isn't done. "We're ashamed that the president of the United States is from Texas," she declares.

The words tumble out of her mouth and a big smile erupts on her face. She looks over to her right as the rest of the band laughs along. The audience applauds wildly. After a few more songs, the show ends. Everyone goes home pleased with the performance, totally unaware of the shitstorm headed their way.

At the same time the Dixie Chicks were expressing their disdain for the president, most of the Nashville country establishment was hitting the recording studios and churning out overblown, patriotic-to-the-point-of-xenophobic anthems in support of 'Merican values and 'Merican policies. Whereas

Maines was ashamed of the president and his administration's hawkish nature, Toby Keith was advocating putting boots in asses on "Courtesy of the Red, White and Blue (Angry American)" while Alan Jackson was proudly admitting that he couldn't tell you "the difference between Iraq and Iran." Mainstream country audiences ate it up gleefully.

It's one thing for Eddie Vedder, Neil Young, Bruce Springsteen, Ian MacKaye or another rock artist to speak out, but Nashville remained firmly behind the president and, for the most part, supported the war. The backlash to Maines's words was swift and harsh. The band's latest single, a cover of Fleetwood Mac's "Landslide" dove from No. 10 in the charts to No. 44 in a single week, then fell out of the rankings completely as radio stations boycotted the Dixie Chicks' music. Lipton, the tour's sponsor, dropped their involvement. The group struggled to fill the large arenas they had booked. Officials in South Carolina went a step further and tried to ban them completely.

President Bush himself weighed in shortly afterward in an interview with NBC's Tom Brokaw. "They shouldn't have their feelings hurt just because some people don't want to buy their records when they speak out," Bush said. "[I] don't really care what the Dixie Chicks said. I want to do what I think is right for the American people, and if some singers or Hollywood stars feel like speaking out, that's fine."

"We don't feel part of the country scene any longer," Maguire admitted to *Der Spiegel* months after the show. "A few weeks ago, Merle Haggard said a couple of nice words about us, but that was it. The support we got came from others, like Bruce Springsteen. So, we now consider ourselves part of the big rock 'n' roll family."

The Dixie Chicks ran a rough road over the next several years. They eventually clawed their way back into the good graces of a large contingent of the audience that spurned them, but they never again reached the stunning highs of their turn-of-the-century peak. Their next album, *Taking the Long Way*, released in 2006, sold millions of copies, but fell far short of the marks they had once set. A short while later, the group went on an extended hiatus, broken only by the spare tour here and there. They have yet to release another album.

Nearly three years after that fateful night in London, the Dixie Chicks returned to Shepherds Bush Empire to kick off their new Accidents & Accusations World Tour. Support for President George W. Bush was nowhere near as high as it once was now that the American invasion had turned into a deep-sinking quagmire. Concertgoers waited with bated breath to hear what Maines had to say.

"I didn't plan anything," Maines admitted to the crowd. "But I thought I'd say something brand-new and say, 'Just so you know, we're ashamed the president of the United States is from Texas.'"

HONORABLE MENTION
Eminem and 50 Cent at Ford Field
Detroit, MI (July 13)

In this corner, you have the master, Eminem, one of music's biggest stars, who had the bestselling album of 2002 with *The Eminem Show*. In the opposing corner, the student, 50 Cent, universally regarded as the "next big thing," who had the bestselling album of 2003 with *Get Rich or Die Tryin'*. Both men are at or near the top of their game. Put them together, and you have a concert for the ages. After touring extensively the year before, Eminem stayed off the road for most of 2003, except for a pair of shows at Ford Field in July. To open the concerts, he enlisted 50 Cent, who had just gotten off his Rock the Mic Tour with Jay Z. 50, along with members of his G-Unit collective, went hard during the show, taking shots at his nemesis, Ja Rule, and running through his hits like "In Da Club" and "Magic Stick." He knew he wasn't going to upstage the headliner, and that was okay with him. "Eminem is number one to me," he proclaimed mid-show. "He gave me my shot." Eminem didn't disappoint the hometown fans either and put together a set as heavy on spectacle as it was on hits. Flanked by his group, D-12, Em put his lyrical talents on display as he ripped through mind-bending takes on songs like "Cleaning Out My Closet," "Without Me," "Sing For the Moment" and the Academy Award–winning "Lose Yourself."

#1 Single of the Year:
"Yeah!"
Usher (Featuring Lil Jon and Ludacris)

2004

#1 Album of the Year:
Confessions
Usher

The Roots, The Fugees, Erykah Badu, Talib Kweli, Common, Mos Def and Kanye West
MADISON SQUARE GARDEN—NEW YORK, NY
SEPTEMBER 18

DAVE CHAPPELLE'S BROOKLYN BLOCK PARTY

As far as tickets go, this was a tough one to come by. Comedian Dave Chappelle, star of *Chappelle's Show* on Comedy Central, had only announced his blowout block party 12 days earlier, but the lineup was one of the most enticing in recent memory. Lauryn Hill was going to be there. So were Kanye West, Mos Def, Talib Kweli, The Roots, Jill Scott, Erykah Badu, Common and Dead Prez. "If all the surprises come through, this cannot be missed," Ahmir "Questlove" Thompson of the Roots promised MTV. Boy, was he right.

The tickets were free. That wasn't the problem. The real issue was the obstacles created by the organizers to obtain them, beginning with an online registry and casting questionnaire. Rapper J. Cole, who was a 19-year-old college sophomore at the time, described the arduous process on Reddit.

"Woke up that morning at 6 am to leave, and it was pouring. Some hurricane level shit," he recalled. After talking it over with his roommate, they decided to brave the weather and make the journey anyway. "Had to walk to the bus stop in the rain, then wait on the bus in the rain. Now we're soaked. Hopped off the bus, hopped on the train. Took the train to the bottom of Manhattan to the secret 'meet-up' point. Some random grocery store by the water. We were the first ones there. People showed up over the next couple of hours. Then finally, they put us all on these yellow school buses to take us to the real secret concert location. A random block in Bed Stuy, Brooklyn." It was a long way to go, but the man behind the event was determined to make it all worthwhile.

2004 was a great time to be Dave Chappelle, at least from an outsider's perspective. He was one of the biggest comedians in the world, flush with cash after signing a new $50 million contract in August with Comedy Central. Internally, however, he was a man torn apart. At a stand-up gig in Sacramento in June, he admitted to a crowd that kept interrupting his set with many of his signature catchphrases—like "I'm Rick James, bitch!"—that "the show is ruining my life."

A planned third season of *Chappelle's Show* never happened. The crush of fame and the stress of turning in a product that met his exacting standards caused him to flee to South Africa in the middle of filming. He later told Oprah Winfrey that he felt that he was "deliberately being put through stress because when you're a guy who generates money, people have a vested interest in controlling you." He added, "The hardest thing to do is be true to yourself, especially when everybody is watching."

Before he reached that breaking point, Chappelle had one other project that he wanted to bring to life. "He had an idea for a kind of city party, something similar to Wattstax," Questlove wrote in his memoir, *Mo' Meta Blues*, referring to a 1972 benefit gig hosted at the Los Angeles Memorial Coliseum. Determined to turn his proposed concert into an era-defining event, Chappelle brought in director Michel Gondry, most notable for his work crafting the film *Eternal Sunshine of the Spotless Mind*, and assembled a roster of impeccable musical talent.

"All these people that are coming to this concert, before I ever met 'em, I was fans of theirs," the comedian said in the subsequent documentary, *Dave Chappelle's Block Party*. "To work with these people, in this kind of setting, is a dream come true. This is the concert that I've always wanted to see."

West is a blur of energy, rapping and dancing as though his life depends on it.

"Sometimes, there's a moment that in retrospect it's, like, 'Oh, wow, that was pretty huge. That was a monumental occasion," rapper Black Thought of The Roots told me. "But Dave Chappelle's Block Party was something that, every step along the way, we could tell it was going to be a legendary affair."

Because of the difficulty securing tickets, the block in front of Arthur and Cynthia Wood's ornate, five-story Broken Angel House is far emptier than anyone anticipated. Only the diehards are present. "Five thousand black people chillin' in the rain," Chappelle observes. "19 white people peppered in." Though the skies remain gray and full of mist, they refrain from opening up completely.

The show begins grandly. Chappelle takes the stage as the sounds of the Central State University marching band come to life down the street. "Throw 'em up!" Chappelle commands. "Give it up for none other than Kanyeezy, aka Kanye West."

Decked out in an oversized checkered blazer and black T-shirt with a large diamond-encrusted gold chain dangling from his neck, West strolls down the block toward the stage, the band trailing in his wake and blasting out "Jesus Walks."

"I thought about how presidential he looked and how the black kids were responding to him," Questlove recalled of West's grand entrance. "I remember having a kind of out-of-body experience and investigation of the thought of my own artistic death. Am I dead already? I wondered. . . . I saw the rest of the plot stretched out before me. Kanye was going to be the new leader, and I was fine with that."

West does his best to steal the show. Backed by The Roots, he rips into a tightly packed set filled with bangers from his debut album, *The College Dropout*. Two songs in and Mos Def appears to bring to life his verse on "Two Words." After that Common and Talib Kweli hit the stage, guesting on "Get 'Em High." They're followed by John Legend, who adds the soul on "Spaceship," then Syleena Johnson appears to provide the hook on "All Falls Down." West is a blur of energy, rapping and dancing as though his life depends on it. His set ends with a performance of "Jesus Walks" that leaves the poncho-adorned audience screaming for more.

After West leaves, Chappelle plays bongos and riffs on fake poetry before Dead Prez takes the stage. That's followed by an incredible set of Afro-soul courtesy of Erykah Badu, Jill Scott and The Roots. "That was one of the rare occasions where we performed our song 'You Got Me' with both Jill Scott, who wrote it, and with Erykah Badu, who made it famous," Black Thought remembered. When they're through they cede the stage to the Black Star duo Mos Def and Talib Kweli, along with Common, who trade songs and verses with one another with an intensity that's stunning to witness.

Then comes the kicker. All day long, Chappelle has been harboring a major surprise. Lauryn Hill was listed as the headliner, and that's whom the crowd expects next, but then the comedian pulls the rug out from underneath them. "We were going to have Lauryn Hill perform tonight, but Columbia wouldn't clear her songs," Chappelle tells the crowd. "So, she came up with a better idea. Ladies and gentlemen, the Fugees!"

As far as shocks go, this is a big one. The group

called it quits seven years earlier, shortly after dropping their multiplatinum monster album *The Score*. Following the runaway success of Hill's even bigger *The Miseducation of Lauryn Hill*, the prospects of a reunion seemed grim. Yet here they are in the flesh, bringing hits like "Nappy Heads" and "Ready or Not" back to life for an audience that can hardly believe what they are seeing.

Writing for the *New York Times*, Kelefa Sanneh observed, "It was a shock and a thrill to see all three of them creeping through 'Fu-Gee-La' once again. A few songs later Mr. Jean rhymed, 'Jay Z said, "The Fugees gon' break up"/He ain't even know, one day we'd make up,' and the crowd ignored the form (the easy rhyme, the clunky meter) in order to cheer the content."

Jean and Pras Michel eventually fade to the background, affording Hill time in the spotlight to croon out a powerful rendition of "Killing Me Softly With His Song." She begins a cappella and builds into a powerful instrumental tour de force, leaving her crying the three-word phrase "singing my life" over and over again. The effect is mesmerizing.

The next moment is even more incredible. With Jean playing acoustic guitar, Hill kicks into "Lost Ones," singing the lines "Miscommunication leads to complication/My emancipation don't fit your equation" right into her former bandmate's face, while Pras feigns anger on the side. It's a moment of shocking self-awareness. "Lost Ones" has always been interpreted as a shot at Jean, and the fact she can sing it directly to him now feels cathartic.

"Holy shit!" Chappelle says after the Fugees come off the stage. With his hands raised in the air like a championship fighter and with the crowd screaming their lungs out, the comedian revels in his glory. "We shook up the world," he declares. "We shook up the world!"

HONORABLE MENTION
Usher at the Phillips Arena
Atlanta, GA (October 3)

2004 was the year of Usher. "Mr. Entertainment" took the world by storm shortly after unveiling his blockbuster fourth album, *Confessions*, that March. The record sold 1.1 million copies in its first week alone. Even more incredible, he held down the top of the singles charts for 25 of the year's 52 weeks with the songs "Yeah!" "Burn," and "My Boo." On August 5, Usher kicked off a tour befitting his status as the biggest thing in the music business. The tour wound its way around the country before landing in Atlanta for the penultimate gig on October 3. After an opening set from Kanye West, Usher took the elaborate stage and gave the hometown crowd all he had. He danced and sang with a beguiling mix of intensity and grace, pouring every ounce of energy he had into songs like "U Got It Bad," "Nice & Slow," "Burn" and "Confessions Part II." As MTV noted in its review, "For all the knocks he gets about coming off arrogant sometimes, he's really that good. . . . For two hours, he keeps the crowd on its feet, makes every song a spectacle, dances incessantly and doesn't miss a note."

#1 Single of the Year:
"We Belong Together"
Mariah Carey

#1 Album of the Year:
The Massacre
50 Cent

2005

Green Day
THE NATIONAL BOWL—MILTON KEYNES, ENGLAND
JULY 18

AN AMERICAN IDIOT IN LONDON

This was the gig that Green Day had been waiting to play for a very long time. Nine months before landing at Milton, Keynes, the Bay Area punk rockers released their seventh studio album, *American Idiot*. As a grandiose, politically charged rock opera, the record touched a major nerve in the zeitgeist. It catapulted Green Day to the top of the charts and to the upper stratosphere of the music elite. The group that was co-headlining with Blink-182 three years earlier was now selling out arenas and stadiums across the globe by themselves.

American Idiot is a concept record about a kid named Jesus of Suburbia as he comes of age in President George W. Bush's America. It's an uncompromising album that rails against the forces of corporate greed and proponents of the Iraq War. Nominated for seven Grammys, *American Idiot* ended up taking home the award for Best Rock Album in 2005.

"This album is about feelings," Green Day front man Billie Joe Armstrong told *Rolling Stone*. "I didn't want to make a Rage Against the Machine record. I wanted to make an album of heartfelt songs."

With the situation in Iraq growing worse by the day and the administration's sluggish response to Hurricane Katrina, many teens and twentysomethings turned to *American Idiot* to vent their frustrations at their political leaders. As Jon Pareles wrote in the *New York Times*, "*American Idiot* did what punk does best: it channeled frustration."

The album sold in the millions, and the subsequent tour grew to outrageous proportions. By the time the band plotted out its next run of dates through Europe in the summer, it was one of the biggest draws on earth. "Punk sometimes has this defeatist attitude where you can't expand," Armstrong told *Entertainment Weekly*. "I look at a band like U2 that started out more or less as a punk band but kept expanding and wound up being one of the biggest bands in the world. And I think it's okay to want that."

To help quell the overwhelming demand for tickets in the U.K., Green Day booked two back-to-back shows at the immense National Bowl. Across two days, they would perform before around 130,000 fans. To put that in perspective, they had played in front of 5,000 people at the Brixton Academy in London just six months earlier. These mega-shows were far and away the biggest of their career and represented a high-water mark for mid-2000s rock 'n' roll as a true cultural force.

As Nick Ruskell put it in his review of the show in *Kerrang!*, "You're watching something that's going to go down in rock 'n' roll history as the moment when Green Day stopped being a huge-selling band and became *the* band of this generation."

A red-hued sun sets low over the National Bowl, just an hour-long car ride away from the heart of London. Overhead, the dramatic sounds of "Also

SET LIST

American Idiot

Jesus of Suburbia

Holiday

Are We the Waiting

St. Jimmy

Longview

Hitchin' a Ride

Brain Stew

Jaded

Knowledge

Basket Case

She

King for a Day

Shout

Wake Me Up When September Ends

Minority

Maria

Boulevard of Broken Dreams

We Are the Champions

Good Riddance (Time of Your Life)

MUSICIANS

Billie Joe Armstrong: Vocals/Guitar

Mike Dirnt: Bass

Tré Cool: Drums

Jason White: Guitar

Jason Freese: Keyboards

Ronnie Blake: Trumpet

Mike Pelino: Guitar

Sprach Zarathustra" from *2001: A Space Odyssey* lends a sense of drama to the occasion. Down below, 65,000 fans chant the name of the band they've waited all day to see. "Green Day! Green Day! Green Day!"

As "Also Sprach Zarathustra" reaches its crescendo, the men of Green Day walk out in front of the massive crowd dressed in matching black short-sleeved shirts with distinctive ties. Armstrong darts to the front of the stage, hops on top of his speaker monitor and puts his hands on his hips like Superman, letting the screams of adulation wash over him. To his left, bassist Mike Dirnt adopts a similar posture, while Tré Cool hams it up behind on the drums.

The recording ceases and Armstrong begins whacking out a few off-kilter notes on his guitar that transform into the opening riff of the song "American Idiot." The fans closest to the stage surge forward as the band whips them into a full punk rock frenzy, inciting them to "do the propaganda." When the solo hits, Armstrong and Dirnt cross paths, running to opposite wings of the stage, raging away on the track's upbeat rhythm. They jump, they shout and they bang away on their instruments with reckless abandon.

"All riiiiiiight Englaaaaaand!" Armstrong screams. "Are you guys ready to sing along?" he asks. "I want you to sing so loud that every fucking redneck in America can hear ya tonight, alright?" While they don't reach across the Atlantic, the English crowd shouts the final verse with a tremendous fury that's punctuated by an explosion of pyro at song's end.

The next number is another sing-along and carries a lot of weight for Armstrong. "For 'Jesus of Suburbia,' when people are singing it back to you, they're not just reflecting the thing about the song you're wrapped up in, but it's also what their lives are wrapped up in too," he explained in the concert film *Bullet in a Bible*. "It's about all the emotional baggage that you come with and that you finally have an outlet for. That's what 'Jesus of Suburbia' is to me and when it's reflected back at you by 65,000 people, it's a feeling you can't even describe."

The band pumps through a bevy of *American Idiot* songs, including the caustic "Holiday," the grandiose "Are We the Waiting" and the warp-speed "St. Jimmy," before playing old favorites like "Longview," "Brain Stew" and "Basket Case."

For a cover of Operation Ivy's "Knowledge," Armstrong brings up a group of teenagers to perform. He asks the guitarist if he's ever been laid, and when the young punk shakes his head, Armstrong responds, "Well, you're gonna get laid tonight!" After the three young musicians finish their ramshackle take on the song, Armstrong playfully shouts, "You were shit. Get off my stage!" then gifts the guitarist with his instrument.

For "King for a Day," the band brings out a full horn section while they whoop it up in an assortment of funny hats. Armstrong is wearing a regal red crown and cape, Dirnt is rocking an oversized foam cowboy hat and Cool is keeping time in a pink, ruffled bonnet. The fun, carefree vibe is carried over into a mad dash cover of the Isley Brothers' "Shout" and then comes to a screeching halt as they slip into the dramatic ballad "Wake Me Up When September Ends."

> *I want you to sing so loud that every fucking redneck in America can hear ya tonight, alright?*

The main set closes with a riotous rendition of "Minority," after which the band departs the stage and the crowd stomps and screams for more. They return and bust out the *International Superhits!* single "Maria," before breaking into the opening chords to "Boulevard of Broken Dreams" and a bombastic cover of Queen's "We Are the Champions." With their triumph secured, the rest of the band heads for the wings, leaving just Armstrong and his worn-down tobacco sunburst Gibson Les Paul Jr. alone in the spotlight.

The front man walks down a flight of stairs to the very lip of the massive stage, and with all eyes on him, plucks out the intro to "Good Riddance (Time of Your Life)." The audience hangs onto his every word, singing it back at twice the volume. After a final dramatic strum from his guitar, a steady blast of fireworks goes screaming into the air. His bandmates jump down to wave goodnight to the adoring English crowd.

"This was the perfect show," BBC Radio DJ Jo Whiley wrote in the *Daily Mail*. "To play Milton Keynes Bowl and own it, to fill the space completely, was pretty impressive." For those lucky enough to have been there, it was the time of their lives.

HONORABLE MENTION
Live 8 at Hyde Park
London, England (July 2)

A live music extravaganza the likes of which may never be seen again, Live 8 was the spiritual successor to the 1984 charity blowout Live Aid. With shows staged on almost every continent, in places like Philadelphia, Berlin, Paris, Rome, Moscow, Johannesburg, Tokyo and Barrie, Canada, it was truly a global event. It was in Hyde Park in London where the biggest highlights took place. Kicking off with a duet of "Sgt. Pepper's Lonely Heart's Club Band" between Paul McCartney and Bono, the lineup was as stacked as any that's ever been assembled, featuring performances by Elton John, Mariah Carey, R.E.M., Snoop Dogg, Sting, The Killers, The Who, Annie Lennox and Madonna. The most galvanizing moment came later in the evening when the classic lineup of Pink Floyd—Roger Waters, David Gilmour, Richard Wright and Nick Mason—appeared onstage together and performed for the first time in almost 25 years.

2006

Daft Punk
THE EMPIRE POLO FIELDS—INDIO, CA
APRIL 29

THE TECHNICOLOR PYRAMID

It's completely dark in the Sahara Tent. The air crackles with electricity. Depeche Mode has just finished their headlining performance on the Coachella main stage and now, at 11:00 p.m., 40,000 people are packed in like sardines underneath a covered structure that's only designed to hold a quarter of that number.

The French EDM duo Daft Punk hasn't performed live in the United States since 1999. Every year, Coachella dangled increasingly tantalizing offers in front of their robot-helmeted faces, and every year they turned them down. Daft Punk reigned as the most requested act on the vibrant, all-important festival message boards.

"I got four calls a week about Daft Punk and my job was just to tell people, 'No,'" booking agent Gerry Gerrard told me. "They told me, 'Playing live is not what we do. We are producers. We work in the studio. We will never play live.'"

For the 2006 iteration of Coachella, the folks at Goldenvoice, the company that runs the festival, made one last pitch: over $300,000 for a single set of music. It was a crazy sum, especially for a non-headliner, but the Hail Mary worked: Daft Punk accepted. Still, there was a catch.

Breaking from festival industry conventions, they wanted most of the money up front. If Guy-Manuel de Homem-Christo and Thomas Bangalter were going to come out of seclusion, they were going to do it with a bang. They wanted to give people something they'd never seen before, and they needed the funds to make it happen.

"For Coachella, they would advance just 10% as a deposit. Take it or leave it, no negotiations," Gerrard explained. "To [Coachella organizer] Paul Tollett's credit he kept advancing them more and more and more until by the time the show happened, I think they had 80% of the fee. They spent every penny of it on that show."

"The whole goal was to make the greatest show on earth," Michaelangelo Matos, author of *The Underground Is Massive: How Electronic Dance Music Conquered America*, told me. "What Daft Punk did was weave together every single technological, visual doodad they could get their fingers on and they put it altogether."

No expense was spared as Daft Punk all but drained the world's supply of LED lights to create their technologically innovative new set piece. Everyone was kept in the dark about what they were building, even members of their own team. If you wanted to see it, you needed to be in that tent.

Five notes ring out over the chatter of the crowd. Da-da-dah-doo-dum. If you've seen the film *Close Encounters of the Third Kind*, you recognize them instantly. The sequence rings out again as the audiences cheers wildly.

The lights in the tent come up enough to reveal the outline of the two robots standing side by side in the middle of a gigantic black pyramid. The sound of a vocoder breaks through the applause and a blue light emanates from out from behind them. Two words repeat themselves in a digital garble: "Robot" and "Human."

The pace quickens. The syncopated rhythm of a high-hat tick-tick-ticks into place. The lights multiply. Daft Punk become more and more exposed until finally, the cacophony is brought to order with a segue into their song "Robot Rock."

"Contrary to popular belief they don't just push play," Paul Hahn, the head of Daft Punk's production company, told *Spin*. Standing in front of them, without being able to see their faces or their hands, it's easy to get that impression, but there's a hell of a lot happening onstage. Those helmets aren't just for show. Loaded with video monitors and microphones, they're used by the Robots to communicate with one another and manipulate the performance.

At their fingertips sits a whole range of virtual synths and Minimoogs powered by a set of computers situated out of view. What seems like a completely scripted program—there are a set list and a multitude or preprogramed audio and visual cues—is a very human performance, marked with moments of subtlety, spontaneity and improvisation.

"It's . . . like a movie in that you focus on an experience rather than the ego of the performer," Bangalter said to *Spin*. "It's not just performing and creating music and images that makes the show, it's God in the middle of [40,000] people."

As they say, God is in the details, and none are too small to escape the notice of Daft Punk. With so many new toys to play with, the duo don't try to blow the audience away in one shot. The full power of the Pyramid—the overall design is an homage to the famous P-Funk Mothership set used by George Clinton while in Parliament Funkadelic—only become realized as the 75-minute set wears on.

SET LIST

Robot Rock / Oh Yeah
Touch It / Technologic
Television Rules the Nation / Crescendolls
Too Long / Stream Machine
Around the World / Harder, Better, Faster, Stronger
Too Long
Face to Face / Short Circuit
One More Time / Aerodynamic
Aerodynamic Beats / Forget about the World
The Prime Time of Your Life / Brainwasher / Rollin' & Scratchin' / Alive
Da Funk / Daftendirekt
Superheroes / Human After All / Rock'n Roll

Before 2006, electronic dance music acts struggled to break through in America because they couldn't meet audience expectations of what a live music event should be. "What you had were people that were expecting a show," Matos said. "They thought, you're at a concert, you're not at a party. That's a significant difference. Dance music was always about parties; it wasn't about concerts. What Daft Punk did was they made it a fucking concert. That being said, it still was a party. You could sit back and watch the thing and be entertained, or you could get up there and dance with everybody. It was like being at the best club in the world."

MUSICIANS

Thomas Bangalter: DJ
Guy-Manuel de Homem-Christo: DJ

As they break into "Technologic," some of the more impressive features of the Pyramid reveal themselves. The entire set glows red as thousands of LEDs come to life, pulsing and scrolling in eye-widening patterns. The motif shifts to a blazing white as they pump up the crowd with "Around the World." It then erupts into a mania of multi-colored swirling light, sending the audience into an absolute frenzy, before Daft Punk hits them with "Harder, Better, Faster, Stronger."

The party is raging at full force now. Every sense of the human body is activated as an array of lasers, 3-D projections and rib-cage–crushing bass tones obliterate your cerebral cortex. Everywhere you look, people are either dancing with complete abandon or are looking to one another with slack-jawed expressions of wonder.

> *They made it a fucking concert. That being said, it still was a party. It was like being at the best club in the world.*

"There were some of the best video people in the world standing next to me just going, 'How the hell did they do that?'" Gerrard said. "They were doing stuff with visuals that no one had ever done before. It was just one of the greatest things I've ever seen."

With midnight having come and gone, Daft Punk dive into the last song of the night, "Human After All." When it ends, the Pyramid becomes a singular, white glowing object. The two robots face one another, applaud the crowd below them and raise a finger in the air.

The impact of this show cannot be overstated. It proved once and for all that EDM could work as a live, concert-going experience, setting the example for artists like Skrillex, Deadmau5 and Major Lazer. As Neal Rahman wrote in *Magnetic Magazine*, "Daft Punk's 2006 Coachella set is to the explosion of dance music in the 21st century what the assassination of Archduke Franz Ferdinand of Austria is to World War I."

HONORABLE MENTION
Sleater-Kinney at the Crystal Ballroom
Portland, OR (August 12)

After a twelve-year run as one of the most exciting rock groups in America, around 2006, the Portland power trio Sleater-Kinney decided to take a break. The endless cycle of new album/tour/new album/tour had left Corin Tucker, Carrie Brownstein and Janet Weiss physically drained and emotionally exhausted. They announced they were going on hiatus and finished up with a pair of hometown gigs in Portland. As Carrie Brownstein remembered in her memoir, *Hunger Makes Me a Modern Girl*, "We wanted to go out in a way that acknowledged our history, and that was also respectful to ourselves and to the fans. But we didn't want to feel like a museum piece." Pearl Jam's Eddie Vedder introduced Sleater-Kinney, who then dove headlong into a monster-sized show that culled the best tracks from their most recent record, *The Woods*; their 1997 breakthrough, *Dig Me Out*; and everything in between. "When we finished the show, there wasn't any real closure," Brownstein remembered. "It just felt like it always does, the three of us trying to pass something on to the crowd, hoping it was good enough."

#1 Single of the Year:
"Irreplaceable"
Beyoncé

2007

#1 Album of the Year:
Daughtry
Daughtry

Led Zeppelin
THE O2 ARENA—LONDON, ENGLAND
DECEMBER 10

ACHILLES LAST STAND

Band reunions are fraught with more tension and hang-ups than the outside observer can fathom. Still, they've become one of the most dependable cash cows in the music industry in the 21st century. Bands just don't stay broken up anymore. The dwindling resources that can be expected from album royalties, combined with the staggering profits to be gained by playing a short string of dates on the road or the festival circuit, has led to even the most impossible reunions.

In 2016, I saw Guns N' Roses fill a football stadium with Axl Rose and Slash snake-dancing back to back, as well as the reborn Misfits with both Glenn Danzig and Jerry Only glaring menacingly into each other's eyes at Riot Fest in Chicago. The year before that I witnessed the renewed Pacific Northwest rockers Sleater-Kinney twice. The year before that I saw the greatest rap duo of all-time, OutKast, come out of retirement for a gig at the Sasquatch Festival in the Gorge. Each of those events seemed totally out of the question even five years beforehand.

For all the improbable band reunions that have taken place over the last quarter-century, the biggest by a mile was Led Zeppelin in 2007. The living members of the British rock group—guitarist Jimmy Page, singer Robert Plant and bassist John Paul Jones—had tried on a few different occasions following the death of their drummer, John Bonham, in 1980 (most notably and abysmally at Live Aid in 1985), but it never worked out.

Maybe without Bonham and his singular, thunderous percussion to drive the whole enterprise forward, Led Zeppelin couldn't take flight anymore. Plant, more than Jones and Page, seemed eager to put his cocksure Golden God image behind him. It seemed like Zeppelin's time had come and gone.

Then tragedy struck. On October 29, 2006, Atlantic Records president Ahmet Ertegun was backstage watching the Rolling Stones play a benefit gig for President Bill Clinton's charity foundation when he fell and hit his head on the concrete floor. Ertegun had given Zeppelin the most lucrative recording contract in music history up to that point in 1968 and was one of their fiercest advocates throughout the '70s.

At first, it seemed like the 83-year-old label head would make it through the incident okay. Then his condition took a turn for the worse. He died on December 14, 2006.

Immediately, talk began of staging a tribute concert in his honor. Ertegun had signed and fostered the careers of many influential artists, from Crosby, Stills, Nash & Young and Ray Charles to Aretha Franklin and Cream. Still, there was one name that overshadowed them all and the question had to be asked: Was it possible that Led Zeppelin would take part?

Jimmy Page was on board. As the founder, producer and latter-day caretaker of the band's legacy, he pushed the band hard for a reunion on multiple oc-

SET LIST

Good Times, Bad Times

Ramble On

Black Dog

In My Time of Dying

For Your Life

Trampled Under Foot

Nobody's Fault but Mine

No Quarter

Since I've Been Loving You

Dazed and Confused

Stairway to Heaven

The Song Remains the Same

Misty Mountain Hop

Kashmir

Whole Lotta Love

Rock and Roll

MUSICIANS

Robert Plant: Vocals

Jimmy Page: Guitar

John Paul Jones: Bass/Keyboards

Jason Bonham: Drums

of the 20,000 tickets. To borrow a phrase from Mel Bush, the man who promoted Zeppelin's five-night run at Earl's Court in 1975, it was "demand unprecedented in the history of rock music."

The press was all over the concert. You could hardly turn on a television or walk past a newsstand without seeing the names and faces of Page, Plant and Jones. The eyes of the world were on them, waiting to see if they'd take flight or fall flat once again.

Out amongst the crowd everyone is having the same conversation. "Holy shit, is this really about to happen?" Suddenly, the giant screen up front comes to life. It's a clip from 1973 of a broadcaster reporting on a stadium concert Led Zeppelin were about to undertake in Tampa Bay, Florida, that would break the Beatles' Shea Stadium attendance record. Inside the O2, everyone shouts with joy at the mere mention of the band's name. Paul McCartney, who is in the front row, smirks at the dated footage.

As soon as the broadcast ends, the room goes black. The only light visible is the galaxy of cell phones held skyward. The clicking of drum sticks tapping together sounds out over the whoops and hollers, and then bang! Two sharp jolts. Bang! Bang! Another set of jolts joined by a pair of intense flashes of yellow light. The lights come up and there they are in the flesh: Led fucking Zeppelin.

The selection for the first song could not be more perfect: "Good Times, Bad Times." Track one, side one, from their self-titled debut album. Plant struts around the stage, crooning his lines about being shown "what it means to be a man" in the "days of his youth." To his right, Page remains the definition of cool in a long black trench coat and dark sunglasses, making duck faces as he slams into the chords of the song's main riff. To Plant's left is Jones, laying down

casions. John Paul Jones was also game. Jason Bonham quickly signed up to honor his father. The only wild card was Plant, who was in the midst of his biggest success yet as a solo artist.

He had just released an album titled *Raising Sand* with country singer Alison Krauss, which became the kind of critical darling he had never enjoyed before during his solo career. At the Grammys that year, *Raising Sand* took home five awards, including the top prize for album of the year. Was he willing to put all that aside and revisit his past? Under a different set of circumstances, the answer likely would have been no, but Plant held a dear place in his heart for Ertegun.

"They were great people, Ahmet and his widow, Mica," Plant said. "When she approached me, I told her I'd do anything for her, for Ahmet."

As soon as the news broke that Led Zeppelin was getting back together to perform a full concert at the newly constructed O2 Arena in London, demand shot through the stratosphere. To this day, the event holds the Guinness record for "Highest Demand for Tickets to One Concert." A staggering 20 million people signed up online for the chance to purchase one

the rhythmic framework on his bass strings.

If we're being honest, all Zeppelin has to do is show up, know their parts and stay reasonably in tune and everyone would come away thinking it's a triumph. The band isn't interested in earning attendance credit, however. For two hours, they play like their legacy is on the line.

A compromise that led to Plant agreeing to take the stage is that most of the self-indulgence from their 1970s shows—like the blues and rock medleys thrown in the middle of "Whole Lotta Love," the 45-minute renditions of "Dazed and Confused" and the 20-minute drum solo on "Moby Dick"—is excised.

For two hours, they play like their legacy is on the line.

Led Zeppelin stick to playing the songs as they were arranged on the album, and frankly it's a wise choice for this occasion.

The energy in the crowd hardly ever flags, with the Zeppelin moving from megahit to megahit, reminding everyone why they were considered one of the most potent forces of live music ever to mount a stage. Though Plant's voice is a little deeper and Page's guitar playing a little more ragged, the energy, the volume and the sheer force of the music blasting out of the speakers remains the same.

The big question going into the show was, "Would they play 'Stairway to Heaven'?" Plant had gone on record multiple times about how much he hated the band's biggest hit. He referred to it as "that wedding song" and swore that he would never perform it again live. But then, 11 songs into the set, Page begins softly picking out the song's first few notes on his massive double-neck guitar.

The crowd goes out of its mind. Maybe they thought that by tucking "Stairway" into the middle of the set that it might lose some of its potency, but that's clearly not the case. The version they perform sounds far grittier than it ever had in the past.

It's possible that Page has his distortion pedals set too high, but the symmetry is perfect. The passage of time seems to have weathered the sound of the song, much as it has the musicians, yet neither has been robbed of their potency.

The climax is tremendously cathartic. Everywhere in the crowd, people look to their left and right so that the person next to them can confirm that what they had just seen had actually happened. The applause goes on for a while. Plant looks skyward and simply says, "Hey, Ahmet, we did it!"

HONORABLE MENTION
Amy Winehouse at Shepherd's Bush Empire
London, England (May 29)

In stark contrast to her storm-threatened set a month later at Glastonbury, this relatively intimate gig finds Amy Winehouse at the top of her game. The beehive-adorned jazz/soul singer's latest album, *Back to Black*, was lighting up the charts, propelled by the singles "Rehab," "You Know I'm No Good" and "Back to Black." For now at least, she relished in the spotlight. Kicking off with "Addicted," Winehouse dove deeply into her signature, sultry, jazz-inspired oeuvre, songs like "Hey Little Rich Girl," "Love Is a Losing Game" and an awesome mashup of "He Can Only Hold Her" and Lauryn Hill's "Doo-Wop (That Thing)." In between numbers, Winehouse reveals herself to be a bit shy and somewhat cowed by the evening's events. When she sings, she reveals herself as a total master of dynamics, mixing a loose, twangy delivery on the verses with incredible bombast during the choruses. It's a signature performance from a singular artist.

2008

Foo Fighters
WEMBLEY STADIUM—LONDON, ENGLAND
JUNE 7

FOOS FIGHTING IN LONDON

"The first time we played Wembley at the Live Earth event, I joked to the crowd we'd be back to play multiple nights," Foo Fighters front man Dave Grohl told *The Sun*. "No way did I think it would come true—I was fucking kidding!"

The new Wembley Stadium is a massive place. Billed as "The Venue of Legends," it's not the same structure that Queen and Michael Jackson rocked in the 1980s. This brand-new, significantly enlarged, state-of-the-art facility opened its doors in 2007. Capable of seating 90,000 people, the new Wembley is the biggest soccer stadium in England and the second biggest in Europe. To fill it once would be an amazing feather in the cap of any entertainer. To fill it twice on consecutive nights is an unbelievable achievement.

As Grohl mentioned, the Foos' first foray at Wembley was for the Live Earth charity event that took place in 2007. That concert featured one of the most impressive collections of music superstars ever assembled: Madonna, Beastie Boys and Metallica, just to name a few. It was a watershed moment for the band, opening Grohl's eyes to the real power of their popularity.

"We showed up that day to Wembley, and we thought, 'Oh, God, how can we possibly entertain this size with this many people?'" he said. "I looked at the lineup and saw that we were after Metallica, we were after the Chili Peppers and the Beastie Boys. . . . I realized that we had five songs and 25 minutes, so we'll play the five songs that everyone knows the chorus to, and I'll get them to sing along with me. And in those 25 minutes I became the front man. And every concert since then has been a little bit easier."

Two months after that gig, the Foos released their sixth album, *Echoes, Silence, Patience & Grace*, to a slew of positive reviews and strong commercial sales. Anchored by singles like "The Pretender," "Long Road to Ruin" and Grohl's emotionally charged tribute to his Nirvana bandmate Kurt Cobain, "Let it Die," the record was heralded as one of the best releases that year. It received five Grammy nominations, taking home the Best Rock Album prize and the Best Hard Rock Performance award for "The Pretender."

Shortly after *Echoes, Silence, Patience & Grace* was released, a tour was booked, taking the band across North America before hitting some of the bigger venues in Europe. When it came time to pick the location for the London stop, the Foo Fighters' booking agent rolled the dice and secured Wembley Stadium. There was a lot of tension within the band and its management about their ability to sell the place out, so they put the tickets on sale six months ahead of the show.

To their utter amazement, they sold every single ticket in just a few hours. A second show was quickly announced, which sold out a few days later. 172,000 Londoners put down their money to see the Foo

SET LIST

The Pretender
Times Like These
No Way Back
Cheer Up, Boys (Your Make Up is Running)
Learn to Fly
This Is a Call
Long Road to Ruin
Breakout
Stacked Actors
Skin and Bones
Big Me
Marigold
My Hero
Cold Day in the Sun
Let It Die
Everlong
Monkey Wrench
All My Life
Rock and Roll
Ramble On
Best of You

Fighters, smashing the new Wembley's attendance record to bits.

When asked about the feat in the weeks leading up to the gigs, Grohl kept up his patented self-deprecating posture. "We have brainwashed your country into thinking we're good enough to play two nights at a stadium," he told *Kerrang!* "I don't know what to expect! But I do know that it's going to be our biggest fucking show ever!"

A guitar that sounds like a billion pissed off killer bees comes hurtling out of the speakers. Dave Grohl, the man behind the cacophony, emerges on the large, round stage set up in the middle of the soccer pitch. He races out onto a catwalk that extends more than a hundred feet into the sea of people, booting a beach ball along the way.

Grohl makes it all the way to the end of the long runway, strumming that single chord the entire time. He stands there with a big smile on his face, drink-ing in the sight, before running back to join his bandmates. Taylor Hawkins taps out a four-count on his hi-hat as Grohl reaches for his microphone.

"Keep you in the dark / You know they all pretend," he drawls.

The audience roars in recognition of the opening lyrics of the Foos' most recent single, "The Pretender." The quiet, minor-key mood of the track's opening moments shatters when the band kicks into the song proper. A mosh pit whirls to life in front of the stage. From the stage, it looks like a scene taken from Dante's *Inferno*, a writhing twist of smashed-together bodies shouting, dancing and waving toward their heroes as they macerate their brains with intense, conjoined head-banging.

Grohl smiles down at the thrashing taking place in front of him, whips his hair back and pushes even harder. "C'mon!" he screams as the Foos thunder away behind. "The Pretender" segues seamlessly into "Times Like These," before giving way to the fist-in-the-air rager "No Way Back."

The set design is impressive. It stands around 100 feet tall and is crowned on top by an LED video display that's arranged like a vertical set of shutter shades. The stage itself rotates to give everyone in the massive venue a proper look at the band throughout the night.

A guitar that sounds like a billion pissed off killer bees.

"HEYYYYY!" Grohl screams after playing "Learn to Fly." He loudly burps into the microphone and asks, "Hi, Wembley, how are you?" The crowd roars. "Tonight, I promise you, we're gonna do something we've never done before at a Foo Fighters show and it's gonna blow your fucking shit right out the door!" he goes on. "This is not only the biggest fucking place we've ever played in this country, this isn't only the biggest fucking crowd we've ever played to, tonight, this is gonna be the show that we're talking about for the next 20 years of our fucking lives."

The show rolls on. The band mixes newer selections from its latest record with older, crowd-pleasing favorites. Nine songs in, they swap out electric guitars for a mini-acoustic set made up of "Skin and Bones," "Big Me," "Marigold," "My Hero" and "Cold Day in the Sun." After that the amplifiers roar back to life and the mosh pit swirls once again.

The main set closes with a charged-up take on "All My Life." The Foo Fighters leave, the lights go down and the stage turns to a brilliant cobalt blue. Everyone in Wembley is chanting in one unified voice, "We want more! We want more!"

Mercifully, the Foo Fighters acquiesce to their pleas. Grohl steps up to the microphone and scans the crowd, drinking in their applause. "First of all, thank you very much. You guys fucking rule," he says. "Playing here at Wembley Stadium . . . " He tries to finish his thought, but the words catch in his throat. He pulls back and ducks his head. When he looks up there are tears in his eyes. "It's an honor."

Grohl keeps talking as two figures emerge from the wings. The one clad in an olive-green jacket takes hold of a sunburst Gibson Les Paul. The other, decked out in all black, straps on a flaming orange bass guitar. "We'd like to invite a couple of very special guests," Grohl says. "Mr. Jimmy Page and Mr. John Paul Jones of Led Zeppelin!"

The crowd loses its ever-loving mind for the two icons. Grohl hops behind the drums, allowing Hawkins to take over on lead vocals. After a quick look around at one another, the foursome kick into Zeppelin's classic "Rock and Roll." Everyone is on their feet. Grohl is bashing the hell out of the kit with a massive smile on his faces as Page and Jones bring the dormant hit back to life. Before the next song Hawkins and Grohl switch places, then everyone launches into "Ramble On" off *Led Zeppelin II*. When it ends, the four men hug and pose for the crowd, and Page and Jones disappear back into the shadows.

"Welcome to the greatest day of my whole, entire life," Grohl says after they depart. The rest of the band slowly reemerges during a cathartic take on "Best of You" to close out the show. Green and red fireworks explode in the sky above.

HONORABLE MENTION

Leonard Cohen at the Playhouse Fredericton, New Brunswick, Canada (May 11)

On May 11, 2008, one of the premiere singer-songwriters of the 20th century staged one of the most stunning comebacks in music history. Leonard Cohen hadn't performed in front of an audience in about 15 years when he arrived at the 700-seat Playhouse in far-flung New Brunswick. In that time away, he retreated as far from the spotlight as any former star had before, becoming a Buddhist monk at the Mount Baldy Zen Center in Los Angeles. Eventually he started writing and recording again, and by the end of the 2000s he decided to return to the stage. The small crowd was treated to two different sets of music as well as a four-song encore. Cohen was spellbinding. Backed by a nine-person band, Cohen crooned his way through a 20-song set-list made up of beloved classics like "First We Take Manhattan," "Bird on a Wire" and "Hallelujah." Of his first foray in front of a crowd, Cohen was effusive. "I was very grateful for the warmth of the audience, the competence of the musicians and the coherence of the group," he told *Rolling Stone*.

2009

U2
CROKE PARK—DUBLIN, IRELAND
JULY 27

360° OF AN IRISH ROCK BAND

Nothing can prepare you for the first time you see "The Claw." Standing at a massive 167 feet tall, it's the largest, most awe-inspiring stage ever built in the history of concert touring. With its four long legs, halo-like outer stage and round inner-stage, it looks like an alien monster that might come to life and stomp out all the thousands of fans splayed out below.

By 2009, U2 were the biggest band on the planet. No one was more popular, and no one had greater drawing power. With that kind of cache, the Irish rockers went for the unprecedented, splurging on a stage show that matched their status. They wanted more height, more lights, better sound—the loudest system ever created—and more spectacle than anything anyone had ever seen before, and they got it.

The vision for the design sprang from the mind of lead singer Bono. "I got these knives and some forks, and a grapefruit, and started mucking around, placing the knives and forks over the grapefruit, trying to build this thing in my head," he said. "I did it on the breakfast table, much to the dismay of my family, who thought I'd lost it."

U2 didn't commission just one of these monsters. For their two-year, 360 Tour, the Irish rock band had three "Claws" built so that it could leap-frog from one city to the next without skipping a beat. To give you an idea of the sheer size of the 200-ton behemoths, it took a fleet of 200 eighteen-wheelers at a cost of $750,000 a day to transport all the components around the world.

Many wondered what the point of all this was. Why put yourself through that kind of logistic nightmare for a two-hour rock concert? "Somebody asked us . . . 'Do you need this stuff?'" bassist Adam Clayton said. "Part of show business is you have to change people's perceptions. You have to find ways to make the songs touch people more, to disorientate people so they're more open to being touched."

"I've always been obsessed with the things that separate you from the audience," Bono added. "I've been in small clubs seeing bands and I've felt a million miles away as there is no connection, no relationship, so it's not always about the size of the venue. It's about how you communicate. That was the breakthrough, realizing that. It's about trying to get in the face of your audience."

The basic concept of the show, as one could surmise from the name, was for U2 to perform in the round. It's something they had wanted to do for years, and came with the bonus of fitting thousands more people into massive football and soccer stadiums, breaking attendance records nearly everywhere they went. By the end of the run, U2 had accumulated a jaw-dropping $730 million in total ticket sales. Seven million people came out to see one of the 110 shows. It's hard to believe that anyone will ever be able to top that mark.

SET LIST

Breathe

No Line on the Horizon

Get on Your Boots

Magnificent

Beautiful Day

New Year's Day

I Still Haven't Found What I'm Looking For

Stay (Faraway, So Close!)

Unknown Caller

The Unforgettable Fire

City of Blinding Lights

Vertigo

I'll Go Crazy if I Don't Go Crazy Tonight

Sunday Bloody Sunday

Pride (In The Name of Love)

MLK

Walk On

Where the Streets Have No Name

One

Bad

Ultra Violet (Light My Way)

With or Without You

Moment of Surrender

MUSICIANS

Bono: Vocals

The Edge: Guitar

Adam Clayton: Bass

Larry Mullen Jr.: Drums

While every stop on the tour has been spectacular, there's something special about seeing U2 perform on their home turf. In addition to the mass of Irish fans who turned out for the shows, people have flown in from across the world—Brazil, Romania, Texas and everywhere in between—to catch this gig. "Playing Dublin isn't even a musical event," Bono said in the months before U2's three-night residency in their hometown. "It's a tribal event. A sociological experiment like a wedding."

The lights go down in the stadium, and the soundman pushes play on David Bowie's classic hit "Space Oddity." U2 walks single-file out of the backstage area and then ducks down out of view into the belly of "The Claw." Mullen emerges first. The drummer makes his way over to his kit and begins the show alone, beating out the opening solo on "Breathe." Moments later, The Edge and Adam Clayton join him to provide rhythm and melody. Finally, Bono strolls out in a patchwork leather jacket and rose-colored sunglasses, grabs hold of the microphone and screams, and the crowd explodes.

The show begins with four songs from U2's latest album, No Line on the Horizon. "Breathe" gives way to the title track, which is followed by the lead single, "Get on Your Boots," and then "Magnificent." It's not what you expect from a band of their size and stature, but U2 has faith in their audience's patience and is rewarded by waves of applause after each song.

The weather is distinctly Irish—gray, overcast and on the verge of raining—but everyone enjoys the fifth song, "Beautiful Day," all the same. Even with the loudest speaker system ever assembled, the conjoined power of 80,000 voices almost overwhelms the sound blasting out of The Claw when Bono reaches the "Touch me / Teach me" part of the song. After that, they break into "New Year's Day," followed by "I Still Haven't Found What I'm Looking For."

"Intimacy on a grand scale," Bono says midway through the show. "That's what we wanted." The sun is setting now, and the gray skies are turning black. The Claw is fully lit up, and a massive cone of LED lights descends from the top portion, nearly engulfing the band, as The Edge picks out the glistening intro notes to "The Unforgettable Fire."

The mood is heavy as Bono sings about the effects of the atomic bombings of Hiroshima and Nagasaki, and it remains that way through "City of Blinding Light." The spell is finally broken when they kick into one of their most blatant and joyous rock songs, "Vertigo." The audience revels in their role shouting back the Spanish words "Hola" and "Dónde está" as Bono's voice and the Edge's guitar pin them to the backs of their seats during the choruses.

The band is hitting its stride, and the qualities

that make Bono such an indelible front man become increasingly evident. While he can't match the energy and enthusiasm he had in his younger days like at Red Rocks or Live Aid, there's an indescribable magnetism to the way he saunters across the stage and engages the audience. You simply can't tear your eyes off him.

For the penultimate song of the main set, Bono commands someone out of view to "Turn my lights down" and then implores the crowd to hold their phones up to "turn this place into the Milky Way." The gargantuan stage is completely dark. The mass out in the field and in the stands blasts the band with thousands of flashes of tiny light. "Wow! That is a really beautiful sight that we will never, ever forget," he remarks as a segue into "One."

> ## Playing Dublin isn't even a musical event. It's a tribal event.

The song is one of the most popular selections in U2's catalog, a wedding day classic, and the crowd relishes in singing along to every word. As "One" ends, the band closes its set with an obscure but cherished gem, "Bad," which Bono croons while clutching an Irish flag someone has tossed onto the stage.

The lights go out, it's dark and the audience steadies itself for the encore they can feel coming. When U2 returns, Bono is decked out in a leather jacket fixed with red lasers, which shoot in different directions. A microphone that looks like a steering wheel drops from The Claw, and he grabs a hold of it and kicks into "Ultra Violet (Light My Way)." After that, "With or Without You," and then finally "Moment of Surrender." It's a three-song explosion of rock 'n' roll catharsis that leaves jaws on the floor and hearts filled with contentment.

"Thank you, God bless you," Bono says after wringing out the final "Oh, oh, ahhhhhh, oh, oh, oh" from the last song of the night. "Goodnight, Croke Park." The band, four tiny figures underneath a behemoth of scaffolding, lights and speakers, step forward, lock arms and take a bow. "Don't forget about us now."

HONORABLE MENTION

Lil Wayne and Young Money at the Toyota Pavilion Scranton, PA (August 9)

Between 2007 and 2009, Lil Wayne reigned as the most lyrically adept and exciting rapper in the world. Verse-to-verse, no one could touch him. You can hear it in his smash, No. 1 album *Tha Carter III*, but the full breadth of his ability becomes evident when you dig into his mixtapes, like *Da Drought 3* and *No Ceilings*. In 2009, Wayne hit the road alongside Jeezy, Soulja Boy and His Young Money labelmates Drake and Nicki Minaj for one of the most star-packed showcases of rap talent that decade. The entire show is a wild dance party, but Weezy's set—complete with fake guitar soloing, heavy pyro, scantily clad dancers and mega-hits like "A Milli," "Lollipop" and "Mrs. Officer"—packs the biggest punch. Drake tore his ACL just before the tour kicked off, so instead of delivering his own set, he aired out some of his early hits like "Best I Ever Had" during his mentor's performance, after being lowered onto the set via an elevator. The night ends with an all-hands-on-deck Michael Jackson tribute.

Arcade Fire
MADISON SQUARE GARDEN—NEW YORK, NY
AUGUST 5

OUT OF THE SUBURBS

There's a convivial feeling to Arcade Fire concerts that's quite unlike most other arena-sized rock shows. It's not by accident. The band actively conspires to create this atmosphere. They want you to have as good of a time as they do onstage. They want you to lose yourself in their music. They want you to free yourself from inhibition. They want you to sing, dance and stomp with your neighbor. They also sometimes want you to show up in costume.

"At every show there's always someone sitting in front of you who's like, 'Can you please not dance?'" Arcade Fire front man Win Butler explained to the audience during the band's second show at Madison Square Garden in 2010. "So politely say, 'It's very nice to meet you. I respect your personal space, but I'm trying to be at a fucking rock show!"

2010 was a milestone year for Arcade Fire. They enjoyed tremendous acclaim following the release of their debut album, *Funeral*, six years earlier but seemed to take a step back with their follow-up, *Neon Bible*. Looking to rebound, they retreated north to Quebec to record their next major project. The resultant album, *The Suburbs*, was an unmitigated triumph.

Audiences loved the band's bombastic arena rock sound, while it's themes about growing up in the staid confines of American suburbia resonated with scores of new fans and old diehards alike. The album shot up the charts, besting Eminem to become the number one record in the U.S. and Canada. It was a major coup for Arcade Fire—and all the rock defenders looking for someone to come along and prove that the genre still carried cultural cache. *The Suburbs* ultimately took home the prize for Album of the Year award at the Grammys.

"We are ambitious, and I think that the general mode of almost all art these days is pretty small-focused," Butler told *Pitchfork* shortly after the album came out. "I remember reading a book where the author was making fun of people who liked [Melville's] *Bartleby, the Scrivener* instead of *Moby Dick*—like favoring a well-crafted short story instead of his flawed, epic thing. But I think we're definitely much more of a *Moby Dick* kind of band, and a lot of bands just aren't."

It was that kind of ambition that led Arcade Fire to book back-to-back concerts at New York City's Madison Square Garden just two days after releasing their album. The idea that, in 2010, a modern rock group touring behind a new record could fill MSG on two different nights seemed ludicrous. But then Arcade Fire has never been a band to do anything small. The white whale was in their sights.

A little after 10 pm, the lights in the historic arena go down and the members of Arcade Fire assemble onstage. A solitary high-pitched synth note hums overhead. Jeremy Gara pounds on his snare

SET LIST

Ready to Start

Neighborhood #2 (Laika)

No Cars Go

Haiti

Empty Room

The Suburbs

Crown of Love

Rococo

Intervention

We Used to Wait

Neighborhood #3 (Power Out)

Rebellion (Lies)

Month of May

Keep the Car Running

Neighborhood #1 (Tunnels)

Sprawl II (Mountains Beyond Mountains)

Wake Up

MUSICIANS

Win Butler: Vocals/Guitar/Percussion

Régine Chassange: Vocals/Accordion/Keys/Drums

Will Butler: Synth/Guitar/Percussion

Tim Kingsbury: Bass

Jeremy Gara: Drums

Sarah Neufeld: Vocals/Violin

Owen Pallett: Violin

drum, and an array of soft yellow lights strobe in time with him. A few beats later and the rest of the band steps out and launches into the second track from their most recent work, "Ready to Start."

At around 6'4" and easily the most physically dominant presence onstage, Win Butler takes all the focus. He's an interesting personage to take in, with one side of his head completely shaved off and the other a flop of hair. He's wearing an ornate blue shirt buttoned up over his chest, with the sleeves rolled up above the elbow. He's here to work.

It's hard to convey how in sync all of the musicians sound stacked together. From a purely visual standpoint, seven people onstage can appear a little decadent. You start to question if this person or that person is necessary. Then the cacophony hits you in the chest and it becomes obvious that the sum is greater than its individual parts. Take away the strings or the second keyboard player and it wouldn't be the same.

The first song ends and the band shifts into "Neighborhood #2 (Laika)" from its first album, then moves on to "No Cars Go" off of *Neon Bible*. After that they dig into "Haiti," a wonderful showcase for the lithe voice and avant-garde dance moves of Régine

Chassange, Butler's wife and songwriting partner. All around, the stage is lit up in an intense shade of green as Chassange "woo oohs" and sashays in front of the microphone.

Near the end, "Haiti" devolves into a wall of amorphous noise, which Arcade Fire uses to shift into "Empty Room." Then Win takes a seat at the piano and plunks out the first chords of "The Suburbs." It's a beautiful, affecting song that brings to life so many memories of mundane surroundings that so many of us came of age in. The places where we "learned to drive." Where we ran through the yards around all those houses they built in the '70s.

The verses beg to be screamed out at full throat, and that's exactly what both Butler and the crowd do.

Win stays behind the piano for the next song, "Crown of Love," before picking up an acoustic guitar and introing "Rococo." Up to this point, everything has come across relatively straightforward. The band seems intent on delivering its songs as close as possible to the version that you hear on record. That all changes with "We Used to Wait." Here they start coming out of their shell a little bit.

Halfway through the song, Win abandons the stage, raises the microphone high over his head and wades deep into the general admission section below with a long red microphone cable trailing behind. At first, the fans make way for him, but as he gets to the first part of the bridge—"Now our lives are changing fast"—they start to clamor around, jumping up and down with the rhythm of the song. Somehow, he's able to extricate himself from the mass just in time to mount the railing and belt out the chorus: "Ooh, we used to wait!"

Four songs later the band ends the main set with "Keep the Car Running." They leave the stage, but then reemerge after a few minutes and slip into "Neighborhood #1 (Tunnels)," which ends with a maelstrom of confetti exploding over the heads of the audience. They launch into a tremendously rousing take on "Sprawl II (Mountains Beyond Mountains)," which finds Chassange stepping out front once again.

Midway through the song, the arrangement comes apart. In the back, seated at a keyboard, Win screams "Fuck it!" bringing everything to a halt. "This is live music," he explains. "Live as shit. Can't get any more live. It is so live that our drum machine fucked up. It's a beautiful song so we're gonna start from the fucking top and it's gonna be awesome." They do, and it is.

For the last number, the band pulls out the song that made people take notice of it in the first place six years back, "Wake Up." The song is as pure an anthem as anything recorded in the 21st century. The verses beg to be screamed out at full throat, and that's exactly what both Butler and the crowd do. When they reach the iconic "Whoa, oh" chorus, the roof practically blows off the place.

"Thank you," Butler says when it's over. "*Merci beaucoup*," Chassange adds. Before leaving the stage, the front man runs to the back, grabs a pair of tambourines with long yellow ribbons attached and flings them into the crowd, along with a set of drum sticks. They wave, they bow and then they leave.

HONORABLE MENTION
Metallica, Slayer, Megadeth and Anthrax at the Sonisphere Festival Sofia, Bulgaria (June 22)

In the summer of 2010, the "Big 4" of thrash metal—Metallica, Slayer, Megadeth and Anthrax—played together for the first time on a short tour through Europe. It was an event as unexpected as it was mind-blowing, with all four groups treating their denim-clad acolytes to an hours-long marathon of head-banging classics. For this one gig in Bulgaria, all four bands shared the stage during Metallica's set for a supercharged take on "Am I Evil?" by the British heavy metal group Diamond Head. "The reason we picked 'Am I Evil?' is because obviously playing a Metallica song would've seemed a little selfish," Metallica drummer Lars Ulrich explained to *Revolver*. "[Megadeth front man Dave] Mustaine and a bunch of these guys obviously knew the riff, too, and it just seemed like a logical choice." It was a galvanizing moment to say the least, something akin to the Mount Rushmore of Thrash coming to life in one ear-popping moment.

#1 Single of the Year:
"Rolling in the Deep"
Adele

2011

#1 Album of the Year:
21
Adele

Kanye West
THE EMPIRE POLO FIELDS—INDIO, CA
APRIL 17

HIS BEAUTIFUL DARK TWISTED COACHELLA COMEBACK

People love a good comeback story. It's why there are seven different *Rocky* movies. It's why grown men weep whenever *Rudy* comes on cable. It's why we rooted for LL Cool J when *Mama Said Knock You Out* came out in 1990, even though he specifically told us *not* to call it a comeback. We knew the score.

I submit for your approval one of the great musical redemption stories of the 21st century: the case of Kanye Omari West. This is the tale of a brash young artist who rose from the South Side of Chicago, grabbed the brass ring of pop superstardom and trashed it in a spectacular televised moment of unmitigated bone-headedness, the likes of which may never be seen again.

It was September 13, 2009, and MTV was hosting its annual Video Music Awards at Radio City Music Hall in New York City. Shakira and Taylor Lautner were about to hand out the award for Best Female Video. Many assumed that the Moon Man would go to Beyoncé for "Single Ladies," which was viewed hundreds of millions of times and touched a nerve in the zeitgeist. When the envelope was ripped open, Beyoncé's name was nowhere to be found. Instead, Taylor Swift won for "You Belong with Me."

"Thank you so much!" Swift said. "I always dreamed about what it would be like to maybe win one of these someday, but I never actually thought that it would happen. I sing country music, so thank you so much for giving me a chance to win a VMA award. I . . ."

Before she could finish her sentence, West leaped out of the crowd and seized the microphone out of her hands.

"Yo, Taylor, I'm really happy for you. Imma let you finish, but Beyoncé had one of the best videos of all time!"

West turned to point to Beyoncé, who looked stunned and embarrassed, mouthing the words, "Oh, Kanye. God!" The crowd pelted West with boos, but he simply shrugged his shoulders, returned the mic to Swift and departed the stage. Swift could only stand there mortified.

She couldn't know it at the time, but Swift's temporary embarrassment turned into the galvanizing moment of her career. It was the end of her phase as the country crossover artist and the beginning of her dominance as global megastar. Things didn't work out as well for West. In the wake of the VMAs, he posted an apology letter on his blog (which he later deleted), posted a second apology, then went on the *Tonight Show* to apologize again. Criticism and condemnation came from all corners. Writers, actors, musicians and television personalities all piled on the beleaguered rapper. Even President Obama called him "a jackass."

For that one, shining moment in 2009, we as a human race could come together in support of one common idea. Despite all our ideological differences

SET LIST

H.A.M.

Dark Fantasy

Power

Jesus Walks

Can't Tell Me Nothing

Diamonds from Sierra Leone

Hell of a Life

Monster

Flashing Lights

Good Life

Love Lockdown

Say You Will

Heartless

Swagga Like Us

Run This Town

E.T.

Homecoming

Through the Wire

All Falls Down

Touch the Sky

Gold Digger

All of the Lights

Stronger

Chariots of Fire

Runaway

Lost in the World

Hey Mama

Across the next year, he bounced around the world from Japan to Italy and numerous places in between. He put his music career on hold, took an internship at the Fendi fashion house, drank away his pain in Tokyo and did the best he could to put his past behind him. When the year was up, he was ready to stage his comeback.

He booked time in a studio in Hawaii, far away from the glare of the media and assembled the greatest collection of rap talent ever put together for one project. His mentors Jay Z and No I.D. were brought in. So were three of the most visible members of the Wu-Tang Clan (RZA, Ghostface Killah and Raekwon) and half of the Clipse (Pusha T), along with Beyoncé, Kid Cudi, Rick Ross, Rihanna, John Legend and an up-and-comer named Nicki Minaj.

All of West's passion, skills and focus went into the project. The ideas, which had ceased flowing the day after the VMAs, were now pouring out of him. When it debuted on November 22, 2010, *My Beautiful Dark Twisted Fantasy* was universally praised as a masterpiece. In a 5-star review for *Rolling Stone*, Rob Sheffield wrote, "[West] makes everybody else on the radio sound laughably meek, but he's also throwing down a challenge to the audience. Kanye West thinks you're a moron if you settle for artists who don't push as hard as he does. And that means pretty much everybody." The album shot to No. 1, and Kanye was once again hailed as one of the greatest pop icons of his generation.

After months of speculation, West announced a series of appearances around the summer festival circuit. The centerpiece of this short run was his head-lining spot at Coachella. It wasn't his first dance out in the desert—he had performed there in 2006—but a lot had changed since then. Coachella was now the premiere live musical event of the year, and hordes of press and influential industry types would be on hand to catch the show. He knew he had to make an impression.

and international disputes, everyone agreed: Kanye West was an asshole. "I feel like Ben Stiller in *Meet the Parents* when he messed everything up and Robert DeNiro asked him to leave," West told *Tonight Show* host Jay Leno. That's exactly what Kanye did next. He left.

A planned co-headlining tour alongside Lady Gaga was scrapped. The rapper went completely off the grid. A little under two years after the death of his mother and a short while after the release of his harrowing, critically panned ode to autotune and personal misery, *808s & Heartbreak*, West was facing a crisis of confidence.

Act 1

After an intensely hot afternoon, the air around the Polo Fields has finally cooled with the setting sun. All around, the grounds are lit up with an array of colorful light, most prominently from the slow-moving Ferris wheel spinning out in the middle distance. The gravity of the festival has shifted toward the north, toward the main Coachella stage. 80,000 people are waiting with bated breath for the arrival of Kanye West.

The sound of manic violins breaks out over the soft murmuring below. Onstage, female dancers dressed like nude phoenixes with wings on their backs weave in and out of view. In the darkness, three men clad head to toe in white stand stoically behind a range of different keyboards and computer screens. Time passes and the sound shifts into the foreboding, operatic chant taken from one of West's recent singles, "H.A.M." A curtain falls from the top of the rafters, revealing a dramatic backdrop of a frieze taken from the ancient, 2nd century B.C. Pergamon Altar in Greece. The crowd gasps.

Suddenly, the chanting stops. A single piano chord rings out across the field and the music shifts to the opening track of West's recent masterpiece, "Dark Fantasy." Then, from out of nowhere, Kanye begins levitating from the middle of the audience with one finger raised in the air. Decked out in a boho-patterned, button-down shirt by French designer Céline, light blue jeans and a heavy gold chain, he floats over the audience on a cherry picker.

"Yeah!" he exclaims. "I fantasized about this back in Chicago / Mercy, mercy me, that Murciélago," West raps while the crane slowly brings him closer to the stage. Waiting for him there is Justin Vernon of Bon Iver, who is providing a melodic, auto-tuned vocal backdrop to Yeezy's bombastic words. Down below, thousands of hands reach up toward him as he journeys onward.

When he gets near enough to the front, West disembarks from his ride and walks like a prizefighter through the audience toward the stage. Suddenly, a synth loudly breaks into the main riff of "Power." Assuming a place in front of the mic stand, he raises his hand once again. The dancers behind him are bowed in supplication. He stands there, still and silent for several moments while the audience chants his name over and over again. "Kanye! Kanye! Kanye!"

Finally, he gives the signal and "Power" begins in earnest. The dancers rise and begin clapping their hands. The crowd shouts back the song's refrain at deafening levels, "Uh-Huh! Yay! Uh-Huh! Yay!" West raps with a fury. "No one man should have all that power!"

It's a spectacular moment, one made even more poignant later in the set when West reveals, "When I was making my last album I kept saying I can't wait to perform 'Power' at Coachella. So, this is the most important show to me since my mama passed." He adds, "There were many times that I thought about not being here, and you all make it all worth it."

For the next 25 minutes, he keeps the energy high, mixing new bangers like "Monster" and "Hell of a Life" with bankable, crowd-pleasing classics like "Jesus Walks" and "Diamonds from Sierra Leone." He finishes with the *Graduation* track "Good Life" and departs the stage.

> *The pain that inspired the art that he's airing out in public is fully realized through his manic, unsettling screeches.*

Act 2

Red fireworks shoot into the sky as a rumble like thunder spreads across the green fields below. The theme from the film *Chariots of Fire* blasts out of the speakers, building anticipation for whatever will happen next. With every dramatic strike of a guitar chord, a well-timed red flame streaks through the air just behind the stage. This continues, until the song dies out and is replaced by the pulsing beat of West's *808s & Heartbreak* track "Love Lockdown."

West comes out and is bathed in a soft white light. Slowly, the dancers reappear behind him, moving as one in a deliberate, interpretative choreography. As the song enters its last harrowing moments, Kanye goes into a full-on John Lennon–style scream therapy mode. The pain that inspired the art that he's airing out in public is fully realized through his manic, unsettling screeches.

The hurting continues across the next two numbers, "Say You Will" and "Heartless." At one point, West turns to the crowd and opens his heart. "To be able to close the festival and see all of you that still love me after everything I read on TV said the opposite, for us to still go platinum, for us to still have number ones, to have fans that were here since 'Through the Wire,' that you ain't believe shit that they said . . . I really appreciate y'all tonight."

Having gotten that off his chest, West goes on a tear through some of his more prominent feature turns, including T.I.'s "Swagga Like Us," Jay Z's "Run This Town" and Katy Perry's "E.T." That last one is prefaced by a slow-morphing rendition of Queen's "We Will Rock You," which explodes out over the audience. Behind him a curtain of silver sparks showers down.

The excitement is ratcheted even higher by the subsequent medley of his earliest hits. The crowd goes crazy as West dusts off songs like "Homecoming," "Through the Wire," "All Falls Down" and "Touch the Sky," before capping it off with "Gold Digger." Then, when it doesn't seem possible for the show to get any more hyped, he hits them with "All of the Lights."

The second act closes with a dramatic rendition of "Stronger." Daft Punk's vocoder-filtered lyrics kick in, and West completely loses it while rapping out the song's chorus.

Act 3

"Act 3." The phrase is projected in white light against the gleaming Greek frieze. This is the home stretch. The grand finale. The final movement of West's dark, twisted fantasy.

Again, the *Chariots of Fire* theme rings out into the open, but this time, the stage in front is a flurry of activity. The dancers, formerly nude phoenixes, are now clad in either tight white unitards or long, flowing silk robes. A giant white tarp is brought out, and they all grab a piece, run to the front and cover themselves in it, creating something that looks like a giant, long, flat igloo.

After a few moments, the tarp is ripped away to reveal West standing defiantly on a white cube, covered from head to toe in red; drenched in sweat. He pauses, adjusts his collar, hops down off his pedestal, and walks over to an Akai MPC 2000 XL sampler.

Ping. West presses down on one of the MPC's soft, rubber pads, eliciting the sound of a single high piano note. Ping. The same note twinkles in the air as West rubs his hands together. Ping. Ping. Ping. Pong. It's the unmistakable opening sounds of one of his most confessional, self-flagellating songs to date: "Runaway."

Bent over at the waist, West's fingers dance across the many pads of the MPC, throwing the song's different samples together in a crazy mishmash, with little in the way of rhyme or reason. A sample of Rick James's voice repeatedly rings out: "Look, look atchya!" The rapper's face is twisted in a determined grimace as he presses his thumb down on the same key over and over again.

"Yeah I always find something wrong," West raps to the crowd. "You been puttin' up with my shit just way too long."

Eventually, Pusha T comes out, clad in white, to spit his acrobatic guest verse while West resumes his place back on the pedestal. The stage itself is now a squirming nest of ballerina dancers alternating poses on the ground. Near the end, West starts ad-libbing lines while a single ballerina performs a high-intensity routine.

After it's over, the crowd begins chanting his name again. It's the ultimate moment of redemption he'd been lusting after. At least in the minds of the people sprawled out before him, he's no longer public enemy number one. He's a rock god of the highest order.

For the dramatic conclusion, Justin Vernon returns to reproduce his portion of "Lost in the World." The phoenixes are back, and when the galloping sound of the drums kicks in, the stage turns into a scene of pure chaos. West doesn't seem to have much left, but he's giving all he's got. By song's end, both he and Vernon are trading off-the-cuff lines, with the rapper leaning heavily on the microphone for support.

The show isn't quite over yet though. Before taking his final bow, West decides to pay tribute to the one person who always believed in him. The one person who meant more to him throughout his life than anyone else. The person who left him far too soon and whose loss sent him down a dark road. With his eyes tightly closed, West unveils his ode to his mother, "Hey Mama."

"I'm finna talk about my mama if you don't mind."

HONORABLE MENTION
Adele at the Royal Albert Hall
London, England (September 22)

Not since Michael Jackson's *Thriller* had one album so thoroughly dominated the charts like Adele's sophomore release, *21*. Not only was it the best-selling album of 2011, it was also the best-selling album of 2012. Millions of people fell hard for her affecting, heartbroken songwriting and incredible pipes. Despite her newly minted status as one of the top pop idols in the world, the British chanteuse eschewed big arenas and stadiums and instead performed in relatively intimate theaters. Nowhere did she put on a better show than in her own backyard at the place she describes as "the Royal Albert fucking Hall." Despite a nagging throat malady that would eventually force her off the road, Adele unleashed the full force of her incredible voice on anthems like "Rolling in the Deep" and "Someone Like You." The Bob Dylan cover "Make You Feel My Love"—which she dedicates to the recently deceased Amy Winehouse, an artist that paved the way for Adele's success—is an especially poignant moment.

2012

Dr. Dre & Snoop Dogg with Kendrick Lamar, 50 Cent and Eminem
THE EMPIRE POLO FIELDS—INDIO, CA
APRIL 15

DRE'S SO-CAL SÉANCE

By the time the second decade of the 21st century rolled around, it had become difficult, bordering on impossible, to find new ways to surprise and impress a crowd. Pyro had been done to death, and so had lasers, confetti, projection screens, LED lights and even inflatable genitalia. You could still count on the unannounced guest spot to add the element of surprise, but outside of that, how else were you going to shock the crowd?

This was the dilemma facing Dr. Dre as he planned his headlining spot at Coachella in 2012. Dre wasn't the kind of guy to do anything small. His entire career had been big. N.W.A had been big. Death Row Records had been big. *The Chronic* had been huge. His work with Eminem was massive. If he was going to perform a show at Coachella, it had to be larger than life.

Then the idea hit him. What if we brought someone back from the dead? Not just someone—what if we brought back one of the greatest MCs ever to hold a microphone or put pen to paper? What if we brought back Tupac Shakur?

First, Dre had to see if such a thing was possible. There were some examples he could draw on for inspiration, like the holographic Japanese character Hatsune Miku in 2007. With so many eyes watching, he knew he had to get this right and make 'Pac appear as realistic as technologically possible. To make it happen, he turned to the special effects production company Digital Domain, which told him that for somewhere between $100,000 and $400,000, they could us projection and reflection technology to bring the legendary MC back to life. It wasn't a hologram in the strictest definition of the word, but in the absence of a better definition, that would do.

For months, the designers at Digital Domain worked on turning their concept into an actual, working form. They were going to utilize a technique pioneered in the 19th century called "Pepper's Ghost" to project the image of Tupac onto a glass surface and make it appear like he was floating in the air. There was a lot of advanced technology that went into the production, but the premise was 150 years old.

Making things even more challenging, Dre wasn't interested in using old footage either. If this was go-

Then the idea hit him. What if we brought someone back from the dead?

ing to come off as believable to tens of thousands of people that night, they had to build the rapper from the ground up and give him a way to interact with the performers onstage. It was a tall order, but if they could pull it off, it'd be the kind of thing that people would talk about for decades to come.

SET LIST
SNOOP DOGG AND DR. DRE

The Next Episode
Kush
Gin & Juice
Deep Cover
Nuthin' but a "G" Thang

SNOOP DOGG

Ain't No Fun
I Wanna Rock
Jump Around
Drop It Like It's Hot
In the Air Tonight
Young, Wild & Free

KENDRICK LAMAR

The Recipe

50 CENT

What Up Gangsta
P.I.M.P.
In Da Club

DR. DRE

Xxplosive
California Love

TUPAC SHAKUR HOLOGRAM

Hail Mary
2 of Amerikaz Most Wanted

EMINEM

I Need a Doctor
Forgot About Dre
'Till I Collapse

SNOOP DOGG AND DR. DRE

Who Am I? (What's My Name?)
Still D.R.E.

When the night arrives, Coachella concertgoers are already excitedly talking about who might show up for Dre's set. The Beats headphones kingpin is set to hit the stage alongside his sidekick Snoop Dogg, but beyond that, the options for cameos seem endless. Former *Rolling Stone* editor Simon Vozick-Levinson was amongst the crowd, and as he told me, "Someone like Dr. Dre and Snoop have such an immense presence in the music industry and there were so many people they've worked with who could have come out. You could almost trace the entire history of rap through what those two guys did and who they worked with."

Dre kicks the show off with a rousing performance of "The Next Episode" from his celebrated sophomore album, *2001*. "La-duh-da-da-da / It's the D-oh-double-G," Snoop raps. It's a stupefyingly funky love letter to marijuana, with multiple references to Tupac's classic "California Love" interspersed throughout. The crowd "La-duh-da-da-da's" right back at Long Beach's favorite son.

"You know who's back up in this motherfucker!" Dre declares. "Coachella! Make some motherfucking noise!"

"Kush" comes next, followed by Snoop's send-up to his favorite drink, "Gin & Juice." "Oh, we just getting started," Dre promises. The duo slips into "Deep Cover," the first track that Dre released after his split from N.W.A. and the title track to a 1992 film by the same name. The audience is receptive but goes off minutes later for "Nuthin But a 'G' Thang."

After that, Dre leaves, allowing Snoop free reign to pay tribute to his friend Nate Dogg, who died a year earlier from multiple strokes, with the song "Ain't No Fun." Then, he goes into full-on crowd-pleaser mode, hitting them with House of Pain's "Jump Around," his club banging hit "Drop It Like It's Hot" and "Young, Wild & Free," during which he brings out Wiz Khalifa.

Having paid homage to older artists, big-upped his own legacy and featured modern hit-makers, when Dre hits the stage again he's out to highlight newer talent. "This man is from my city," Dre proclaims. "He's from straight outta Compton. Please make some noise for Kendrick Lamar!"

A young, pre–*Good Kid, M.A.A.D. City* Lamar emerges from the shadows to tag-team with his mentor on their song "The Recipe." Lamar is hyped for the occasion and brings a welcome youthful exuberance to the festivities. When it's over Dre can only laugh and say, "Kendrick motherfucking Lamar, man," as he walks off.

The sound of gunshots explodes out of the large speakers, cutting through the hush. The projection screen in the back displays a series of bullet holes, through which bright rays of light shine through. You know that phrase "This person needs no introduction." Dre takes it literally, because all of a sudden, there stands 50 Cent.

50 launches into "What Up Gangsta," expending an incredible amount of energy that leaves him a little gassed as he tries to follow it up with "P.I.M.P." and then "In Da Club." Fortunately, Snoop is on hand to help fill in some of the gaps and keep the crowd hyped.

After 50's mini-set, Dre and Snoop kill some time asking where people in the crowd are from. East Coast, Miami, Australia, Dirty South, Canada, the Midwest, etc. Finally, the duo arrives at Los Angeles and up on the screen they project a clip of Frank Sinatra singing "L.A. Is My Lady." When it's over, Dre demands, "Okay, California, let's go!"

The unmistakable opening to Tupac's "California Love" erupts like a volcano. Dre raps his immortal opening verse welcoming everyone "to the wild wild west / A state that's untouchable like Eliot Ness." As promised, the track hits the crowd's eardrums like a slug to the chest. Everyone goes crazy for the ultimate West Coast banger.

The song ends and the field is blanketed by darkness. A thunderclap crashes out, giving way to a symphonic minor key orchestration that's punctuated by the steady mournful toll of church bells. And then, there he is: Tupac Shakur.

It takes a moment for people to register exactly who, or what, they're seeing. As the realization dawns, the audience breaks out into a rolling wave of screams. The shirtless apparition, with Tupac's iconic "Thug Life" midriff tattoo exposed to offer proof of identity, raises its hands to the sky.

"Yeah! You know what the fuck this is!" it announces. "Whaddup, Dre?"

"I'm chilling. What's up, Pac?" he replies.

"What up, Snoop?" Tupac asks.

"S'up my nigga!"

"What the fuck is up, Coachellllllaaaaa?"

No one can believe what they are seeing and hearing. "The vibe was surreal," Vozick-Levinson said. "You have to remember this is at the end of a long weekend in the desert out in the sun. People have been drinking, maybe smoking a little weed and then onstage this ghost appears like a dream and says, 'What the fuck is up, Coachella?' There was a moment of shock and then people roared in excitement and happiness."

After giving the people a few moments to unscramble their brains, Tupac launches into his posthumous hit single, "Hail Mary," a song that came out four months after he was gunned down on September 7, 1996. It is an inspired choice, making the seemingly impossible that much more extraordinary.

After finishing "Hail Mary," Tupac is joined by Snoop, who asks him to "Let these motherfuckers know what kind of party they at now." The pair trade verses on "2 of Amerikaz Most Wanted" from Shakur's greatest work, *All Eyez on Me*. It's a bit baffling watching a living performer go back and forth with a dead guy.

Tupac is the perfect candidate for this type of surprise. For years, rumors swirled that he survived the shooting in Las Vegas that supposedly took his life and had gone into hiding. Sightings had been reported intermittently, and the sheer volume of his post-death output was taken as proof by some that he was bunkered down somewhere, still committing flows to tape.

It was the first time anything like this had been tried on this scale. This apparition looked like Tupac, walked like Tupac and rapped like Tupac. In the moment, that he wasn't actually Tupac didn't matter.

Everyone is more than willing to suspend reality and throw a middle finger in the air.

As "2 of Amerikaz Most Wanted" ends, Tupac moves back to the middle of the stage and stands stark still, before exploding into a ball of light. Just like that, he's gone again. RIP.

The show still isn't over, though the question begs, "How do you follow the ghost of one of the most celebrated rap artists of all time?" Dre answers by bringing out the best-selling rapper of all time: Eminem.

The Detroit MC bursts out from backstage decked in black and launches into a three-song mini-set comprised of "I Need a Doctor," "Forgot About Dre" and "Till I Collapse." It is a magnanimous move to lay into a set of music that entirely big-ups his mentor, but Em has always acknowledged Dre's role in pushing him to the highest echelons of the rap stratosphere.

Almost 80 minutes after it began, the set ends in perhaps the most appropriate fashion possible: with Dr. Dre and his ride-or-die Snoop standing side by side, going back and forth on his comeback single, "Still D.R.E." Indeed, he still is Dre. Still bringing together the best collection of talent on the planet. Still wowing crowds. Still dipping with Snoop. Still taking his time to perfect the beat. "Still got love for the streets."

As great as the entire show was, the legacy of Dre's night at Coachella will forever be the holographic revival of Tupac Shakur. In the wake of that performance, plans have been sketched out for whole tours put on by deceased music icons. The prospect opened an entirely new revenue stream for the estates of some of the biggest acts ever to step foot on a stage, and many heirs are eager to cash in.

Some argue that the holographic resurrection is a repulsive money grab. Others counter by saying if the demand is there, who is it hurting? Regardless, for one night in Southern California at least, it was just cool to see one of the greatest of all time do his thing one final time.

"Looking back years later, Hologram Tupac wasn't a herald of the future, it wasn't a cash grab or a business plan, it was just this entity that came out onstage, lived and died again one night in the desert," Vozick-Levinson said. "Hologram Tupac was too rare to live."

HONORABLE MENTION

12-12-12: The Concert for Sandy Relief
Madison Square Garden
New York, NY (December 12)

In late October, Hurricane Sandy hit the Northeastern portion of the United States with a meteorological fury that hadn't been experienced in years. The damage was catastrophic, running around $71 billion. In the wake of the destruction, the same organizers who put on the Concert for New York City after 9/11 spun through their Rolodexes and began plotting a benefit show to help those most in need. The lineup they put together on December 12 was as stacked as anything anyone had seen thus far in the 21st century, featuring short sets by Bruce Springsteen, Roger Waters, Bon Jovi, Eric Clapton, The Rolling Stones, Alicia Keys, The Who, Kanye West, Billy Joel, Chris Martin of Coldplay and Paul McCartney, who brought out the living members of Nirvana to play their new song, "Cut Me Some Slack." There were so many British rock icons invited that night that at one point, Mick Jagger cracked a joke to the New York audience that, "If it rains in London, you've gotta come help us."

#1 Single of the Year:
"Thrift Shop"
Macklemore & Ryan Lewis (Featuring Wanz)

2013

#1 Album of the Year:
The 20/20 Experience
Justin Timberlake

Kanye West with Kendrick Lamar
KEY ARENA—SEATTLE, WA
OCTOBER 19

YEEZUS SEASON APPROACHING

Many thoughts were running through my mind while standing outside of Key Arena on October 19, 2013. Kanye West was set to kick off his hotly anticipated Yeezus Tour in Seattle that night, except he was running late. Extremely late. I was there to report on the show for *Rolling Stone*. It was my first assignment for the publication I had revered since I was a kid, and I was beginning to worry that it wasn't going to happen.

The printed start time was 10:00 pm, but it was already 9:45 and the doors to the basketball arena were still shut tight. Did I mention it was cold? Not cold for say, a Chicagoan, a Minnesotan or a New Yorker, but Arctic by Pacific Northwest standards. I was dressed in a light black hoodie and could only look on in sympathy as girls in barely-there crop tops and miniskirts huddled together to achieve some measure of warmth.

About 15 minutes and two cigarettes later, the prolonged wait and chilly night air compelled me to pull out my phone and dial the number for my on-scene contact. "Yeah, the show is still going on, don't worry," he told me. "They're just having a problem getting the mountain to fit properly into the venue. Key Arena is a little smaller than the Staples Center or Madison Square Garden." *Did he just say mountain?*

A few moments later the security staff finally opened the doors. Everyone tried to shove their way in all at once and then make a mad dash over to the merch table to swipe up all the Confederate flag and Indian skull T-shirts that West had printed up for the occasion. I copped a ghoulish garment myself and then walked over to my assigned seat on the east side of the arena to get a feel for what I was in for.

To my right, sure as I was told, was a giant mountain, maybe 30 to 40 feet tall, solid white and with a winding pathway leading to the top. Hanging above it, a massive, circular projection screen titled forward just so. In front of that, a catwalk that led to a smaller triangular-shaped stage in the center of the general admission pit.

After a short wait, the lights go out and the screen on the stage is illuminated by the image of the van taken from Kendrick Lamar's latest album, *Good Kid, M.A.A.D. City*. The Compton MC, decked out in all black, his face obscured by a hood pulled low over his head, makes his entrance to huge applause.

If you've been to many rap shows, you know that in a live setting, a lot of rappers allow the pre-recorded backing tracks to do most of the work for them. I can't tell you how many times I've been to gigs where MCs essentially jump around onstage like in-person hype men for their recorded selves. Kendrick Lamar is not one of these rappers. His flow is impeccable, and for a guy who writes densely layered, intricate verses, it's a true achievement that he hardly misses a word throughout his entire time onstage.

SET LIST

On Sight

New Slaves

Send It Up

Mercy

Power

Cold

Black Skinhead

I Don't Like

I Am a God

Can't Tell Me Nothing

Coldest Winter

Hold My Liquor

I'm In It

Drunk and Hot Girls

Guilt Trip

Heartless

Blood on the Leaves

I Wonder

Runaway

Hey Mama

Street Lights

Lost in the World

Heard 'Em Say

Stronger

Through the Wire

Jesus Walks

Flashing Lights

All of the Lights

Bound 2

The high point of Lamar's set comes with the song "m.A.A.d. city," where he enlists the audience to perform the thunderous "yack, yack, yack" refrain. He plays two more songs and then departs. The wait resumes. The wait for what, we don't know, but it'd have to be something spectacular to top the performance we just saw.

Just before midnight, the house lights go out again and a slow, steady succession, of a dozen or so women covered in white robes march out two by two to the triangular stage in the middle of the arena. They assume their predetermined positions and stand there motionless. Suddenly, a grating, industrial noise cuts through the crowd chatter and the giant, circular screen comes to life to display an image of dark storm clouds.

Everyone, myself included, is on their feet as the opening notes to "On Sight" break through the speakers. West, wearing a long, gray tank top and a bejeweled mask that covers his face, makes his way to the tip of the triangle and just stands there drinking in the applause. When his cue arrives, he transforms from the picture of stoicism to the definition of mania. "Yeezy season approachin' fuck whatever y'all been hearin'," West raps. Yeezy season is no longer approaching. It is here, and the thousands gathered are eager to celebrate.

By the second and third songs, "New Slaves" and "Send It Up," it's clear that this isn't going to be a run-of-the-mill concert. No, this is a full-on stage production beyond the scope of anything you're likely to see on Broadway. You may be thinking, "Wasn't there just a chapter about Kanye West two years back? How good can he be to have two shows spaced so close together?" The answer: Really, really good.

In all honesty, no one around can match him in terms of hype, energy and eye-popping spectacle. He's not only got the songs, he assembles the visuals and deploys the pyrotechnics while bringing something wholly unique to the stage. In the annals of the 21st century live music experience, Kanye stands alone.

Despite the late hour and the pains it took to get this show off the ground, West is amped all the way up. At certain points he practically turns the triangular stage up front into a diving board as he hurtles himself up and down on its wooden frame.

After that intense opening salvo, West disappears from view and a narrator's voice cuts through the silence, spouting some kind of psychobabble over an instrumental passage from "Hold My Liquor." When he returns, he's on top of the mountain thanks to an obscured hydraulic lift. With his arms outstretched and with the women, now in nude bodysuits, down below, he launches into a bracing rendition of "Power" that leaves jaws on the floor.

Over the course of the night, West performs every single song off his most recent album. On older material, he toys with the arrangements slightly so that they better fit into the aesthetic of his *Yeezus* material. Some songs, like his *Graduation*-era hit "Stronger," are stripped to the bones, while others, like the bombastic set-closer "Lost in the World," are left completely untouched.

No one around can match him in terms of hype, energy and eye-popping spectacle.

From time to time, he retreats backstage for a short stretch, only to reemerge in a different location, in a different outfit or donning a different Margiela-designed mask. As a spectator, you're kept constantly on your toes, wondering what might happen next. At one point, while West stands near the front, draped in a long canvas coat, an Abominable Snowman–type creature with large, glowing red eyes leaps onto the mountain, points its finger out and scans it across the audience. What the hell is that supposed to symbolize?

Near the end of the show, the mountain cracks open to reveal that it wasn't a mountain at all, but a volcano. Out pour the women in a plume of smoke, dressed head to toe in white, carrying various items of religious iconography: The Virgin Mary, a swinging thurible spewing incense and a crucifix. West joins them soon after.

All night, people speak in hushed whispers about the rumor of a major guest popping up at some point during the show. The rumors are true. Jesus Christ appears . . . well, an actor portraying the son of God. For the first time in nearly two hours, West strips off his mask and kneels before the false Father. Jesus bends down and touches a loving hand on the rapper's head.

West quickly jumps up to declare how insane it is that Jesus showed up to his concert. "I've been looking for you," he exclaims to the pretend savior. "I've been here all along," Christ replies. After their détente, West launches into "Jesus Walks" before rounding out the encore with "Flashing Lights," "All of the Lights" and the last track off *Yeezus*, "Bound 2."

As "Bound 2" comes to an end, Jesus reemerges on top of the reassembled volcano. The dancers in white turn toward him and fall to their knees. As all eyes go skyward. Kanye bows his head. Over the speakers, the child-like refrain from "On Sight" bellows off the walls of Key Arena: "Oh, you give us what we need / It may not be what we want." He leaves for the final time.

It's around 2 a.m. when I exit through one of the big glass double doors. I only have three hours left to put together my review of the show because of the East Coast/West Coast time difference. I brought my laptop along with me and left it in the trunk of my car, so on the way home, I peel off the highway into a grocery store parking lot and start typing. The words pour out of me as I replay the night's events in my mind. Before I know it, I am finished. I send the review to my editor and then drive the rest of the way home.

It was one of the greatest nights of my entire life.

HONORABLE MENTION

Lady Gaga at Rodgers Arena
Vancouver, British Colombia, Canada (July 11)

Lady Gaga envisions concerts as sensory over-loading events that need to be felt as much as they are seen or heard. In 2013, she hit the road with her biggest production yet, the Born This Way Ball, which touched down for the first time in North America on January 11 in Vancouver, British Columbia. Not to sound too much like Bill Hader's character Stefon from *Saturday Night Live*, but this show had every-thing: a medieval castle, a couch made of meat . . . a highway unicorn. *What's a highway unicorn?* Well, it's that thing where someone dresses like the evil Lord Sauron from *Lord of the Rings* and sings while on a puppet horse. Of course, the show also had Lady Gaga, who at that moment was traveling the world and bringing with her a positive message about self-empowerment. Say what you want about her over-the-top persona; you can't deny that she's got a world-class set of pipes, and she nearly blew the roof off the place during songs like "Poker Face," "Bad Romance" and "Born This Way."

#1 Single of the Year:
"Happy"
Pharrell Williams

2014

#1 Album of the Year:
Frozen (Soundtrack)
Various Artists

Jay Z and Beyoncé
STADE DE FRANCE—PARIS, FRANCE
SEPTEMBER 13

BONNIE & CLYDE

On May 5, 2014, after attending the extravagant Met Gala in New York City, Beyoncé; her husband, Jay Z; and her sister Solange, entered the elevator together at the Standard Hotel. In footage leaked to TMZ, Solange was seen yelling at Jay about something. Then, as the doors closed, she attacked him, swinging wildly at the tuxedo'd Roc Nation president. Jay defended himself from the attack, while a body guard came from behind Solange to restrain her. With her arms trapped by her sides, she continued to kick wildly at Jay while the two yelled at one another. Beyoncé did not intervene.

After the video was made public, the three artists did their best to pour cold water on the story. They released a joint statement saying, "Families have problems and we're no different. We love each other and above all we are family. We've put this behind us and hope everyone else will do the same." The public wasn't as eager to let the incident go.

In 2014 Jay Z and Beyoncé were easily the biggest celebrity couple in the world. They also cultivated two of the most carefully managed public personas. As much as they wished to put the embarrassing incident behind them, the spotlight refused to move away from their personal turmoil.

Speculation ran wild about the status of their relationship. Did he cheat on her? Was their union a sham? Was there any real love left between them? What did Jay do to piss her sister off so bad?

At the same time as this controversy was brewing, Jay and Bey were in the middle of preparing their first co-headlining tour together. Fans had been anticipating this kind of run for years, but now a venture that once seemed like a no-brainer was thrown into doubt. Faced with the proposition of either going into seclusion or getting in front of the people, the couple chose the latter option. Jay Z had just released his 12th album, *Magna Carta Holy Grail*, and Beyoncé was riding high on her critically adored self-titled release. It wasn't the time to bunker down.

To help drum up publicity and guarantee sellouts in all the massive outdoor stadiums they were determined to fill, the couple adopted a genius marketing strategy. If what the public wanted to talk about was the precariousness of their relationship, they would give them something to talk about. Overnight, gossip columns and Internet websites were flooded by inside reports that Jay and Bey were on the verge of calling it a day. For two people known for handing out nondisclosure agreements like they were candy, this new leak-filled reality couldn't be a coincidence.

Every single stop along the way felt like it could be their last. I caught the show with my wife at Safeco Field in Seattle, and up until the moment we took our seats in the upper deck, we were still having the "Will they or won't they show up?" conversation. It felt like the divorce papers might drop any day.

In retrospect, the anxiety seems silly. Jay Z and

SET LIST

'03 Bonnie & Clyde

Upgrade U

Crazy in Love

Show Me What You Got

Diamonds from Sierra Leone

I Just Wanna Love U (Give It 2 Me)

Tom Ford

Run the World

Bow Down

Flawless

Yoncé

Jigga My Nigga

Dirt Off Your Shoulder

Naughty Girl

Big Pimpin'

Ring the Alarm

On to the Next One

Clique

Diva

Baby Boy

U Don't Know

Ghost

Haunted

No Church in the Wild

Drunk in Love

Public Service Announcement

Why Don't You Love Me

Holy Grail

Fuckwithmeyouknowigotthis

Beach Is Better

Partition

99 Problems

If I Were a Boy

Ex-Factor

Song Cry

Resentment

Love on Top

Izzo (H.O.V.A.)

Niggas in Paris

Single Ladies (Put a Ring on It)

Hard Knock Life (Ghetto Anthem)

Pretty Hurts

Part II (On the Run)

Young Forever

Halo

Beyoncé both understand better than anyone the power of imagery and how much you can say by not saying anything at all. They knew exactly which buttons to push to get the public to come out in full force for their concerts, and they pressed them in the perfect sequence.

The *On the Run Tour* wound its way through North America from June into August, culminating with a two-night stand at AT&T Park in San Francisco. That wasn't the end, however. For the *piece de resistance* of their real life/fake life melodrama, Mr. and Mrs. Carter booked a pair of shows at the Stade de France in Paris, which were filmed by HBO for a documentary. The stakes were at an all-time high, and both man and wife were determined to deliver the performance of a lifetime.

The lights go down over the 80,000 people gathered in the football stadium. Above the massive stage, the words "THIS IS NOT REAL LIFE" flash on the screen. A telling disclaimer. In the next instant, Beyoncé's image graces the screen, looking gorgeous in a simple striped shirt. The caption reads, "THE QUEEN." Cut to Jay Z looking debonair decked out in black, while gripping a fat, smoldering cigar. Under him: "THE GANGSTER."

The clip has a light and breezy air, adopting the feel and tone of a vintage World War II–era romance film. The mood is shattered when a gun appears and fires a shot. In the next frame a fearsome, black muscle car roars into view. Beyoncé enters the car decked out in a badass leather jacket embroidered with the word "TEXAS" in metal studs on the back. In her hands, an AK-47. The images are coming faster now:

Beyoncé, aiming her weapon skyward at an unseen target.

ON

A suitcase stuffed with cash tossed onto a motel room bed.

THE

A windshield shattered by bullets.

RUN

Suddenly, the gigantic screen slides open and from the middle Jay Z and Beyoncé enter the stadium as if busting out from the film itself. They stand there for a moment letting the screams wash over their heads until Jay looks over and asks, "You ready, B?"

"Let's go," she replies. Side by side they step forward into the light and launch into the first song, "'03 Bonnie & Clyde."

Together, they look like the coolest people on the planet. Jay is rocking a black and white American flag tank top. Over his shoulders, a blazer. Around his neck, a heavy gold chain. Beyoncé is in full Sasha Fierce mode in her lace and leather onesie with a custom-made net stocking mask wrapped around her face. She looks like a cross between an Amazonian warlord and an S&M dominatrix. Everything about her screams, "Don't fuck with me."

"'03 Bonnie & Clyde" is technically a Jay Z song, and he does most of the heavy lifting. Beyoncé, standing to his right, enacts a series of sensual, suggestive dance moves while joining him on the choruses. "All I need in this life of sin is me and my girlfriend," he sings. "Down to ride 'til the very end, just me and my boyfriend," she answers.

The next two songs, "Upgrade U" and "Crazy in Love," find her in the driver's seat. She hits her choreographed marks with precision, blasting the front row with the full force of her tremendous voice. The mask is off now. She stomps, sashays and twirls her hair with abandon while backup dancers move behind her in perfect unison.

When her part is over, Beyoncé departs, allowing Jay to remind everyone that he isn't a "businessman, he's a business, man" over the Kanye West song "Diamonds from Sierra Leone." After that he dives into "I Just Wanna Love U (Give It 2 Me)" and "Tom Ford." When he's done, the lights go out, and Beyoncé comes back out to prove that girls run this motherfucker on "Run the World." "Bow Down" comes next, followed by a surprise appearance from Nicki Minaj, who joins Bey on a remix of her gender equality anthem "Flawless."

This tag team approach remains in place for the next two and a half hours. Jay takes over to run through some of his biggest hits like "Big Pimpin'," "99 Problems," "Dirt Off Your Shoulder" and "Izzo (H.O.V.A.)" before ceding the stage back to Beyoncé for songs like "If I Were a Boy," "Single Ladies (Put a

It feels like the curtain has dropped and behind it is a real family that truly loves one another.

Ring on It)," "Ring the Alarm" and "Baby Boy." Their paths frequently cross, most spectacularly on "Drunk in Love," but they allow each other the room to bask in the spotlight

In between set changes, there are more film clips. For the audience, it's total sensory overload. The Carters clamor for your attention and refuse to give you a second to slip off to the bathroom or look down at your phone.

For the last thirty minutes, the blueprint is tossed out the window and the couple appears together again, hand in hand, backing each other up and pushing each other forward. As big as he is—and Jay Z is unquestionably one of the three biggest rap stars of all time—he's no match for the outsized profile of his wife. Onstage, there's almost no one better in the world than Beyoncé. He would probably be the first to admit it.

As the show races toward its final moments, they both walk through the crowd to a small stage in the middle of the general admission area. Beyoncé begins to softly sing the '80s synth pop hit and graduation classic "Forever Young." As the song unfurls, Jay raps out his verses from his own track that samples it, "Young Forever."

All around, the stadium is illuminated by thousands of individual bits of light. People are holding their cell phones high in the sky, waving them to and fro with the rhythm of the song. The screen behind them goes black, and the words "THIS IS REAL LIFE" flash across it.

Clips of Shawn Carter and his wife, Beyoncé Knowles, along with their daughter, Blue Ivy, filter in and out. There they are at a birthday party. There they are lounging out on a yacht in some far-flung paradise. There they are getting matching IV tattoos on their ring fingers.

The moment Beyoncé's pregnant stomach is displayed, she stops singing. They both turn away from the crowd to look at the screen. Behind them, the audience loses it as they gaze lovingly on their daughter, watching as she grows from an infant to a toddler.

It's a preplanned moment, one they've duplicated 20 times over the tour. It might have felt contrived—another example of the power couple cashing in on their relationship to get a cheap pop from the crowd—but it doesn't play that way. It feels, at long last, like the curtain has dropped and behind it is a real family that truly loves one another.

Suddenly, Beyoncé breaks into her song "Halo." She's not singing to anyone but Blue Ivy now. Next to her, Jay Z is mouthing the words with his arm wrapped around his wife's back. Just before she hits the first chorus, he gives her a soft kiss on the forehead. A crowd singalong ensues, and then it's all over.

"We did it!" Jay screams. Beyoncé laughs, jumps into the air and clicks her heels together, then falls into his arms and gives him a kiss. They walk out together, hand in hand.

Honorable Mention
Miley Cyrus at Bridgestone Arena
Nashville, TN (August 7)

2013 was the year that Miley Cyrus killed her Disney TV alter-ego Hannah Montana. The act began with the release of her fourth album, *Bangerz*, and was completed the moment she twerked up against Robin Thicke's crotch at the VMAs. 2014 was the year that she took her newfound, parent-enraging, over-the-top identity out on the road. Cyrus put together a show that mirrored that aesthetic perfectly, using a wide range of zany props like an oversized, floating hot dog and a giant tongue slide, along with some eye-popping outfits like a barely-there red leotard and a marijuana-leaf–emblazoned onesie. For all the spectacle surrounding Cyrus, the most intriguing part of the show was her actual voice, a versatile yet husky instrument she deployed beautifully on songs like "Wrecking Ball" and "Party in the U.S.A." and a sublime cover of Dolly Parton's "Jolene." It was a perfect mixture of mania and musicianship.

2015

Drake
MOLSON CANADIAN AMPHITHEATRE
TORONTO, CANADA
AUGUST 3

CHARGED UP

Heading into the sixth annual OVO Fest in Toronto, Aubrey Drake Graham had two goals in mind. One: to establish, unequivocally, his status as the reigning king of the rap game. Two: to burn Philadelphia rapper Meek Mill's career to the ground. By the end of the night, he accomplished both objectives in stunning fashion.

2015 was a banner year for Drake. On February 13, he dropped his mixtape/album hybrid *If You're Reading This It's Too Late* with almost no warning. Then he watched as it not only topped the Billboard 200 but also became one of the first albums ever to log over 1 billion streams online. The Toronto rapper—excuse me, 6 God—grabbed a hold of the zeitgeist and refused to let go.

Drake headlined Coachella in April and made headlines around the world for his cringe-worthy make-out session with Madonna. Shortly thereafter he kicked off a run of shows with Atlanta trap rapper Future. Drake later hooked up with him in the studio to record a collaboration mixtape titled *What a Time to Be Alive*, which came out in September and became his second No. 1 of the year.

Just as it seemed like nothing could go wrong for Drake, his world was rocked by some serious charges made by a former friend. Philadelphia rapper Meek Mill, perhaps looking to drum up a little bit of buzz about his album *Dreams Worth More Than Money*, wrote on Twitter asking for people to "Stop comparing Drake to me . . . He don't write his own raps! That's why he ain't tweet my album because we found out!" Meek Mill followed that up by claiming, "He ain't even write that verse on my album and if I woulda knew I woulda took it off my album . . . I don't trick my fans!"

More than in most genres, authenticity is an important element in rap. Listeners expect rap artists to deliver lines from the heart, and if they feel that their favorite rapper isn't the genuine article, they are quick to turn their backs. Beats matter, but lyricism is king. If you aren't writing your own material, what's the point?

Drake couldn't afford to take Meek's shot lying down. For years, he had battled back against charges of being "soft," stemming from his turn as the wheelchair-bound Jimmy Brooks on the Canadian high school drama *Degrassi: The Next Generation*, as well as his propensity to sing most of the hooks on his songs himself. He had recently gotten past most of that, and he couldn't allow questions about his authenticity and abilities as a writer to erode his image.

Just ten days after Meek's tweet, Drake dropped a diss track titled "Charged Up." Most were unimpressed, and Meek himself tweeted out that the song was "Baby lotion soft." The world waited with baited breath for Meek to hit back with a record of his own, but before he got the chance, Drake unleashed a second song titled "Back to Back."

SET LIST
DRAKE

Charged Up
Back to Back
6 God
Trophies
We Made It
6 Man
Shutdown
Star 67

FUTURE

March Madness
Real Sisters
Trap Niggas
Fuck Up Some Commas

KANYE WEST

Stronger
Power
Black Skinhead
All Day
Niggas In Paris
I Don't Like
Upper Echelon
Antidote
Mercy
New Slaves
Can't Tell Me Nothing
Blessings

In this song, Drizzy went after Meek without mercy. He addressed his pettiness, "trigger fingers turn to Twitter fingers." Even more savagely, he called out his nemesis's relationship with rapper Nicki Minaj and their disparity in celebrity: "Is that a world tour or your girl's tour?" It didn't help Meek that the song was a sub-woofer–bursting club banger. "Back to Back" cemented Drake as the winner of the feud, but many expected him to deliver one final, knockout blow at OVO Fest. He wouldn't miss.

SET LIST CONTINUED
DRAKE

My Way
Tuesday
Hotline Bling
The Motto
Truffle Butter

PHARRELL WILLIAMS

Drop It Like It's Hot
Frontin'
Get Lucky
Alright
Freedom

DRAKE

0 to 100
HYFR (Hell Ya Fucking Right)
Started from the Bottom
10 Bands
Energy
Know Yourself
Back to Black
Legend

The 15,000 people gathered in the Molson Canadian Amphitheatre can't wait to see what their hometown idol has in store. Drake tipped his hand by showing up to the venue wearing a "Free Meek Mill" T-shirt, which had been en vogue when Meek was incarcerated around 2014. This is going to be good.

Hanging above the stage is a giant projection screen, which depicts an iPhone whose battery life steadily rises. The moment it hits 100 percent, Drake races out, wearing a black jacket and jeans. He furiously raps the first lines of his song "Charged Up." The crowd goes wild.

The enthusiasm is hardly unexpected. This is Drizzy's crowd, his people. Few artists represent their hometown as vocally as Drake has in the last few years. From his role as an ambassador for the Raptors basketball team, to the many interviews and songs where he shouted out the city and its importance in his rise, the love affair between Drake and Toronto is very real.

After "Charged Up," Drake segues into "Back to Back." Up top, the iPhone is replaced by a slideshow of Meek-disparaging Internet memes. Some are savage and some are stupid; most are pretty funny. It may have been a juvenile move, a bit heavy-handed, but the crowd loves it and laughs uproariously. Onstage, Drake looks like he's having a blast. He flashes a big, white smile as he looks back toward the screen.

I won't let nobody disrespect my city and everything that we stand for.

After finishing "Back to Back," Drake's feud with Meek is all but settled. "You did it to yourself, boy," he chides his nemesis. "I won't let nobody disrespect my city and everything that we stand for."

In the weeks that follow this show, the Philly rapper would try to swing the momentum back his way, to no avail. He messed with the biggest dog in the yard and got bit hard. Eventually he'd violate his probation and be ordered into house arrest, effectively silencing him.

With one objective achieved, Drizzy turns his attention to his other, larger goal of the night: world domination. In the six years since its inception, Drake had managed to turn his annual Toronto extravaganza from another in a long list of regional festivals into a can't-miss event. Half the fun of the show is the pervading sense that anything could happen and that anyone might show up.

As *Noisey* writer Bryan Espiritu remembered, "I heard Drizzy was bringing [WWE wrestler] The Undertaker out. I heard N.W.A was gonna be here. I heard Kendrick. Kanye. Will Smith." The options were endless.

In that opening salvo, Drake busts out several tracks from his most recent release, *If You're Reading This It's Too Late,* including "Star 67" and "6 God." The latter, which alludes to his status as the king of Toronto, gets an explosive response. For the second-to-last number in this opening set, he brings out his first guest of the night, British grime rapper Skepta, who launches into his hit of the moment, "Shutdown."

With the crowd primed, Drake departs, ceding the limelight to his collaborator and friend Future, who puts on his own dynamic four-song showcase, culminating with his *Monster* mixtape standout, "Fuck Up Some Commas." When it's over, Drake gives Future a shout-out and then introduces his "idol," Kanye West.

A gigantic lighting rig slowly descends from the rafters. Yeezy emerges, clad in camo, to the sloweddown strains of "Stronger." For the next half-hour, West attempts to steal the show by running through a 12-song set of his most incendiary bangers, like "Black Skinhead" and "All Day." In a surprise move, he brings out Travi$ Scott, who had just been released from jail to perform "Upper Echelon." For the last song, Drake comes back out to duet with West on the Big Sean track "Blessings," after which Yeezy leaves.

If he seemed energized before, Drake is absolutely buzzing now. The crowd is fully into it and pops huge when he slips into his newest hit, "Hotline Bling." Two songs later, Drake goes into another short monologue about idols before bringing Pharrell Williams to the stage. Clad in a sailor's cap and blue jacket, Williams rips into some of his biggest crowd-pleasers, like "Freedom" and the Daft Punk song "Get Lucky." Drake tells Pharrell, "The music you make, the way you dress, we appreciate you. We look up to you. And now you're on a mission to change the world. Thank you."

After Pharrell leaves, Drake resumes his place in front of his people, ready to deliver the evening's coup de grâce. Opening with "0 to 100," he practically sprints through the biggest, self-aggrandizing anthems he has at his disposal. "Started from the Bottom" is followed by "10 Bands," which is followed by "Energy." There's hardly a moment to catch your breath.

Then, at long last, he tees up "Know Yourself." The crowd has waited all night for this moment, and when he reaches the Toronto-boosting line "I was running through the six with my woes!" they explode. In that one shining moment, there's no denying who reigns as the king of rap. As he says during the last song of the night, "All I know, if I die, I'm a mother-fuckin' legend."

Honorable Mention

Taylor Swift at the Staples Center
Los Angeles, CA (August 24)

If the 1989 World Tour was Taylor Swift's victory lap as the new queen of pop music in the mid-2010s, then her five-night stand at the Staples Center in Los Angeles was the coronation ceremony. The promise of hearing Swift sing her way through an immense catalog of hits like "Shake It Off," "Bad Blood" and "Blank Space" would have been more than enough to pack the basketball arena many times over. She took things a step further by inviting a coterie of famous faces to join her onstage night after night. At the first show, Kobe Bryant came out to present a banner celebrating her achievement of selling out the venue 16 times over. Mary J. Blige showed up the next night, with St. Vincent, Beck and John Legend three nights later and Selena Gomez and Justin Timberlake for the final show. It was the third concert, however, that takes the cake, with Natalie Maines appearing to sing "Goodbye Earl" and Alanis Morissette showing up for "You Oughta Know." On the whole, the show was a welcome celebration for positive, independent womanhood.

The Rolling Stones, Paul McCartney, Roger Waters, Neil Young, The Who and Bob Dylan
EMPIRE POLO FIELDS—INDIO, CA
OCTOBER 7-9

A DESERT TRIP THROUGH THE PAST

I was somewhere around Barstow, California, on the edge of the desert, chewing up asphalt at 80 MPH in a white Camaro I borrowed from my brother-in-law. It was nearing 100 degrees outside, but the top was down and the tunes were cranked. My stomach had just been satiated by the culinary miracle that is the In-N-Out Double-Double cheeseburger, Animal Style of course. Life couldn't get any better.

I left Las Vegas two hours earlier and was about halfway toward my destination: Indio, California. Earlier that year, Goldenvoice, the same company behind the Coachella Music Festival, announced a once-in-a-lifetime concert featuring six acts: Paul McCartney, The Rolling Stones, Bob Dylan, Roger Waters, Neil Young and The Who. The crème-de-la-crème of the baby-booming, post-WWII rock 'n' roll generation. Less charitable observers called the event "Oldchella"—the average age of the performers was around 72—its official name was Desert Trip.

2016 had been a dismal year for music fans. David Bowie succumbed to cancer in January, just days after releasing his final album, *Blackstar*. He was followed a few weeks later by Glenn Frey of the Eagles. Then came Paul Kantner of Jefferson Airplane, Phife Dawg of A Tribe Called Quest, Merle Haggard, Prince, Leonard Cohen and George Michael.

With each stunning loss, the concept of Desert Trip grew less ridiculous. As the months wore on, it became clear that this event might be the last big blowout of the '60s classic rock class. I sure as hell wasn't going to miss out on the party.

October 7

I arrive at the Empire Polo Fields just as Bob Dylan is hitting the stage. I abandon my car in a grassy lot and race breathlessly through the entranceway, catching him midway through his opening number, "Rainy Day Women #12 & 35." In that instant one of my biggest questions is answered.

Dylan had spent the last year or so on the road playing Sinatra standards almost exclusively. It was a cruel joke, having one of the greatest songwriters of all time—a few days later it was announced that he'd won the Nobel Prize for Literature—eschew his entire canon in favor of a wide berth of Tin Pan Alley cuts. For this singular event, he gives the crowd what they want: hits, baby, hits!

At 75, Dylan is no spring chicken. His voice, once a subversive, nasal wail, has transformed into a gravel-encrusted croak. On this night, he sounds far better than he did the last time I caught him in concert six years earlier. Not that the crowd cares much one way or another. Everyone is content to cheer along as Dylan treats us to a collection of old favorites like "Highway 61 Revisted," "Simple Twist of Fate," "Tangled Up in Blue" and "Ballad of a Thin Man," forgiving the fact that the songs sound far more weathered than they do in our digital libraries.

Dylan's Western-appareled visage is projected on the football-field–sized LED video screen during the first six songs and then disappears for the rest of his set, replaced by a tableau of classic film clips. Apparently, he doesn't like the way he looks up there. There is no playful banter. No, "Hey, how ya doing?" He chooses to remain, as he has throughout his career, an enigma—an artist willing to give you a tantalizing piece of himself before locking it back up.

No act is more diametrically opposed to this approach than the night's headliners, The Rolling Stones. Whereas Dylan is all shadow and intrigue, Mick Jagger and company have made their bones through a singular brand of 1,000,000-watt showmanship. Subtlety has no place here. To wit: the show begins with an incredibly forceful rendition of "Start Me Up," punctuated by massive explosions of pyro.

The effects of time seem impervious to the Rolling Stones. The wrinkles on their faces tell the story of long lives lived to the fullest. But the charisma and energy that each member exudes—minus drummer Charlie Watts, who remains as gracefully above it all as ever—is superhuman. Jagger remains the perfect, preening, cocksure front man, full of verve and ready to shake his ass. "Not gonna make any age jokes, but welcome to the Palm Springs Retirement Home of Genteel English Musicians," he says with a knowing smile.

For the most part the Stones, like their opening act, stick with the hits, including "Sympathy for the Devil," "Gimme Shelter," "Brown Sugar" and "Midnight Rambler, but they also bust out a handful of seldom played cuts like "Mixed Emotions," "Little T&A" and a cover of the Jimmy Reed song "Ride 'Em on Down," which they haven't performed since their earliest days at the Marquee Club in 1962. There's a nice homage to the next day's headliner, Paul McCartney, with a bluesy take on the Beatles' "Come Together."

If the Stones don't have anything left to say at this point, they still play like a group with something to prove. They're the only act across all three days to acknowledge—and challenge—the "Oldchella"

barbs. No way is Mick Jagger going to let you take the piss out of him. He is going to beat you to the punch and put on a show that would leave rock bands a quarter of his age panting in his wake. As the last blast of fireworks erupt into the night sky at the end of their signature song "(I Can't Get No) Satisfaction," you know that you've just witnessed the greatest rock 'n' roll band on the planet.

October 8

Saturday begins a little easier. The lot around the Polo Grounds is filled with campers who lazily filter through the security checkpoints and into the venue at their leisure. Onstage, the crew is setting up an array of teepees and canvas backdrops for Neil Young's stage show. Leave it to "Shakey" to cover up a state-of-the-art, ginormous video screen with a couple of brown tarps.

This is my first opportunity to walk the grounds and get a feel for the place, and from the upscale restaurants (I had one of the best bowls of Ramen of my life) to the bathroom facilities (real flushing toilets!), Desert Trip makes Coachella, Bonnaroo and Lollapalooza look like neighborhood block parties. The field is divided into two sections: the general admission area in the back and ticketed seating in the front. There's a pit filled with folding chairs arranged in front of the stage that extends back the length of two football fields, with two grandstands set up for additional seating on the sides. I spend the weekend in a second-row seat on the North Grandstand.

At around 6:30, Young emerges by himself and without saying a word, sits down at an upright piano and plunks out the first gorgeous notes of "After the Gold Rush." The crowd is enraptured. They fall even deeper under his spell a few moments later when he transitions to an acoustic guitar for "Heart of Gold" and "Comes a Time." Of all the singers who take the stage that weekend, Young is the one whose voice escapes the effects of time the best. That signature, high-pitched whine retains all the potency it had going back to his earliest days in the 1960s with Buffalo Springfield.

After that incredible three-song opening salvo, Young introduces his newest band, The Promise of the Real, a group that a curmudgeon seated in front of me derides as "Straight outta central casting. You know? Bradley Cooper, Brad Pitt." The band is comprised of a collection of twentysomethings and is led by Willie Nelson's sons Lukas and Micah. Together, they imbue their leader's music with an edge and an energy that's been missing in years past.

Both elements are on full display during the back-to-back performance of "Powderfinger" and "Down by the River." As soon as Young straps on his trusted Gibson Les Paul "Old Black," you know something savage is about to go down. Still, I'm totally unprepared for the sheer ferocity blasting out from the stage. Across nearly 30 minutes, "Down by the River" crests over and over again in tidal waves of guitar fury that actually force the phrase, "Are you fucking kidding me?" out my mouth, to no one in particular. I feel bad for Paul McCartney for having to follow that kind of display.

My fears turn out to be warranted, if only slightly. McCartney is one half of the greatest songwriting duo of all time, a Knight of the British Order and a damn Beatle; there is no way he isn't going to deliver the goods. In any other context, it would have been a performance for the ages, but when stacked up against Dylan, the Stones and his incendiary opening act, Neil Young, Macca falls a little flat.

Having seen him three times in the last four years, I am disappointed that McCartney refuses to change almost anything about his act. I'm not just talking about the same songs delivered in the same order. He makes the same jokes, about Eric Clapton tuning Jimi Hendrix's guitar in 1967 and a Russian minister telling him that he learned to speak English from Beatles records. Each time he's about to deliver the punch line, to his obvious consternation, he's preempted by his own devoted audience.

Still, it's incredible to hear one of the greatest collections of songs ever recorded, presented live by the man who penned them. "Live and Let Die," with its over-the-top fireworks show, is a crowd-pleaser,

as are "Helter Skelter," "Hey Jude" and the famous *Abbey Road* suite he uses to close the show. "We know what songs you like hearing," McCartney says. "It lights up with your phones like a galaxy of stars during certain songs, like Beatles ones. When we play one you don't know, it's like a black hole." Needless to say, the three-hour set is packed with galaxy-inducers.

The real gems are the moments when McCartney breaks free from the status quo and gives the crowd something different, like when he busts out the pre-Beatles Quarrymen demo "In Spite of All the Danger" or when he returns the favor to the Rolling Stones by playing "I Wanna Be Your Man," a song that he and John Lennon wrote and gifted to them in 1963.

In the middle of the set, Young comes onstage ready to kick some ass on "A Day in the Life," "Give Peace a Chance" and, for the first time ever live, "Why Don't We Do It in the Road?" It's a much-needed injection of energy and intrigue, and the audience cheers wildly as both men trade licks on their guitars.

October 9

The final day of Desert Trip can be summed up in two words: volume and vision. The former comes courtesy of The Who, who explodes onto the stage with the force of an atomic blast. The latter from Roger Waters, who unveils a show as visually stunning as anything I have ever seen.

First, The Who. The London Mod rockers—Mockers, if you will—are down to just two members: lead singer Roger Daltrey and guitarist Pete Townshend. The group of fill-ins behind them don't lack musicianship, though, especially Ringo Starr's son, Zak Starkey, on drums. At 72, Daltrey looks outstanding, easily one of the most in-shape individuals you'll find in Indio, while Townshend has lost nothing from his violent windmill guitar attack or his sharp tongue.

"Well, here the fuck we are," Pete says after the first number, "I Can't Explain." It's a toss-off comment but a welcome reminder that rock 'n' roll is meant to be vulgar and more than a little tongue-in-cheek. There are many more moments like that to come, like when he refers to the front row as a bunch of cunts or his departed bandmate and drummer Keith Moon as a wanker. Pete remains Pete.

The piss-taking attitude between songs would ring hollow if their musical performance can't measure up, but thankfully, The Who brings the house down. They sound tight, focused and, most importantly, loud. The Who's music isn't designed to be consumed through headphones or home audio systems. It's meant to be heard at 100 dB+ and more in a field full of head-banging, fist-pumping maniacs. Desert Trip finds the band at home in its natural habitat.

Townshend provides most of the highlights on classics like "Behind Blue Eyes," "We're Not Gonna Take It," "Eminence Front" and "Love Reign O'er Me," but Daltrey sounds far better than he has in well over a decade. His recent surgery to remove pre-cancerous growths from his throat has done wonders for his voice. His iconic scream on "Baba O'Riley" sends chills up and down my spine.

If nobody could match the jet engine volume of The Who, no one came close to surpassing the stunning display put together by Roger Waters. The lights around the field dim to an incandescent blue, as the image of a galaxy packed with stars fills the gigantic screen up front. The camera slowly pans forward over what appears to be the surface of the moon as a large, glowing orb grows larger in the distance. The unmistakable sounds of clanking cash registers ping from every direction until the band explodes into view onstage and slips into the song "Breathe."

Eyes go wide as the image of The Pink Floyd front man is projected onto the screen behind him in a twisted mess of psychedelic colors. For the next hour, a jaw-dropping array of exhilarating visuals engulf the crowd as Waters dives headlong into his impressive oeuvre, songs like "Set the Controls for the Heart of the Sun," "Time" and "Money." Just after finishing "Wish You Were Here," everything goes black and the air is filled with the sound of alarms. A rendering of

the Battersea Power Station pictured on the cover of *Animals* hones into view as four smoke-spewing towers slowly rise from behind the stage.

2016 is an election year, and with less than a month to go until the votes are cast, Waters utilizes his time—to the chagrin of some in the audience—to attack Republican nominee Donald Trump. During "Pigs (Three Different Ones)," some of the real estate mogul's most offensive comments are splashed across the screen. Overhead, a large inflatable floating pig, adorned with Trump's face, glows a menacing shade of red. On the side is emblazoned the phrase, "Ignorant Lying Racist Sexist *Pig*—Fuck Trump and His Wall," alluding to the real-estate mogul's plan to build a wall between Mexico and America. "I toned it down a lot," Waters later told *Billboard*. "It used to be 'Trump is the c-word.'"

Waters's show overwhelms almost every sense of the human body. Between the quadrophonic pinging sounds echoing between the numerous speaker towers during "Another Brick in the Wall Pt. 2," the laser light pyramid after "Brain Damage" and the vast, pungent clouds of marijuana smoke that flutter in and out with the shifting breeze, there's hardly a moment to let your mind rest from the overwhelming spectacle unfolding before you. It all ends with "Comfortably Numb." On top of the vast video screen, a second singer and the lead guitarist take turns belting out the classic song, while the audience watches in amazement.

"It's great to be here," Keith Richards said between long drags on a cigarette during the Rolling Stones' set on the first day. "It's great to be anywhere!" he added as a rejoinder. That statement floated into my mind as I drove back to my hotel around 2 am after Waters's stunning set. I thought about all the performers that had taken the stage and all the music that they'd given me through the years. I thought about specific moments in my life that music had lent itself to, gifting it with poignancy it would have lacked otherwise.

As I mentioned, 2016 was a rough year filled with

a lot of losses in the music industry. On the flip side, it may have been one of the best years for new releases so far this century. We got huge event records from Frank Ocean, Kendrick Lamar, Kanye West, Drake, Beyoncé, Bon Iver, Rihanna and Radiohead, along with outstanding albums from the next generation of artists like Car Seat Headrest, ScHoolBoy Q, Sturgill Simpson and Anderson .Paak, as well as poignant farewells from David Bowie, Leonard Cohen and A Tribe Called Quest. Though there's a huge Prince-shaped hole in our universe, there are many promising new talents ready and eager to fill the void. Where there is loss, there's also renewal. The music industry—and the concert industry—will endure.

It's possible that I'll see some of the artists from the Desert Trip lineup in concert again someday, but maybe I won't. The memory of this weekend will stick in my brain for as long as I'm around to relive it. If there's a better mark of a great show, then I don't know what it is.

SET LISTS
BOB DYLAN

Rainy Day Women #12 & 35
Don't Think Twice, It's All Right
Highway 61 Revisited
It's All Over Now, Baby Blue
High Water (For Charley Patton)
Simple Twist of Fate
Early Roman Kings
Love Sick
Tangled Up in Blue
Lonesome Day Blues
Make You Feel My Love
Pay in Blood
Desolation Row
Soon After Midnight
Ballad of a Thin Man
Masters of War

THE ROLLING STONES

Start Me Up
You Got Me Rocking
Out of Control
Ride 'Em on Down
Mixed Emotions
Wild Horses
It's Only Rock 'N' Roll (But I Like It)
Come Together
Tumbling Dice
Honky Tonk Women
Slipping Away
Little T&A
Midnight Rambler
Miss You
Gimme Shelter
Sympathy for the Devil
Brown Sugar
Jumpin' Jack Flash
You Can't Always Get What You Want
(I Can't Get No) Satisfaction

NEIL YOUNG

After the Gold Rush
Heart of Gold
Comes a Time
Mother Earth (Natural Anthem)
Out on the Weekend
Human Highway
Neighborhood
Show Me
Harvest Moon
Words (Between the Lines of Age)
Walk On
Texas Rangers
Powderfinger
Down by the River
Seed Justice
Peace Trail
Welfare Mothers
Rockin' in the Free World

PAUL McCARTNEY

A Hard Day's Night

Jet

Can't Buy Me Love

Letting Go

Day Tripper

Let Me Roll It

I've Got a Feeling

My Valentine

Nineteen Hundred and Eighty-Five

Maybe I'm Amazed

We Can Work It Out

In Spite of All the Danger

I've Just Seen a Face

Love Me Do

And I Love Her

Blackbird

Here Today

Queenie Eye

Lady Madonna

FourFiveSeconds

Eleanor Rigby

Being for the Benefit of Mr. Kite!

A Day in the Life

Give Peace a Chance

Why Don't We Do It in the Road?

Something

Ob-La-Di, Ob-La-Da

Band on the Run

Back in the U.S.S.R.

Let It Be

Live and Let Die

Hey Jude

I Wanna Be Your Man

Helter Skelter

Golden Slumbers

Carry That Weight

The End

THE WHO

I Can't Explain

The Seeker

Who Are You

The Kids Are Alright

I Can See for Miles

My Generation

Behind Blue Eyes

Bargain

Join Together

You Better You Bet

5:15

I'm One

The Rock

Love, Reign O'er Me

Eminence Front

Amazing Journey

Sparks

The Acid Queen

Pinball Wizard

See Me, Feel Me

Baba O'Riley

Won't Get Fooled Again

ROGER WATERS

Speak to Me

Breathe

Set the Controls for the Heart of the Sun

One of These Days

Time

Breathe (Reprise)

The Great Gig in the Sky

Money

Us and Them

Fearless

Shine on You Crazy Diamond (Parts I-V)

Welcome to the Machine

Have a Cigar

Wish You Were Here

Pigs on the Wing 1

Pigs on the Wing 2

Dogs

Pigs (Three Different Ones)

The Happiest Days of Our Lives

Another Brick in the Wall Part 2

Mother

Run Like Hell

Brain Damage

Eclipse

Why Cannot the Good Prevail

Vera

Bring the Boys Back Home

Comfortably Numb

HONORABLE MENTION

The Tragically Hip at the Rogers K-Rock Centre Kingston, Ontario, Canada (August 20)

In 2016, lead singer of The Tragically Hip Gord Downie announced that he had terminal brain cancer. The appeal of The Tragically Hip remains a mystery to most Americans and Europeans, but for Canadians, there's hardly anyone bigger. The prospect of losing the Hip forever became a national crisis. Rather than hang up his guitar and call it a day, Downie and company hit the road for one last tour that culminated with a final blowout in their hometown of Kingston, Ontario. Every show of the tour sold out within minutes, as thousands of Canucks clamored to pay their respects and hear the songs of their youth live for the final time. The last show of the run was all but a national holiday. The prime minister showed up for the gig, and those that couldn't make it watched the livestream in their homes and at outdoor viewing parties across the country. The whole thing had the vibe of a Viking funeral, going out in flames as the final notes of "Ahead by a Century" burst out of their amplifiers and then died away, never to be heard again.

NOTES

1960:

The Autobiography, Chuck Berry, Harmony Books, 1989

"50 Years Later, Still Swingin' in Newport" *Cape Cod Times*, Charles J. Gans, July 19, 2004

Newport Jazz Festival: The Illustrated History, Burt Goldblatt, *Dial Press*, 1977

Can't Be Satisfied: The Life and Times of Muddy Waters, Robert Gordon, Little, Brown, 2002

Deep Blues: A Musical and Cultural History of the Mississippi Delta, Robert Palmer, Penguin Books, 1982

Brown Eyed Handsome Man: The Life and Hard Times of Chuck Berry, Bruce Pegg, Routledge, 2005

At Newport 1960, Muddy Waters, Chess, 2001

"Riot in Newport, 1960," *The Wall Street Journal,* Marc Myers, July 1, 2010

"Riot in Newport Puts End to Jazz Festival," *Chicago Tribune,* Staff Writer, July 4, 1960

1961:

"Presley Show Brings In $52,000," *The Honolulu Advertiser,* Buck Buchwach, March 26, 1961

Coltrane "Live" at the Village Vanguard, John Coltrane, Impulse! Records, 1997

The King on the Road: Elvis on Tour: 1954-1977, Robert Gordon, St. Martin's Press, 1996

The Last Train to Memphis: The Rise of Elvis Presley, Peter Guralnick, Back Bay Books, 1994

Careless Love: The Unmaking of Elvis Presley, Peter Guralnick, Back Bay Books, 1999

The Colonel: The Extraordinary Story of Colonel Tom Parker and Elvis Presley, Alana Nash, Chicago Review Press, 2004

Elvis – Word For Word: What He Said, Exactly as He Said It, Jerry Osborne, Osborne Enterprises, 1999

John Coltrane: His Life and Music, Porter Lewis, University of Michigan Press, 2000

Such a Night in Pearl Harbor, Elvis Presley, Memphis Recording Services Limited, 2012

1962:

Live at the Apollo, James Brown, King, 1990

James Brown: The Godfather of Soul, James Brown and Bruce Tucker, Da Capo Press, 2003

Brother Ray: Ray Charles' Own Story, Ray Charles and David Ritz, Da Capo Press, 2004

Live in Paris 1961-1963, Ray Charles, Fremeaux, 2013

The James Brown Reader: 50 Years of Writing About the Godfather of Soul, George Nelson, Plume, 2008

"Being James Brown" *Rolling Stone*, Jonathan Lethem, December 2006

"James Brown *Live at the Apollo* [Expanded Edition]" (Album Review) Pitchfork, Dominque Leone, March 30, 2004

Ray Charles: Man and Music, Michael Lydon, Riverhead Books, 1999

Kill 'Em and Leave: Searching For James Brown and the American Soul, James McBride, Spiegel & Grau, 2016

"The Apollo, Uptown's Showbiz Incubator," *New York Times,* Edward Rothstein, February 7, 2011

"The Godfather Fills the Apollo One Last Time," *The Washington Post*, David Segal, December 28, 2006

The One: The Life and Music of James Brown, RJ Smith, Gotham, 2012

"Music History: James Brown at the Apollo Theater," *Huffington Post,* David Weible, July 30, 2015

1963:

Live at the Harlem Square Club, Sam Cooke, RCA Records, 2005

Nina Simone at Carnegie Hall, Nina Simone, EMI Import, 2005

Dream Boogie: The Triumph of Sam Cooke, Peter Guralnick, Back Bay Books, 2006

"Sam Cooke's Wild Side," *Mother Jones*, Joe Kloc, January 24, 2011

What Happened, Miss Simone? A Biography, Alan Light, Crown Archetype, 2016

"A Night Out With Sam Cooke: 'Harlem Square' Turns 50," NPR, Scott Simon, January 12, 2013

The Life and Times of Little Richard: The Quasar of Rock, Charles White, Harmony Books, 1985

You Send Me: The Life and Times of Sam Cooke, Daniel J. Wolff, William Morrow & Co., 1995

What Happened Miss Simone?, Directed by Liz Garbus, Netflix, 2015

1964:

Live at the Regal, B.B. King, ABC, 1997

Jerry Lee Lewis: Lost and Found, Joe Bonomo, Continuum Pub Group, 2009

Blues All Around Me: The Autobiography of B.B. King, B.B. King, It Books, 2011

Jerry Lee Lewis: His Own Story, Rick Bragg, Harper, 2014

Sam Phillips: The Man Who Invented Rock 'n' Roll, Peter Guralnick, Little, Brown, 2015

Live at the Star Club, Hamburg, Jerry Lee Lewis, Bear Family, 1999

"Jerry Lee Lewis: Live at the Star Club," *Rolling Stone,* Milo Miles, 2002

Hellfire: The Jerry Lee Lewis Story, Nick Tosches, Grove Press, 1998

1965:

The Beatles Anthology, Paul McCartney, John Lennon, George Harrison, Ringo Starr, Chronicle Books, 2000

The Beatles: The Authorized Biography, Hunter Davies, McGraw-Hill, 1968

Ticket To Ride: Inside the Beatles' 1964 Tour that Changed the World, Larry Kane, Running Press, 2003

The Beatles Across the Universe: John, Paul, George & Ringo on Tour and on Stage, Andy, Neill, Haynes Publishing UK, 2010

Shout! The Beatles in Their Generation, Philip Norman, Touchstone, 2005

Secrets of a Sparrow, Diana Ross, Villard, 1993

"Shrieks of 55,000 Accompany Beatles," *New York Times,* Murray Schumach, August 16, 1965

The Beatles at Shea Stadium: The Story Behind Their Greatest Concert, Dave Schwensen, North Shore Publishing, 2013

Lennon Remembers, Jann Wenner, Verso, 2001

The Supremes at the Copa [Expanded Edition], The Surpemes, Motown, 2012

The Beatles Anthology, Directed by Geoff Wonfor, EMI Records, 1995

The Beatles: Eight Days a Week: The Touring Years, Directed by Ron Howard, Apple Corps, Imagine Entertainment, White Horse Pictures, 2016

1966:

Bob Dylan: The Essential Interviews, Jonathan Cott, Wenner, 2006

The Bootleg Series, Vol. 4: Bob Dylan Live 1966, The "Royal Albert Hall" Concert, Bob Dylan, Columbia, 1998

The 1966 Live Recordings, Bob Dylan, Sony Legacy, 2016

Chronicles Vol. 1, Bob Dylan, Simon & Schuster, 2005

"Bob Dylan Unleashed," *Rolling Stone*, Mikal Gilmore, September 27, 2012

Bob Dylan: Behind the Shades Revisited, Clinton Heylin, Harper Entertainment, 2003

Judas!: From Forest Hills to the Free Trade Hall: A Historical View of the Big Boo, Clinton Heylin, Route, 2016

"Fan Who Called Dylan 'Judas' Breaks 33 Years of Silence," MTV News, Chris Nelson, March 9, 1999

The Rolling Stones: A Life on the Road, The Rolling Stones, Avery, 1998

Yardbirds: The Ultimate Rave-Up, Greg Russo, Crossfire Pubns, 2001

Dylan Goes Electric!: Newport, Seeger, Dylan, and the Night That Split the Sixties, Elijah Wald, Dey Street Books, 2015

Eat the Document, Directed by D.A. Pennebaker, ABC Television, 1972

No Direction Home: Bob Dylan, Directed by Martin Scorsese, Capitol, 2006

1967:

Room Full of Mirrors: A Biography of Jimi Hendrix, Charles Cross, Hachette Books, 2006

"Monterey International Pop Festival," *Monterey Herald,* Joe Fitzpatrick, June 17, 1967

Aretha: From These Roots, Aretha Franklin, Villard, 1999

A Perfect Haze: The Illustrated History of the Monterey International Pop Festival, Harvey Kubernick, Santa Monica Press, 2011

"Lou Adler on Monterey Pop," *Los Angeles Times,* Irene Lacher, June 12, 2012

Ultimate Hendrix: An Illustrated Encyclopedia of Live Concerts and Sessions, John McDermott, Hal Leonard Corporation, 2008

"Soul Survivor," *The New Yorker,* David Remnick, April 4, 2016

Respect: The Life of Aretha Franklin, David Ritz, Little, Brown, 2014

"Aretha Franklin Is Still The Queen, And The Keeper, Of Soul," *Chicago Tribune ,* Jessi Roti, March 30, 2017

Monterey Pop, Joel Selvin, Chronicle Books, 1992

Crosstown Traffic: Jimi Hendrix and the Post-War Rock 'N' Roll Revolution, Charles Shaar-Murray, St. Martin's Press, 1992

"Jimi Hendrix: I Don't Want to Be a Clown Anymore," *Rolling Stone*, Sheila Weller, November 15, 1969

Jimi Hendrix at Monterey, Directed by D.A. Pennebaker, Geffen Records, 2007

1968:

Hellraiser: The Autobiography of the World's Greatest Drummer, Ginger Baker, John Blake, 2010

Composing Himself: The Authorized Biography, Jack Bruce, Jawbone Press, 2010

At Folsom Prison (Legacy Edition), Johnny Cash, Columbia Records, 2008

Cash: The Autobiography, Johnny Cash, HarperOne, 2003

Clapton: The Autobiography, Eric Clapton, Broadway Books, 2008

Johnny Cash: The Life, Robert Hilburn, Back Bay Books, 2014

Eric Clapton – Day By Day: The Early Years 1963-1982, Marc Roberty, Backbeat Books, 2013

Cream: How Eric Clapton Took the World By Storm, Dave Thompson, Virgin Books, 2010

Cream: The Legendary Sixties Supergroup, Chris Welch, Backbeat Books, 2000

Cream's Farewell Concert, Directed by Tony Palmer, Image Entertainment, 2005

1969:

Room Full of Mirrors: A Biography of Jimi Hendrix, Charles Cross, Hachette Books, 2006

Long Time Gone: The Autobiography of David Crosby, David Crosby and Carl Gottlieb, Doubleday, 1988

Woodstock: Three Days That Rocked the World, Mike Evans and Paul Kingsbury, Sterling, 2010

Fortunate Son: My Life, My Music, John Fogerty, Back Bay Books, 2016

Bill Graham Presents: My Life Inside Rock and Roll and Out, Bill Graham and Robert Greenfield, Da Capo Press, 2004

The Beatles Anthology, Paul McCartney, John Lennon, George Harrison, Ringo Starr, Chronicle Books, 2000

I Want to Take You Higher: The Life and Times of Sly & The Family Stone, Jeff Kaliss, Backbeat Books, 2009

The Road to Woodstock, Michael Lang, Ecco, 2010

Woodstock: The Oral History, Joel Malkower, Excelsior Editions, 2009

Wild Tales: A Rock & Roll Life, Graham Nash, Three Rivers Press, 2014

The Universal Tone: Bringing My Story to Light, Carlos Santana, Little, Brown, 2014

Barefoot in Babylon: The Creation of the Woodstock Music Festival 1969, Bob Spitz, Plume, 2014

The Beatles: The Biography, Bob Spitz, Back Bay Books, 2006

Prisoner of Woodstock, Dallas Taylor, Thunder's Mouth Press, 1994

Who I Am: A Memoir, Pete Townshend, Harper Perennial, 2013

Woodstock: Three Days of Peace & Music [Director's Cut], Directed by Michael Wadleigh, Warner Home Video, 2009

The Beatles Anthology directed by Geoff Wonfor, EMI Records, 1995

1970:

Elton: The Biography, David Buckly, Chicago Review Press, 2009

"The Who Live at Leeds: 40th Anniversary," *The Quietus*, Stevie Chick, December 2, 2010

Moon: The Life and Death of a Rock Legend, Tony Feltcher, It Books, 2014

Never a Dull Moment: 1971 The Year Rock Exploded, David Hepworth, Henry Holt and Co., 2016

"Elton John's American Debut: August 25, 1970," *Performing Songwriter*, Lydia Hutchinson, August 25, 2010

"The Who: Live at Leeds," *Rolling Stone*, Greil Marcus, July 9, 1970

Before I Get Old: The Story of The Who, Dave Marsh, Plexus Publishing, 2015

The Who: 50 Years: The Official History, Ben Marshall, Harper Design, 2015

Who I Am: A Memoir, Pete Townshend, Harper Perennial, 2013

Amazing Journey: The Story of The Who, Directed by Murray Lerner, Universal Studios, 2007

Live at Leeds [Super Deluxe Edition], The Who, Geffen Records, 2010

1971:

The 1971 Fillmore East Recordings, The Allman Brothers Band, Mercury, 2014

My Cross to Bear, Gregg Allman, William Morrow Paperbacks, 2013

So Many Roads: The Life and Times of the Grateful Dead, David Browne, Da Capo Press, 2016

Bill Graham Presents: My Life Inside Rock and Roll and Out, Bill Graham and Robert Greenfield, Da Capo Press, 2004

Live at the Fillmore East and West: Getting Backstage and Personal with Rock's Greatest Legends, John Glatt, Lyons Press, 2014

One Way Out: The Inside History of the Allman Brothers Band, Alan Paul, St. Martin's Griffin, 2015

Skydog: The Duane Allman Story, Randy Poe, Backbeat Books, 2008

"Rousing Soul to Soul," *The New York Times*, Howard Thompson, August 19, 1971

"BAM Celebrates Bill Graham," *Bay Area Magazine*, Kenny Wardell, January 12, 2015

Soul to Soul, Directed by Denise Sanders, Rhino, 2004

1972:

The True Adventures of the Rolling Stones, Stanley Booth, Chicago Review Press, 2000

"Marvin Gaye's Homecoming Concert Remembered at the Kennedy Center," *Washington Post*, Roger Catlin, April 27, 2012

"The Rolling Stones: They Need Us; We Need Them," Robert Christgau, *Newsday*, July 1972

What's Going On [Deluxe Edition], Marvin Gaye, Motown, 2016

Bill Graham Presents: My Life Inside Rock and Roll and Out, Bill Graham and Robert Greenfield, Da Capo Press, 2004

Exile on Main St., A Season in Hell With the Rolling Stones, Robert Greenfield, Da Capo Press, 2008

S.T.P.: A Journey Through America With the Rolling Stones, Robert Greenfield, Da Capo Press, 2002

Life, Keith Richards, Back Bay Books, 2011

Divided Soul: The Life of Marvin Gaye, David Ritz, Da Capo Press, 2003

According to the Rolling Stones, The Rolling Stones, Chronicle Books, 2009

"Rolling Stones Fans Enter Lottery For Madison Square Garden Tickets" *Rolling Stone*, Rolling Stone Staff, July 20, 1972

"The Rolling Stone Interview: Jagger Remembers," *Rolling Stone*, Jann S. Wenner, December 14, 1995

Ladies and Gentlemen: The Rolling Stones, Directed by Rollin Binzer, Dragonaire Ltd., 1974

1973:

"On 'Astral Weeks,'" in *Stranded: Rock and Roll For a Desert Island*, Lester Bangs, Edited by Greil Marcus, Da Capo, 2007

The Man Who Sold the World: David Bowie and the 1970s, Peter Doggett, Harper, 2012

"David Bowie: How Ziggy Stardust Fell to Earth," *Rolling Stone*, Mikal Gilmore, February 2, 2012

"Starman! – The Story of Bowie's Ziggy Stardust," *NME*, Tom Howard, January 11, 2016

"David Bowie On the Ziggy Stardust Years: 'We Were Creating the 21st Century in 1971'" *Fresh Air*, Terry Gross, NPR, January 11, 2016

Bowie: The Biography, Wendy Leigh, Gallery Books, 2014

"Ziggy Stardust: How Bowie Created the Alter Ego that Changed Rock," *Rolling Stone*, Alan Light, June 16, 2016

The Complete David Bowie, Nicholas Pegg, Titan Books, 2016

On Bowie, Rob Sheffield, Dey Street Book, 2016

Ziggy Stardust and the Spiders From Mars, Directed by D.A. Pennebaker, 20th Century Fox, 1983

It's Too Late to Stop Now, Van Morrsion, Warner Bros., 2015

It's Too Late to Stop Now...Volumes II, III, IV & DVD, Van Morrison, Warner Bros., 2016

1974:

"Crosby, Stills, Nash, Young & Bert," *NME*, Roy Carr, August 31, 1974

CSNY 1974, David Crosby, Stephen Stills, Graham Nash, Neil Young, Rhino, 2014

Long Time Gone: The Autobiography of David Crosby, David Crosby and Carl Gottlieb, Doubleday, 1988

"Crosby, Stills, Nash & Young Carry On," *Crawdaddy*, Cameron Crowe, October 1974

"Stephen Stills Interview," *Creem*, Cameron Crowe, September 1974

"CSNY's Reunion: A Show of Strength," *Rolling Stone*, Ben Fong-Torres, August 15, 1974

Can You Feel the Silence? Van Morrison: A New Biography, Clinton Heylin, Chicago Review Press, 2004

Bill Graham Presents: My Life Inside Rock and Roll and Out, Bill Graham and Robert Greenfield, Da Capo Press, 2004

"The Oral History of CSNY's Infamous 'Doom Tour,'" *Rolling Stone*, Andy Greene, June 19, 2014

CSNY 1974 Liner Notes, Pete Long, Rhino, 2014

Shakey: Neil Young's Biography, Jimmy McDonough, Anchor Books, 2003

Wild Tales: A Rock & Roll Life, Graham Nash, Three Rivers Press, 2014

Waging Heavy Peace, Neil Young, Blue Rider Press, 2012

4 Way Street: The Crosby, Stills, Nash & Young Reader, Dave Zimmer, Da Capo Press, 2004

1975:

LZ – '75: The Lost Chronicles of Led Zeppelin's 1975 American Tour, Stephen Davis, Gotham, 2010

Led Zeppelin: The Oral History of the World's Greatest Rock Band, Barney Hoskyns, Wiley, 2012

"No. 1 in Rock...And How They Roused Those Eerie Wastes of Earl's Court to Frenzy," *Daily Mail*, Roderick Gilchrist, May 26, 1975

Led Zeppelin: Concert File, Dave Lewis, Omnibus Press, 2005

"The Story of Led Zeppelin's Historic Five-Night Residency at Earls Court," *Ultimate Classic Rock*, Corbin Reiff, May 17, 2015

Led Zeppelin – Day By Day, Marc Roberty, Backbeat Books, 2016

Led Zeppelin: 1968-1980, Keith Shadwick, Backbeat

Books, 2005

Bob Marley: A Life, Gerry Steckles, Interlink Books, 2008

Light and Shade: Conversations With Jimmy Page, Brad Tolinski, Crown, 2012

When Giants Walked the Earth: A Biography of Led Zeppelin, Mick Wall, St. Martin's Griffin, 2010

Catch a Fire: The Life of Bob Marley, Timothy White, Holt Paperbacks, 2006

Led Zeppelin DVD, Directed by Dick Carruthers, Atlantic, 2003

1976:

The Last Waltz [40th Anniversary Edition], The Band, Rhino, 2016

The Last Waltz, Directed by Martin Scorsese, MGM, 2006

"Why The Band's 'The Last Waltz' is the Greatest Concert Movie of All-Time," *Rolling Stone*, David Fear, November 25, 2016

Bill Graham Presents: My Life Inside Rock and Roll and Out, Bill Graham and Robert Greenfield, Da Capo Press, 2004

This Wheel's on Fire: Levon Helm and the Story of The Band, Levon Helm, Chicago Review Press, 2013

Across the Great Divide: The Band and America, Barney Hoskyns, Hal Leonard, 2006

"'The Last Waltz' Is The Greatest Thanksgiving Movie Ever Made," *UPROXX*, Steven Hyden, November 23, 2016

Autobiography, Morrissey, Penguin Classics, 2014

I Swear I Was There: The Gig That Changed the World, David Nolan, John Blake, 2006

Testimony, Robbie Robertson, Crown Archetype, 2016

England's Dreaming: Anarchy, Sex Pistols, Punk Rock, and Beyond, Jon Savage, St. Martin's Griffin, 2002

1977:

"The Curse of the Ramones," *Rolling Stone*, Mikal Gilmore, May 19, 2016

"Kiss Forever," *Rolling Stone*, Brian Hiatt, March 26, 2014

KISS: Behind the Mask: The Official Authorized Biography, David Leaf, Grand Central Publishing, 2005

On the Road With the Ramones, Monte Melnick, Bobcat Books, 2007

Ramones at 40, Martin Popoff, Sterling, 2016

Lobotomy: Surviving The Ramones, Dee Dee Ramone, Da Capo Press, 2016

Commando: The Autobiography of Johnny Ramone, Johnny Ramone, Harry N. Abrams, 2012

Nothin' to Lose: The Making of KISS (1972-1975), Ken Sharp, It Books, 2014

Alive II, KISS, Island/Def Jam, 1977

It's Alive!, The Ramones, Sire, 2005

End of the Century: The Story of the Ramones, Directed by Jim Fields, Magnolia Pictures, 2003

Ramones: It's Alive 1974-1996, Directed by George Seminara, Rhino, 2007

1978:

"How Cheap Trick Put the Budokan on the Map," *Japan Times*, Philip Brasor, April 18, 2008

Bruce, Peter Ames Carlin, Touchstone, 2012

At Budokan, Cheap Trick, SBME Special MKTS, 1979

"Springsteen: Local Boy Makes Good," *The Aquinas*, Paul Dwyer, September 21, 1978

"The History of Cheap Trick's Breakthrough 'At Budokan' LP," *Ultimate Classic Rock*, Jeff Giles, February

2, 2016

Bill Graham Presents: My Life Inside Rock and Roll and Out, Bill Graham and Robert Greenfield, Da Capo Press, 2004

"Greetings From the Capitol," *The Montclarion*, Kevin Malmud, September 20, 1978

Bruce Springsteen On Tour: 1968-2005, Dave Marsh, Bloomsbury USA, 2006

Talk About a Dream: The Essential Interviews of Bruce Springsteen, Christopher Phillips, Bloomsbury Press, 2013

"Springsteen's Golden Age: 1978," *The New Yorker*, David Remnick, July 20, 2012

Racing in the Street: The Bruce Springsteen Reader, June Skinner Sawyers, Penguin Books 2004

"Cheap Trick: For Us, Budokan Was Like Winning the Lottery," *Team Rock*, Ken Sharp, October 15, 2008

Born to Run, Bruce Springsteen, Simon & Schuster, 2016

The Promise: The Making of Darkness on the Edge of Town, Directed by Thom Zimmy, Sony Legacy, 2011

1979:

"Van Halen's Big Rock," *Rolling Stone*, Terry Atkinson, June 14, 1979

Everybody Wants Some: The Van Halen Saga, Ian Christie, Wiley, 2008

Paul McCartney: Many Years From Now, Barry Miles, Holt Paperbacks, 1998

Van Halen Rising: How a Southern California Party Band Saved Heavy Metal, Greg Renoff, ECW Press, 2015

Crazy From the Heat, David Lee Roth, Vintage, 2000

Slash, Slash and Anthony Bozza, It Books, 2008

"Backstage With Van Halen at the Califfornia Word Music Festival," *Van Halen Newsdesk*, Staff Writer, April 8, 2014

Concert For The People Of Kampuchea, Various Artists, Atlantic, 1981

Van Halen: A Visual History: 1978-1984, Neil Zlozower, Chronicle Books, 2007

Eddie Van Halen, Eddie Van Halen, Chronicle Books, 2011

1980:

Comfortably Numb: The Inside Story of Pink Floyd, Mark Black, Da Capo Press, 2008

"How Pink Floyd's 'The Wall' Almost Became a Deadly Disaster," *Music Aficionado*, Alan Di Perna, October 7, 2016

AC/DC: Maximum Rock & Roll: The Ultimate Story of the World's Greatest Rock-and-Roll Band, Murray Engleheart, It Books, 2008

The Youngs: The Brothers Who Built AC/DC, Jesse Fink, St. Martin's Press, 2014

"How Pink Floyd's Short-Lived Tour For 'The Wall' Re-Invented the Rock Concert, *Ultimate Classic Rock*, Dave Lifton, February 7, 2015

Inside Out: A Personal History of Pink Floyd, Nick Mason, Chronicle Books, 2005

The Complete Pink Floyd: The Ultimate Reference, Glenn Povey, Sterling, 2016

"Pink Floyd Stages Lavish Show on 'Wall,'" *The New York Times*, John Rockwell, February 26, 1980

The Making of Pink Floyd: The Wall, Gerald Scarfe, Da Capo Press, 2010

Saucerful of Secrets: The Pink Floyd Odyssey, Nicholas Schaffner, Delta, 1992

Highway to Hell: The Life and Death of AC/DC Legend Bon Scott, Clinton Walker, Verse Chorus Press, 2007

Is There Anybody Out There? The Wall Live 1980-1981, Pink Floyd, EMI, 2000

1981:

"The Clash – 30 Years Since Bond's on Broadway," *The Huffington Post*, Salvatore Bono, June 21, 2011

The Clash, The Clash, Grand Central Publishing, 2008

From Here to Eternity: Live, The Clash, Epic, 2008

"For The Clash, Music Is Part of the Message," *New York Times*, Debra Rae Cohen, May 24, 1981

Passion For Fashion: The Real Story of The Clash, Pat Gilbert, Da Capo Press, 2005

"Flashback: The Clash Take New York in 1981," *Rolling Stone*, Andy Greene, March 14, 2013

"The Clash, Quartet," *New York Times*, Stephen Holden, May 30, 1981

Glow: The Autobiography of Rick James, Rick James, Atria Books, 2015

"The Bloom Has Faded at Small Rock Clubs," *New York Times*, Robert Palmer, May 29, 1981

Redemption Song: The Ballad of Joe Strummer, Chris Salewicz, Farrar Straus and Giroux, 2006

Street Songs [Rarities Edition], Rick James, Motown Records, 2010

The Future is Unwritten, Directed by Julian Temple, Sony Legacy, 2008

1982:

Not Dead Yet: The Memoir, Phil Collins, Crown Archetype, 2016

Without Frontiers: The Life and Music of Peter Gabriel, Daryl Easlea, Overlook-Omnibus, 2014

"Ozzy Osbourne: I Had Nothing to Lose," *The Guardian*, Rob Fitzpatrick, June 16, 2011

"Flashback: Peter Gabriel Reunites With Genesis in 1982," *Rolling Stone*, Andy Greene, April 7, 2015

Crazy Train: The High Life and Tragic Death of Randy Rhoads, Joel McIver, Jawbone Press, 2011

"Everything you need to know about Ozzy Osbourne biting the head off a bat in Des Moines," *The Des Moines Register*, Kyle Munson, January 20, 2016

"Hang 'Em Short, Says Ozzy," *Georgia Straight*, Steve Newton, June 18, 1982

I Am Ozzy, Ozzy Osbourne, Grand Central Publishing, 2011

Speak of the Devil, Directed by Ozzy Osbourne, Eagle Rock Entertainment, 2012

1983:

"A Musical Perfect Storm: U2 Live at Red Rocks," *Nikkei View*, Gil Asakawa, June 4, 2008

Bono: In Conversation With Michka Assayas, Riverhead Hardcover, Michka Assayas, 2005

"U2 Show Still Echoes at Red Rocks," *Denver Post*, Ricardo Baca, May 21, 2008

"U2's Gamble at Red Rocks," *Rolling Stone*, Damien Cave, June 24, 2002

"The Police: Alone at the Top," *Rolling Stone*, Christopher Connelly, March 1, 1984

The Police: 1978-1983, Lynn Goldsmith, Little, Brown and Company, 2007

U2: The Definitive Biography, John Jobling, Thomas Dunne Book, 2014

U2 by U2, Neil McKormick, It Books, 2009

"The Police Perform For 70,000 at Shea Stadium," *New York Times*, Jon Pareles, August 20, 1983

"U2: Under a Blood Red Sky," *Pitchfork*, Scott Plagenhoef, September 29, 2009

U2 Live at Red Rocks: Under a Blood Red Sky, Directed

by Gavin Taylor, 1984
Under a Blood Red Sky, U2 Island, 2008

1984:
Our Band Could Be Your Life, Michael Azerrad, Back Bay Books, 2002
"The Replacements: The Greatest Band That Never Was," *Rolling Stone*, Jon Dolan, September 22, 2014
"Everybody Is a Star: How the Rock Club First Avenue Made Minnesota the Center of Music in the '80s," *Pitchfork*, Michaelangelo Matos, March 14, 2016
Trouble Boys: The True Story of the Replacements, Bob Mehr, Da Capo Press, 2016
"Revisiting the Replacements 'Let it Be,'" *Slate*, Stephen Metcalf, December 17, 2009
"1984 Michael Jackson Tour," *Newsweek*, Staff, July 15, 1984
"Going Down With The Replacements," *The Village Voice*, RJ Smith, December 11, 1984
Michael Jackson: The Magic, The Madness, The Whole Story, 1958-2009, J. Randy Taraborelli, Grand Central Publishing, 2010
Walsh, Jim, *The Replacements: All Over But the Shouting: An Oral History*, Jim Walsh, Voyageur Press, 2009
"The Story of the Jackson Family, NFL, and the Disastrous Victory Tour," *Tampa Bay Times*, Kevin Wuench, November 21, 2015

1985:
"U2's Bad Break: 12 Minutes at Live Aid That Made the Band's Career," *Rolling Stone*, Gavin Edwards, July 10, 2014
"For Prince's Concert, It's a Reign of Rock," *Los Angeles Times*, Robert Hilburn, February 20, 1985
"Prince Talks: The Silence is Broken," *Rolling Stone*, John Karlen, September 12, 1985
Let's Go Crazy: Prince and the Making of Purple Rain, Alan Light, Atria Books, 2014
"Live Aid: 30 Things You Never Knew About the 1985 Concert," *Mirror*, Steve Mayall, July 13, 2015
"Prince: The Oral History of 'Purple Rain,'" *Spin*, Ben Raferty, July 2009
Prince: Inside the Music and the Masks, Ro Ronin, St. Martin's Press, 2011
"Prince's Historic 1984 Purple Rain Tour," *About*, Ken Simmons, April 21, 2016
I Would Die 4 U: Why Prince Became an Icon, Touré, Atria Books, 2013
Prince: The Man and His Music, Matt Throne, Agate Bolden, 2016
Live Aid, Directed by Vincent Scarza, Rhino, 2004

1986:
"Flashback: Queen Steals the Show at Live Aid," *Rolling Stone*, Andy Greene, February 5, 2013
Lady Gaga: A Monster Romance, Flame Tree Publishing, Hugh Fielder, 2012
A Light That Never Goes Out: The Enduring Saga of The Smiths, Tony Fletcher, Crown Archetype, 2012
"Queen's Tragic Rhapsody," *Rolling Stone*, Mikal Gilmore, July 7, 2014
Mercury: An Intimate Biography of Freddie Mercury, Lesley-Ann Jones, Touchstone, 2012
Bowie: The Biography, Wendy Leigh, Gallery Books, 2014
Set the Boy Free: The Autobiography, Johnny Marr, Dey Street Books, 2016
Autobiography, Morrissey, Penguin Classics, 2014
Somebody to Love: The Life, Death and Legacy of Fred-

die Mercury, Marr Richards and Mark Langthorne, Weldon Owen, 2016
"Queen Turns 40: How Rare was Freddie Mercury," *Consequence of Sound*, Michael Roffman, July 14, 2013
Queen: Live at Wembley Stadium, Directed by Queen, Eagle Rock Entertainment, 2012

1987:
My Appetite For Destruction: Sex, Drugs & Guns N' Roses, Steven Adler and Lawrence Spagnola, It Books, 2011
Reckless Road: Guns N' Roses and the Making of Appetite For Destruction, Marc Canter and Jason Porath, Shoot Hip Press, 2008
Def Jam, Inc. : Russell Simmons, Rick Rubin, and the Extraordinary Story of the World's Most Influential Hip-Hop Label, Stacy Gueraseve, OneWorld, Ballantine, 2005
"Guns N' Roses' 'Appetite for Destruction': Filthy, Sexy, Cool," *Rolling Stone*, Brian Hiatt, August 9, 2007
It's So Easy: And Other Lies, Duff McKagan, Touchstone, 2012
"Rock: 'Def Jam 87,' Rap at the Garden," *New York Times*, Robert Palmer, September 5, 1987
Slash, Slash and Anthony Bozza, It Books, 2008
"Guns N' Roses Glam Slams With Noisy Aggressiveness," *Los Angeles Times*, John Voland, December 28, 1987
W.A.R.: The Unauthorized Biography of William Axl Rose, Mick Wall, St. Martin's Griffin, 2008

1988:
"Lee Brings Michael Jackson's 'Bad' Magic to Big Screen," *Reuters*, Mike White-Collett, August 13, 2012
"Everybody Say AAOW!," *Q Magazine*, Paul Du Noyer, November 1987
"A Principle Boy in Total Control, *The Observer*, John Peel, July 17, 1988
Michael Jackson: The Magic, The Madness, The Whole Story, 1958-2009, J. Randy Taraborelli, Grand Central Publishing, 2010
"Depeche Mode's Concert For the Masses Rose Bowl Show, 25 Years Later," *Radio.com*, Jay Tilles, June 18, 2013
"A Piece of History: Michael Jackson Live at Wembley Stadium," *Huffington Post*, Joe Vogel, September 13, 2012
"'When was I last really happy? Being Michael Jackson's backing singer on his Bad tour': Inside the head of... Sheryl Crow," *The Daily Mail*, John Wilde, January 15, 2014
Michael Jackson Live at Wembley, July 16, 1988, Directed by Andrew Morhan, Sony Legacy, 2012
Depeche Mode: 101, Directed by D.A. Pennebaker, Mute Film 1989

1989:
Ruthless: A Memoir, Jerry Heller, Gallery Books, 2006
"Ice Cube Keeps Cool . . . Chills Clash," *L.A. Times*, Robert Hilburn, March 25, 1989
Dr. Dre: The Biography, Ro Ronin, Da Capo Press, 2007
"Remembering N.W.A's Infamous Concert 25 Years Ago in Anaheim," *O.C. Weekly*, Gabriel San Roman, March 27, 2014
Enter Night: A Biography of Metallica, Mick Wall, St. Martin's Griffin, 2012
Original Gangstas: The Untold Story of Dr. Dre, Eazy-E, Ice Cube, Tupac Shakur, and the Birth of West Coast Rap, Ben Westoff, Hachette Books, 2016

Live Shit: Binge & Purge, Metallica, Elektra, 2002

1990:
Out of the Madness: Strictly Unauthorized Biography of Janet Jackson, J. Randy Taraborelli and Bart Andrews, Headline Books Publishing, 1995
My Life With My Sister Madonna, Christopher Ciccone, Simon Spotlight Entertainment, 2008
"The Time Toronto Police Nearly Arrested Madonna," *Toronto Sun*, David Friend, May 28, 2016
"Madonna Pumps it Up With 'Blond Ambition,'" *Los Angeles Times*, Robert Hilburn, May 14, 1990
"On the 25th Anniversary of 'Madonna: Truth or Dare,'" *The Museum of Modern Art*, Izzy Lee, August 23, 2016
"25 Reasons Madonna's Blond Ambition Tour Still Rules, 25 Years Later," *People*, Drew Mackie, April 13, 2015
The Mammoth Book of Madonna, Morgan Michaelle, Running Press, 2015
"Madonna Moments: Pope Calls For Live Boycott," *Digital Spy*, Reynolds Simon, August 13, 2008
"Top 10 Vatican Pop-Culture Moments: Madonna, Over and Over," *Time*, Frances Romero, October 20, 2010
"Janet Jackson's Dance of Community," *Los Angeles Times*, Chris Willman, April 23, 1990
Madonna: Truth or Dare, Directed by Alek Keshishian, Miramax Films, 1991

1991:
Our Band Could Be Your Life: Scenes From the American Indie Underground, Michael Azerrad, Back Bay Books, 2002
"Lollapalooza Proves the Most Successful Tour of the Festival Season," *Rolling Stone*, David Fricke, September 19, 1991
"Reflecting On Jane's Addiction and the First Lollapalooza at Irvine Meadows," *OC Weekly*, Lina Lecaro, September 22, 2016
"The Day the Music Didn't Die," *Seattle Weekly*, Chris Nelson, October 9, 2006
Cinderella's Big Score: Women of the Punk & Indie Underground, Maria Raha, Seal Press, 2004
"Lollapalooza, A Woodstock For the Lost Generation," *New York Times*, Simon Reynolds, August 4, 1991
"Lollapalooza 1991: The Underground as a Community," *PopMatters*, Dennis Shin, October 20, 2011
International Pop Underground Convention, Various Artists, K Records, 2004
"The Five Best (And Five Worst) Lollapalooza Lineups Ever," *Spin*, Dan Weiss, July 31, 2013
"An Oral History of the First Lollapalooza," *Spin*, Jonathan Zwickel, May 17, 2011

1992:
Come As You Are: The Story of Nirvana, Michael Azerrad, Three Rivers Press, 1993
"Nirvana, Public Enemy, Beastie Boys Cross the Pond For Reading Festival," *Rolling Stone*, Michael Azerrad, October 29, 1992
"Going For Baroque," *Spin*, Mark Blackwell and Jim Greer, July 30, 2015
Heavier Than Heaven: A Biography of Kurt Cobain, Charles Cross, Hachette Books, 2002
"Dave Grohl on Nirvana's 'Disastrous' Reading Gig," *Spin*, William Goodman, November 25, 2009
It Crawled From the South: An R.E.M. Companion, Marcus Gray, Da Capo Press, 1997

"Strange Love: The Story of Kurt Cobain and Courtney Love," *Vanity Fair*, Lynn Hirschberg, September 1, 1992

At Reading, Nirvana, Geffen Records, 2009

"Peace Buzz: Rice's Tour is Delaying Her Viewing of Dracula," *Atlanta Journal-Constitution*, Don O'Brient, November 20, 1992

"R.E.M. Played Sole 'Automatic For the People' Concert 20 Years Ago Today, *Slicing Up Eyeballs*, Staff Writer, November 19, 2012

Nirvana: The Biography, Everett True, Da Capo Press, 2009

"Gig of a Lifetime: Nirvana, Reading Festival 1992," *Penny Black Music*, Paul Weller, March 13, 2012

1993:
Unbelievable: The Life, Death, and Afterlife of the Notorious B.I.G., Cheo Hodari Coker, Vibe Books, 2013

Holler If You Hear Me, Michael Eric Dyson, Civitas Books, 2006

"For Whitney Houston, Showy Doesn't Count: The Show is the Voice," *New York Times*, Stephen Holden, July 22, 1993

Remembering Whitney," Cissy Houston and Lisa Dickey, Harper, 2013

Tupac Shakur: The Life and Times of an American Icon, Tayannah Lee McQuillar, Da Capo Press, 2010

"After Further Review #2: Tupac/Biggie Freestyle," *Soul-Sides*, O-Dub, November 27, 2013

1994:
"Looking Back on Woodstock 1994, Twenty Years Later," *The Gothamist*, Jen Carlson, August 13, 2014

"Flashback: Nine Inch Nails Play Mud-Caked Set at Woodstock '94," *Rolling Stone*, Andy Greene, June 6, 2013

"Review: Lollapalooza," *Variety*, Bruce Haring, July 11, 1994

Nine Inch Nails, Martin Huxley, St. Martin's Griffin, 2007

"Woodstock '94: Music, Moshing, Mud . . . And Bob Dylan," *Ultimate Classic Rock*, Frank Mastropolo, August 12, 2015

"Lollapalooza '94 Opens in Las Vegas," *New York Times*, Jon Pareles, July 9, 1994

"Woodstock '94: The Overview," *New York Times*, Scott Janny, August 15, 1994

Nine Inch Nails, Tommy Udo, Bobcat Books, 2008

"The Five Best (And Five Worst) Lollapalooza Lineups Ever," *Spin*, Dan Weiss, July 31, 2013

1995:
Selena's Secret: The Revealing Story Behind Her Tragic Death, Maria Celeste Arrarás, Atria Books, 2015

"Pearl Jam: Taking On Ticketmaster," *Rolling Stone*, Eric Boehlert, December 28, 1995

Ticket Masters: The Rise of the Concert Industry and How the Public Got Scalped, Dean Budnick and Josh Baron, Plume, 2011

"Brokering the Biggest Deal of All," *Chicago Sun-Times*, Jim DeRogatis, September 14, 2003

"Just Play, Baby," *Chicago Tribune*, Greg Kot, July 12, 1995

"Pearl Jam Versus Ticketmaster," *Seattle Weekly*, Fred Moody, November 2, 1994

Five Against One: The Pearl Jam Story, Kim Neely, Penguin Books, 1998

Pearl Jam 20, Pearl Jam, Simon & Schuster, 2011

"15 Best Moments From Selena Quintanilla Iconic Houston Astrodome Concert in 1995," *Latin Times*, Jessica Lucia Roiz, February 26, 2016

"Ten Past Ten," *Spin*, Eric Weisbard, August 2001

Live: The Last Concert, Selena, EMI, 2002

1996:
Oasis: Supersonic, Directed by Mat Whitecross, Mint Pictures, 2016

...There and Then, Directed by Dick Carruthers, Sony Music Distribution, 1996

"Zero Worship," *Spin*, Craig Marks, June 1996

Take Me There: The Oasis Story, Paul Mather, Overlook Books, 1997

"Liam Gallagher Interview: Remembering 'Dribs and Drabs' of Oasis' Supersonic Years," *Dorkshelf*, Noah R. Taylor, October 24, 2016

"Oasis @ Knebworth: 20 Years On," *Drowned in Sound*, Derek Robertson, August 11, 2016

"Oasis at Knebworth: 20 years since Britpop's biggest gigs," *BBC News*, Mark Savage, August 10, 2016

Live/Smashing Pumpkins Brixton Academy, London," *The Independent*, Ryan Gilbey, May 16, 1996

"Pop Will Eat Itself: Oasis As Mass-Catering Phenomenon," *The Quietus*, Roy Wilkinson, June 14, 2010

1997:
"The Greatest Gig I Ever Saw: Radiohead at Glastonbury, 1997," *Sabotage Times*, Craig Campbell, June 25, 2014

"Thom Yorke Interview," *Interview Magazine*, Daniel Craig, July 15, 2013

"Rage Against the Machine's Revolution Rock," *Rolling Stone*, Matt Hendrickson, September 4, 1997

"Whatever Happened to Alternative Nation Part 8: 1997: The Ballad of Oasis and Radiohead," *A.V. Club*, Steven Hyden, January 25, 2011

"We Have Lift-Off," *Mojo*, Jim Irvin and Barney Hoskyns, September 1997

"Radiohead: OK Computer," *Rolling Stone*, Mark Kemp, July 10, 1997

"Press Your Space Next to Mine, Love," *MOJO*, Nick Kent, July 1997

"20 Sets That Shook Glastonbury: The Stories Behind Worthy Farm's Most Memorable Ever Performances," *NME*, Al Horner, June 22, 2015

"Meeting People Is Easy," *Melody Maker*, Neil Kulkarni, November 1998

Exit Music: The Radiohead Story, Mac Randall, Delta, 2000

"Rage Against the Machine/Wu-Tang Clan Review," *Spin*, Jeff Salmon, November 1997

Glastonbury: An Oral History of the Music, Mud & Magic, John Shearlaw, Ebury Press, 2005

"Live Report: Rage Against the Machine and the Wu-Tang Clan in New Jersey," *Rolling Stone*, Staff Writer, August 22, 1997

"The Making of OK Computer," *The Guardian*, Tony Wadsworth, December 20, 1997

"Classic Review: Radiohead, *OK Computer*," *Spin*, Barry Walters, May 8, 2016

1998:
Elliott Smith, Autumn De Wilde, Chronicle Books, 2007

"Rock Is Deader...or Maybe It's Just Unconscious," *Star Tribune*, Tiffany Funk, November 1, 1998

"Largo Nights," *The New Yorker*, Dana Goodyear, May 19, 2008

"Keep the Things You Forgot: An Elliott Smith Oral History," *Pitchfork*, Jayson Greene, October 21, 2013

"Off Camera: Jon Brion on Legendary Largo Shows," Sam Jones, YouTube Video, June 22, 2016

"Marilyn Manson Kicks Off Tour," MTV News, Staff, October 28, 1998

"Elliott Smith Launches Tour in Support of XO," MTV News, Chris Nelson, September 21, 1998

"At Coronet, Largo Tries a New Space on For Size," *Los Angeles Times*, Natalie Nichols, May 18, 2008

Torment Saint: The Life of Elliott Smith, William Todd Schultz, Bloomsbury USA, 2015

Marilyn Manson: The Unauthorized Biography, Doug Small, Omnibus Press, 2008

1999:
"Gary Tovar Has His Goldenvoice," *LA Weekly*, Vickie Chang, December 15, 2011

"Inside 'The Miseducation of Lauryn Hill,'" *Rolling Stone*, Laura Checkoway, August 26, 2008

"Woodstock '99 Burns Its Own Mythology," *Rolling Stone*, Jenny Eliscu, July 26, 1999

"Paul Tollett, Goldenvoice Team on the Struggle and Ultimate Success of Creating Coachella," *Billboard*, Andrew Flanagan, November 9, 2012

"Woodstock '99: The Day the Music Died," *The San Francisco Chronicle*, Jane Ganahl, July 28, 1999

"Triumph of the Anti-Woodstock," *Los Angeles Times*, Robert Hilburn, October 12, 1999

"Hill Moves to Higher Ground," *Los Angeles Times*, Robert Hilburn, February 22, 1999

"Let's Revisit the Chaos of Woodstock '99: 'The Day the Music Died,'" *Huffington Post*, Matthew Jacobs, July 23, 2014

"Coachella Festival to Offer Beck, Tool, Pavement," MTV News, Gil Kaufman, August 6, 1999

"Lauryn Hill Finds Her Place in the World," *Chicago Tribune*, Greg Kot, February 7, 1999

"19 Worst Things About Woodstock '99," *Rolling Stone*, Daniel Kreps, July 31, 2014

"Coachella: Musical Oasis in the California Desert," *Rolling Stone*, Steven Mirkin and Marlene Goldman, October 11, 1999

"Coachella Provided an Antidote to Woodstock '99's Hangover," *Rolling Stone*, Steven Mirkin and Marlene Goldman, October 11, 1999

"Paul Tollett, Coachella Founder – Renman Live #91" YouTube Video, Steve Rennie, Posted February 22, 2014

"Woodstock '99: Rage Against the Latrine," *Rolling Stone*, Rob Sheffield, September 2, 1999

2000:
"Why 'Stankonia' is the Most Important OutKast Album," *Complex*, Brandon Caldwell, October 31, 2015

"Jesus Saves," *The Village Voice*, Robert Christgau, March 21, 2000

"Melody Makers of Hip-Hop," *New York Daily News*, Isaac Guzman, October 22, 2000

"End of the Ice Age?" *Spin*, Sacha Jenkins, March 2001

"100 Greatest Albums: 1985-2005," *Spin*, Michaelangelo Matos, July 2005

Third Coast: OutKast, Timbaland, and How Hip-Hop Became a Southern Thing, Roni Sarig, Da Capo Press, 2002

Mo' Meta Blues, Ahmir Thompson, Grand Central Publishing, 2015

"D'Angelo Is Holding Your Hand," *Rolling Stone*, Touré, May 11, 2000

"OutKast's Powerful Words Stir House of Blues Crowd," *Los Angeles Times*, Marc Weingarten, October

28, 2000

Dirty South: Outkast, Lil Wayne, Soulja Boy, and the Southern Rappers Who Reinvented Hip-Hop, Ben Westoff, Chicago Review Press, 2011

2001:

Decoded, Jay Z, Spiegel & Grau, 2011

"Jay Z Vs. Nas: The Story Behind The Last Great Rivalry in Hip Hop History," *Uproxx*, Daniel Figueoa, December 8, 2014

"The Oral History of Hot '97s Summer Jam," *Complex*, Thomas Golianopoulos, June 5, 2015

"Nine Years Ago Today, Jay Z and Nas Officially End Their Beef at 'I Declare War,'" *Uproxx*, Eddie Gonzales, October 27, 2014

"Ralph McDaniels on 20 Years of Hot 97's Summer Jam," *Village Voice*, Chaz Kangas, May 31, 2013

"Kanye West Violinist Miri Ben-Ari Debuts," *Rolling Stone*, Loolwa Khazzoom, September 23, 2005

"Jay Z's Special Guest a Thriller For Summer Jam Crowd," MTV News, Shaheem Reid, June 29, 2001

"Nas a No-Show at Summer Jam, Denies Planned Mock Lynching of Jay Z," MTV News, Shaheem Reid, June 27, 2002

"Review: The Concert For New York City," *Variety*, David Sprague, October 21, 2001

"Concert For New York City Raises Over $30 Million," MTV News, Jon Wiederhorn, November 2, 2001

The Concert For New York City, Directed by Louis J. Horvitz, Sony Legacy, 2002

2002:

"The Making of the Strokes," *Rolling Stone*, Jenny Eliscu, April 11, 2002

"Strokes, Stripes Paint NYC Red," *Rolling Stone*, Tony Gervino, August 16, 2002

"Live—I Kissed Meg White!: White Stripes/Strokes at Radio City," *The Fader*, Drew Goldberg, 2002

"The White Stripes Interview," *Spin*, Chuck Klosterman, October 2002

"Wilco's Shot in the Arm," *Chicago Tribune*, Greg Kot, August 15, 2001

Wilco: Learning How to Die, Greg Kot, Three Rivers Press, 2004

"Fader Cover Story: The White Stripes," *The Fader*, Knox Robinson, Spring 2002

"POP REVIEW; Coming Home on Crutches and Filling Radio City," *New York Times*, Kelefah Sanneh, August 17, 2002

"The Strokes and the White Stripes Rock Radio City Music Hall," *Rolling Stone*, Austin Scaggs, September 19, 2002

"The Strokes: The Rebirth of Cool," *Spin*, Marc Spitz, January 2003

2003:

Dixie Chicks: Shut Up and Sing, Directed by Barbara Kopple and Cecilia Peck, The Weinstein Company, 2006

Whatever You Say I Am: The Life and Times of Eminem, Anthony Bozza, Three Rivers Press, 2004

"Full Text: Bush's Speech," *The Guardian*, George W. Bush, March 17, 2003

"Full Text of Brokaw's Interview with Bush," *New York Times*, Tom Brokaw, April 25, 2003

"The Gig of a Lifetime," *The Guardian*, Martin Clarke and Imogen Tilden, June 29, 2003

"Dixie Chicks: Shepherd's Bush Empire, London," *The Guardian*, Betty Clarke, March 12, 2003

"Old Hands Make Light Work of Set Pieces," *The Guardian*, Akin Ojumu, June 29, 2003

"Effect That Turns Tritiest Trundlers into Perky Philosophers," *The Guardian*, Alexis Petridis, June 30, 2003

"Full Text of Colin Powell's Speech," *The Guardian*, Colin Powell, February 5, 2003

"Eminem Gets Some Hometown Love, 50 Cent Make Em Fans Believers at Rare Show," MTV News, Shaheem Reid, July 14, 2003

"It's Dixie Chicks Vs. Country Fans, But Who's Dissing Whom?" *New York Times*, Kelefa Sanneh, May 25, 2006

"You Can Take the Chick Out of the Country..." *The Washington Times*, Staff Writer, October 2, 2003

From Pieces to Weight, 50 Cent, MTV Books, 2006

2004:

Dave Chappelle's Block Party, Directed by Michel Gondry, Bob Yari Productions, 2005

"Chappelle Open to Comedy Return," CBC News, CBC Staff, February 3, 2006

"Usher's Wild Ride," *Rolling Stone*, Vanessa Grigoriadis, May 13, 2004

"How Dave Chappelle's Block Party Charted Hip-Hop's Evolution," MTV News, Julian Kimble, March 2, 2016

"Why Dave Chappelle Should Never Come Back," *Esquire*, Sean Manning, August 26, 2013

"Usher Tells 'The Truth,'" *Daily Press*, Sam McDonald, August 1, 2004

"Usher Proves He's 'The Truth' at Tour Kickoff," MTV News, Staff, August 6, 2004

"Chappelle Throwing a Block Party with Kanye, Lauryn, Others," MTV News, Joseph Patel, September 7, 2004

"Fugees—Yes, Even Lauryn—Reunite For Dave Chappelle's Block Party," MTV News, Joseph Patel, September 20, 2004

"Dave Chappelle's Rise From Rick James to Radio City: A Timeline," *Rolling Stone*, Staff, June 17, 2004

"The Weather Makes Way for a Reunion," *New York Times*, Kelefa Sanneh, September 20, 2004

Mo' Meta Blues, Ahmir Thompson, Grand Central Publishing, 2015

"Dave Chappelle Inks $50 Million Deal," *Today*, Andrew Wallenstein, August 3, 2004

"The Story of the Fugees' Bitter Breakup and Unforgettable Legacy," UPROXX, Carl Williott, 2016

2005:

Bullet in a Bible, Directed by Samuel Bayer, Reprise, 2005

"Working Class Heroes," *Rolling Stone*, John Colapinto, November 17, 2005

Green Day: A Musical Biography, Kjersti Egerdahal, Greenwood, 2009

"Green Day and the Palace of Wisdom," *Rolling Stone*, Matt Hendrickson, February 24, 2005

"Geldof's Live 8 a Triumph," *CNN*, Graham Jones, September 2, 2005

Nobody Likes You: Inside the Turbulent Life, Times and Music of Green Day, Marc Spitz, Hachette Books, 2007

"Green Day: Milton Keynes Bowl, Sunday, June 19," *NME*, Staff, September 12, 2005

"Green Day—Milton Keynes Bowl 2005," *Virtual Festivals*, Mr. Jasinski, July 6, 2005

"The Morning After 'American Idiot,'" *New York Times*, Jon Pareles, April 29, 2009

"Review: Live 8," *The Guardian*, Alexis Petridis, July 3, 2005

"Green Day Live at Milton Keynes, June 18, 2005," *Kerrang!*, Nick Ruskell, June 25, 2005

"Jolly Green Giants, How Green Day Saved Rock—And Their Own Career," *Entertainment Weekly*, Tom Sinclair, February 11, 2005

"David Bowie to Beyoncé: Ten of the Greatest Live Performances," *Daily Mail*, Jo Whiley, November 2, 2011

2006:

Hunger Makes Me a Modern Girl, Carrie Brownstein, Riverhead Books, 2016

The Underground Is Massive: How Electronic Dance Music Conquered America, Michaelangelo Matos, Dey Street Books, 2015

"The 20 Best Coachella Sets of All-Time," *LA Weekly*, John Ochoa, January 14, 2016

"A Glorious Ending to Sleater-Kinney," *Los Angeles Times*, Ann Powers, August 14, 2006

"Ten Years Ago: Daft Punk @ Coachella 2006," *Magnetic Magazine*, Neal Rahman, April 29, 2016

Daft Punk: A Trip Inside the Pyramid, St. Martin's Press, Dina Santorelli, 2014

"Daft Punk," *Spin Magazine*, Andrew Vontz, January 2008

"Sleater-Kinney: Return of the Roar," *Rolling Stone*, Jonah Weiner, January 20, 2015

Daft Punk Unchained, Directed by Hervé Martin-Delpierre, BBC Worldwide France, 2015

2007:

"One Step Closer to Heaven," *The Observer*, Kitty Empire, December 16, 2007

"Led Zeppelin Reunite: The Full Report From David Fricke," *Rolling Stone*, David Fricke, December 11, 2007

"The Return of Led Zeppelin," *Rolling Stone*, David Fricke, December 13, 2007

Led Zeppelin: The Oral History of the World's Greatest Rock Band, Barney Hoskyns, Wiley, 2012

"Led Zeppelin, The O2 Arena, December 10, 2007," *Uncut*, John Mulvey, September 13, 2012

"Led Zeppelin Finds Its Old Power," *New York Times*, Ben Ratliff, December 10, 2007

Led Zeppelin—Day By Day, Marc Roberty, Backbeat Books, 2016

Light and Shade: Conversations With Jimmy Page, Brad Tolinski, Crown, 2012

When Giants Walked the Earth: A Biography of Led Zeppelin, Mick Wall, St. Martin's Griffin, 2010

Celebration Day, Directed by Dick Carruthers, Three P Films Limited, 2012

Amy, Directed by Asif Kapadia, Film 4, 2015

Amy Winehouse: I Told You I Was Trouble: Live in London, Directed by Hamish Hamilton, Island, 2007

2008:

This Is a Call: The Life and Times of Dave Grohl, Paul Bannigan, Da Capo Press, 2013

"Flashback: Leonard Cohen's Miraculous Resurrection In 2008," Rolling Stone, Andy Greene, April 24, 2014

"Exclusive Q&A: Leonard Cohen On New Tour, 'Old Ideas,'" *Rolling Stone*, Andy Greene, January 30, 2012

"Foo Fighters, Wembley Stadium, London," *Independent*, Nick Hasted, June 9, 2008

Dave Grohl: Times Like His, James Martin, John Blake, 2016

"Leonard Cohen's Return To The Stage Started With A Flavorful Stop In Fredericton," *The Global News*, Jeremy Keefe, November 11, 2016

"Foo Fighters Play 'Biggest Ever Show' at Wembley Stadium," *NME*, Staff, June 6, 2008

"Hotter Than Hell: Summer Gig Preview—Foo Fighters," *Kerrang!*, Staff, 2008

I'm Your Man: The Life of Leonard Cohen, Sylvie Simmons, Ecco, 2013

"Foo Fighters Frontman Dave Grohl on Glastonbury Nerves, Kanye West and 20 yrs of Performing," *The Sun UK*, Jacqui Swift, June 11, 2015

Foo Fighters: Live at Wembley Stadium, Directed by Nick Wickham, RCA, 2008

2009:

"Lil Wayne, Young Jeezy, Drake Announce 'Young Money' Tour Dates," *Billboard*, Mariel Concepcion, June 15, 2009

"Lil Wayne Kicks Off 'America's Most Wanted' Tour," *Spin*, William Goodman, July 28, 2009

"U2, Live From Outer Space: Launching the Biggest Tour of All-Time," *Rolling Stone*, Brian Hiatt, April 11, 2011

U2: The Definitive Biography, John Jobling, Thomas Dunne Books, 2014

From the Ground Up: U2 360° Tour Official Photobook, Dylan Jones, Random House UK, 2012

"U2—Croke Park—Saturday" *State Magazine*, Dave Roberts, July 26, 2009

"U2 Croker Sell-Out Sees Bono Breathe Sigh of Relief," *Irish Examiner*, Staff, March 21, 2009

U2 by U2, Neil McKormick, It Books, 2009

"U2 Reinvent Stadium Rock Shows With 360 Tour," MTV News, Jocelyn Vena, March 9, 2009

U2360° at the Rose Bowl, Directed by Tom Krueger, Mercury, 2010

2010:

"The Unstoppable Ambition of Arcade Fire," *Rolling Stone*, David Fricke, February 14, 2011

"Interview: Arcade Fire," *Pitchfork*, Ryan Dombal, October 4, 2010

"Live: The Arcade Fire Basically Own Madison Square Garden," *The Village Voice*, Rob Harvilla, August 5, 2010

"Arcade Fire Go Big at Madison Square Garden," *Rolling Stone*, Will Hermes, August 5, 2010

"The Story of The Big 4, 'Am I Evil?'" *Revolver*, Kory Grow, August 27, 2011

"Arcade Fire: 'The Cliché Rock Life Never Seemed That Cool to Us," *The Observer*, Sean O'Hagan, November 27, 2010

"The Arcade Fire: Beyond Indie," *The New York Times*, Jon Pareles, July 28, 2010

"Arcade Fire Triumph at Madison Square Garden," *American Songwriter*, Even Schlansky, August 6, 2010

"Arcade Fire at Madison Square Garden," *Huffington Post*, Avi Sinesky, August 6, 2010

The Big 4: Live From Sofia, Bulgaria, Directed by Nick Wickham, Warner Bros., 2010

2011:

Adele: Live at the Royal Albert Hall, Directed by Paul Dugdale, XL, 2011

Kanye West: God and Monster, Mark Beaumont, Overlook-Omnibus, 2015

"The Triumph of Adele," *Rolling Stone*, David Browne, October 11, 2012

"Kanye West: Project Runaway," *Complex*, Noah Callahan-Bever, November 22, 2010

"Kanye West Slays Coachella Festival's Last Night," MTV News, Mary DeMeglio, April 18, 2011

Your Favorite Band Is Killing Me, Steven Hyden, Back Bay Books, 2016

"Kanye's Bold Greek Tragedy Closes Coachella," *Spin*, William Goodman, April 18, 2011

"Coachella 2011: Kanye West Doesn't Play It Safe as He Closes the Indio Fest," *The Los Angeles Times*, Todd Martens, April 18, 2011

"Kanye West Delivers One of the Greatest Hip-Hop Sets of All Time at Coachella," *Hollywood Reporter*, Jeff Miller, April 18, 2011

2009 MTV Video Music Awards, Directed by Hamish Hamilton, MTV, September 13, 2009

"At Coachella, Every Note Is Writ Large," *The New York Times*, Ben Ratliff, April 18, 2011

"Adele Opens Up About Her Inspirations, Looks and Stage Fright," *Rolling Stone*, Touré, April 28, 2011

2012:

"Snoop Dogg and Dr. Dre Revive a Golden Era at Coachella," *Rolling Stone*, Steve Appleford, April 16, 2012

"Tupac Hologram Wasn't a Hologram," *Gizmodo*, Sam Biddle, April 17, 2012

"Coachella's Paul Tollett Recalls Journey to Mainstream," *The Desert Sun*, Bruce Fessier, April 7, 2015

"Hologram Tupac Was Inevitable," *The Atlantic*, Jack Hamilton, April 17, 2012

"Dr. Dre & Snoop Dogg's Coachella Set: Hits, Guests and a Tupac Resurrection," *Billboard*, Jason Lipshutz, April 16, 2012

"Opinion: The Problem With The Tupac Hologram," *Billboard*, Jason Lipshutz, April 16, 2012

"Coachella 2012: Dr. Dre, Snoop Dogg and . . . Tupac Wrap Sunday in Style," *The Hollywood Reporter*, Jeff Miller, April 16, 2012

"Tupac Coachella: Behind the Technology," CBS News, Cheda Ngak, November 9, 2012

"Tupac' Live and Onstage," *New York Times*, Russell Potter, April 19, 2012

"How the Tupac 'Holgram' Works," *Washington Post*, Hayley Tsukayama, April 18, 2012

2013:

"Behind Kanye's Mask," *New York Times*, Jon Caramanica, June 11, 2013

"Kanye West Announces 'Yeezus' Tour," *Rolling Stone*, Erin Coulehan, September 6, 2013

"Lady Gaga Shows She's Impossible to Top in Vancouver," *The Straight*, Michael Mann, January 12, 2013

"Review: Lady Gaga Rules Over Her Little Monsters in Vancouver," *Vancouver Sun*, Francois Marchand, January 12, 2013

"Lady Gaga's Born This Way Ball Heads to North America in 2013," *Spin*. Chris Martins, September 5, 2012

"Kanye West Brings on Jesus For Yeezus Tour Kickoff," *Rolling Stone*, Corbin Reiff, October 20, 2013

"Kanye West's Masked 'Yeezus' Tour Opener in Seattle Brushes Off Idea of 'A Fun Night Out,'" *Spin*, Douglas Wolk, October 20, 2013

"The Teaches of Yeezus: Kanye West's Los Angeles Concert," *Grantland*, Emily Yoshida, October 28, 2013

2014:

"Beyonce & Jay Z's Street-Fab 'On the Run' Tour Opens in Miami: Review," *Billboard*, Leila Cobo, June 26, 2014

"Beyoncé and Jay Z On The Run in Paris," *Digital Spy*, Lewis Corner, September 13, 2014

"Miley Cyrus: Confessions of Pop's Wildest Child," *Rolling Stone*, Josh Eells, September 24, 2013

"Beyonce, Jay Z Announce On The Run Summer Stadi-

um Tour," *Billboard*, Andrew Flanagan, April 28, 2014

"Jay Z Allegedly Attacked By Solange After Met Gala," *Rolling Stone*, Kory Grow, May 14, 2014

"Jay Z, Beyonce, Solange Issue Statement After Met Gala Fight," *Rolling Stone*, Kory Grow, May 15, 2014

"Beyonce & Jay Z: On The Run—Stade de France, Paris," *The Line of Best Fit*, Thomas Hannan, September 14, 2014

"Beyonce and Jay Z's On The Run Tour Opener: A Collaborative Spectacle," *Rolling Stone*, Daniel Kreps, June 26, 2014

"Beyoncé and Jay Z On The Run Tour—Paris Review," *Huffington Post*, Carina Maggar, November 16, 2014

"Miley Cyrus Is Naughty and Nice in Return to Nashville," *Associated Press*, Chris Talbott, August 8, 2014

On the Run Tour: Beyoncé and Jay Z, Directed by Jonas Åkerlund, Black Dog Films, 2014

2015:

"OVO Fest 2015 Review: Drake Proves He's a '6 God,'" *Toronto Sun*, Julia Alexander, August 4, 2015

"OVO Fest 2015 Recap," *Hypebeast*, Josephine Cruz, August 5, 2015

"Everything That Happened at Drake's OVO Festival 2015 in Toronto," *High Snobiety*, Chris Danforth, August 4, 2015

"Here's Everything That Happened at Drake's OVO Fest," *Complex*, Justin Davis, August 3, 2015

"I Watched Drake Become a Legend For Years, Then Saw the Results at My First OVO Fest," *Noisey*, Brian Espiritu, August 4, 2015

"Ellen, Alanis Morissette and Natalie Maines Join Taylor Swift Onstage in L.A.," *L.A. Times*, Randy Lewis, August 25, 2015

"Meek Mill Vs. Drake: A Full Timeline of the Rap Beef & Who Weighed In," *Billboard*, Erika Ramirez, July 31, 2015

"Taylor Swift Tells Sold-Out Staples Center Crowd, 'I'm Kind of in Love With You,'" *Variety*, Malina Saval, August 26, 2015

2016:

"How Desert Trip Made History," *Forbes*, Steve Baltin, October 17, 2016

"Gord Downie, Tragically Hip Singer, Has Terminal Cancer," *CBC News*, Laura Fraser, May 24, 2016

"Desert Trip: How Classic Rock Mega-Fest Proved Doubters Wrong," *Rolling Stone*, David Fricke, October 13, 2016

"Tragically Hip: Canada Waves Goodbye to a National Treasure," *Rolling Stone*, Jared Lindzon, July 20, 2016

"Surviving Oldchella: Scenes From the Ultimate Classic Rock Rager," *Pitchfork*, Jillian Mapes, October 11, 2016

"Gord Downie Thanks Crowd 'For Keeping Me Pushing' In Stage Farewell," *The Star*, Nick Patch, August 20, 2016

"Coachella Classic: A Festival For Rock Giants and Their Aging Fans," *The New York Times*, Ben Sisario, September 28, 2016

"Desert Trip Founder Paul Tollett Explains Pulling Off McCartney, Stones & Dylan Lineup," *Billboard*, Ray Waddell, October 6, 2016

"Roger Waters Shares What He Really Wanted to Say About Trump (And Clinton) at Desert Trip," *Billboard*, Chris Willman, October 14, 2016

ACKNOWLEDGEMENTS

Writing this book has been a dream of mine for many, many years, and it took a lot of amazing people to turn that dream into a reality. I'd first like to thank my agent, Jim Fitzgerald, for sticking with me and being an incredible advocate. I'd like to thank my editor, Michael Croland, for your tremendous wisdom, impeccable advice and willingness to hear out all my ideas no matter how stupid they sounded. I'd also like to thank Jacob Hoye for his insight and knowledge and for seeing the promise in this book.

I couldn't have gotten to this point if not for a tremendous number of writers and editors who've given me a shot through the years or simply offered advice and a friendly ear. There are so many that it's impossible to name them all, but I'd like to mention Tessa Jeffers, Chris Kornelis, Mark Baumgarten, Dusti Demarast, Marah Eakin, Mike Ayers, Nick Murray, Hank Shteamer, Simon Vozick-Levinson, Jeff Kitts, Brad Tolinksi, Matthew Wilkening and Edwin Ortiz. To all the rest that I didn't name, you know who you are and I can't thank you enough.

I want to thank Peter Guralnick, Stephen Thomas Erelwine and Annie Zaleski for their valuable input. I also want to thank David Greenwald for putting together the website.

I need to thank Andy Cirzan, Big Daddy Kane, Bob Gruen, Butch Trucks, Black Thought, D.A. Pennebaker, David Crosby, Dickey Betts, Elvin Bishop, George Wein, Gerry Gerrard, Gregg Allman, Greg Kot, Kelefa Sanneh, Larry Crane, Marc Geiger, Michaelangelo Matos, Mister Cee, Monte Melnick and Sam Coomes for sharing your memories and observations.

This book wouldn't have been possible if not for the tremendous support of my friends and family. I'd like to thank my brother, Cameron; his wife, Heather; and my niece, Winnie, for giving me the encouragement that kept me going through the long days and even longer nights writing. I'd like to thank Cameron especially for being my sidekick to some of the best rap shows I've ever seen. Did we really catch Future four times together? We did, didn't we?

I'd like to thank my dad, Ruben, for instilling in me a tremendous work ethic, while also teaching me to enjoy the little things in life. I'd like to thank my mom for encouraging my love of music. I want to thank my dad for buying my first Gibson Les Paul and then taking me to meet the man himself. I'd like to thank my sister, Payton, a country music fan who went with me to see Alice in Chains and Cheap Trick, and her husband, Morris, for not talking her out of it. I'd like to thank my spectacular in-laws: Ed and Wendy, Karin and Rich, Mandy, Sarah and Daniel and their families for your support and belief in me.

I'd like to thank Nathan Feutz for being the best friend a guy could ask for and the wingman to that first Nine Inch Nails concert. I want to thank my uncle Tom Pluth for having a copy of *The Song Remains the Same* in the middle of all his Brooks & Dunn and Toby Keith CDs. I also want to thank my uncle Jim and his wife, Annie, for their encouragement to pursue a career in music.

Finally, and most importantly, I need to thank my wife, Jenna. You are the light of my life. You've made me a better writer and a better man. Only you and I know the sacrifices it took to make this possible. I love you so much. This book is for you.